A HISTORY OF MODERN YEMEN

Yemen's history is unique and deserves to be better understood. Divided in the nineteenth century between Ottoman and British spheres of influence and by local connections which reached as far afield as Java, Yemen had a long tradition of imagined unity which reached political fruition in the form of a single state only in 1990. North Yemen, under the Zaydī Imamate, was the one fully independent Arab government after World War I. South Yemen was a British protectorate. Both Yemens were at the centre of Arab politics in the 1960s, and the South then became the Arab World's only Marxist state; the North was the site of intense Saudi interest. Yemen's belated union in May 1990, as the Yemen Republic, was shaken by the Gulf Crisis and by civil war in 1994. Drawing on his skills as an anthropologist, Paul Dresch handles the story deftly, using poetry, quotations from local sources, and personal experience to evoke what the events of the twentieth century meant to Yemenis, who today form Arabia's largest national population. With its fast-moving narrative, the book provides an easy introduction to a little known slice of Arabia's modern history, and experts will find much here that is new.

PAUL DRESCH is University Lecturer at the Institute of Social and Cultural Anthropology, University of Oxford. He is author of *Tribes, Government and History in Yemen* (Clarendon Press, 1989) and of many articles on Yemen.

A HISTORY OF MODERN YEMEN

PAUL DRESCH

University of Oxford

CAMBRIDGE
UNIVERSITY PRESS

PUBLISHED BY THE PRESS SYNDICATE OF THE UNIVERSITY OF CAMBRIDGE
The Pitt Building, Trumpington Street, Cambridge, United Kingdom

CAMBRIDGE UNIVERSITY PRESS
The Edinburgh Building, Cambridge CB2 2RU, UK
40 West 20th Street, New York, NY 10011–4211, USA
477 Williamstown Road, Port Melbourne, VIC 3207, Australia
Ruiz de Alarcón 13, 28014 Madrid, Spain
Dock House, The Waterfront, Cape Town 8001, South Africa

http://www.cambridge.org

First published 2000
Reprinted 2002

Printed in the United Kingdom at the University Press, Cambridge

Typeface Monotype Baskerville 11/12.5 pt *System* QuarkXPress™ [SE]

A catalogue record for this book is available from the British Library

Library of Congress Cataloguing in Publication data

Dresch, Paul.
A history of modern Yemen / Paul Dresch.
p. cm.
Includes bibliographical references and index.
1. Yemen–History–20th century. I. Title.
DS247. Y48 D74 2000
953.305–dc21 00-029266

ISBN 0 521 79092 1 hardback
ISBN 0 521 79482 X paperback

For Melinda Babcock,
with a great many thanks for patience

In every croft, somehow, there lives and persists the dream of something better; for a thousand years they have imagined that they will rise above penury in some mysterious manner and acquire a large estate and the title of landed farmers, the eternal dream. Some consider that it will only be fulfilled in heaven.

. . . it was a good man indeed who could stand immovable as a rock in these times, when everything, including money and views of life, was afloat and swirling . . .

Halldor Laxness, *Independent People*

Contents

Illustrations

Maps and figures

Preface and acknowledgements

The series this book forms part of is defined by nation states, thus by modern politics. State politics must dominate the lay-out. I am not sure we would do this anymore for Europe or much of Asia (I am fairly sure we might not in fact) and my own predilection would make rulers and states less central. Perhaps that is prejudice: my first experience of North Yemen in the 1970s included people, though admittedly few, who did not know who the President was and could scarcely have cared less, for government remained inside the Sanaa ring-road and theories of government were abstract fantasy. That has all gone and Government is now everywhere. The political story is worth telling but I hope both historians and ethnologists will recover other stories, for Yemenis of all sorts have tales to tell and often fascinating theories of how the world works.

Even political history presents problems. For the North we have predominantly Zaydī sources, which obscure much of Shāfiʿī life; for the South we have British views and local views that oppose them, both of which obscure what ordinary people thought; for Ḥaḍramawt we have a literature of learning and politics. Modern works, worst of all, work in modern terms. Yemeni writers have begun to include in their books photostat documents, which are one important path to a better history leaving work such as mine redundant, but there are no central archives from which to recover past forms of life save those of the British, whose views were a small part of what affected Yemenis.

I have used such terms as North, South and Ḥaḍramawt throughout the book. The meaning should be clear. Arab Nationalist rhetoric and Islamic rhetoric before it portray all difference whatever as derived from error or from foreign plots, but well before 1900 there were separate cultural and political foci just as there are in many countries. For those with the patience to read sources thoroughly, recent nomenclature ("South Yemen", "the Arab South") proves anyway more labile than advertised. The shifts may be fun to track but they are not worth a lot of arm-waving. Yemenis know where Yemen is and one must simplify in some degree to write a history.

The complexities are large. I have tried to ease the burden by providing maps, and thanks are due to Jonathan Rae for help producing them. Other works on modern Yemen provide ample graphs and tables, so these I have kept to a minimum. The definite article, meanwhile, is dropped or retained for ease of reading (Ḍāliʿ, al-Ḍāliʿ; it doesn't matter) but most personal and place names are otherwise transliterated fully (hence Ḍāliʿ or al-Ḍāliʿ, for instance, not Dhala), with the exception of Sanaa, which as Ṣanʿāʾ looks outlandish in frequent transliteration, and Aden. Not everyone always agrees on vowelling or pronunciation, however, and in Arabic short vowels are usually not shown. Thus, the family name Muḥḍār in Ḥaḍramawt, for instance, becomes Miḥḍār further west, while the North Yemeni name al-Ḥibshī is Ḥabshī or even Ḥabashī in Ḥaḍramawt. In the South compound vowels differ, so *dawlah* for example is pronounced *dôlah*; more strikingly Shuʿayb, always written that way, is pronounced by many as Shāʿib, and Shaʿīrī as Shāʿirī. The value of consonants sometimes differs too. In most of Upper Yemen *qāf* is pronounced as a thick /g/ and *jīm* as /j/, while in parts of Lower Yemen *qāf* is /q/ and *jīm* or *gīm* is /g/, and near the border between North and South *qāf* is /gh/ – so *mā ghult* for *mā qult*, "What did you say?" I have tended to the classical, which makes names at least easier to look up.

Such details can produce confusion. In 1965, for instance, an important political meeting was held at Khamir, dominated by Northern tribal shaykhs most of whom were quite conservative. Several authors imply a meeting of radical Southern socialists in the following year was held at the same place, which would surely give pause for thought as if the Fourth International had met on the Duke of Beaufort's property, but the second meeting was actually at Ḥumar (in Arabic there's a dot's worth of difference on the consonant; I hope I have the vowels right) near Qaʿṭabah on the North–South border.

Published literature remains weak on many scores. One finds oneself interrogating again and again, from this angle and that, the same range of sources, and all manner of basics on, for instance, land tenure remain informed guess-work. (When the Turks took Sanaa in 1872 they acquired the "registers" from which they would learn "the administration of the country and its resources". What were those registers? Where did they go? What else is there?) But there are secondary sources which already cover the course of politics. The works of Wenner (1967), Stookey (1978,

1982) and Bidwell (1983) are all good, though the last hides its light beneath a bushel: few references are given, yet it turns out to rest on very detailed reading of, for instance, pamphlet literature. Gavin's *Aden Under British Rule* (1975) is a fine piece of history despite the misprints. Peterson's account of the republican state in North Yemen (1982) remains the best. The late Leigh Douglas's work on "Free Yemenis" (1987) is superb. To go further would risk playing favourites among colleagues, but there is now a good deal of interesting work in European languages and Auchterlonie (1998) is a sound guide.

Yemeni writing I can only hint at in a book intended mainly for Western readers, particularly in the present format. When I first began work in the North, however, there were maybe six Arabic books on the modern period one really had to read and now there are hundreds, of which many are excellent and nearly all are of real interest. Readers with Arabic, please note. There is simply not space to present and explain what in one sense is real history, but I should mention two major references. I have not cited *The Encyclopaedia of Yemen* (ʿAfīf et al. 1992) but I have used it constantly; the same goes for al-Ḥajrī's *Areas and Tribes of Yemen* (1984), whose spelling I have usually followed.

All who write on Yemen feel we oversimplify. Social classes, tribes, regions, sects appear all too often as objects, not as words and ideas experienced or used by people, while the "grass-roots" Yemeni view is often of individual people linked by kinship or vicinity but interacting as if power and wealth were a personal creation. The problems are not unique to Yemen. Sixty years ago the most interesting historian of modern England (George Dangerfield) wrote: "It is the habit of contemporary philosophy to mesh every succeeding crisis in the ordered and apparently inescapable nets of economic theory; but when the nets are dragged brimful into the light of day, one thing seems to have evaded them . . ., the human soul, . . . [the] irrational side of human nature." Economism is misleading, he argues, even for so "economic" a time and place as England before World War I. It would certainly be so for Yemen. So also would too simple a "political" frame. Unifying forms of history work well for unifying institutions – ministries, states, standardised school systems – but Yemen works largely in other terms. The pretence is maintained that everyone knows everyone else or knows someone who potentially knows them and might thus provide an introduction, and that pretence is as effective politically as the claims of, say, the Central Bank.

Qadi al-Akwa's five-volume compendium of learned places (al-Akwaʿ

1995) consists of hundreds of short biographies. As one browses among these, following the different connections, one gains an intimate feel for part of Yemeni life: one finds that *qāḍī* families of no great importance are prominent here, that *sayyid* families get short shrift, that certain stories one expects to find are not present, and so on. It is a deeply "engaged" piece of work. Nor are my views those of the learned Qadi. But a similar compendium of small farmers, another of officers, a third of political party members, a fourth of migrant workers, a compendium of house-wives (we shall never get that, I fear), and the total would be a start on history. The themes of "modern" writing would remain between the lines. To do such a view justice within a narrative is difficult.

While writing, I have checked and discussed what I can with those I could reach from Oxford. Help was sought from and freely given by all the following: Ḥusayn al-ʿAmrī, Noel Brehoney, Sheila Carapico, Fred Halliday, ʿAbd al-Rabb al-Ḥabīlī, the learned Bernie Haykel, Peter Hinchcliffe, the learned Engseng Ho, David Ledger, Godfrey Meynell, Khadījah al-Salāmī, ʿAbduh Ṣāliḥ, John Shipman, Zayd al-Wazīr, Robert Wilson, and ʿAlī Muḥammad Zayd. Fred Halliday and James Piscatori were also kind enough to read a complete draft. None of them is responsible for what I say, and most may disagree with much of it. There are scores of Yemeni friends and acquaintances over twenty years whose views inform this book and on balance they are better left unnamed: "History only matters," said one of them, "to people who are angry". That is not true for me but it may be for some of them and for those who rule them.

Lastly, Yemeni books of traditional cast had more interesting titles than do ours. I am grateful for wild suggestions. "The Raging Torrent of Historical and Social Comment" seemed too broad – too Zaydī as well for those who know the literature. Certain others focused too much on a particular tradition, area, or group, and some were too frivolous as well ("The Fragrant Orange Peel Concerning Ḥāshid and Bakīl" – thank you, Robert). A proper neutrality suggests the following, though it only works in English: "The Camel Trotting Heavy Laden with News of Ḥaḍramawt, Sanaa and Aden", for which again thanks to Robert.

The Trotting Camel is dedicated to my wife.

Abbreviations

ATUC	Aden Trades Union Congress
EAP	Eastern Aden Protectorate. A shorthand British expression for Quʿayṭī and Kathīrī sultanates of Ḥaḍramawt, plus Mahrah. Sometimes reckoned to include the Wāḥidī Sultanate, adjacent to Bayḥān and ʿAwlaqī
FG	Federal Guard
FLOSY	Front for the Liberation of Occupied South Yemen, Egyptian backed coalition of nationalists in South Yemen, 1966–7
FRA	Federal Regular Army
GNP	gross national product
GPC	General Popular Congress (*al-muʾtamar al-shaʿbī al-ʿāmm*), North Yemeni state institution to displace party politics. Established 1982
HBL	Hadrami Bedouin Legion
IMF	International Monetary Fund
MAN	Movement of Arab Nationalists (*ḥarakat al-qawmiyyīn al-ʿarab*)
MECO	Military Economic Corporation (since renamed the Yemeni Economic Corporation), a vast governmental apparatus through which Northern army officers became rich
NDF	National Democratic Front; from early 1976 the main leftist grouping within the North, active mainly in Lower Yemen
NLF	National Liberation Front, anti-colonial movement in the South established first by Egypt but later at odds with Egypt and FLOSY
OECD	Organisation for Economic Co-operation and Development, a club of wealthy, industrialised nations
OPEC	Organisation of Petroleum Exporting Countries, the cartel of oil states which in the 1970s was dominated by Middle Eastern countries and which itself for a while seemed to dominate world finance

PDRY People's Democratic Republic of Yemen (the South, which from November 1967 to December 1970 was the People's Republic of South Yemen)

SAL South Arabian League (*rābiṭah abnā' al-janūb*, literally "League of the Sons of the South")

UAR United Arab Republic; from 1958 to 1961 Egypt and Syria together, from 1961 just Egypt

WAP Western Aden Protectorate (the little states of the Aden hinterland)

YAR Yemen Arab Republic (the state in the North, declared in 1962)

YD Yemeni dīnār, the currency of the PDRY (a little less than $US 3 in 1980). 1 dīnār = 20 dirhams

YR Yemeni riyāl, the currency of the YAR (a little more than $US 0.2 in 1980)

YSP Yemeni Socialist Party

CHAPTER ONE

Turkey, Britain and Imam Yaḥyā: the years around 1900

The borders of most states in the Middle East were drawn by colonial powers and many countries such states represent are themselves in some degree inventions. Once invented, they acquire history. Iraq, for instance, before the British produced a state of that name, was little but a geographical expression yet its ruler in recent times has harked back to Babylon; Jordan dates also from 1921, yet Roman and Nabatean ruins form part now of Jordan's past. Yemen is an oddity for the history in a sense is real. Traditions of Yemen before Islam are at the heart of Islamic literature (the collapse of the Ma'rib dam is mentioned in the Holy Qur'ān; references to Yemen in Traditions of the Prophet are numerous), and local works through the centuries since then have repeatedly defined themselves as "Yemeni".[1] Unwritten tradition is as prominent. To do the subject justice would require extensive cross-referencing to imitate at least the "feel" of Yemen, that endless overlapping of local knowledge which makes life there, and not least political life, richly textured.[2]

Since the rise of Islam, if not well before, the idea of Yemen as a natural unit has been embedded in literature and local practice. Unified power has not. Political structures through the nineteenth century were defined by reference to religion or dynasty, not territory, and a list of rulers would be indefinitely long for their claims overlap in both time and space. The wish for a single Yemeni state emerged in a context shaped by outside powers. Much of Yemen's history through the twentieth century connects with efforts to form that state, which was finally established in 1990. Before that there were two states, North and South, with their capitals at Sanaa and at Aden, each with its view of the country's past and future, and in the years around 1900 there were myriad little centres of power – hence myriad different histories, were there space to give them – and a few great claimants, two of which were foreign empires.

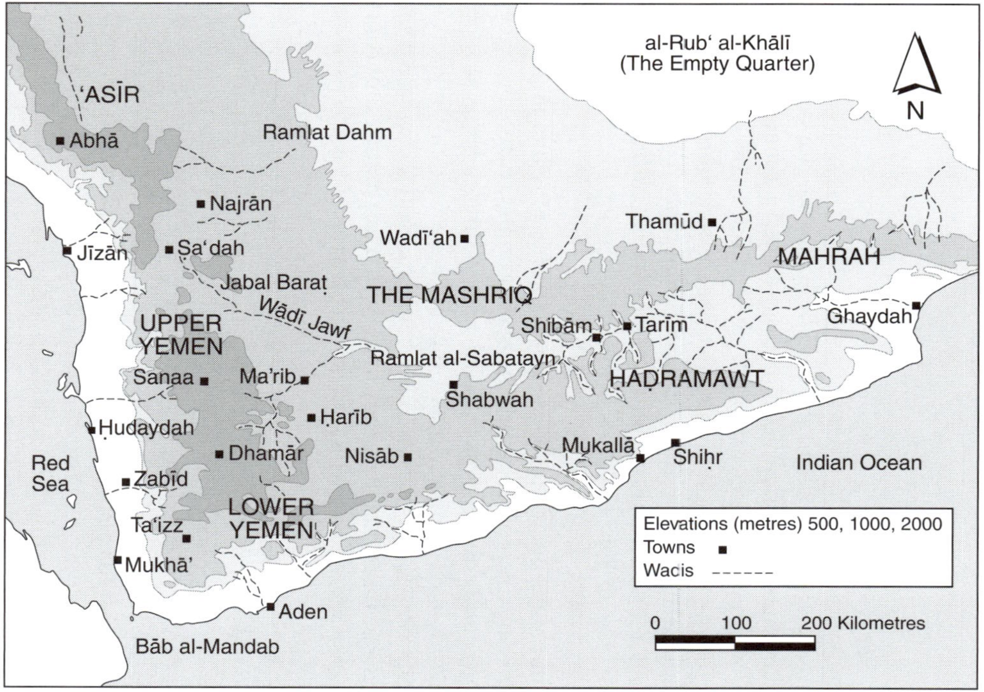

Map 1.1. Yemen circa 1900

IMPERIAL DIVISIONS

In 1839 Captain Haines took Aden for the East India Company's Bombay Presidency. The reasons, as is usual with politics, were muddled. One pressing reason, however, was the presence further north of troops belonging to Muḥammad ʿAlī Pāshā, the ruler of Egypt, whose service for the Ottoman Sultan as nominally a vassal, ambitions against the Ottomans, and troubles with underlings whom the Sultan encouraged, led him, after crushing the Wahhābīs in Central Arabia (the ancestors of what later would be a Saudi state), to send his forces south along the Red Sea coast of Yemen. In 1837 he acquired the southern highland town of Taʿizz. The British warned him off from moving further and in 1839 they occupied Aden themselves by force.[3] As part of a broader policy that was not to do with Yemen but with grand strategy, the British forced Muḥammad ʿAlī back under Ottoman suzerainty, thus aborting the prospect of Egypt as an autonomous Middle Eastern power: in 1840 they forced him out of the Levant and, less directly, out of all Arabia. Despite this, they remained in Aden.

The Ottomans established a presence on the Red Sea coast in 1849. An immediate attempt on Sanaa came to nothing (the Ottoman force, although invited in, was largely massacred) and through the decades following, ʿAsīr, further north, was repeatedly up in arms against Turkish rule. Only after the Suez canal was opened (1869) did the Turks make a serious commitment to the central highlands. In 1872 they took Sanaa, the present capital of Yemen, controlling fairly quickly the areas south of there around Taʿizz and with far less success pushing northwards also. Two empires, the Ottoman and the British, thus had lodgements with administrative centres 300 km apart – 450 km or so as the routes then ran – or in terms more appropriate to the time, perhaps two weeks on foot or by mule across the plateaux and the mountains (Map 1.1).

Beneath and between, or off to one side of, two foreign empires were 3–4 million Yemenis, most of whom were Sunnis attached to the Shāfiʿī school of Islamic law. The next largest group were Zaydī Shiʿites, and in places there were small groups of Ismāʿīlīs. A few Indian traders had once been prominent and Yemen's Jews claim roots far preceding the Islamic era, but Yemen overall was a Muslim country and in the view of most Yemenis always had been. The Prophet's own "supporters" at Medina had been Yemeni, which readily elides in the popular view with a general tradition of Arabic letters that Yemenis are the "original Arabs" (*al-ʿarab al-ʿāribah*), all others are people who "became Arabs" (*mustaʿrabīn*), and a region at the margins of global economy in the nineteenth century was felt by its inhabitants to be the centre of a lost history. Aden, to take a specific case, had a population of only about 1,000 when the British seized it but was said to be the oldest town on earth or "the oldest of the Arabs' markets".

Most political language at first was couched in Islamic terms, and its forms were various. In the 1840s Aden was twice attacked in *jihāds* led by men claiming supernatural power. Later Zaydī writers said the first and more famous of these, the Faqīh Saʿīd, claimed to be the Awaited Mahdi – a sure sign of impiety or madness – and a Zaydī Imam of the day had him executed, while twenty years later "Sufi sorcerers", again in the Zaydī view, had Raymah and Ānis up in arms. Jewish millenarianism had briefly swept up Muslim tribes near Sanaa. But those who claimed to defend more orthodox and Islamic order failed to establish peace.

The mid-to-late nineteenth century is known to Yemeni historians as "the time of corruption". The coffee trade which had once made the country prosperous had decayed (Mocha is named for a Yemeni town; plantations elsewhere in the world, however, brought the price down sharply before 1800), and the Red Sea ports from which highland rulers continued drawing revenue from local trade had all been lost. Ḥarāz, west of Sanaa and itself a partly Ismāʿīlī region, was dominated by Ismāʿīlīs from Najrān, northeast of Ṣaʿdah; the highland agricultural zone near Taʿizz was in the hands of tribes from Baraṭ. Few places were in the grip of government, for as Muḥsin al-Ḥarāzī said near the time, the State could not be put right without soldiers, soldiers were only ruled by money, and in the treasury there was no money. As early as the 1830s Sanaa was littered with corpses of the starved. The Qāsimī state (ruled by descendants of the Zaydī Imam al-Qāsim, d. 1620), which earlier had held the highlands firmly and been a regional power of some importance, simply fell apart as rival claimants to the Imamate warred among themselves in a maelstrom of shifting alliances and famine and disease ravaged much of Yemen. The Turks' second move to the highlands, unlike their first, won effective support locally.[4]

When the Turks again took Sanaa, in 1872, al-Mutawakkil Muḥsin moved north and sustained his claim as Imam in accordance with the Zaydī (Shiʿite) school of Islamic law. Though it had once, in the seventeenth century, produced the Qāsimī dynastic state or *dawlah*, Zaydism had usually been a tradition of the anti-state: the collapse of the Qāsimīs, indeed, was rationalised by saying they were less like Imams than Kings. Righteousness had mattered more than power. Nor did most Zaydī scholars accept dynastic succession. An Imam had to be of the Prophet's kin and a man of learning, but his duty was "coming out" (*khurūj*) against oppression and his legitimacy was in effect by *faḍl*, by God's preference. In Zaydī terms the Qāsimī *dawlah* had been something of an aberration. Yet the shape of that state lingered in people's imaginations still,[5] perhaps particularly among Sanaanis and those descended from al-Qāsim.

Several claimants to the Imamate were active. In Zaydism it is possible in theory as well as practice to have more than one Imam at once, but in 1904 the Imamate passed to Yaḥyā Muḥammad Ḥamīd al-Dīn, whose father before him had claimed the title since 1890, and Yaḥyā took the regnal name al-Mutawakkil ʿalā Allāh, "He who relies on God". Though none in his particular line before his father had been Imam, the family were descendants of al-Qāsim and, as it happened, Yaḥyā's theology was of Qāsimī form.[6] His claim in correspondence, like that of all Imams, was to descent from his ultimate ancestor, the Prophet of God; his duty was to wage the *jihād* against oppression. Like his father, he launched a rising in northern Yemen, and all the old calumnies against the Turks from the last time that "Turks" ruled Yemen, in the sixteenth century, were redeployed: that they were corrupt, allowed the drinking of wine, had a taste for small boys, exploited the poor, failed to uphold God's law and, in short, were scarcely Muslims.

The details of the fight were complex. So were the issues fuelling it. The Turks at most points had Yemeni supporters: indeed by then there was something of a local bureaucracy staffed by Yemenis, many judges and clerks spoke Turkish well, several Yemeni delegations had travelled to Istanbul, and not everyone near Sanaa or even among the Prophet's kin supported the Imam.[7] The little towns far south of Sanaa remained quiet, as too did the countryside around them, while Sanaa itself was by most accounts prosperous and well ordered. The revolt was in the northern countryside. Many tribes there, like many learned persons, had taken stipends since the Turks arrived, but offences against their leaders' status, interference with their land, attempts to tax them, and famine induced by recurrent drought all provoked opposition.[8]

Turkish administration was often corrupt. Yet the Shāfiʿī regions of Lower Yemen far south of Sanaa, which must surely have borne the brunt of excess taxation for there was the only source of revenue, remained quiet while the Zaydī areas of Upper Yemen (around Sanaa and northwards) rose, we are told, "as one man". In the midst of a general famine Sanaa surrendered in 1905: "its markets were destroyed, its houses empty, and only a few of its inhabitants were left".[9] Fighting went on as far south as Qaʿṭabah, but little towns in Lower Yemen, such as Ibb, mainly stood with the Ottomans even when Sanaa fell. The Turks landed thousands of fresh troops, retook their capital, and pushed north to the mountain stronghold of Shahārah where they were beaten with heavy losses. In the course of that year they lost 30,000 men. Fighting the Idrīsī ruler of ʿAsīr, meanwhile, they lost more troops than their opponent mustered in his whole army. Yemen was "the graveyard of the Turks".

To address the difference between Zaydī and Shāfiʿī can nowadays be difficult and to mention the topic may be held by nationalists to be in doubtful taste. The theologies of power were different, however; the fact that Turks were fellow-Sunnis had its effect also. But the natural ecologies of these regions, as we shall see, are different, and the relation of ecology to power is perhaps a key. In Lower Yemen the Turks co-opted successfully local magnates, dominating systems of inequality on their own ground and granting notables such titles of respect as Pāshā, while in Upper Yemen there is little to exploit.[10] But certain families among the tribes of Ḥāshid and Bakīl in Upper Yemen own land elsewhere. Around Ḥajjah, for instance, in the western mountains, shaykhs from the barren plateau further east own extensive property; so they do in Lower Yemen. When control of such wealth was threatened by the Turkish presence they could call on their tribesmen, who themselves, without a source of patronage in grain or cash, lived on the edge of famine. For tribesmen swept up in Yaḥyā's following it was war to the knife.

In 1906–7 a mission of religious scholars from Mecca was sent by the Turks to mediate, and Yaḥyā's reply to them deserves quoting for its mix of Islamic righteousness with proto-national feeling. The Ottoman claim to broader suzerainty is accepted in some degree (the ruler of the Empire is addressed throughout such correspondence as "Sulṭān al-Islām"; the term "Caliph" is reserved to the Imam) but the right of Imams to rule all Yemen brooks no argument.

> The land of Yemen was in the hands of our ancestors, the most noble family [i.e. the Prophet's kin], from the third century [of Islam] to the present, and never has there not been a claimant to that right, whether ruling all Yemen or part of it, as is known from the chronicles of Yemen. There were constant battles between our ancestors and those who opposed them, thus opposing the wish of the people (*ahl*) of Yemen to be ruled by their lords and the sons of their Prophet, may God be pleased with them . . . They have no desire save to order the right and extirpate what is loathsome and reprehensible, to establish the *sharīʿah*, set straight him who strays, and advise the ignorant . . .[11]

Plate 1.1. Turks and Yemenis before World War I.

The "ordering of what is right" (*al-amr bi-l-maʿrūf . . .*) is a timeless obligation on Zaydīs. The mention of dates – "from the third century to the present" – however, has a ring both modern and dynastic. Similar language had been used by Yaḥyā's father, and this "nationalist" elision of territory and legitimate rule might provisionally be dated to the period 1890–1910.

In 1911 there was another vast rising and the Turks again had to fight their way back in.[12] The Imam and the Ottomans, both aware that Italy was then invading Libya, agreed a truce, the terms of which were largely those suggested in 1908 by Yaḥyā. The Imam claimed the right to appoint judges for the Zaydī school of law (the government could appoint even non-Yemeni judges for other schools if it wished, though non-Muslims were not to be placed above Muslims); the *waqf*, or property gifted for religious ends, was to be under Yaḥyā's control; Zaydīs were to pay their taxes to him, directly or through local leaders, and he was to submit a tithe to the Turkish government; neither side was to attack the other's borders. What "borders" meant is unclear, for the British soon found the Imam's influence extending to areas beyond the Zaydī fold.[13] But in practice the Turks retained control of majority

Shāfiʿī areas such as Taʿizz and al-Ḥugariyyah, and the Sanaa-based government became something of a condominium.

Yaḥyā appointed new agents to several regions. He retained, however, the Shaykh al-Islām (the highest Zaydī judge but himself) whom the Ottomans had recognised in Sanaa, Qadi Ḥusayn al-ʿAmrī.[14] Qadi Ḥusayn, who once taught Imam Yaḥyā, had mediated the truce discussions. He had previously been the Ottomans' supervisor of *waqf* (religious property) and was now appointed president of the Appeal Court, an institution which perhaps echoes earlier Qāsimī forms but accords more directly with Ottoman views of judicial order and, from 1911 onwards, carries through the discontinuities of political control until our own day. In a small way, a new state administration was taking form. In the countryside, meanwhile, the Imam's own affairs were simply run. Tiny sums of money were assessed and disbursed by Yaḥyā personally:

> [Seal] Commander of the Faithful, He who Relies on God.
> Receipt to brother ʿAlī Aḥmad Muḥammad al-Ḥusaynī for one quarter, one eighth and a half an eighth of a riyāl in respect of God's due [the *zakāt*, or religious tax prescribed for Muslims] which God accepted from him. May sundry good things befall him. Issued Ṣafar 1331 [February 1913]

In another scribbled note the Imam complains that the expenses of *jihād* were enormous and people were unwilling to pay even their *zakāt*. The allotment, a month later, of 20 riyāls to his governor in Khamir (the main town of the Ḥāshid tribes, about two days north of Sanaa) has the appearance of a major outlay, while a note goes back to a shaykh near Radāʿ, four days journey southeast of Sanaa, acknowledging payment of one riyāl, a quarter *qadaḥ* of red sorghum and an eighth of a *qadaḥ* of barley.[15]

Attention to detail should not suggest Yaḥyā lacked wide perspective. He claimed, and doubtless felt on occasion, that the whole Islamic World was threatened, and events close at hand were addressed in these wider terms. His treaty with the Ottomans was not recognised by the Idrīsī, for instance, a separate (Sunni) ruler of ʿAsīr to the north and west. The Idrīsī instead allied with the Italians against the Turks, and in 1912 Yaḥyā issued a proclamation which addressed "all the people of Yemen, Zaydī and Shāfiʿī, in the highlands and the lowlands", setting this in global context:

> the Christians decided upon taking Islamic lands . . . such as Bulgaria, Crete, Bosnia-Hercegovina, the land of Fez [Morocco] whose ruler was called Commander of the Faithful, a man named ʿAbd al-Ḥafīẓ, and then Iran, which is the land of Inner Iraq whose ruler is Shah of the Persians . . . Then the

Italians fell upon the land of Western Tripoli [Libya], killing and driving out its people . . . When they failed to take it . . . the Italians asked the Idrīsī for help in Yemen. What is more reprehensible than aiding the unbelievers against the Muslims and Islam?[16]

This language of righteousness, of *jihād* indeed, had been used against the Turks themselves before 1911; nor had it prevented Yaḥyā approaching the infidel British for help against them.[17] But when Europe's powers fell to fighting, in 1914, Yaḥyā stood quietly by the Ottomans. Not everyone in Yemen did so.

Astrological predictions to the effect that Britain would replace Turkey had been heard in places as different as the Jawf and Ḥugariyyah, and the British in Aden were courted by several factions. Yaḥyā, on the other hand, made no contribution to the volunteer force from Lower Yemen (about 6,000 Shāfiʿī soldiers) which accompanied the Turks on their march against the British base.[18] While the Ḥijāz revolted against the Turks, however, most of Yemen remained quiet; the Imam's position was consolidated. World War I collapsed the Ottoman Empire, with repercussions throughout the Middle East, and when the Turks withdrew from Yemen in 1918–19, Yaḥyā expanded his influence southward with Turkish encouragement into what had been their domain, that is into largely Shāfiʿī areas (we shall look at this in Chapter 2). His predecessors as Imams, not least the Qāsimīs in the seventeenth century, had also expanded southward. But Yaḥyā did so in a politically different world. The rules of this new world order, to borrow a recent phrase, were those of European-style states which identify legitimate power with territory and historical continuity, and part of Yemen, with the Ottoman demise, now had a place in this. A modern Egyptian author identifies Yaḥyā with "the establishment of modern Yemen".[19] He is right to do so.

In the North tremendous things had happened, pregnant with implications, but in the South at the level of formal politics much less had happened. The East India Company which had taken Aden town in 1839 had given way to the (British) Indian Empire, and the initial lodgement in Aden had been expanded by acquiring water-wells and land across the bay. Apart from that, all the British did was make treaties with outlying notables. In accordance with British–Indian practice, the "rulers" (actually few of them were rulers in an Indian or in a British sense; most were prominent for other reasons) were eventually accorded different ranks and thus salutes of different numbers of cannon as if on a list of protocol around Delhi:[20]

Name of tribe etc.	Estimated population	Name of ruler	Salute to which entitled
ʿAbdalī	15,000	Sultan Sir Aḥmad Faḍl	9 guns
ʿAqrabī	800	Shaykh Faḍl Bā Ḥaydarah	. . .
Ḥawshabī	6,000	Sultan ʿAlī Manīʿ	. . .
Faḍlī	20,000	Sultan Ḥusayn b. Aḥmad	9 guns
Amir of Ḍāliʿ	12,000	Amir Shāyif b. Sayf	. . .

Agreements sometimes overlapped with and contradicted each other. For most of the notables, however, the only real tie with Aden before World War I was an annual visit to collect a small stipend and presents from the British of rifles and ammunition.

Aden port, meanwhile, had developed as a coaling point on the route to India. With the growth of Suez canal traffic, post-1869, the town itself began to grow, attracting a diaspora-colonial population of, for instance, Indians (already about 40 per cent of Aden's people in 1856) and the beginnings of a Yemeni migrant population from further north who slaved in the coaling trade. By the 1890s half of Aden's population was Arab, mainly from Ḥugariyyah and al-Bayḍāʾ, but few workers came from the immediate hinterland. (This pattern will be important later; between the port and its source of labour there lay a gap.) Near Aden, people grew vegetables and fodder for the town. The port itself, however, connected most immediately in Britain's maritime empire with Suez and India, London and Singapore, while relations between town and hinterland were largely between officials and what became known as the "treaty chiefs".

The treaty system, as with most things British, "just growed", but connections with these notables figured in grand strategy when, in 1873, a note was sent to Istanbul warning the Ottomans off from Aden and claiming nine "tribes" as under British protection. From 1886 formal Treaties of Protection were signed.[21] The Sultan or Shaykh or Amir (no standard terminology existed) pledged not to alienate territory to any foreign power without Britain's permission; and Britain extended in return "the gracious favour and protection of Her Majesty the Queen-Empress" or later the King-Emperor. Turkey and Britain, between 1902 and 1904, drew a line dividing their separate areas.[22] The line was agreed in 1905. In due course the two imperial powers laid a ruler on the map and drew a further line from near Ḥarīb northeast across Arabia to somewhere near Qaṭar.

The compound line from the coast at Bāb al-Mandab inland was ratified in March 1914. This defined not sovereignty or administration but merely areas where each power, British and Ottoman, agreed the other should not trespass: in other words, "spheres of influence". In the long term, long after both powers had left, it defined two Yemens. At no point did Yaḥyā accept its validity, claiming always the right to rule all Yemen, and the signatories to the agreement were themselves very soon at war. As of 1915, their border line seemed a dead letter.

PREMODERN YEMEN

Traditionally, in Arabic literature, Yemen reached from the Indian Ocean and Red Sea coasts in a huge parabola across the middle of all Arabia, which was roughly the extent of pre-Islamic kingdoms such as Saba' and Ḥimyar and their client tribes. To anyone well read in Arabic the idea would have been familiar.[23] This was not a world of settled frontiers, however, nor yet of state power in the modern form. In the years around 1900, sundry practical connections made parts of Yemen real and immediate but political uniformity was not among them, nor would legend by itself, no matter how embedded in Islamic learning, explain the course of politics. What, then, was Yaḥyā claiming?

John Wilkinson, the great geographer and historian of Oman, provides an answer.[24] Throughout the history of Arabia, he argues, large-scale divisions have been recognised, each attaching to a circulation system. Oman, for instance, faces the Indian Ocean and its history has turned on the combination of oceanic trade to East Africa and South Asia with hinterland support. Central Arabia traditionally is Najd. Its connections face northward through the Syrian *bādiyyah* (countryside, steppe; the place where badu live) and towards Iraq. The Ḥijāz, on Arabia's western edge, by contrast, abuts the Red Sea and connects primarily with Sinai and Egypt, and even now, under Saudi government, Najd and Ḥijāz are really quite distinct.

Yemen is the Peninsula's southern part. It is separated from Oman by a sparsely populated belt of territory where people speak languages other than Arabic and pursue ways of life distinct from their neighbours' (a border in the modern style was drawn amicably between Yemen and Oman in 1991; one could have drawn it a little west or east without upsetting anyone), while north of Ḥaḍramawt and east of Ṣaʿdah is a sea of sand. A few specialists were able to cross this but no-one lived there. It cuts the more densely settled areas of Yemen off from those of Najd as clearly

Plate 1.2. The *zaptiyeh* or local gendarmerie.

as the sea cuts Britain off from Holland, and only recently has anyone thought to draw political lines. The Red Sea and Indian Ocean define Yemen's other flanks. The one direction in which Yemen might connect with or merge into something else is along the mountains of Ḥijāz, up the Red Sea coast – but there one comes to Mecca and thus, since the rise of Islam, to discontinuity. The area has usually been held by Islamic empires or local powers standing outside the larger forms of politics.[25]

Separated from the Peninsula's other regions by natural and political barriers, Yemen faced its neighbours across the Red Sea. Links with India, the East Indies and East Africa have also been important. Yemen, like Scotland or Ireland, has often exported population, and in Islam's first centuries Yemeni names spread through much of the known world with the result that there are "Yemenis" real or imagined in many places across Africa and Eurasia. Mostly, however, the country's history has been its own. There is just enough there in the way of natural resources to sustain an autonomous history and sufficient mix of ecologies to make this complex.

Yemen's "bread basket" was the mountainous region around Taʿizz, Ibb, and Jiblah: together with the less fertile area of Ḥugariyyah, this is

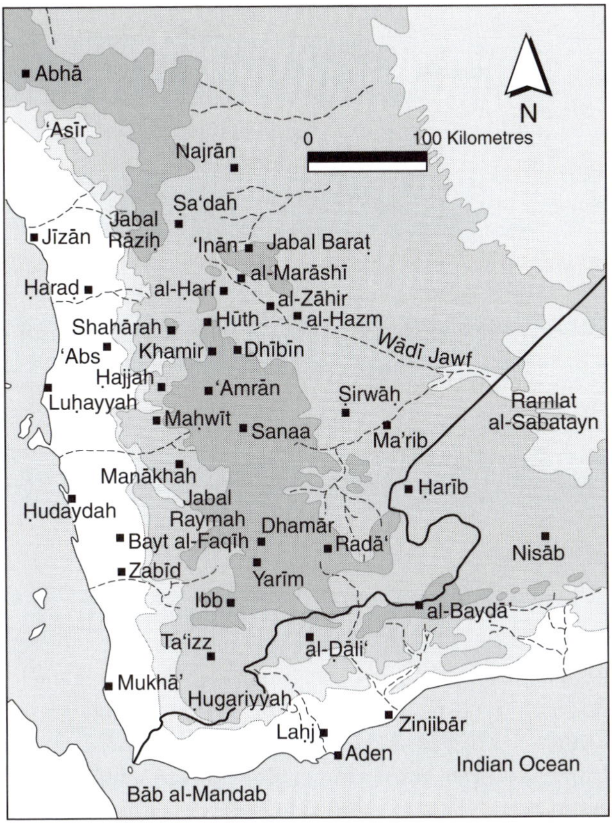

Map 1.2. Yemen in detail, north and west

Lower Yemen (Map. 1.2). Rainfall near Ibb is almost 1,000 mm per annum. The mountains are terraced, the productive capacity is immense, and the agricultural wealth of the region, if nothing else, makes this the "real" Yemen. It was here and in the mountains west of Sanaa that coffee was once so important. People further north will often say Yemen and mean Lower Yemen, which etymologically is easy to follow for "Yemen" once perhaps meant "to the right of" and hence usually "south of" Central Arabia.[26] But people further south again may also say Yemen and mean the same mountain farming area around Ibb and Taʿizz. Further still to the south lies the port of Aden, the "eye" of Yemen as it was sometimes called, which potentially ties southwest Arabia into oceanic trade.[27] States that held the port and the agricultural zone would

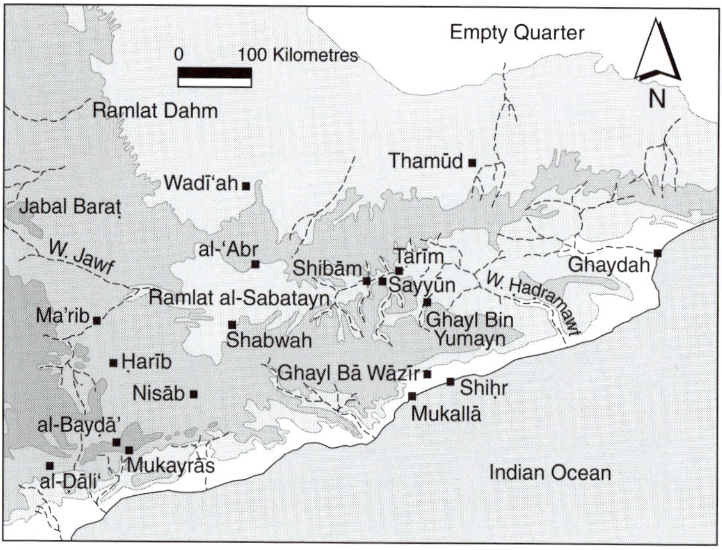

Map 1.3. Yemen in detail, south and east

have the makings of a solid tax-base, though no-one since the fourteenth-century Rasūlid dynasty had exploited that potential to have Lower Yemen dominate other areas.

Northwards is Upper Yemen, an ecologically much poorer region that includes Sanaa; and Ṣaʿdah, seven days' march north again of Sanaa, was the original centre of the Zaydī Imams. Much of Yemeni history concerns the north–south axis along the mountain spine from there to the agricultural zone near Taʿizz. Sometimes northerners had invaded the south; more often they had drifted south under pressure of scarce resources (average rainfall at Ṣaʿdah is a quarter of that near Ibb) and simply integrated into Lower Yemen. People did not move the other way, however. The relation between the highlands' two poles was not symmetrical, and among the great landlords of Lower Yemen in the years around 1900 were families from further north.

To the east of the mountain chain lies Wādī Jawf and Ma'rib, the site of a great pre-Islamic city but in 1900 hardly more than a village on the edge of the nomad, desert world (Yaḥyā claimed control of Ma'rib in 1909), and further east again lies the valley system of Wādī Ḥaḍramawt (Map 1.3). The plateau through which the valley runs is barren, but the wadi itself allows intensive cultivation and Ḥaḍramawt's particular history ties in closely with India and Southeast Asia: the Foreign Minister of Indonesia for many years, ʿAlī al-ʿAṭṭās, came from an old Ḥaḍramī family. Such connections go back to the fifteenth century. The number of Ḥaḍramīs in the Dutch East Indies, and then also in Singapore, rose enormously in the nineteenth century, however, and made parts of the wadi rich, while other Ḥaḍramīs were elsewhere in the Arab World, East Africa or India. Perhaps a quarter of the population (nearly all of them male) were overseas. Without migrants' remittances, states in the area were not viable, but with those remittances certain families were wealthy by European standards.[28]

The less productive areas of Ḥaḍramawt were the site of a vigorous tribal system, as too were the areas around Sanaa and northwards which for centuries were dominated by Zaydī (Shiʿite) Imams. The crux of Zaydism was that legitimate rule descends through the Prophet's line, the line of his daughter Fāṭimah and son-in-law ʿAlī bin Abī Ṭālib. Such descendants of the Prophet are usually called *sayyid*s (also sometimes *sharīf*s; or ʿAlawīs, after ʿAlī bin Abī Ṭālib). Their venture in the northern parts of Yemen was launched in AD 896 around Ṣaʿdah by the first Imam, al-Hādī, and on occasion they had ruled enormous areas, Imams being properly men of the sword as well as of the book and righteousness: the Qāsimīs in the seventeenth century had briefly held most of Yemen (even Ḥaḍramawt for some years), and certain earlier Imams less enamoured of state forms had also been conquerors. The *sayyids* were important further south too, especially in Ḥaḍramawt. There the *sayyid* presence was established in AD 952 by a migrant from Iraq named Aḥmad ʿĪsā, but the venture he began was very different from that in the far north and the Shāfiʿī (Sunni) style of Islam, unlike the Zaydī, launched no great bids for power: *sayyid* influence was local, often built around mediation and sacred tombs, although family connections and connections of learning reached beyond particular towns or tribes. Lower Yemen (Taʿizz, Ibb and Ḥugariyyah) was Shāfiʿī also.[29] When families moved there from Upper Yemen they often simply became Shāfiʿī, and doctrinal markers such as forms of prayer were seldom a great issue.[30]

Along the Red Sea coast runs a plain called the Tihāmah which now is marginal to Yemen's politics (a standing joke runs, "Name an important Tihāmī politician"),[31] yet highlanders who have worked there enthuse, shamefacedly, about Tihāmī honesty and kindness. These people too are Shāfiʿīs. One of their towns, Zabīd, was still through the early twentieth century a centre of religious learning. It was famous also for its weaving and its indigo dyeing, and quite prosperous by the standards of the time with a population of perhaps 8,000, though its trade was being drawn towards Ḥudaydah port.[32] Certain lowland tribes, most importantly the Quḥrā and the Zarānīq, were powerful and the Turks never did control them, but they had not for a long time posed a threat to highlanders as the highlanders did to them.

The western mountains, which are Zaydī in the north, Shāfiʿī in the south, overlook the Tihāmah, and along the terraced mountain ridges run little villages built of stone, usually the same three- or four-storey fortified houses that characterise the highlands from Ḥūth down through Taʿizz and ʿAwdhalī: grain and livestock were kept on the ground floor, while the family crammed in to little rooms of the upper storeys. Northwest to southeast behind this, from Ṣaʿdah and Najrān out to Ḥaḍramawt, runs a multi-storey architecture of packed mud. Along the Red Sea coast runs a third architectural complex where low mud and coral houses or compounds built of brush and thorn resemble dwellings on the coast of Muslim East Africa. Nowhere were there many tents, however. Some tribes in the east, such as Dahm of Bakīl, overlap with the North Arabian nomadic world, and certain tribes of North Arabia claim Yemeni origins, but Yemen was primarily a farming country and most pastoralists were subordinate or marginal to farming tribes who themselves often owned significant amounts of livestock.

In Wādī Ḥaḍramawt and at a few sites elsewhere date-palms were grown intensively. The Wādī was spate-fed (that is, run-off came as flash floods), as also were the wadis running south to Laḥj, east to Maʾrib, and westward from the mountains to the Red Sea coast, where a major crop was often millet (*dukhn*) or sorghum (*dhurah*). Sorghum is drought resistant. One finds it nearly everywhere in Yemen, including the highlands, for nearly everywhere the rains are unreliable and drought was a constant fear. In the highlands one also finds wheat and barley. Besides small quantities of vegetables, sesame for oil, indigo for dye, some tobacco in the lowlands as a cash crop, Yemen depended largely on grain, and bread or porridge was what most people lived on. Around the coast people fished. In the mountains the better off ate mutton.

In the highlands one other cash crop deserves noting, *qāt*. This is a mildly narcotic leaf which Yemenis have been chewing among themselves for centuries, and as the value of coffee declined so *qāt* sometimes took its place. Around 1900, probably, most people lacked the means to chew all that much, but if they could, men chewed as they always had done at afternoon parties where affairs of all kinds are discussed and one's contacts maintained with kin and neighbours. Such a party is called a *maqīl* (or *maqyal*, as some have it), an occasion for "talk", and it was customary before lunch and *qāt* to make a *dawrah*, a "round" of the neighbourhood to admire the view and work up a taste for chewing.

Women's parties were sometimes called *tafrīṭah*s, and we hear little of them. Nor are we meant to, for the privacy of women was a key motif in manners. Muḥammad al-Akwa's mother, for instance, who died young in about 1908, was remembered by her husband as a paragon of virtue and wifely competence, and he told a story about her against himself, recounted here by their son Muḥammad:

> He used to say his noon prayers each day at the appropriate time in the mosque at the upper end of Dhārī village, and sometimes he would hear the sound of my mother laughing, really very clearly. The mosque in question was some way off. He was shamed and embarrassed in front of people . . . My father would come back embarrassed and upset, and he'd blame her and tell her off. He used to say to her that a woman's voice is shameful . . . She would face him, laughing out loud still, and laugh even more, saying jokingly, "Chastity's guarded [Dear?] and your secrets are safe with me".[33]

The idea that a woman's voice was shameful occurred in jurisprudence: in an ideal male world, women's voices should not have been heard by unrelated men. "Wishful thinking!", says Martha Mundy. One imagines that a hundred years ago Yemeni women were as forceful as they now are, but to turn history inside out and write in a female voice would require sources no-one yet commands.

Separation of the sexes, forms of greeting, conventions of dress and deference, made up an elaborate moral order in the countryside and towns alike. That order rested on weak foundations. Al-Akwaʿ, remembering Turkish times from the vantage of old age, relates how the major grain harvest came all at once in late summer, when as the saying went, "there is nothing yet and nothing left"; before the harvest was gathered, all last year's may have been used up. People fell into debt. A rich landowner might open his grain-pits (*madāfin*), weighing out and writing down all that was loaned to poorer farmers, and in the process perhaps gaining lien on their land, but "if it happened that the shaykh did not open the grain-pits, there was great commotion and grief, and they would return broken-hearted, dumb-founded, overcome with sorrow and misery . . ."[34] In many years people starved. When the rains came, by contrast, people celebrated: everywhere in rural areas star-lore, work-songs and proverbial wisdom about crops and animals formed the texture of everyday life, and the chronicles, with an eye to the towns and the state of the country generally, often mention grain prices. The sale of produce was handled through middlemen. But all over Yemen were rural markets, each held on a particular day of the week, and al-Akwaʿ remembers one near his own village where thousands of people would gather each market day: "the road was like a village of ants".

The variety of tradition and practice in Yemen was immense. Yet the regions were tied together. The routes where local trade ran were the same routes along which incense moved in pre-Islamic times and dates, salt, and pilgrims have moved at most times since; the traditions, partly set in literature, of South Arabian genealogy were known in fragments everywhere (the names of places and of major groups, save the Prophet's kin, all attach to Qaḥṭān, "the father of the Southern Arabs"). More than this, there were similar institutions in different areas. In most of the southern and eastern parts of Yemen, for instance, all the way out through Ḥaḍramawt, there used to be protected towns and markets called *ḥawṭah*s, which often were associated with saints or holy families. They provided a kind of neutral space in which people from different tribes could meet freely, and around them were built systems of trade and arbitration. North of Sanaa one found *hijrah*s. Saints there were not the norm, for veneration of the dead was often thought anathema by Zaydī scholars, but the *hijrah*, like the *ḥawṭah*, was a protected place where tribes used to meet and trade and arbitration centred.[35]

POLITICAL CONNECTIONS

From the Imam's point of view, soon after 1900, there were few natural limits to his ambition. Historically, Zaydī Imams had occasionally held all Yemen and seldom more than that, but the high pan-Islamic hopes of their ancestors circa AD 900 lingered still in their title "Commander of [all] the Faithful". The Ottomans, while their presence lasted, never formally ceded their own right to rule the Islamic World, of which Arabia, including Yemen, formed a vital part as the "cradle of Islam". The British in Aden hardly aimed so high. They wanted a strategic base, then as it turned out a coaling station, then a prosperous port, and then, at the end of their time (in the 1960s), a strategic base again. Their tenure throughout was fraught with trouble over who in the British system decided policy. But they also faced brute geography.

> To hindsight there were only two valid alternatives: either the whole hinterland should have been subjected to outright occupation and imperial disciplines, or Aden should have been isolated from it but rendered impregnable, leaving the

interior to its own (or Ottoman or Yemeni) devices. Neither alternative was adopted.[36]

The second option would have been difficult. Aden, the rock fortress, has no water supply. Nor can one grow much in Aden town. One has to be involved with the hinterland to survive, and the "Aden hinterland", to adopt a view from this tiny foothold the British held, in fact connects with all of Yemen.

The man Captain Haines opened talks with in the 1830s was the Sultan of Laḥj, a town just north of Aden (properly the town is al-Ḥawṭah, the protected place). The Sultan used to own the port. Negotiations before the British seized Aden involved the ʿAbdalī Sultan of Laḥj requesting arms to see off his neighbours, the Faḍlī Sultans and tribes; a later Laḥj proposal was that stipends they had paid to outlying tribes should now be paid by the British through them, thus affirming their paramountcy. Haines was drawn willingly into Laḥj politics. But even these were not strictly localised. In 1871, for instance, a sultan of Laḥj asked for British help to occupy Taʿizz and Ḥugariyyah, which were coffee areas north of the later Anglo-Turkish line. Laḥj depended heavily on trade revenue. Why not cut out the middleman, own the coffee, own the route, and also have access to a major port? To advance his scheme he secured a vast loan from Muḥsin al-ʿAwlaqī.[37] The ʿAwlaqīs are a tribe to the east and north of Aden, and Muḥsin himself was then a *jemadar* (officer) with the Nizām of Hyderabad in India. The British note to the Ottomans in 1873 claiming nine "tribes" was an expression of a Laḥj sphere of influence; but the mention of India suggests how far abroad others within that sphere had their own connections. And none of this mapped as concentric circles.

In the 1840s, the British Resident in Aden conspired with an Imam of the day against Sharīf Ḥusayn of Abū ʿArīsh, who held much of the Tihāmah, the land along the Red Sea coast. Abū ʿArīsh is enormously far north, nowadays in Saudi Arabia. The Imam, in dire straits, had offered Captain Haines the whole of Tihāmah, Taʿizz and Ḥugariyyah. Later Imams held Lower Yemen (the object of Laḥjī and ʿAwlaqī designs) with tribesmen of Dhū Muḥammad and Dhū Ḥusayn from Jabal Baraṭ, a region at almost the latitude of Abū ʿArīsh but inland near the desert. The Yāfiʿī tribes, much nearer to hand and south of the Anglo-Turkish line, had also an interest in Lower Yemen: often they were used as mercenaries against Dhū Muḥammad and Dhū Ḥusayn. They spread the other way too, west to east into Ḥaḍramawt, while Ḥaḍramī merchants and scholars had themselves migrated east to west into towns such as Ibb and Taʿizz. Within "Natural Yemen" there were simply no natural boundaries.

There were, however, certain shapes of history, and the map of Yemen around 1900 shows the calcified trace of earlier upheavals. The great shaykhly families of Upper Yemen (the leading families of major tribes named Ḥāshid and Bakīl), for instance, date to the early Qāsimī period, circa 1700; Imams had then overrun most of Yemen, their troops had been tribesmen, and the shaykhs won land beyond their own sparse territory. That non-tribal land they often still owned. As the Qāsimī state collapsed it was northern tribes who fought for the rival claimants, but the tribes' leading families did not claim power in their own names and in this respect the South was different. The *dawlah*s or petty states of the South had split off from the Qāsimīs (the ʿAbdalī Sultans of Laḥj did so in 1728) and had been there ever since, as had their connections with specific tribes. Yāfiʿ, for instance, had a memory of expelling the Imams:

> Your fathers before you,
> Who passed on in early times,
> Red of cheek expelled the Turks and Zaydīs.
> Qaḥṭān took it all
> From Maʿsāl to the coast of Aden.[38]

The Sultans of Yāfiʿ, intermarried with the ʿAbdalīs of Laḥj, claimed descent from learned rulers of the sixteenth century. The Amirs of Ḍāliʿ held documentary proof of their importance from the same period.

There were long established families in the North too, and the Sharaf al-Dīns, who just predate the Qāsimīs, were still addressed as "princes" of Kawkabān, a little north and west of Sanaa. But no-one else in Upper Yemen claimed to be a *dawlah*. Nor did anyone in Lower Yemen, the region around Ibb and Taʿizz. There one had certain great families who controlled wide areas, as most still do, but the *dawlah* in their world was the Qāsimī Zaydī *dawlah* and many people loathed its memory: in Ibb, for instance, the Faqīh Saʿīd, whom a Zaydī Imam had executed as in effect a heretic, "is a popular figure in local oral history . . ."[39] There were no recent *dawlah*s well spoken of in Lower Yemen save that of the Ottomans. What there were instead were Sufi orders and tombs of saints. Ibn ʿAlwān near Taʿizz, for instance, was venerated far afield (well south of the Anglo-Turkish line) and his devotees were everywhere known by their drums and iron-shod staves. He died in 1267. Many thought he had ruled a *dawlah*. In Taʿizz itself are the tombs of several kings and saints; in Jiblah is the tomb of Queen Arwā (d. 1137). The shadows of past greatness did not inspire coherent attempts at self-rule but rather forms of piety and memory which left power to the (Sunni) Turks.

To the north and west lay a ruler of more recent provenance, Muḥammad al-Idrīsī. His family – relatives of the Sanūsīs who after World War II were Kings of Libya – came originally from Morocco, and this branch established itself in ʿAsīr, a Sunni region, after study and residence in Mecca.[40] Aḥmad al-Idrīsī (d. 1837) had a reputation as a holy man and worker of miracles. His grandson Muḥammad al-Idrīsī we have seen rejecting Yaḥyā's truce with the Ottomans, but the region he dominated was very much part of Zaydī history for the "Mikhlāf Sulaymānī", which takes its name from a governor of the Banī Ziyād (c. AD 1000), was controlled for centuries by collateral relatives of the Imam ʿAbdullāh bin Hamzah.[41] After the truce of 1911 the Idrīsī attracted shaykhs of several nominally Zaydī tribes. Rival Zaydī Imams, one of whom endured around Ṣaʿdah until 1923, never threatened Yaḥyā's support to the same degree and through World War I the Idrīsī was Yaḥyā's main rival. The only other claimants to prominence, apart from Britain and Turkey, were far away.

ʿAwlaqī families, as we saw, were involved not only with Laḥj and Lower Yemen but also with India as mercenaries, specifically with Hyderabad. So were other families such as the Quʿayṭīs and Kathīrīs of Ḥaḍramawt and Yāfiʿī families from further west (in the orbit of Taʿizz and of Aden) who, apart from their Indian connections, spread through Ḥaḍramawt as soldiers. Two Yāfiʿī factions held the ports of Shiḥr and Mukallā. In the mid-1800s ʿUmar ʿAwaḍ al-Quʿayṭī (himself from a wealthy dynasty of Yāfiʿī mercenaries) began to build a state – very clearly a *dawlah* – in Ḥaḍramawt and was opposed by Ghālib Muḥsin al-Kathīrī.[42] A full-scale war developed, with shifting alliances among Quʿayṭīs, Kathīrīs, ʿAwlaqīs and different groups from Yāfiʿ, sustained by money, weapons and even troops from India. The British were drawn in, partly because of India and shipping, partly to forestall the Ottomans. By the end of the nineteenth century the Quʿayṭī Sultanate held nearly all the coastline with a lesser Kathīrī state inland, and each had a stretch of Wādī Ḥaḍramawt, while to their east, filling most of the margin of what traditionally was Yemen, lay Mahrah.[43] Nominally this attached to the Sultan of Soqotra, an island in the Indian Ocean, but there was no administration in Mahrah, nor structures of formal learning.

FORMS OF LIFE

Western literature depicting a "forbidden kingdom" is misleading, for trade and learning alike have always linked Yemen to wider patterns in Islam,[44] but engagement with Europe's world produced specific changes and British authors concerned with the rural South stress the influx of modern weapons:

> when I first entered the country twelve years ago [1896?] I got to know every rifle by sight . . . There have been no intermediate stages . . . No, there was a direct leap from the old 'bindok' [matchlock musket] to carbines and rifles of Le Gras, M.H., and Snider patterns . . . In the hands of most members of a ruling house you will now find high velocity small-bores and smokeless ammunition.[45]

The British thereafter, right down through the 1960s, saw this as spinning old squabbles out of all control. There is something in what they say. Tribes are far from slaves of weaponry, however,[46] and the fate of Southern tribes, who around 1900 were indeed in a state of chronic warfare, remains to be explained fully. In the North, Imam Yaḥyā was to cut through the weapons issue with scant problem. But on neither side of the imagined line was there ever an age of pre-governmental bliss.

Turkish government of most Northern areas was sparse. The *zaptiyeh* or "gendarmerie", in which some hundreds of Yemenis served, offered a certain model of discipline and order, and administrative divisions established by the Ottomans have often lasted until the present day. Until World War II the Imam's own state would retain a mildly Turkish flavour, requiring foreign visitors, for instance, to wear Ottoman *kalpak*s or lamb's-wool caps as court dress. Even now, Turkish words still linger in Yemen's vocabulary. Perhaps the most important technical innovation, changing more obviously forms of politics, was the telegraph, which linked Taʿizz to Sanaa, for example, from 1902 or so: "at a time when the people still used camels, donkeys and horses . . . and the distance between Taʿizz and Sanaa was known as eight days, suddenly the telegraph shortened this to moments".[47] The rather primitive nineteenth-century "ground return" system of wires and buzzers was to be an important part of rule in the North until the 1960s, but outside the major towns Turkish hopes for reform made little progress.

Tribal areas north of Sanaa were grim when Glaser visited in the late nineteenth century and remained so until near our own time. The minor shaykhs there had tobacco and *qishr* (a drink made from spiced coffee-husks) and could even serve mutton to a guest; but the staple was bread or sorghum porridge, and bodily luxury meant smearing oneself with often rancid butter. "Oil lamps of the most primitive type provide light, and only the better shaykhs have a large, but very old fashioned candelabra with two candles." The windows were tiny. One would have lived in semi-darkness, and bugs and fleas apart, the squalor of life is easy to imagine: the memory is of half the children dying at birth or in infancy, the women would have toiled for hours to bring water from often foul and half-dry cisterns, and Glaser depicts a world among the men of constant disputes and armed panics.[48] The houses served as forts against one's neighbours. People seldom had enough to eat, and what Trevaskis later said of the South could be said of most tribal areas, the North included: "to look across the great thirsty expanse of rock, stone and sand with their few pathetic ribbons of dampness . . . is to feel the fear of famine".[49]

Elsewhere was agriculturally richer. Muḥammad al-Akwaʿ (born 1903) grew up in al-Dhārī, nine hours south of Dhamār. This is not the lush heartland of Ibb and Taʿizz, but the memoir mentions birds and trees and wadis more full of crops than one would usually see in ʿAwlaqī or north of Sanaa. The author's father was a minor judge, a cut above the peasantry. He bought in his *qāt* from elsewhere, and a lunch for important guests ran to meat and chicken, wheat-based bread which the author's mother made, *samn* (clarified butter) "of a soothing smell", white honey and eggs. That, however, required the mother to call in all her debts and good deeds among the neighbours. She was known as a good woman. Female networks of this kind, whereby meals appear that males find inexplicable (pots and pans pass around, meat is contributed, bread is baked), are the stuff of the everyday but seldom of explicit history. Nor are they egalitarian. Poorer people never fed so well.

Even a judge's family lived always in the shadow of death, and al-Akwaʿ knows his birth date because his father made a note of family movements at a time he himself almost died of fever. The author's mother died young in childbirth, which his father noted sadly in the margins of a standard work of Zaydī law, as Americans and Europeans used to list their deaths in the family Bible. His stepmother, for whom the author still said prayers in his seventies, died early too; and the memoir is littered with still-births, deaths in infancy and deaths later from disease. Smallpox swept the area. People's skin collapsed on itself like the mud on a fresh wall, and all one could do was lay them on finely sieved dirt or dust, hold their hands to prevent them touching their eyes (the disease often caused blindness) and fumigate them with smoke from dung.[50] One "depended on God".

Among al-Akwaʿ's memories are the locust hunts. Locusts were roasted as a feast, and in the course of the chase boys and girls could meet away from their parents' eyes. But if locusts swarmed in a wadi where crops were growing

> people would rush out wailing as if it were a funeral. They would come quickly from their homes not bothering about anything else, the children with the children and the women and the men in a yelling mob, carrying cane sticks with cloths tied on them, and they would rush through the farmland yelling at the top of their voices, "God's locusts, let God take care of you! Go away! Don't come back!"[51]

Often locusts stripped everything; a crop could be lost entirely. Nor did political disorder help. The author remembers the Turks and the Zaydī tribes fighting around Yarīm and people fleeing to mountain caves. The usual tales are related of tribesmen eating soap which they thought was sugar and shooting at their own reflections in mirrors, which supposedly they had never seen before, and al-Akwaʿ saw a tribesman driving a cow laden down with loot from the town's pillage. Townspeople, scholars and non-tribal farmers alike regarded "the tribes" as savages.

The labels "shaykh" and "tribesman" (*qabīlī*, pl. *qabāʾil*) were used widely of people in rural areas, as indeed they still are, but in many areas the tribesmen, so called, did not belong to really much of a tribe. Their relation to their local shaykhs was largely that of peasants to greater landowners. In the ecologically richer areas of the western mountains from Rāziḥ through Maḥwīt and Raymah to Wuṣāb this was common, as it was more intensely in Lower Yemen. In the dryer areas of Upper Yemen, dominated by major groupings of tribes named Ḥāshid and Bakīl, however, one is dealing with something different, as one is in, for instance, ʿAwlaqī or Yāfiʿ in the South. Here tribal divisions were of real importance. Shaykhs usually did not control tribesmen's land. They sometimes owned extensive land elsewhere (as Ḥāshid and Bakīl shaykhs owned land west or south of their homelands), or there were localised areas of more intensive production within tribal territory worked largely by non-tribesmen while tribesmen held less fertile land and worked it for themselves (this was common in the South, the Aden hinterland).[52] The "real" tribes, by local reckoning, lived in areas that produced little economic surplus; the more productive areas had social structures a later generation would paint as "feudal" and populations spoken of long before that as "subjects" (*rāʿyā* or *raʿiyyah*). We can fairly say peasants as opposed to tribesmen.[53]

Tribal identity is often expressed, through a loose metaphor, in kin

Plate 1.3. Dhamār in 1911.

terms. One does not in those terms stand with outsiders against one's immediate relatives: one makes history instead against more distant "relatives", the tribe or section of a tribe next door. Such contests among people in the same moral system are sometimes all that matters, and states, even empires with their grand pretensions, become pawns in games of local interest. This is something of a theme in Yemen's history. Within the local world one can also, as linguists say, "shift register", and in the name of Islam or the nation or revolution, not tribalism, one can turn against immediate kin and neighbours. Two brothers at odds may seek help, perhaps, from different governments.

Amidst the tribes, who were mainly farmers and whose unwritten histories were made locally against their neighbours, were the towns, not least Sanaa. Sanaanis had sometimes, when public order collapsed, acted as a tribe of their own against others, but here, despite punctilious differences of rank among families and professions, was a bloc of people with a less confrontational vision of events ("unwarlike, yet rancorous", said an English visitor, "always ripe for sedition, yet shrinking from its bloody issue"; the Yemeni view, one might note, was and is of a city full of subtle humourists).[54] The Old City was set around with a vast mud wall. Within this were famous mosques, gardens, and extraordinary mud-brick houses, sometimes five or six storeys high, picked out in whitewash and elaborate brickwork. The Jewish quarter lay about 1.5 kilometres southwest of there, and in the nineteenth century a wall had been thrown around the whole area, connecting Qāʿ al-Yahūd to the Old City. The space between, known as Bīr al-ʿAzab, filled with farms and gardens where Turkish officers and functionaries had their houses. Sanaa's place as a Turkish capital made it prosperous. It recovered quite quickly from the disaster of the 1905 siege, and its inhabitants by late in World War I were probably almost as numerous as in 1900 (perhaps 40–50,000), drawing wealth not so much from the city's hinterland as from Turkish Yemen.

Towns elsewhere in the North were small. In Upper Yemen (the Zaydī part) were Ṣaʿdah, Ḥūth, Shahārah and ʿAmrān; all but the last were centres of Islamic learning. In Lower Yemen (the Shāfiʿī part) were Taʿizz, Ibb and Jiblah. In Ḥaḍramawt (also Shāfiʿī) were the port of Mukallā and such inland towns as Shibām, Sayyūn and Tarīm, the last of which is popularly said to have so many mosques – most very small, of course – that one could pray in a different one each day of the year. In the late 1930s Mukallā was thought to number about 15,000 people and the inland wadi towns close to 10,000 each: even if one halved the numbers for 1900, as almost certainly one should, these would still have been major centres. Ḥudaydah, on the Red Sea coast, is hard to estimate, for it seems to wax and wane freely with passing trade, but in 1913 was prosperous: "the wealthier classes live in tall, white houses, and pervade the sandy streets in flowing robes, silk waistcoats and expensive turbans – all imported from Europe or India".[55] Aden, meanwhile, was already by 1900 almost as large as Sanaa, with some 40,000 people. But while Aden in its modern form was still a shanty town – the squalid bloom of new economic forces – Sanaa with its decorated tall mud houses, winding streets and famous mosques was the battered expression of a much older moral order which according to tradition reaches back to the sons of Noah.

The world outside the towns was as complex as that within them. Tribesmen, the vast majority of many regions' population, bore arms. Most were farmers, a few were nomads, nearly all were extremely poor. Their chiefs or shaykhs were occasionally leaders, more often arbitrators, but the position ran in families and a few of these were powerful because of land elsewhere; the shaykhs of most peasant areas, by contrast, were not powerful far afield but their local dominance was considerable.

*Sayyid*s (descendants of the Prophet) claimed everywhere a certain precedence. In the South there were also *mashāyikh*, religious families of a different descent, and in the North families of *qāḍī*s (non-*sayyid* "judges") were as prominent. Everywhere one found "weak" people who lacked either tribal or religious honour and whose men were not permitted to bear arms: some were share-croppers, some were artisans, others (the lowest of the low) were butchers, messengers and sweepers. People, despite their poverty, owned slaves. Here and there were communities of Jews, some engaged in craft manufacture but many simply farming like their Muslim neighbours.[56] The distinctions of rank were endless and a great deal depended on descent.

The position of *sayyid*s – descendants of the Prophet and themselves rather specialists in descent, for they maintained broad, detailed genealogies of a kind no-one else did – was ambiguous nearly everywhere in Yemen: some were poor, some were rich, some were learned and others not. They were scarcely a class in the modern sense. But generally they exacted a degree of respect and they refused to have their women marry non-*sayyid*s, a principle which was challenged first in 1905 among Ḥaḍramīs in Singapore. In 1915 the challenge took form, again overseas, in Java, as the Irshādī movement, of which we shall see more in Ḥaḍramawt later on. In the North, by contrast, at about the same time, the rise to power of Imam Yaḥyā (himself, of course, a *sayyid*) gave many *sayyid* families a stake in what emerged as a *dawlah* – a state, and then a dynasty, which far outweighed the little *dawlah*s of South Yemen and claimed a place of its own on the world map.

CHAPTER TWO

Yaḥyā and the British: 1918–1948

In World War I Britain's "sphere of influence" was not defended. British forces were pushed back even from Laḥj – "the Turks are on the golf course" ran a signal from Aden's garrison – and there they stayed until 1918, concerned with sea routes from India to Suez. Against Imam Yaḥyā after World War I Britain showed more resolution. Yaḥyā himself, between 1918 and 1934, conquered much of Yemen and built a state in the North to which, as R. J. Gavin suggests, the South emerged gradually as an antithesis; the state in the North meanwhile had to be invented, morally as much as otherwise, in circumstances new to Yemenis.

CONTROL OF YEMEN

Early in December 1918 Yaḥyā was informed by the Turkish Governor that Ottoman troops must be withdrawn and that "Franks" (Europeans) would occupy the Empire. Yaḥyā garrisoned the western approach to Sanaa and two days later entered Sanaa himself, staying at the house of Ḥusayn al-ʿAmrī – the *qāḍī* who had once been his teacher and who in 1911 had mediated with the Turks. Within weeks the British were landing at Ḥudaydah. Colonel H. F. Jacob left from there in August 1919 for Sanaa, but the Quḥrā tribe of the Tihāmah, fearful of what deal he might do with the Imam, imprisoned him and the Imam's attempts to buy him out (thus to discover what was going on) all failed. After Jacob's release, the British left Ḥudaydah not to Yaḥyā, as he thought they had promised, but instead to his rival the Idrīsī, and he ordered his own troops to hold Shuʿayb, Quṭayb and Ḍāliʿ. All these were south of the old Anglo-Turkish line and the garrisons were drawn from Zaydī tribes near Sanaa.

Later Shāfiʿī writers, such as Muḥammad Aḥmad Nuʿmān, depict the period as a Zaydī conquest of Shāfiʿī territory. It was not so simple. There were ample disputes among local leaders south of Sanaa, and some who were prominent under Turkish rule hoped for independent power (a meeting of Shāfiʿī notables at al-ʿAmāqī came to nothing; in places the Turkish flag was raised). Many more, however, fought for position under Yaḥyā's suzerainty. Yaḥyā's campaign against the Ḥubayshīs at Makhādir, north of Ibb, for instance, was supported by shaykhs of Ibb and al-ʿUdayn. A dispute between two shaykhs (one a Sufi leader) from Jabal Ṣabir beside Taʿizz, both of whose influence extended to Mukhāʾ on the Red Sea coast, led to serious fighting; one was opposed by the shaykhs of Āl Nuʿmān, great Shāfiʿī landowners of Ḥugariyyah who had flourished under Turkish rule, and when a lesser shaykh attempted to escape Nuʿmān "authority" (*sulṭah*) the Imam supported Āl Nuʿmān. The brutality of the fighting is in little doubt. Powers, to start with, however, were confirmed and co-opted in Lower Yemen more than overturned.[1]

Zaydī tribes disputed Yaḥyā's control as they had always done, and through the 1920s as many skirmishes were fought against "rebels" (*bughāh*) north of Sanaa as south. Ḥāshid, for example, had supported the Imam against the Turks in the fighting of 1910–11 and Yaḥyā had lived among them through much of World War I; in December 1924, however, Imamic forces fought their way into Ḥāshid's main town, Khamir, and "set their affairs in order", taking hostages from Banī Ṣuraym and Khārif and billeting troops on them "as is done to subjects other than them in all the Imamic lands" (the urban chronicler's satisfaction is plain here, though committed to print three decades later; the term "subjects" denies any difference between tribes and peasants). Arḥab, a Bakīl tribe nearby, had also to surrender hostages. Al-ʿUṣaymāt and ʿIdhar, two Ḥāshid tribes in the region near Shahārah where Yaḥyā first claimed the Imamate in 1904, were left alone after swearing their nominal allegiance.

Not until 1928 was all Ḥāshid under the Imam's control, and not until the 1930s did he control the east around Maʾrib – such tribes as ʿAbīdah and Murād, importantly – or the northeast near Jabal Baraṭ, the homeland of Dhū Muḥammad and Dhū Ḥusayn. His progress around Taʿizz was more rapid. When a number of Lower Yemeni leaders conspired in the 1920s (perhaps specifically against Zaydī rule; the sources obscure the issue) Yaḥyā had large numbers of shaykhs sent in chains to Sanaa where few survived.[2] But the most important did so. Indeed ʿAbd al-Wahhāb Nuʿmān, the great baron of Ḥugariyyah, re-emerged for a time as governor of Bilād al-Bustān near Sanaa. The pattern throughout was of negotiation, blandishments and severity of a kind hard to summarise, for one shaykh was used against another, one tribe against another, amid shifting complexities which the language of *jihād* obscures. In the midst of this the rudiments of state power emerged. A shaykh of Hamdān, just north of Sanaa, felt he deserved more consideration and Yaḥyā asked him angrily, "Who made you a shaykh?" "The same as made you Imam", came the answer; but Yaḥyā gained means before long to have ʿAlī Muṭlaq chained in a dungeon for twenty years.[3]

In 1919, two thousand men were levied from tribes near Sanaa and trained "according to the rules of the Turkish army". (A good many Turks individually had elected to stay on.) A Yemeni historian does justice to the novelty:

> The army was divided into numbered *ṭābūr*s, or "detachments", so the first was called the first *ṭābūr*, the second called the second *ṭābūr*, and so on. Three *ṭābūr*s together were called a *liwāʾ*, and three *liwāʾ*s were called a *firqah*, and the whole together was called the Victorious Regular Army. Every *ṭābūr* was made up of four *bloc*s . . . and each of them had its number, the first and the second and so forth.[4]

Unlike tribal levies, this army had a fixed pay scale. The officers were mainly Turkish – indeed, instruction remained in Turkish until the 1930s; some, though, were Yemenis who had been to Turkish schools and command was given to ʿAbdullāh Ḍumayn, a *sayyid* from the Jawf who had served with the Turks in the rank of *bekbāshī*. "The Imam expended the utmost effort on this and showed enormous interest", and in the next year four *ṭābūr*s more were raised around Taʿizz. The number of regulars rose to 15–20,000. A school for telegraphists was opened, allowing the Imam's care for detail to reach everywhere.

Yaḥyā's claim was to "establish the true *sharīʿah*" and such divisions as tribes proved to count for little, for greater shaykhs could be by-passed in favour of lesser or the great could be turned in the name of religion against each other. Epithets such as "evil ones" and "servants of idols" were used of people who themselves served as allies in God's cause against their neighbours, and from those whose obedience mattered the Imam took hostages (by the 1930s there were probably about 4,000). At family level there was often resentment. All larger identities were irrelevant when the call was made, however, for there were no other forms of claim to righteous order, nor means to organise, and Yaḥyā at first had only one effective rival.

Muḥammad ʿAlī al-Idrīsī, based in ʿAsīr, had been at odds with Yaḥyā since the 1911 truce. In 1915 the British signed a treaty with him against the Turks (from 1917 they paid a stipend), and after the war he gained from them Ḥudaydah; but he also signed an agreement with ʿAbd al-ʿAzīz Ibn Saʿūd, then Sultan of Najd, late in 1920. Ibn Saʿūd at this date seemed a long way from Yemeni concerns. The Idrīsī himself, however, attracted wide support, not least from Bayt al-Aḥmar the paramount shaykhs of Ḥāshid (ʿAlī Daḥḥān al-Aḥmar and Nāṣir Nāṣir al-Aḥmar in turn both went to him), and just after World War I, Yaḥyā al-Shāyif of Dhū Ḥusayn at Baraṭ, among the greatest of Bakīl tribes, had appeared in Aden as his spokesman, promoting a "confederation" to include, as the British were told, "Zaydīs and Shāfiʿīs and Ismāʿīlīs".[5] After 1918 many of Yaḥyā's battles in the fertile mountains overlooking the Tihāmah – from Rāziḥ in the north, through al-Ḥaymah and Raymah, to Wuṣāb in the south – were contests with the Idrīsī state.[6]

Muḥammad al-Idrīsī died in 1923 and the British, more concerned with the Imam, abandoned the Idrīsīs to their fate. The Imam was scarcely privy to British policy, however. Before World War I the Italians had supported the Idrīsī against the Turks, for which Yaḥyā condemned him as a *kāfir* (infidel), but with Britain to face near Aden and the Idrīsīs seeking British help, Yaḥyā himself now signed a treaty with Italy (1926), which had colonies across the Red Sea.[7] The Italians sold him an arms workshop and machinery to strike a handsome new coinage, the silver riyāl being marked "Commander of the Faithful, al-Mutawakkil ʿalā Allāh (he who relies on God)". He sent his favourite son, Muḥammad, on a mission to Italy. A little later the eldest son, Aḥmad, arrived in Sanaa from Ḥajjah: "There went out to meet him the princes and learned men, the nobility and merchants, and all the people. The soldiers and bandsmen went out, and he arrived in a huge procession . . . When he left Ḥajjah each tribe in turn received him until he arrived at Sanaa with a vast gathering."[8]

Connections of religious learning provided governors and judges, the greatest of whom were from famous *sayyid* families. ʿAbdullāh al-Wazīr, for instance, who had aided Yaḥyā at Dhamār in 1915, was a leading figure in the conquest of Lower Yemen, cleared the province of al-Bayḍā' in the Zaydī cause, and fought Ḥāshid at Khamir: he emerged as Governor of Ibb and later of Ḥudaydah. ʿAlī al-Wazīr, who had acted for Yaḥyā in the siege of Sanaa (1911), was from 1920 Governor of Taʿizz, where his court rivalled that of the Imam.[9] Such major figures held the title "commander" or "prince" (*amīr*). Another of the al-Wazīrs, Muḥammad, governed Dhamār for a time. But the other imposing figure already by the 1920s was Aḥmad, son of Yaḥyā. More a warrior than his father yet also a wit and poet, he terrified most people: his appearance was alarming, his ferocity a by-word and his temper volatile. There are stories of how, as a young man still studying the rudiments of law, he forced his age-mates at knife-point to promise one day to support him as Imam.[10]

The shaykhs of northern (Zaydī) tribes, who in 1918 had entered Sanaa beside Yaḥyā, were less important. Many had given daughters to great *sayyid* houses. They retained their lands and a certain precedence, and many received a percentage of tax they gathered. But their independence, once the Idrīsī disappeared as a balance to the Imam, was circumscribed.[11] Abū Ra'ṣ of Dhū Muḥammad and al-Shāyif of Dhu Ḥusayn, for instance, though their tribes in the far north remained beyond Yaḥyā's control for years yet, were in Lower Yemen simply landowners among others and Shāfiʿī shaykhs such as Aḥmad Pāshā of Taʿizz or Muḥammad ʿAlī Pāshā al-Jamāʿī of ʿUdayn were more important there. Other northern (Zaydī) shaykhs, not least the al-Aḥmars of Ḥāshid, held land near Ḥajjah. It was this which Aḥmad had been "setting in order", constraining the shaykhs and dismantling Idrīsī influence exactly where disputes with the Turks in the nineteenth century first launched the Imam's family, Bayt Ḥamīd al-Dīn, to power.[12] Tribesmen there were turned on the coastal lowlands. So were the Regular Army and levies from Lower Yemen. Famously the Zarānīq, around Bayt al-Faqīh, were crushed in a brutal campaign (1927–9) where Aḥmad played a major role, and many of them died in highland dungeons.

By 1930 Yaḥyā controlled the Tihāmah to the latitude of Ṣaʿdah. But a small Idrīsī state under Saudi protection remained in ʿAsīr, and by 1924 Ibn Saʿūd had seized most of North Arabia (Map 2.1). When the Saudis – or Wahhābīs as Yemenis saw them, and perhaps most still saw themselves – enquired about borders, in 1927, Yaḥyā declined to discuss the issue:

> The land of ʿAsīr is indivisibly part of Yemen. The Idrīsīs had only usurped an area which they cut off from Yemen's lands when under Turkish rule. He reinforced what he said with books of history that show the Mikhlāf Sulaymānī was always under the influence of Yemen's Imams before the Turks arrived, and he stressed that the Sharīfs of Abū ʿArīsh [before the Ottomans] derived their principality from Imams of Yemen.[13]

When a further delegation came, he assured them ʿAsīr was Yemeni and always had been but he himself had no expansionist aim. The same position emerged on the southern front. Yaḥyā seems never to have demanded Aden Port; he did claim everything else, however (it was all

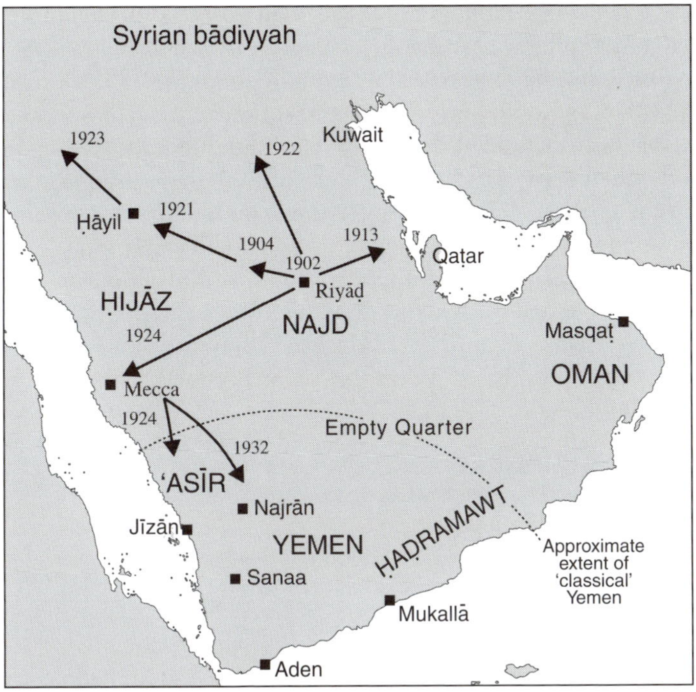

Map 2.1. Saudi expansion and "classical" Yemen

part of "Greater Yemen"), and as the British came to oppose him he maintained his formal claim while in practice, by 1930, leaving Britain's protégés fairly undisturbed. The British threat and the Saudi were symmetrical.[14]

At first, when the Turks withdrew from Aden's hinterland there was no British presence there. The Colonial Office and Colonel Jacob argued that none should be established and that Yaḥyā should be acknowledged as paramount beyond Laḥj,[15] but the Imam moved very quickly to consolidate power, attacking areas that had not known Zaydī domination for two centuries: 3,000 Zaydīs took Shuʿayb, for instance, "to wrest it from the hands of Yāfiʿ," killing 250 men in battle and another dozen they had taken prisoner. The Quʿayṭī Sultan in Ḥaḍramawt (himself from a Yāfiʿ family) sent his minister Sayyid Ḥusayn al-Muḥḍār to mediate, supposedly with a purse of 20,000 riyāls.[16] Half ʿAwdhalī was taken by the Imam's men and forced to surrender hostages. Hostages were taken from al-Ḍāliʿ. Some were held for a decade while their leading families invoked claims to British protection conceived in a different setting.

The Ottomans, a generation earlier, had been turned back by diplomatic pressure (a polite phrase for threats elsewhere) but when immediate power was at issue the British had retreated into Aden. Now, hesitantly, they armed the treaty chiefs, and in 1922, using aircraft, to which Yaḥyā had no effective counter, they bombed the Imam's men out of Ḥawshabī south of Ḍāliʿ. Negotiations in 1926 came to little, and in 1927 Qaʿṭabah (just north of the old Anglo-Turkish line) was bombed and machine-gunned for five days, at which stage the Imam's men were 50 kilometres from Aden. Even Ibb, 100 kilometres north again from Qaʿṭabah, was strafed and Taʿizz itself was bombed. Yaḥyā al-Iryānī's poem is well known:

> This is barbarism
>   when you come with what we don't have.
> A fight would be a fight
>   were you warriors who do not fear soldiers.[17]

The Imam pulled back. But a treaty became likely only as the Saudi threat intensified to Yaḥyā's north.

In mid-1932 Yaḥyā's forces moved up to Baraṭ, the homeland of Dhū Muḥammad and Dhū Ḥusayn. Baraṭ itself was taken. The usual mix of fighting and negotiation, of righteous proclamation and proffered hostages, led through Wā'ilah, the next tribe north, to Wādī Najrān which was occupied after fighting with supporters of Ibn Saʿūd. Najrān figures prominently in the story of Yemen's first Imam a millennium before and in much of Zaydī history. It was home to, among other groups, the Ismāʿīlīs of Yām who had often supported their co-religionists west of Sanaa; men from Yām, more recently, had sought service in Yaḥyā's army. Now the Wahhābīs, however, were there in Najrān also. War on two fronts was not sustainable, and a settlement with the British was concluded hurriedly: indeed, levies from Lower Yemen (presumably mostly Shāfiʿī troops) were marching north through Sanaa as the document was signed. This suspended discussion of sovereignty and agreed an administrative division along roughly the Anglo-Turkish boundary – the Treaty of Sanaa, February 1934.

Talks with the Saudis went less well. Najrān by itself was not cause for war, but west of there in ʿAsīr, in November 1933, part of the Idrīsī family threw off its allegiance to Ibn Saʿūd (contracted to in 1920, then again in 1926) and sought refuge in Yaḥyā's domain. When people from

Najrān fled to ʿAsīr for help, talks collapsed and the Saudis struck south. A delegation of Muslim notables intervened: Muḥammad ʿUlūbah Pāshā and ʿAzīz Pāshā of Egypt, Hāshim al-ʿAtāsī of Syria, Amīn al-Ḥusaynī of Palestine, and Shakīb Arslān. The settlement was hailed as a model of affairs between Arab states and the Saudis agreed a boundary in ʿAsīr equivalent to that they had guaranteed the Idrīsī, thus withdrawing voluntarily from 100 kilometres of coastal plain. With less restraint they expelled Yaḥyā's forces from Najrān and drew a line just south of there – the Treaty of Ṭāyif, May 1934.

Yaḥyā's claims to all Yemen were never formally surrendered – the treaty with the British was to run for forty years and that with the Saudis for only twenty at a time – but *de facto* by mid-1934 the Imam's own domains had boundaries north and south.[18] His position *de jure*, meanwhile, was established in other respects with foreign powers, and the treaties with Britain and with Ibn Saʿūd alike, on the model of that with Italy (1926), are in the name of His Majesty (*jalālat-hu*) Imam Yaḥyā Muḥammad Ḥamīd al-Dīn, King of Yemen.

ADEN'S HINTERLAND AND ḤAḌRAMAWT

In 1927 the Air Ministry took responsibility for defending Aden.[19] This soon involved not only intimidating Yaḥyā but enforcing "air control" over tribes in the hinterland. The range of aircraft was limited, so landing strips were required "up country", and their use required people on the ground where the British had scarcely gone before to negotiate, cajole and threaten. To replace British–Indian troops the Aden Levies were raised; in 1934 the first political officer was appointed, small forces of Tribal Guards were raised, and then another force of 200 men, the Government Guards, was established in 1937 to escort the Political Officer. An adviser was appointed to the Western Protectorate (the original "nine tribes" plus their neighbours) and another to the Eastern Protectorate (the Quʿayṭī and Kathīrī domains of Ḥaḍramawt, plus Mahrah). Between 1934 and 1941 the number of political officers rose from two to twelve.

This "forward policy" was associated with Bernard Reilly, who served as acting Aden Resident in the 1920s, then as Resident in the 1930s (he negotiated with Yaḥyā the 1934 treaty); he was Governor 1937–40, and from London played a part in Yemen's affairs through the 1950s. Keeping out the Imam was not enough in his view.[20] Good order and sound administration seemed an obligation – as much so as "establishing the

Plate 2.1. British airpower, "the wireless transferred from aeroplane to camel".

true *sharī'ah*" seemed to Yaḥyā – and in those terms the treaty chiefs were a disgrace: '"Government" is a misnomer for the type of misrule that prevails . . .; there has been no attempt on the part of these chiefs to improve the conditions of their followers and subjects. They are almost all self-seeking, obstructive, suspicious and only interested in enriching themselves, which they do by taxation and repression."[21] An image grew up of "feudal" figures whom the British should reform in the name of progress. Ironically, the same image decades later was to prove compelling to Arab nationalists who expelled the British, although feudalism was a poor description – to say the least – of the region's political economy.

In 1934 Harold Ingrams was sent by Reilly to explore Ḥaḍramawt (discussions with Ibn Sa'ūd raised questions about the "Protectorate's" precise extent). Late in 1936 he began to build a network of truces around the Kathīrī and Qu'ayṭī Sultans. Their domains were only loosely defined and, within these, "holy families" – mainly *sayyids*, but *mashāyikh* also – were associated with a plethora of *ḥawṭahs* or protected places guaranteed by tribes and associated often with tombs of saints. Within the *ḥawṭah* violence was forbidden. Beyond its bounds the *sayyids* or *mashāyikh* could intervene by invitation to form truces, but neither they nor the State, the *dawlah*, had standing authority. Many areas were paralysed by feuds, highway robbery was common, and in some places people had not dared leave the house for years or had to reach their fields through trenches – if the fields were not in rifle shot. Yet in the midst of this were splendid palaces, funded from wealth in the East Indies.

A "peace board" was set up, which nominally was headed by the two sultans but in practice was paid for and supported by noted *sayyid*s, most importantly the Āl al-Kāf. A tribe called the Bin Yamānī were summonsed for blockading an al-Kāf road. They were fined 10 camels, 30 rifles, 100 goats and twice what they had stolen, and when they failed to pay, warnings were issued and their villages bombed by British aircraft. Other tribes began signing the general truce, and within three months a three-year agreement covered the whole region:

> In some cases one chief's signature was enough to bind several thousand armed men; there was at least one case where a signature bound only a dozen, but it was thought necesssary to obtain it . . . There were also several hundred autonomous towns of unarmed men . . . and *ḥawṭah*s or sanctuary towns. . . . Altogether I calculated there were about 2,000 separate 'governments' in the Ḥaḍramawt . . .[22]

As Ingrams goes on to say, only two of these, the Quʿayṭī and Kathīrī, were recognised by Britain. The "peace", he claimed, was an Arab solution to an Arab problem and the British were only to advise discreetly, but common sense led Ingrams "on and on" in support of the Quʿayṭīs. In the decade from 1934, the Quʿayṭī revenue spent on medical services went from 4,400 (Indian) rupees per annum to 74,000, the amount for education went from 6,000 rupees to 154,000. The three-year truce was extended in 1940 to last for ten years.

The Western Protectorate proved more difficult. The terrain was more severe, certain tribes were more extensive, the "rulers" recognised by Britain were far more numerous, and local relations among chiefs, tribesmen and non-tribal share-croppers were in places deeply involuted. Al-Ḍāliʿ is an obvious case. British maps often say "Amīrī", but the *amīr*s or "princes" at Ḍāliʿ were merely one large family. "Amīrī territory" contained a fertile plateau worked partly by tribespeople, partly by non-tribal share-croppers, and this, along with tolls on trade, was the source of the *dawlah*'s income. Doreen Ingrams calls the Amirs "feudal chiefs".[23] The mountains nearby, however, also marked Amīrī, held a scattering of minor tribes who, a report of 1909 had cautioned, owned the Amir only "nominal allegiance" – the tribes of Radfān, for instance, include the Quṭaybīs. "That the Amir of Ḍāliʿ had any influence over the Quṭaybī tribe was a delusion of the Aden secretariat."[24]

The mountains of Radfān connect with Yāfiʿ. Much of Yāfi's territory is extremely rugged and there is little feudal there at all: families each have small terraced holdings of their own. Upper Yāfiʿ and Lower Yāfiʿ subdivide extensively. Each had a sultan (apart from the plethora of section shaykhs) whose family was called the *dawlah* locally and claimed vague precedence, though various of the shaykhs themselves had treaties independently with Aden and none obeyed the others, while the Lower Yāfiʿ Sultan was associated primarily with a sacred drum and the ability to make rain. To describe the importance of these persons in British terms of sovereignty was not possible. East of Yāfiʿ is ʿAwdhalī, divided among productive and less productive areas and by a 1,000-metre sheer escarpment called the *kawr*. East again is ʿAwlaqī. In certain of these areas, as in Ḥaḍramawt, *sayyid* families were influential (the al-Jifrīs, for instance, attempted to promote a peace in ʿAwlaqī), but no-one had the funds to succeed as the al-Kāfs did further east and the notables with whom the British signed treaties remained largely arbitrators with their men, contestants among themselves, and potentially enemies of their close kin: "They were given rifles to restore order in their territories. They used them in the prosecution of private feuds, they sold them to the highest bidder and on several occasions they gave them away as bribes. They did not appear to understand the word 'rule'. They were in fact shy of ruling . . ."[25]

In the North the Imam was a ruler straightforwardly. Hostages, fines and punitive action produced, in this ideal, public order. Authority was not devolved in bureaucratic style: rather, claims to prominence overlapped, rivalries were not discouraged, and the Imam in person intervened as he saw fit. One key to his success in Upper Yemen was that, among these rivalries, he favoured the lesser shaykhs over major figures from such families as al-Aḥmar, al-Shāyif or Abū Raʾs; in Lower Yemen the power of shaykhs was more localised and less a threat. In both domains, however, the Imam appropriated existing structures. Around Ḥūth, for instance, a *hijrah* or "protected place" in Ḥāshid's territory, Yaḥyā took over a system of guaranty in 1928 (this is the year in which Ḥāshid as a whole comes under his control), and where each "guarantor" or *kafīl* had been answerable to his fellows for the peace of the market, now all were made answerable to Imam Yaḥyā and a nucleus of jurisdiction by Islamic law inserted amidst tribal custom.[26]

Such *kafīl*s were used for many things. To be a soldier in the army, for instance, one needed a guarantor, and the same idea was apparent in the hostage system where the conduct of groups or persons determined if a hostage lived in comfort – perhaps receiving an education, for most were young – or was fettered in a rank dungeon. Minor squabbles continued among tribes (the official gazette of the time and the chronicles, meanwhile, list Islamic punishments for individual offences of murder, adultery and wine-drinking) but the peace of the Imam was real and was highly valued. It reached to the desert east: "the roads were secure to the point where the traveller from the Jawf to Ma'rib needed only one escort, though the distance is about six days and previously one could not cross it except in large groups".[27]

Merchants who travelled through Yaḥyā's domain in safety were subject when they entered the "Protectorate" to extortion, robbery and murder. The British attempted through air action to secure the trade routes. Access by political officers was enforced in some places (Lower ʿAwlaqī, for instance, was bombed to this end in 1936), but no grand truce spread; instead tribes were forced into sullen, temporary compliance with unwanted "rulers", cutting loose when the chance offered, and the Western Protectorate remained ever after a dangerous place where ambitions of "sound administration" locked bitterly against politicking among chiefs and tribes.

The Eastern Protectorate was a different world. Although there was scant British presence until Ingrams arrived, the British had long been part of Ḥaḍramī politics, along with the Ottomans, the Dutch, the Nizām of Hyderabad, the Germans briefly, Ibn Saʿūd, the Shaykhs of al-Azhar in Cairo, and Imam Yaḥyā. Yaḥyā corresponded with Ḥaḍramī *sayyids* as early as 1912. First he received a letter, postmarked Singapore, from Muḥammad bin ʿAqīl (a learned, much-travelled Ḥaḍramī millionaire) and a poem from Sayyid ʿAbd al-Raḥmān al-Saqqāf, *muftī* of the Ḥaḍramī lands as the Zaydī account calls him. The Imam replied. A set of letters was later published in Egypt. Yaḥyā supported the *sayyid*s against the Irshādī movement, based initially on Singapore and the Dutch East Indies, who denied in the name of Islam a special place to the Prophet's kin.[28] As early as 1916 he had some practical design on Ḥaḍramawt, and in 1922 he renewed his claim, much as with ʿAwdhalī, Ḍāliʿ and indeed all Yemen.[29]

In 1923 certain Ḥaḍramī *sayyid*s, continuing a long connection, appealed to Yaḥyā for support, while the Irshādīs, whom later socialists in South Yemen claim as ancestors, looked more to the Wahhābīs and Ibn Saʿūd. Among both parties modern terms of debate were used in

Plate 2.2. Conference in Laḥj, 1930.

ways unimaginable in Sanaa or Aden, let alone in the western hinterland. In 1927, for instance, one finds reference to "our blessed Ḥaḍramī homeland" and "popular unity" (*al-waḥdah al-qawmiyyah*, a phrase to conjure with elsewhere in the 1950s), and an accession speech in 1936 expressed the wish to set up an agricultural college.[30] The British in supporting "state building" (1936 onwards) found themselves supporting particular *sayyid* families, who themselves by then were broadly in alliance with the Quʿayṭī ruler, against a plethora of groups some of whom claimed Irshādī ideals and some simply independence. The speed with which the pattern changed is striking.

"Ingrams' peace" could as well be called the al-Kāf peace. The Kathīrī state, centred on the Wādī near Sayyūn and with no coastal towns, hence no customs dues, was bank-rolled in effect by Sayyid Bū Bakr al-Kāf whose personal expenditure on charitable works was huge: his wealth came from Singapore, where his fortune was estimated at £25 million. The road around which the "peace" was first built was his doing and ran in the end all the way from the coast to Tarīm in the upper Wādī. In Tarīm, later, one finds a movement to elide the Kathīrī and Quʿayṭī sultanates, in part to avoid double taxation. Sayyid Ḥāmid al-Muḥḍār, Wazīr in Mukallā of the Quʿayṭīs' growing state, later still took up this movement; but from interest in the Imam he shifted soon to internal Quʿayṭī politics and fell foul in the end of the rival al-ʿAṭṭās family and of Ingrams' policy. From late 1936 Ḥaḍramawt slips wholly from Yaḥyā's influence.[31]

A GEOGRAPHICAL INTERSECTION

Maps of Yemen show two axes of high ground: the mountains north to south, down which Yaḥyā's power spread, and the *kawr* and the *jôl* running west to east out through Ḥaḍramawt. Between them lies an angle of semi-desert, the East or *mashriq* (Map 2.2). A shared genealogy connects families of Sharīfs (again descendants of the Prophet) in Ma'rib, Ḥarīb, the Jawf and Bayḥān; some would also claim a relation with parts of Dhū Ḥusayn at Baraṭ, and Dhū Ḥusayn's own connections reach far eastwards.[32] In 1936 H. St. John Philby, an English acolyte of Ibn Saʿūd, cut the corner by motoring across the desert from Najrān to Shabwah and then Mukallā, collecting as he went protestations of enthusiasm for Wahhābī rule. Ibn Saʿūd declined involvement. Then, in 1938, Yaḥyā himself confronted Britain by sending ʿAlī Nāṣir al-Qardaʿī to take Shabwah – the junction point of what were rapidly becoming separate zones of politics.

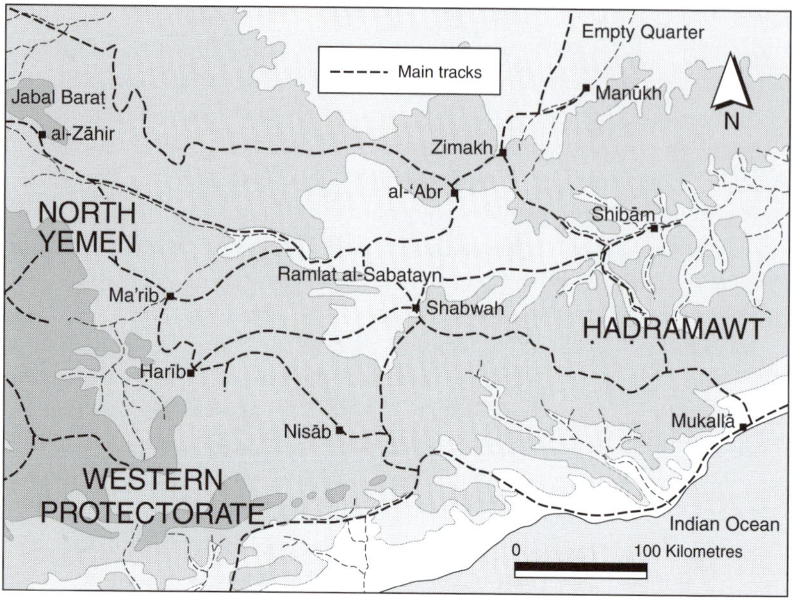

Map 2.2. The Mashriq, 1938

Al-Qardaʿī was a shaykh of Murād, just south of Ma'rib. Certain shaykhs there had agreed to the Imam's dominion in 1927 but only in 1930 had connections with Yaḥyā begun to take solid form, and between those dates ʿAlī Nāṣir was detained in Sanaa. He was established as governor of Ḥarīb, then imprisoned again, and escaped to live as a rebel in the East before Yaḥyā again made peace with him and sent him off to wrest Shabwah from the Christians. His poems tell the story vividly:

> We covered the ground on camel by night,
>   By the star heading out to the east directly.
> In Shabwah sweet things turned sour in our mouths,
>   And we said, O Hidden One, mercy preserve us.[33]

The British political officer, with his own band of tribesmen but also with air support, squeezed al-Qardaʿī out. Shabwah, said the British, was part of Ḥaḍramawt, ʿAlī Nāṣir's homeland was part of Yemen. The Anglo-Turkish line of 1905–1914, they claimed, defined two countries.

The only newspaper in the North apart from the official gazette (both were run from the Imam's press) responded predictably:

God has ordained that Yemen's natural boundaries should not be obscure and ambiguous. The Yemen is encircled by sea from the west, south and east. All that is included within these boundaries up to the tip of southern Ḥijāz is the cradle of Yemen. Ḥaḍramawt is not an island in the Indian Ocean so as to consider Shabwah as part of Ḥaḍramawt and not of Yemen.[34]

More striking is a poem from the man on the ground, ʿAlī Nāṣir. He starts by lamenting a lost world:

I was a badawi, utterly free,
Not asking permission, my country likewise
. . .
We sought Abū l-Ḥasan in every trouble,
Our Caliph who orders all my affairs.

Abū l-Ḥasan here is Imam Yaḥyā. But then in traditional form al-Qardaʿī sends an imagined messenger, in this case to the Sharīf of Bayḥān, and in a second poem the list extends to Upper Yāfiʿ, Ḥumayqān, Mukayrās and Lower ʿAwdhalī regardless of the Anglo-Turkish line. States, borders, the ending of tribal autonomy all come together, for between modern governments in al-Qardaʿī's view there was little any more to choose:

They're all in agreement from Sanaa to London
All in it together, Sayyids and Christians.
They're dividing the land, each setting up idols,
Apportioning Yemen to headmen and Sultans.
If I tried to complain, I'd not know to whom.
My trust has collapsed in my friends and my fellows . . .

Everywhere states were forming.

THE DYNASTIC STATE

The Qāsimī state or *dawlah* left in the North an image of political order. In its day (1650–1750 was the high point) it had taken over grand forms of governance, with the Imam processing to Friday prayers among his troops, court officials as "gate keepers", and documents stamped with the ruler's seal, much of which persisted or had been revived. Certain Turkish forms were then appropriated after World War I and so were "international" forms whereby Arab rulers became Kings, although the Holy Qur'ān says, "Kings when they enter a town [or village] ruin it and make the mightiest of its people lowly . . ." (Qur'ān 27:34). One can see the sensitivity of the issue in two editions of the same book, al-Wāsiʿī's famous *History of Yemen*. The first edition (1928) contains an explicit note:

> The kings of this age are accorded the title His Majesty King So-and-So. Since people of good taste find the title upsetting I have avoided in my book using the title Majesty of our lord the Imam of Yemen. He himself rejects it, for he is bound by high piety, learning, refinement, and adherence to the morals of his ancestor the Lord of Messengers, peace be upon him and the blessings of God. Except for what I found in the treaty with Italy [1926], which I copied exactly, I have been content to use the title he himself uses, that of his forefathers the Imams of Yemen – Commander of the Faithful . . .[35]

The second edition (1948) refers to His Majesty without comment as if "people of good taste" (Zaydī scholars of a certain bent) had not existed. Even the first edition refers to the "Crown Prince", Yaḥyā's son Aḥmad, and several later works backdate the title as if succession by a son were natural, which in Zaydī terms was not so.

It had often happened that Imams were succeeded by their sons. But nominally on grounds of learning and righteousness, not descent.[36] Late in the Qāsimī period, circa 1800, Imams had been recognised who were sons but lacked the formal qualities of pious learning, thus producing under Zaydī (Shiʿite) auspices a Sunni system – within broad limits, temporal and dynastic order was valued above righteousness. Not everyone accepted the theory then. Not everyone did so now, and the document in which certain *ʿulamāʾ*, in 1924, petitioned for Aḥmad to be made Crown Prince shows signs of men aware they are forming doctrine in line with that of other states but perhaps not as clearly so with their own inheritance.[37] The Traditions of the Prophet it cites are not of righteousness but of obedience: "who rebels against a Sultan by so much as a hand's breadth will die a death of the age of ignorance".

A key figure in arranging this petition was Qadi Ḥusayn al-ʿAmrī, the Shaykh of Shaykhs whom Yaḥyā had confirmed in place during Turkish times. Yaḥyā, we might remember, had once studied with him; he himself had studied with a pupil of Shawkānī, the man from whom Sunni-like theories of the state all derive circa 1800. Ḥusayn's son, ʿAbdullāh al-ʿAmrī, came to be *raʾīs al-dīwān* (Head of Chancery, to translate freely; perhaps Chief Secretary) which was understood by some to mean Prime Minister.

The succession excluded other *sayyid* families, particularly the al-Wazīrs whose senior members had subdued and administered Lower Yemen. But Aḥmad's rule was not imminent and certain of his brothers seemed likely to be claimants in due course, not least al-Ḥusayn who reputedly was the most learned of Yaḥyā's sons and was certainly among the nicest.[38] Others talked with possible claimants beyond the family. Yaḥyā himself provided ambivalent support for Aḥmad over many years, encouraged in 1927 by Muḥammad bin ʿAqīl of Ḥaḍramawt.[39] One likely claimant, ʿAlī Ḥamūd Sharaf al-Dīn (a kinsman had been Imam before Yaḥyā's father; 1879–90), was manoeuvred into demanding signatures from two others, the leading al-Wazīrs, as late as 1936, and when he failed to win complete success lost his post as governor of Ḥudaydah; one of the al-Wazīrs (their ancestor too had claimed to be Imam, 1854–90) never did sign, and several *ʿulamāʾ* around Ṣaʿdah avoided doing so. Whether Muḥammad Ḥūriyyah of Ṣaʿdah ever sought the Imamate is unclear, but he was accused of wishing to and was thrown in the dungeons.

The wealth at Yaḥyā's disposal was greater than in Turkish times, for he now controlled the revenue of Lower Yemen, and that in itself spelt power. The style of his administration, however, hardly changed at first. This is Amīn al-Rīḥānī's account from 1922:

> No furniture, no desks, no chairs; the secretaries sit cross-legged on cushions and write with the knee supporting the left hand, in which the paper is held . . .; every letter written, no matter how unimportant, is placed before the Couch of State and His Eminence [the Imam], after reading it and adding a word at the end in his own hand . . . gives it to the soldier before him, who applies to it the seal and then hands it to the addressing scribe . . .
>
> About midnight, the telegraph clerk comes with a packet of telegrams, which are given precedence to the business at hand . . . But the Imam and the First Secretary remain sometimes until the early dawn . . .[40]

Someone complains of a neighbour's donkey kicking the wall at night, and the Imam orders the beast chained up between dusk and daylight. A thousand silver riyāls of tax money are counted one by one in Yaḥyā's presence; each morning the Imam sits outside beneath a tree and deals with petitioners before walking about Sanaa accompanied by admiring crowds.[41] At the centre of the country was a single man (he never laid eyes on the sea to the west nor Maʾrib to the east) directing affairs with the aid of scribes and counsellors.

The American anthropologist Carleton Coon sketched a similar picture in 1933. But by now the Imam's health was failing (he was 64 years old) and the demands of the state had perhaps also grown more complex, for although Coon failed to grasp this, an attempt was being made to delegate: "The complainants coming to us from all directions have increased, to the point where it takes up all the time we have . . . If officials did their jobs, no complainant at all would come to us. We have now forbidden any complainant coming from anywhere with an *ʿāmil* or *ḥākim* [a governor or judge] unless they have first put their complaint to the *ʿāmil* or *ḥākim* of the area."[42] Delegation of responsibility surely lessened the magic of Yaḥyā's rule, where blame attached to local governors and praise to the Imam's justice, but blame was on the increase and by the end of the decade (1940) an Iraqi military mission could report that corruption and bribery had become "almost official".[43] There was not enough revenue to go around.

Few Islamic rulers avoid the problem that *zakāt* is small and *maks* (non-canonical tax) is offensive in the sight of God. Yaḥyā when he first took power ended Turkish road and market tolls. He soon had to reinstate them. In 1930 internal market taxes were again abolished but customs dues were raised to 8 per cent, with luxuries like tobacco, wool, and spices at 15 per cent; the expenses of the state kept growing and a "*jihād* subvention" might in any case be thought legal to support the new military.[44] After the Saudi war of 1934 the army was reinforced with a vast militia, the *jaysh difāʿī*. The burden of taxation on Lower Yemen was becoming unbearable (a witness in the 1930s mentions payments from the al-Wazīrs to Sanaa of a million riyāls a time), and tax-farming made the problem worse, not to mention recurrent famine, with the result that Lower Yemenis emigrated in increasing numbers.

The standard literature identifies labour migration with Shāfiʿīs, but in fact it affected Zaydīs too. Ḥusayn al-Maqbalī, for instance, whose father was "of the middling sort", a village preacher near Yarīm whose own father owned a camel and two plough oxen, wanted to go to Aden when he was about thirteen (this would be the late 1930s): "My mother's three brothers, ʿAbdullāh, Muḥammad, and ʿAlī were migrants in Sudan. My father's brother, Yaḥyā, was a migrant in Ethiopia. There was hardly a house in the village that did not have a migrant or two outside the country. Most young men were migrants."[45] From Aden some moved on not only to Africa, but to America, Britain, Indonesia, or even, by way of French Djibouti, to Vietnam. At home there was insufficient land, taxes were heavy, and "justice" was meanwhile administered by soldiers who charged their victims for the privilege of arrest or imprisonment.

Shāfiʿīs speak of Yaḥyā's rule as "sectarian", which it was. But his Zaydism was scarcely that of the sect's founders. The theory of the State was all but Sunni now, save the ruler had to be a *sayyid*, and the Imam himself ruled against the concept that *sayyid* women could marry only *sayyid* men. He celebrated each year the first day of Rajab, a festival closer to Shāfiʿī hearts than to Zaydī, as well as Yawm al-Ghadīr, to which Zaydī *sayyid*s were attached,[46] and several Shāfiʿīs praise his honesty in appointing judges. Nor yet was he oppressive on points of doctrine: the al-Wazīrs, not the Ḥamīd al-Dīn, forced the Shiʿite call to prayer on Sunni Ibb. But many Shāfiʿīs felt, whatever the Imam's intention, that they were treated as "infidels in interpretation" (*kuffār taʾwīl*) by a Zaydī state.

The distinction between Zaydī and Shāfiʿī was akin to an "ethnic" difference, marked for instance by regional accents, and the literature depicts those who spoke Taʿizzi as farmers and merchants, those who spoke Sanaani as shaykhs and soldiers. Actually there was no shortage in the 1930s of Shāfiʿī shaykhs or of Zaydī merchants, and Shāfiʿīs were probably the majority of army regulars through the 1940s, but freelance (*barrānī*) soldiers from the Zaydī north attached themselves to officials as enforcers and tax-collectors, and these are remembered in Lower Yemen still as a "Zaydī army". Even soldiers were unhappy. They were poorly paid and assumed that the treasury (*bayt al-māl*) was bulging: "How much is there in the Bayt al-Māl – *khayrāt* (untold wealth)! . . . How many Bayts has the Imam? One in every city, and every one is full of wheat and corn and everything. But the people of Yemen except the *sayyid*s have nothing . . . The *sayyid*s have everything."[47] A Ḥijāzī visitor was told the same years later. "The soldier said that we ought to obey the Imam's orders, but the Imam does not pay us much. We are poor. No *zalaṭ*, money." The country was assumed, meanwhile, to be full of hidden treasure-chests: "They said he is keeping them in Shihar [Shahārah], a high mountain, but nobody knows the way to these treasures."

Failure in the Saudi war encouraged opposition, and some whisper of a plot began at once among army officers, the Imam's son ʿAlī, and Ghālib al-Aḥmar of Ḥāshid. The al-Wazīrs were discontented also. But most importantly, in the view of later Yemeni writers, young *sayyid*s and *qāḍī*s began to think of reform, drawing on such modern classics of the Arab World as Kawākibī, Muḥammad Rashīd Riḍā, Muḥammad ʿAbduh and al-Afghānī. Reading circles grew up that were circles of dissent. A later literature depicts "movements" on the model of political parties,[48] and this is where one first hears of such figures as Muṭīʿ al-Dammāj, ʿAbd al-Salām Ṣabrah and ʿAbd al-Raḥmān al-Iryānī, but the real significance of their networks is as markers of a widespread mood. The problem to which the mood responded only sharpened as power became concentrated in the Imam's family, a process which shows in formal nomenclature. Noted commanders and the sons of past Imams alike had the title Sword of Islam: as the older men died off, however, the title became restricted to Yaḥyā's sons, all of whom now bore it regardless of competence as if it meant "prince of the royal blood".[49]

ʿAlī al-Wazīr, the Taʿizz Governor, was kept in play with a marriage between his son and Yaḥyā's daughter, while three of Yaḥyā's sons took up residence at al-Wazīr's home village in Banī Ḥushaysh near Sanaa. Certain of the sons nurtured relations between the two great families, others moved quietly in support of Aḥmad, and the al-Wazīr domain in Lower Yemen was washed away by stages. In 1937 "ministries" were announced, all headed by Yaḥyā's sons. The main governorates were soon held by them also: Aḥmad in Taʿizz (he also retained control of Ḥajjah), Ḥasan in Ibb, ʿAbdullāh in Ḥudaydah. The succession formed one focus of dissent, and a circular letter appeared advising the Imam "to proclaim al-Ḥusayn as his successor and initiate him, in the Imam's lifetime, into the work of government with the assistance of a council of notables. Among the members of such a council should be two Muslim leaders or upright men from Syria, Egypt or Iraq."[50]

Yaḥyā, by contrast, on the basis of God's preference, felt himself rightly the sole ruler, and a document from the Appeal Court referring to "what Brother So-and-So said" brought the furious riposte – "*Whose* brother . . . you asses?!" for the Imam was not as other men. Nor was the work of government quite that of Syria. On occasion Yaḥyā would ensure the proper ordering of his realm by decreeing that all young people at once get married, sending soldiers to enforce this, but developing roads or the like was not pursued with equal vigour: the Imam himself lived simply – his greatest extravagance was having fresh fish brought up to Sanaa in jerry-cans by camel – and his notorious personal meanness extended to state expenditure. An old tribesman turned up seeking charity and held forth on how he had fought the holy war with Yaḥyā against the Turks. "To the labourer his troubles," said the Imam dismissing him, "and to the donkey his proper wage." Wealth was drawn to Sanaa as taxes and seemed never to reappear.[51]

Yaḥyā acquired several "palaces" (they were not all that grand in fact) and extensive land; what divisions there were between state property and his own were listed in a notebook no-one saw but him, and his sons' wealth was as problematic to those beyond family circles. ʿAbbās bin Yaḥyā acquired land in al-Abnā, Yaḥyā bin Yaḥyā in Banī Ḥushaysh, al-Ḥasan in al-Baṭanah (between Shahārah and Ḥūth); al-Qāsim's wealth was from the Ministry of Health, so called, and ʿAbdullāh spent Ḥudaydah's treasury on trips abroad. Meanwhile, a recent author contends, people were dropping from hunger.[52] The 1940s were years of drought; 1943 saw a smallpox epidemic, and a report in 1945 speaks of Aḥmad in Taʿizz simply "gouging" Lower Yemen. Supposedly as people starved around him, he supported the export of grain for cash.[53] A feeling that the Imamate no longer worked became widespread, and although there were probably fewer hostages than ten years earlier (the number may have halved, indeed), a great many men, whether farmers or notables, now routinely spent time in prison.

In 1946 Sayyid Zayd bin ʿAlī al-Daylamī, the Sanaa appeal judge of the day, submitted a memorial to Yaḥyā, demanding that *zakāt* be given voluntarily and not extorted by force, that un-canonical taxes be abolished, that political exiles be pardoned, and that public officials (not least princes of the royal house) be prohibited from exploiting people through trade.[54] Initially his demands were phrased in terms common to all Islam. His later dissent, however, was couched in terms specific to the Zaydī school, whose older theology of power had by now almost disappeared. According to one story, al-Daylamī ceased attending Friday prayers.[55] Congregational prayer, ran Zaydī theory, was valid only under a true Imam – which Yaḥyā by implication no longer was. Yet neither was he fully a modern King.

MODERNIST CONTRADICTIONS

Al-Wāsiʿī's *History* (1928) shows intriguing features. For all the colour of "strange events", the layout of the work is modern: the telescoping of the distant past to situate recent history, for instance, the mirroring of Yemeni concerns in reports from foreign newspapers, and the "ethnographic" section which lists customs and traditions, place-names, and such gems as "the colour of women in the towns".[56] The second edition (1948) reverses the order: the ethnology comes first, the events year by year come second, and it gives more space to the country's pre-Islamic roots, even listing the Ḥimyarite alphabet. A later historian spells out the implication of a wider project which the Imam promoted: "knowledge of the society's history is itself one of the greatest factors in progress, especially if in the society's history there are excellent and glorious accomplishments".[57] Such history encompassed all Greater Yemen (*al-yaman al-kubrā*). The idea of Yemen – not just people who were Yemenis – as an historical subject was new, and the backbone of such accounts was the succession of Imams "from the third century [of Islam] to the present", that is, through a thousand years.

A chronicle from the ʿAbdalīs of Laḥj, which stresses Yāfiʿī connections and how early former Zaydī rule had been thrown off, was one response:[58] it presents itself as no less Yemeni but rejects the equation of Yemen with a single state. A whole alternative tradition was meanwhile developing in Ḥaḍramawt where the ʿAlawī-Irshādī debates, first overseas, which involved the Shaykhs of Cairo and the Zaydī Imam led also to the writing of a new kind of history and a distinctively modern form of Ḥaḍramī self-consciousness. Ṣalāḥ al-Bakrī, from a Ḥaḍramī Yāfiʿī family which had moved to Java (he himself was a teacher with the Egyptian government), published a two-volume *Political History of Ḥaḍramawt* in 1935–6. In Irshādī style it marginalises the *sayyid*s and speaks of their influence as "spiritual authority" (*sulṭah rūḥiyyah*), a phrase unimaginable where political discourse was only of "establishing the true *sharīʿah*". Certain *sayyid* authors wrote in the opposite vein, elaborating genealogies and tales of righteousness. From there, through the 1950s, builds a Ḥaḍramī literature in which the North figures marginally when at all.[59]

Yaḥyā formed a "history commission" in 1937. He also promoted geographical work. He made great play with publishing Yemeni manuscripts abroad (several Zaydī classics saw print in Cairo) and at home with formal schooling, where certain schools he took over from the Turks and others he suppressed. Others still he founded for his own reasons. The Orphans' School, whose students were issued with yellow jackets, produced clerks, for instance, while the Scientific School, whose students were distinguished by the dress of learned men (turbans and long robes), produced functionaries equipped with judicial knowledge; a military school appeared, and a teacher training school. The Imam, as Muḥammad Nuʿmān says, wanted officials on the Turkish model.[60] To depict him as a "traditional ruler" is as misleading in this connection as in connection with his building a standing army, and within the language of the state itself one finds ideas of "progress" as well as more traditionally of justice. Modernity required expertise, however, which lay elsewhere.

In a much quoted passage Yaḥyā tells a Syrian visitor that other countries had been colonised because they allowed in foreigners to develop their resources: "I would rather that my people and I eat straw than let foreigners in."[61] But the idea of Yemen as a forbidden kingdom (very salient in British writing) omits the fact that it was part of the Arab

Islamic World, and the string of nationalist and learned visitors to the Imam's domain in fact is long, from ʿAbd al-Raḥmān al-Kawākibī in the time of Yaḥyā's father through Rīḥānī, al-Thaʿālabī, al-ʿAzm and Shakīb Arslān. Yemenis had travelled for political ends in the Ottoman period; from the 1890s Yemen was a prominent subject in the Arab press. Yaḥyā himself issued proclamations intended for a much wider audience than Yemen, and immediately after World War I the Imam was the only Arab ruler not either under Western control or at least on a Western payroll. When the Ottoman Caliphate ended, Muḥammad Rashīd Riḍā for a time wished Yaḥyā to declare himself Caliph for all Islam.

The standard histories attach perhaps undue importance to missions sent to Iraq in the 1930s in search of technical expertise. These missions, sent after the Saudi war, were partly military and partly civil. Their members, very prominent in later history, relate discussions abroad on Arabism and Islam and their own imprisonment as suspect modernists when they returned to Yemen, all of which is true and was symptomatic; but the argument was already going on.[62] One finds oneself in mind of Lenin's "weakest link". The contradictions of a whole system – the Arab World in face of a modernity dominated by Western powers – were concentrated in one place, which was Yaḥyā's domain of Yemen, and not surprisingly for a Muslim country, education was a focus of dispute.

Al-Maqbalī, whose family was at the edge of poverty (his mother like al-Akwa's a generation earlier died young), grew tired of ploughing behind grandfather's camel:

> I saw a *qāḍī* from Iryān riding a mule, his head covered by a *shāl* [a wool head-cloth] as well as an *ʿimāmah* [the turban of learned men] and holding an umbrella to cool the heat of the sun . . . This *qāḍī* didn't work at ploughing the soil – he judged among people, he rode a mule, he was followed by a soldier and a servant. How could I . . . be a *qāḍī* and judge among people?[63]

The route out of poverty was learning. Al-Maqbalī got to study in Dhamār and then Sanaa; al-Akwaʿ had taken a similar route twenty years before. Juzaylān's memoirs mention equally schools and schooling. Schools beyond the level of a village Qurʾān school were not widespread but they existed. The question was what to teach.

Aḥmad Nuʿmān (a nephew of the landowner ʿAbd al-Wahhāb), born 1909 and educated at Zabīd in traditional form by Shāfiʿī teachers, helped set up a "modern school" at Dhubḥān in Ḥugariyyah, just south of Taʿizz: "This school became widely famous for it was the first to teach modern sciences such as geography, arithmetic . . . and physical education."[64] Around it swirled rivalries and doubts among princes of the

Plate 2.3. The Imam's "Prime Minister", ʿAbdullāh al-ʿAmrī, with the Iraqi delegation to Yemen, 1944.

Ḥamīd al-Dīn and provincial governors. Several notables in Sanaa and Taʿizz supported such initiatives but the Imam in the end sent a traditional teacher of the Zaydī sciences to supervise Nuʿmān's efforts, for modernist forms of education seemed to some to be the devil's work and to attach such concerns to more popular alarms was not difficult: "God protect the Yemen from foreigners," cried an old man near Taʿizz, "God keep them away from the Yemen." The number of Yemenis abroad in the foreign world was meanwhile expanding rapidly.

In 1937 Nuʿmān moved to Cairo, where he was taken under the wing of Shakīb Arslān. ʿAlī al-Wazīr was squeezed from his position as governor of Taʿizz in 1938 and went on the Mecca pilgrimage; his son ʿAbdullāh, squeezed from his own post in Dhī Safāl, went also on the pilgrimage that year and arrived in Cairo in 1940 accompanied by Muḥammad al-Zubayrī, a promising young poet. Nuʿmān and Zubayrī in Cairo formed a group called *al-Katībat al-ūlā* ("the First Battalion"), a name suggesting links with the Muslim Brothers, and when Zubayrī returned to Yemen, in 1941, full of ideas of progress as much as Islamic justice, he presented a memorial entitled in traditionalist form, "The First Programme of Young Men for Enjoining the Good and Prohibiting Evil". His intention, no doubt, was to align his hopes with the Imam's values, for *al-amr bi-l-maʿrūf wa-l-nahy ʿan al-munkar* is the timeless claim of Zaydī righteousness. The Imam, however, had him thrown in prison.[65]

Many "young men" were locked up. The story was put about that they were altering the Holy Qurʾān, and proceedings were started to have Zubayrī executed. The board of *ʿulamāʾ* convened for the purpose, including Zayd al-Daylamī of the Sanaa appeal court, refused to find him guilty, but suspect young men were nonetheless held for months afterwards. When released, many moved to Crown Prince Aḥmad's court in Taʿizz. That relationship lasted two years, until Aḥmad one day in 1944 burst out with "I pray God I do not die before I colour my sword here with the blood of these modernists" and Nuʿmān, Zubayrī and several others fled to Aden. Certain dissidents such as Muṭīʿ al-Dammāj had already moved there. A great many people were now jailed at home. Jāzim al-Ḥirwī, a Shāfiʿī merchant with interests in Ethiopia, had his house destroyed, while Aḥmad Pāshā of Taʿizz, a pillar of the local administration, quietly supported the exiled "Liberals" or "Free Yemenis".

Aḥmad Nuʿmān, in an earlier spell in Aden (1940), had defined one aspect of what some reformers thought their problem: "we define ignorance as a lack of knowledge of Islamic jurisprudence, grammar, morphology . . . [Our] institutions have over the past centuries produced hundreds of knowledgeable *qāḍīs* . . . However, it is not possible to find a doctor, . . . there are no experts in agriculture, . . . and no industries."[66] Not even new technologies of power were adopted. In 1926, for instance, with the Italian delegation, the first ever aircraft had appeared in the skies of Sanaa. Qadi Yaḥyā al-Iryānī composed a long poem. The Italians agreed to provide further aircraft and train Yemeni aviators. Yemen bought two more planes from Germany, and they flew over Sanaa to the delight of Sanaani ladies: "In God's good morning there came to us a flyer", ran their song, "And left all the women trembling with love." But two young *sayyids*, al-Kibsī and al-Sarājī, immolated themselves and two Germans in a crash and, precisely as the British changed the regional balance of power by the use of aircraft, the Imam forbade such experiments as too dangerous. "When we went out to look at the plane that had crashed one of the onlookers said, 'That's al-Sarājī's blood, and that's the Christian's blood. It hasn't mixed with al-Sarājī's.' "[67]

THE COUP OF 1948

The lights of Aden port were visible from Nuʿmān domains in Ḥugariyyah. But Aden (ruled from India until 1937) offered little at first for most Yemenis except the chance to earn money under rough conditions. Migrants lived in shanty towns on the slopes of Crater (Map 2.3). Medical services were rudimentary, labour conditions in the 1930s were reckoned by a later British governor to be "disgraceful", and education was as much an issue as in the North. Less than 1,000 pupils were enrolled in government schools, with another 2,000 elsewhere, and few even of these were Arab children: "What has India done for us? Nothing. We are backward . . . You have seen the schools, you have seen the Indians who teach. Where are the Arab teachers?"[68]

The headmaster of the first Arab secondary school in Aden, Muḥammad Luqmān, was a leading reformer, raising money abroad from Arab rulers to send students to Baghdad and Cairo. Zubayrī and Nuʿmān had gone to Cairo; missions of students had been sent from Sanaa to Baghdad. In Cairo in 1937 one found Northerners, Southerners and Ḥaḍramīs all together, but links existed closer home as well. ʿAlī al-Wazīr, "Prince of Taʿizz" until the late 1930s, corresponded with Aḥmad al-Aṣnaj, President of the Arab Islamic Reform Club in Aden. Zubayrī, the Wazīrs and Aṣnaj met on the 1938 pilgrimage, and

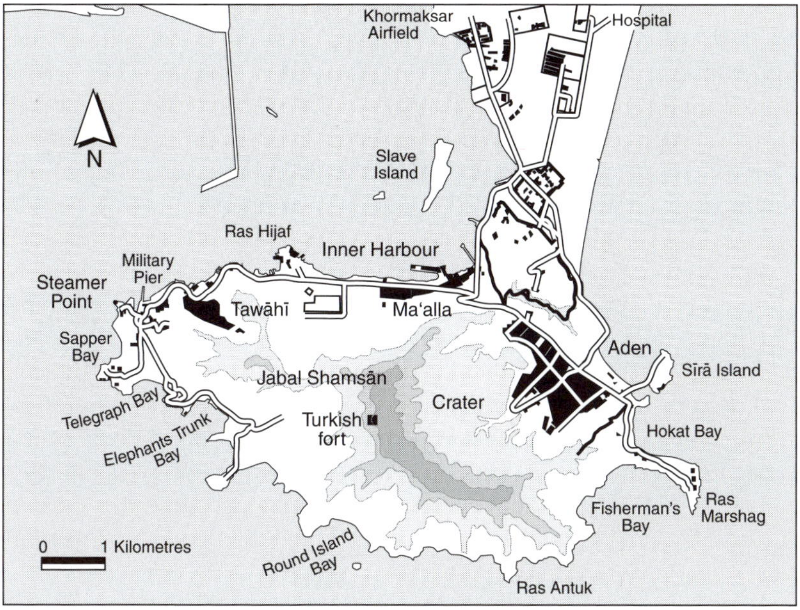

Map 2.3. Aden circa World War II

it was Aṣnaj who smuggled to the North copies of al-Kawākibī's *The Nature of Oppression*, a book whose importance some Yemenis compare with that of Rousseau's works for the French Revolution.[69]

Other movements receive less notice in the literature. Ḥusayn al-Dabbāgh of Mecca, however, at about this time, "shook Yemen and put fear in the Aden Government".[70] He visited the North, then Italy, Ethiopia, Britain and India before arriving in Ḥaḍramawt where he set up a school. From Mukallā he moved to Laḥj, where he set up another, and to Aden where he founded yet a third. In late 1939 he set off for the North with twenty-four of his students "all with their uniforms and drums" but settled for a time in Yāfiʿ where he proclaimed himself "he who summons to God". He set up yet another school. The shaykhs of al-Bayḍā' and Radāʿ, in the Imam's domain, then asked for him and in late 1940 he marched north with his followers and his drum and bugle corps only to have the Imam's army drive him back across the border. He retired to Radfān, where the Quṭaybīs flocked to him. With a British reward out for his arrest he moved back in 1942 to Ḥaḍramawt, where Ingrams returned him forcibly to Aden *en route* for Jiddah. How many movements like this linked the parts of Yemen one cannot tell.

When Zubayrī and Nuʿmān reached Aden (1944) they joined an existing ferment not only of Arab Nationalism but of specifically Yemeni Nationalism – a reformist complement to Yaḥyā's vision. They arrived at a crucial juncture, for the British base in wartime drew in workers from everywhere and these workers set up for themselves "village associations" connecting Aden with Lower Yemen, Yāfiʿ and Ḥaḍramawt. Nor was an intellectual focus lacking: Muḥammad Luqmān's *Fatāt al-jazīrah* ("Youth of the Peninsula"), a newspaper established in 1940, treated "South Arabia" or Yemen as culturally a single entity and it was Luqmān who encouraged Nuʿmān and Zubayrī to name their Party of Free Yemenis "The Greater Yemen Association" (*Jamʿiyyat al-yaman al-kubrā*). But the North was the pressing problem. The only state that was wholly Yemeni was, as modernists saw it, backward and oppressive. When the Arab League was founded (1945) Ḥusayn al-Kibsī was sent as Yaḥyā's delegate and was not allowed to say anything of Yemen or even of the Arab World without his master's agreement: indeed the catch-phrase "*anā kibsī*" was taken up to mean "I have no ideas, I have no opinions".

A mix of Adenis, Northerners and Muslims elsewhere shared concerns with "reform" (*iṣlāḥ*) in Yemen. The word meant to some "setting right" the affairs of Muslims as Yaḥyā once had against the Turks. To others it meant a constitution, and a document was secretly drawn up called "The Sacred National Charter" which in its final version named ʿAbdullāh Aḥmad al-Wazīr as Imam but "on the lines now followed by the most advanced nations of the civilised world . . ."[71] A parliament of some form was envisaged. The Muslim Brothers' emissary to Yemen, al-Fuḍayl al-Wartalānī, arrived in 1947 and the Charter was partly of his drafting; but ʿAbdullāh ʿAlī al-Wazīr, back from Cairo after almost eight years away, may perhaps have been the driving force to kill Yaḥyā. Finally, ʿAlī Nāṣir al-Qardaʿī agreed to assassinate the ageing Imam, though only after Sayyid Ḥusayn al-Kibsī gave a *fatwā* that it was just to do so.

The coup was precipitated by a false report in Aden. The Free Yemenis there (the Brothers in Cairo too) published the list of proposed government members, and no one in the North was ready. Al-Qardaʿī and men from Banī Ḥushaysh killed Yaḥyā, but the plan to murder Aḥmad in Taʿizz miscarried and the Crown Prince reached Ḥajjah, where he summoned the tribes and sought help from Ibn Saʿūd (probably he received none) while al-Wazīr despatched a telegram:

From the Commander of the Faithful, al-Dāʿī li-Dīn Allāh (he who summons to God's religion), ʿAbdullāh bin Aḥmad al-Wazīr to brother Sword of Islam Aḥmad, may God preserve you. Our condolences upon the death of your father Imam Yaḥyā and his sons, may God show them mercy. On account of this, those who loose and bind [i.e. the notables] have decided to choose us for the Imamate and have charged us to take it up . . . You shall have with us position, respect and peace.

Aḥmad's reply simply lists his lineage: "From the Commander of the Faithful, al-Nāṣir li-Dīn Allāh, Aḥmad son of the Commander of the Faithful al-Mutawakkil ʿalā Allāh Yaḥyā son of the Commander of the Faithful al-Manṣūr Billāh Muḥammad son of Yaḥyā Ḥamīd al-Din, to the wretched and despicable traitor . . . I am advancing on you with God's helpers."[72]

There was no general language yet in which a popular rising could be encouraged, and one doubts many people beyond Sanaa ever heard of the "Sacred Charter" or, if they did, cared what it said. The comment of an old man from Ḥāshid a generation later is probably near the truth: "It was 'God preserve the Imam!' and off we went. What did we know?"[73] Yaḥyā's murder repelled many, Aḥmad's presence attracted more, and the revolution was crushed within four weeks. Not only the conspirators but hundreds of suspected "Liberals" were cast in jail: "Imprison every wearer of a turban," yelled the mob, "and Allāh will find a way out for the innocent."[74] In (Shāfiʿī) Taʿizz at Aḥmad's victory parade

people stood on both sides of the road outside town shouting their blessings and approval. Even the women did not hang back from competing with the men, trilling wildly with joy at the procession of the Crown Prince . . .

People said that in the retinue before him were flocks of birds that the city had never seen before and no-one knew their names . . . From the time the birds left the city until the present day they have never been seen again.

If it was like this in Taʿizz, what must it have been like in the north?

Those close to ʿAbdullāh al-Wazīr (fellow *sayyids*, *qāḍīs*, but also friends and in-laws from shaykhly families such as Abū Raʾs of Dhū Muḥammad and al-Shāyif of Dhū Ḥusayn) were executed. So too was the "liberal Imam" himself whose severed head, by one account, was shown to the late Imam Yaḥyā's women-folk before being thrown on a rubbish tip. Sanaa was looted by tribesmen over a period not of days but of several weeks, and the new Imam Aḥmad, al-Nāṣir li-Dīn Allāh ("The Protector of God's Religion"), established himself in Taʿizz.

CHAPTER THREE

A new form of politics: the 1950s

The dominant language in Yemeni affairs through the 1940s was of Islam. After World War II, nationalist concerns became more immediate and from early in the 1950s Gamāl ʿAbd al-Nāṣir of Egypt launched mass appeals to the Arab World. Combined with societal shifts in the British zone, this new style of politics changed the nature of Yemeni events. When Kennedy Trevaskis arrived in Aden in 1951 the issue of the day was a move to East African shillings from Indian rupees; a dozen years later when, as governor, Trevaskis had a grenade thrown at him, Yemen's older politics had all unravelled.[1] We shall follow events to September 1962.

CHANGES IN THE SOUTH

World War II produced a boom in Aden. In October 1946 the first census since 1931 showed a 72 per cent increase in population from 47,533 to 82,359, only one-third of whom were "Aden-born Arabs". Almost as many (24,500) were Arabs from elsewhere, mainly from the Imam's domain, while the non-Arab population was made up largely of Indians, Jews who even then were trying to get to Palestine, and Somalis. This was the Crown Colony, an area of less than 200 square kilometres connected primarily with world trade. A surge in schooling had occurred, and in 1946 boys at the government secondary school boycotted classes to protest that the anniversary of the Arab League, founded the year before, was not a holiday.

Indians and Europeans dominated Aden's administration to the disgust of nationalists, who soon claimed "the Arab citizen lived at the margin of life in his own country".[2] Prejudice focused first on migrants from the North but then, more intensely, on Indians, and "Aden for the Adenis" (1949–50) was an early manifestation of bitter disputes over jobs and influence which increased through the 1950s as the port expanded, the migrant population grew, and the British introduced reforms. Nationalism, as David Holden remarks, was "a mirror image of the colonial power, and the more the British intervened . . . the more vigorous the image became". Between the port and its growing labour force, meanwhile, there remained a gap. Aden residents from the hinterland in 1946 numbered 6,500.

The Protectorates "up-country" are tagged on the end of the *Annual Report* for Aden. In the Eastern Protectorate in 1946

> All local States had a successful financial year; . . . and for the first time the Kathīrī State faces the future with a well balanced budget . . . It is regrettable that the year saw the first strikes in the Ḥaḍramawt; one in Mukallā in protest against the report of the Anglo-American Commission on Palestine, and the other in Sayyūn against new taxation.[3]

The Kathīrī and Quʿayṭī administrations were sound financially. Ḥaḍramawt overall was not. The Japanese invasions of 1941–2 had cut off remittances from Southeast Asia (in the war years, which were years of drought, thousands starved when landowners lacked means to employ or feed them), and the privileged position of Ḥaḍramīs in the Far East was unlikely to be re-established. Bū Bakr al-Kāf, whose personal wealth made the peace of 1937, had need by 1943 of British financial help and had given away all he had.

The alliance between great *sayyid* families and sultans had grown, however. ʿUbayd Bin ʿAbdāt, a shaykh at al-Ghurfah who supported the Irshādīs (those who challenged *sayyid* exclusivity), opposed the extension of *sayyid* and Kathīrī influence. He contested renewal of Ingrams' truce in 1940 and tried briefly to establish his own truce around Tarīm, but in 1943, in the midst of famine, he refused access to British food relief, thus confirming administrators' worst suspicions of "callous, avaricious chiefs", and in 1945 they drove him out by force, in effect extending the Kathīrī Sultanate. Wādī ʿAmd, meanwhile, was subdued by the Quʿayṭī Sultan, who attempted to tax palm-cultivation and ban the carrying of arms. Both moves were resisted. The 1946 *Report* deals briefly with such matters under the heading "Tribal, etc.".[4]

With the imposition of order backed by British air power, old relations of protection, arbitration and patronage in Ḥaḍramawt became meaningless. Local followings were less important now than state bureaucracy, and when the Quʿayṭī Sultan at Mukallā, in 1950, appointed a Sudanese as state secretary a riot broke out, stimulated by the newly-formed National Party. About twenty people died. Through the 1950s one finds a plethora of local movements, from the *sayyid*-centred Ḥaḍramī Reform

Association to a Social Democratic Party to the People's League Party, concentrated in the coastal towns.[5] In the countryside in 1953 Ingrams found apathy: "In tribal villages people sat or wandered aimlessly . . . The beduins too were listless and idle. Though they liked the peace, they complained that promises to protect their camel traffic had gone unfulfilled . . . There were murmurs that corruption and injustice went unchecked . . ."[6]

The meaning had gone out of people's lives, said Bū Bakr al-Kāf. Debt among agriculturalists was severe, however, and the British, paralysed by a cult of indirect rule, failed to address the problem.[7] The discontents of tribes, though never threatening to state administration, were not resolved either. Meanwhile migrants were forced home in increasing numbers. India squeezed out many Yemenis at independence (1947); in 1954 Indonesia forbade remittances; funds from East Africa were soon threatened too. The old diaspora world was everywhere collapsing and a parochial claim of "Ḥaḍramawt for the Ḥaḍramīs", like Aden for the Adenis, came to match petty nationalisms elsewhere.

In the Western Protectorate the 1946 *Report*'s bland line on "shepherding and stimulating new State Administrations" hides as radical an issue. In the aftermath of Ingrams' success in Ḥaḍramawt (1937) the old Treaties of Protection were changed where possible to Advisory Treaties. The impetus was "sound administration" and the language often Kiplingesque. Bayḥān, for instance,

> prior to 1943 had been in a state of anarchy and disruption which defies description . . . Today [1945] that area is a peaceful and organised community; schools have been opened, law courts function for the first time and taxes are paid to the Ruler. In September 1944, for instance, the monthly revenue . . . exceeded £230 – the first time that revenue had ever been collected.[8]

The new form of treaty, which promised more direct colonial support than previously, required signatories to accept advice on "welfare and development". By 1946 five out of the eleven main "rulers" in the Western Protectorate had signed such treaties, and three of the five were soon deposed by the British who had pressured them to sign.

Confusions in British thinking are evident from the language of post-war reports (such terms as "insolence" and "disobedience" become common, though the chiefs were supposedly independent) and from the direction of air action, which became fiercer. In March 1947 the Manṣūrīs in Lower ʿAwlaqī were bombed for cutting a road. In November that year the Quṭaybīs were bombed. The intention "to force

[them] to submit to government with the least possible delay" – government here meaning the Amir of Ḍāliʿ – was achieved, temporarily, by overwhelming force: 66 tons of bombs and 15,000 lbs of rockets were used in three days,[9] and in 1948 similar attacks were launched on the Bal Ḥārith near Bayḥān who "by refusing to bring in salt (on which tax is paid to the Central Administration) have endeavoured to bring financial ruin to the Sharīfate".[10]

Chiefs were the crux of policy. The idea of reaching lower, to encourage local councils or the like, was not developed, for it was always "too late"; the chiefs were "all we had to work with"; and sheer lack of money meant no decisive initiatives could be pursued. The old imperial forms were being challenged by colonial forms wherein officials took responsibility for progress, but co-ordination was scant among departments of London's government. Aden itself had strategic worth. The Treasury in 1953, however, felt "no obligation" to fund hinterland social services. An almost despairing application was made in the following year for £250,000 to fund development administration: "Conscience demands that a very great improvement must be made to the economic and social conditions in the Protectorate. Such improvements are also a political and practical necessity . . ."

The contradictions sharpened as the area became subject to the nationalist rhetoric of Gamāl ʿAbd al-Nāṣir, whose influence would be difficult to overstate: "from 1952 till his death in 1970 he simply bestrode the Arab World . . . His top political priority was to rid the Arab World of the relics of British domination and his voice carried, literally and metaphorically, to the furthest peasant hut and bedouin tent."[11] Local rulers in the South who opposed his aims were condemned as imperialist stooges. At home they were blamed, by relatives if no-one else, for the process of reform. The British and Egyptians shared a similar impatience with local practice – the term "feudal" was used of Yemeni affairs by both – but strategically were quite at odds, and the chiefs of the South were trapped.

Some rose to the challenge. The ʿAwdhalī Sultans, for instance, came to run their affairs effectively, and in Faḍlī there grew up a prosperous and complex administration. The Sharīf of Bayḥān made his state *sui generis*. Others, such as Ḍāliʿ and ʿAwlaqī, however, were a standing reproach to British aims, where rulers' income was disbursed on the basis not of administrative needs but of recipients' "importance" – a euphemism, thought Trevaskis, for nuisance potential. A minor shaykh thus complained of "oppression" because a sultan, at British urging, would no longer give presents of ammunition: the man's honour was slighted. A dirt road northeast from Aden to ʿAwlaqī violated the sovereignty of tribes it crossed, threatening their right to protection money, so they cut the road.[12]

THE ADEN HINTERLAND

Whoever in the hinterland felt slighted, be they chiefs or tribesmen, could appeal to the Imam for help or even move to his domains (those discontented with the Imam sometimes moved to British-protected chiefs). As Amir of Taʿizz, Aḥmad had been involved with the borderlands and with, for instance, the Quṭaybīs, east and south of Ḍāliʿ, long before his father's murder (1948); that murder he suspected was with British connivance; and the claim, voiced so often by Yaḥyā, that the Protectorate was part of Greater Yemen formed for Aḥmad a compelling truth which in the end was to leave him bankrupt. Intermittently he waged war against the British South, and Egypt's revolution (July 1952) gave him powerful allies who vilified not the "Christians", as in Yaḥyā's time, but "colonialism".

When the ruler of Ḍāliʿ, Ḥaydarah bin Naṣr, was driven from office in 1947, he and his son fled to North Yemen. Ḥaydarah, based near the border in Qaʿṭabah, remained a thorn in the British side thereafter, and when Naṣr died in 1954, Ḥaydarah's son Muḥammad was ignored and one of Ḥaydarah's nephews, Shaʿfal bin ʿAlī, was made Amir at British urging. Several members of the family were as dissatisfied with this as was Ḥaydarah and joined him in Qaʿṭabah, from where they encouraged "dissidence" among tribes near Ḍāliʿ.[13] These "Amīrī" tribes, so-called on British maps, no more considered themselves subjects of Ḍāliʿ than the Amirs considered themselves subjects of greater powers: indeed the year before Ḥaydarah fled North to get away from the British, the Shāʿirīs (around Ḍāliʿ itself) had fled North to get away from Ḥaydarah. With Ḥaydarah gone, they all came back again. But they refused to pay taxes to the new Amir any more than to the old, and in 1950 a group of them tried to assassinate the political officer. In 1956, supplied with money and guns from the Imam, they backed Ḥaydarah against the British and the new Amir. Parochial and divided though their aims may have seemed to others, Cairo Radio (Voice of the Arabs) called them nationalist *mujāhidīn*.

Through the British record runs a sense of grievance that whatever seemed for the general good was read otherwise. The Khanfar-Abyan scheme is an obvious case. Lower Yāfiʿ and Faḍlī had been at odds since at least the 1870s over what had once been spate-fed land, the land was out of production, and files on the dispute had become legendary. In 1943, in the midst of famine, Khanfar was taken under direct control. The British developed 600 acres. By 1947, when cotton-growing was promoted, this expanded to 5,000, and by 1954 to 45,000 acres where little had grown before; the Abyan Development Board by then employed 150 staff and the farming population had increased tenfold, an obvious success in British eyes.[14] Less obvious were the implications of cash-cropping and new forms of finance. By the mid-1950s "exploitation" was a nationalist issue, fuelled by complex uncertainties: "the construction of a road must raise land problems arising from such matters as the demand for trading sites; irrigation works give rise to survey, land and settlement problems . . . Such problems become part of the day to day lives of the people . . ."[15]

The colonial guise of the 1950s was shorts and white shirts in the service of "development". Yemenis in the South usually wore cotton *fūṭah*s (the skirts elsewhere called sarongs); but in photographs of the time the crisp shirts of such modernists as school-teachers are exactly those of colonial reformers. In their very resemblance each loathed the other, and as early as 1956 there were anti-British demonstrations by schoolboys in Laḥj, Jaʿār and Abyan where "the most extreme nationalist spirit prevailed". Not all local concerns were exclusively pan-Arab, however. A handbook of the time speaks, for instance, of "growing xenophobia among the Lower Yāfiʿ, who resent the grant of tenancies in land to immigrants and the employment of non-Yāfiʿīs by the Abyan Board. This growing sense of Yāfiʿī 'nationalism' is lent encouragement by the large Yāfiʿī colony in Aden . . ."[16]

Laḥj was paid more for cotton than was Abyan (the debt-structure of the projects differed), and it was widely assumed the British were extracting great wealth from agriculture; in the British view, meanwhile, the Protectorate States absorbed £1,000,000 per annum in free hand-outs. The British, in paternal mode, simply "knew" what needed doing to achieve development, and their certainties gave offence. In 1957 Muḥammad ʿAydarūs of Lower Yāfiʿ, who was Yāfiʿī *nāʾib* or deputy in Abyan and served on the development board, withdrew to the mountains in disgust. He raided Abyan for a time and remained at odds with the British thereafter. Cairo Radio referred to him also as one of many *mujāhidīn* promoting national, pan-Arab, revolution.

Not only could Cairo Radio support dissent but so could Imam

Plate 3.1. Schooling in Jaʿār.

Aḥmad, as when a plan for federation among rulers in the Western Protectorate was floated in 1954. Federation threatened his political claim to Greater Yemen. The arch-reactionary in the eyes of his domestic opponents (no development was taking place in the North; reformers were in chains and shackles) here swam the tide of Arab Nationalism:

GOD IS GREAT, GLORY TO GOD AND HIS PROPHET
A warning which concerns every zealous Yemeni.
Broadcasts continue . . .; the Voice of the Arabs exposes the Coloniser and his lackeys and warns our brothers, the people of the South, from falling into the trap set for them by the British . . .

Beware of selling your consciences for a vile price and for polluted money for you will pay heavily in the end . . .

By God, by your country, by your brothers, by your patriotism, by your religion, let not the hated aggressive Coloniser terrorise you with his arms . . .[17]

The British treated much of this cynically. Aḥmad, they felt, was a "mediaeval" figure whom no-one could take seriously; and no Shāfiʿī, they told themselves, wished Zaydī rule.

AḤMAD'S DOMAIN

The Republic which succeeded Aḥmad stressed his tyranny, and documentary sources from which to think further remain in private hands. Yet during his reign (1948–62) changes occurred which matter. For example, formal slavery largely disappeared.[18] So did local practices of a kind modern Islamists find reprehensible. Among certain eastern tribes, for instance, men and women used to dance at weddings and the like in closely opposed lines, while among tribes far north of Sanaa they sat in groups at opposite ends of the same room, the women satirising the men, usually cruelly and often lewdly, in verse, and the men twitting back the women. This all disappeared in the 1950s. How and why are not known. What we have are discussions of personalities.

Modern literature depicting anonymous social change obscures how willing people were to deal with personal power and how readily holders of power responded. The "Liberals", for example, jailed in huge numbers in 1948, petitioned the Imam and pinned their hopes on Aḥmad's son al-Badr Muḥammad;[19] indeed they pinned hopes on Aḥmad still. Through family connections or a well-turned poem most Liberals were unshackled within two years of the coup and some were soon released (others remained in prison longer, about thirty had been beheaded). Aḥmad Nuʿmān, a major progressive figure jailed in 1948, was brought to Taʿizz from the dungeons of Ḥajjah on the second anniversary of the coup's collapse, and his speech in praise of the Imam "is reported to have been so excellent that the Imam and others of the audience were reduced to tears".[20]

Sayyid Aḥmad al-Shāmī, also in Ḥajjah, wrote a panegyric in 1953 placing Imam Aḥmad in a world of historic figures, of Plato, Bacon and Nietzsche, of Napoleon and Bismark, of Hitler, Mussolini and Churchill, Saʿd Zaghlūl of Egypt "and other sons of our modern age". Aḥmad's genius would lead Yemen forward. Nuʿmān wrote the introduction:

> In so far as Yemen is subject today to the developments of the age . . . one of the first things it acquired, in the period of the late Imam Yaḥyā, was a governmental system with the formation of ministries, a council of ministers, the system of [having] a Crown Prince, a Royal *dīwān*, and the establishment of modern schools . . .
>
> All this . . . broadened out in the time of the Imam al-Nāṣir [Imam Aḥmad] . . . and the post of Prime Minister was given to Sword of Islam Ḥasan without dispute or opposition; . . . Not a thing changed of what had been instituted by

Plate 3.2. "Victory Day", Taʿizz, 1950.

the late Martyr Imam [Yaḥyā], and the position of Crown Prince was accorded Prince Sword of Islam al-Badr as it had been accorded the Imam al-Nāṣir in the time of his father, and likewise with all improvements considered new in Yemen that are close to systems worldwide.[21]

Progress, runs this attempt at persuasion, is in the nature of the governmental system and North Yemen's was already of a kind with those of countries such as Syria or Egypt.

Aḥmad was more open to the world than Yaḥyā – he was criticised, indeed, by his brother Ḥasan for "letting in foreigners" – but was no more willing to change governmental practice. Aviation, as in Chapter 2, provides an illustration. Aḥmad when he came to power bought a couple of DC-3s and a pair of smaller aircraft, and on "victory day" 1950 his speech was dropped in leaflet form. Al-Wazīr in 1948, said the text, had "communicated with the enemies of Islam asking them to come out with aircraft and tanks to take possession of the country" (that the claim was untrue hardly robbed it of effect), but now, under Aḥmad's guidance, Yemeni aircraft flew above Sanaa. In 1951 he bought another DC-3. They were all at Aḥmad's personal disposal, however, and when the (Swedish) crews received orders they took off immediately for fear he would change his mind.[22] Paperwork and petitions were centralised as whimsically: "Everything hangs upon the King's nod," wrote a governor of Aden, "Yet his situation is pathetic, for he knows he has no friends . . ."

The country was no wealthier than in Yaḥyā's time. In 1950 beggars appeared in Aden from the North, where starvation was widespread on account of drought. Cotton-growing was tried in the Tihāmah from about 1951; the old Turkish salt-works at Ṣalīf were revived. However, Aḥmad from early in his reign was desperate to secure financial help, and an American mission visited Taʿizz in 1950. Expansion of the port at Ḥudaydah was discussed, and a road from there to Sanaa (the trip by truck took at best about 18 hours), yet agreement was baffled through a whole decade, for the Americans needed some indication of where funds might be applied while the Yemenis had constantly to refer to Aḥmad, whose governance remained as Rīḥānī described for Yaḥyā. For a government truck to be moved in Taʿizz, or even for mules to receive their fodder, required the Imam's decision.[23]

Those who knew Imam Aḥmad say his moods depended on fear of death and thus of imminent divine judgement. Often he consulted astrologers. His paranoia was not helped by morphine, for the pain of rheumatism, and a mix of other drugs, and he was subject, it was said, to "fairly regular mystical crises during which he lost touch with the world, absorbing himself in fasting and prayer. During such periods – eight days, fifteen days, whatever it was – one could not hope for anything from him, for nothing at all got through."[24] Physically he was unforgettable, and Ingrams' picture from 1941 applied through the 1950s:

> His most alarming feature was his great bulging eyes set off by a forked beard, one prong shorter than the other. He seemed the 'Bluebeard' of my youth come to life. He was short and stout, reeked of scent and was dressed in flowered satin with a large turban wound on a cap several sizes too small and perched precariously on his round bullet-head.

As a Yemeni author mentions, "This intelligent, even genial, man (for how else to explain his reign lasted fourteen years)" was nicknamed "the Djinn".

His household differed from his father's in the role of important women. If any of Yahyā's womenfolk are mentioned it is usually an ageing wife known for her simplicity of manner. Aḥmad, however, although protocol required that her name not be used publicly, entrusted a niece named "Amat Karīm" with his seals and much of his correspondence.[25] Supposedly when a marriage was proposed, Aḥmad said her husband would have to move in with her, not vice versa, for she was indispensable. Two of Aḥmad's daughters also had their husbands live with them in Taʿizz "palaces". A whole female world was gathered there with Aḥmad as head of, literally, the Royal House, and the patrimonial style of Yaḥyā's day was centralised still further while the nominal equality of male family-members (Aḥmad had brothers to consider where Yaḥyā had only sons) was dealt with by excluding them.

Aḥmad, as Yaḥyā had done, gave the brothers "ministries". Unlike his father, he did not retain them long as provincial governors where power lay. Nor were fellow *sayyid*s of other houses as prominent as before. Ḥasan for years was "viceroy" of the north, but provinces were in the end largely placed under men from *qāḍī* families: al-Bayḍāʾ under Muḥammad al-Shāmī, Ibb under Aḥmad al-Sayāghī, Ṣaʿdah under ʿAbd al-Raḥmān al-Sayāghī, Ḥudaydah under Aḥmad al-ʿAmrī. Ḥasan is supposed to have said, "From now on we must never put ʿAlawīs [*sayyid*s, the Prophet's kin] in great positions for they will challenge our sovereignty as ʿAbdullāh al-Wazīr did, to whom Imam Yaḥyā gave high positions . . . And the Imam agreed with his brother's thinking."[26]

Ironically, a rhetoric of Qaḥṭānīs against ʿAdnānīs ("native" Yemenis such as *qāḍī*s against the Prophet's kin) began to spread at precisely the time non-*sayyid*s became prominent and some Zaydīs complained of "Shāfiʿī government". Taʿizz, not Sanaa, was now the capital. The shift recapitulated that of the Qāsimīs 250 years before, when the *dawlah* or dynastic state, unlike its charismatic founders, moved south of Sanaa, and the very distinction between Upper and Lower Yemen should be treated cautiously: the Abū Ra's family, for instance, were shaykhs of Baraṭ in the far northeast but their politics were very much bound up with Taʿizz, and Bayt Dammāj near Ibb, although originally from Baraṭ too, were Shāfiʿī notables. Court affairs account for what occurred far more than does theology.

Before he was Imam, Aḥmad had razed the tomb of Ibn ʿAlwān near Taʿizz. Many Shāfiʿī divines were as suspicious of venerating saints as were Zaydīs, and this seems, perhaps oddly, not to have been a burning issue (the best remembered protest in fact was from the Zaydī poet al-Zubayrī). Nor was Aḥmad tolerant of Zaydī extremism. In early 1952 Aḥmad Bā Salāmah of Ibb gave a sermon in which he praised the first four Caliphs of Islam, thus offending some Zaydī listeners for whom the three apart from ʿAlī were of doubtful worth. They attacked him. The Imam had them all arrested, however, sending twelve to the Ḥajjah dungeons.[27] The difference between "sects" was seldom doctrine. Rather, as a British observer found, most soldiers in Taʿizz (though oddly Aḥmad's bodyguard were Zarānīq) were now Zaydīs, the civil population Shāfiʿī.

In spite of this division . . . there is an almost universal loyalty to the Yemen, if not to the person of the Imam . . . They consider their country to be one of the most blessed; they want it to be one of the most respected and renowned . . . they imagine . . . their land more fertile than any other, and the mineral resources of their country to be unlimited.[28]

In 1940, an Iraqi had complained that Yemenis had "no national or patriotic feeling": they spoke not of Arabism but always of Islam, which they thought corrupted everywhere except Yemen. Their pride in the 1950s now took more plainly secular forms, as did the dynastic state itself where authority was "stripped of its fairy-tale disguises" – the Imam was King. His portrait in Taʿizz was illuminated by neon or electric light bulbs.

The appointment of Aḥmad as Crown Prince had been morally problematic; the appointment of his son, al-Badr, never raised such issues and the older Zaydī distrust of settled power had now been marginalised,[29] but the immediate problems were just as sharp. Al-Badr was widely held to be incompetent. His period as governor of Ḥudaydah, for instance, was marred by binge drinking while he struggled over Tihāmah land-deals against his uncle ʿAbdullāh. The younger of al-Badr's uncles – al-Qāsim, ʿAlī and Ismāʿīl – also drank, and at a function at Ṣalīf in 1953, ʿAlī "had forcibly to be escorted back to Sanaa after arriving totally inebriated and quite out of his senses". Ḥasan bin Yaḥyā was more solid. He had enormous influence in the far north and ran Sanaa independently, refusing Aḥmad even access to the Sanaa treasury; ʿAbbās was influential in the north also, while ʿAbdullāh had experience of the wider world. In the early 1950s there were rumours that ʿAbdullāh and ʿAbbās intended poisoning Ḥasan, and such rumours soon connected the world's great powers, none of which seem in fact to have been interested, with minutiae of local intrigue as if global affairs all centred upon Yemen. Politics turned on talk of plot and counter-plot among the Imam's family.

Land owned by the family had attracted comment in Yaḥyā's time. In the Tihāmah alone they were thought now to own 9,000 hectares, with another 2,700 in Wādī Surdud. There were other great holdings too. Large areas of Wādī Mawr (perhaps 15,000 hectares) were owned by Hādī Hayg, a Shāfiʿī baron of the lowlands whom the Turks had made a *pāshā* and whose links with Ibn Saʿūd were strong. The al-Jabalī family, one of whom was Aḥmad's commercial agent, owned perhaps 2,250 hectares. In the highlands individual holdings were not so large, but continuities of power (Muḥammad Aḥmad Pāshā, for instance, was *ʿāmil* of Taʿizz as his father had been in Turkish times; ʿAlī Muḥsin Pāshā al-Jamāʿī, though jailed in 1948, re-emerged as *ʿāmil* of Ibb and his family at ʿUdayn were as prominent as ever) went usually with continuities of landed wealth.

The aristocracy, if we wish to call it such, was vast and sprawling. A survey largely done in the Tihāmah estimated that 90 per cent of the peasantry between them possessed only 20 per cent of the farming land, but al-ʿAṭṭār suggests that in the highlands 60 per cent of farmland might be closer the mark[30] and more recent and detailed work suggests huge variation of a kind almost calculated to fragment unhappiness. Rather than direct domination of the many by a few on the model of feudal Europe one was dealing often with overlapping forms of dominance. The small land-holder exploited by the larger might himself exploit others on some second plot of land and in any case feel proprietary interest in the land he worked: wage-labour was thought demeaning but share-cropping remained ambiguous. To maintain control of scattered holdings, great landowners needed influence at court (apart from taxation and military support, the Imam often judged their disputes over marriage and inheritance), while small landowners thought primarily in terms of landlord against landlord and discontent took the form of purely local misery or a wish to emigrate.

The growing Northern diaspora of workers and small traders overlapped with a spread of students. The "famous forty", for example, sent abroad before Yaḥyā's death to learn modern administration, spent school-days in Lebanon and Egypt. Others reached Cairo by themselves.[31] There and in Aden, expatriate Liberals flourished. Aden schools saw a constant thin stream of Northern students, and from Aden to the North moved pamphlets and satirical broadsheets criticising Aḥmad's rule. There were soon further sources of work near home, for Saudi Arabia's oil economy was growing (by the mid-1950s about 40,000 Egyptians worked there) and in 1955 the Saudi government decreed for the first time that Yemenis could enter without permits, which attracted Zaydīs as well as Shāfiʿīs. In the North some trade spread. Paraffin, lamp-oil and cotton cloth came in from Aden, where the Yemeni population was growing also; trucks moved between there and Sanaa over rough tracks. A few traders began to cluster in towns such as Ibb and Taʿizz, and some acted as correspondents for a man named ʿAbduh Shūlaq who established himself in Jiddah as a remittance agent.[32] But commerce scarcely opened up the country. Aḥmad taxed emigrant labour (if men failed to pay then soldiers were billeted on their families at home), and in a manner reminiscent of recent times he controlled flows of key goods.

In 1950 a Yemen Trading Company had been formed to deal in sugar, flour, rice and tobacco. Almost 12 per cent of the shares were divided among "merchants" – unfortunately we do not have their names – and 10 per cent among various princes. Al-Ḥasan and the Imam's adviser, Qadi Ḥusayn al-Ḥalālī, received each a small bloc, and ʿAlī al-Jabalī, Aḥmad's commercial agent in Aden, received 6 per cent. Over 50 per cent was allotted to Imam Aḥmad. Sugar soon cost twice in the North what it did in Aden. (The monopoly was formally revoked; the practice seems not to have reverted.) In 1956 a deal for oil and mineral exploration with a US-based corporation upset certain northern shaykhs, but "the Imam replied that though the land might be theirs it was his too, that the money was his and that he was going to keep it, and that they were going to prison". Fifteen were locked up.[33] Their followers, it appears, did nothing. Peasants politically, as Marx once wrote, are usually like potatoes in a sack, not a unified body; and tribes are more divided still. Within North Yemen there was no urban proletariat, but in Aden there was by now and its members were largely Northerners.

THE NEW POLITICS

Aden colony connected less with Yemen in many respects than with world commerce and the remnants of imperial strategy. Iranian oil, for instance, was shipped to Aden. British Petroleum set up an oil-refinery at Little Aden, in 1952, whose construction drew in a large work-force from Shāfiʿī areas of the Imam's domain (mainly from Ḥugariyyah); and shipping increased, because of bunkering on the Europe–Far East route, to the point where, by 1958, Aden was said to be the second busiest port in the world after New York. Population rose almost exponentially (Fig. 3.1). The 1955 census gives a total of 138,000 of whom 37,000 were reckoned Adeni. Close to 50,000 now were Northerners, mostly unaccompanied men. Forms of politics changed. In 1948 there were strikes over wages; soon there were strikes over living standards. 1956 saw seventy strikes which "produced the first warnings of what repercussions might arise from conditions prevailing in the Middle East generally",[34] and at the end of that year Britain invaded Suez, forfeiting what standing it retained in the Arab World.

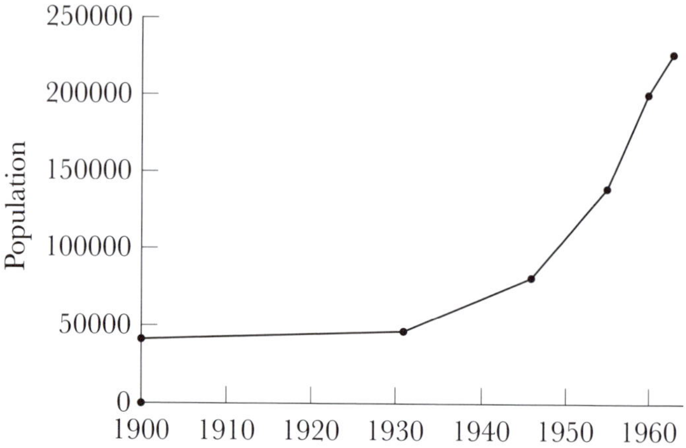

Figure 3.1. Aden population, 1900–65

The number of unions rose, meanwhile, with colonial encouragement, from two that were registered in 1953 to twenty-five affiliated with the Aden Trades Union Congress (ATUC) by March 1959. Some were small and some odd: the Civil Contractors Union as of 1956 had eight formal members, the Qāt Sellers Union had no figures available. But already by then the Technical Workers Union numbered 4,300, and by 1959 15,000 men were unionised.[35] In the climate of the time local discontents and pan-Arabism coincided readily, while a "new class" of young clerks and intellectuals in Aden came to organise urban workers who themselves were nearly all small farmers from territory ruled by Imam Aḥmad. Not surprisingly, the colonial government denied the migrants voting rights. Without them no politics was viable, however, for "Aden-born Arabs", as the British called them, were outnumbered by workers from Lower Yemen and increasingly also from the hinterland. In 1955, after BP's expansion, migrants from the hinterland were close to 14 per cent of the population, almost 19,000 people.

Among the Aden Arabs were important families – Makāwī, Luqmān, Ḥasan ʿAlī, Girgirah – whose position is well described by Gavin: Aden for more than a century had been a diaspora trading town, and their particular trade was in "the arcana of accumulated family knowledge – their own image of Aden's reality" with which they mediated between global and local interests.[36] In 1949–50 they had formed the Aden Association ("Aden for the Adenis"). They demanded self-rule within the Commonwealth, and when elected seats were first provided on Aden's

Plate 3.3. Aden Airways at Mukayrās.

Legislative Council (1955) they willingly contested these, for orderly if tardy progress to independence was the promise held out everywhere to British colonies. In 1956 that promise was revoked. London announced that Aden was too important for "any fundamental relaxation" of Britain's hold, and the Association was left stranded. It broke up in an argument about restricting *qāt*.

The view of old Aden families differed from that of the new class, some of whom were Aden citizens. Aḥmad al-Aṣnaj was mentioned in Chapter 2 as president in the 1930s of an Aden-based reform club. The family were Northerners by origin. Aden in the 1930s was a provincial town in Britain's Indian empire where such families might rise to colonial obscurity, but ʿAbdullāh al-Aṣnaj, who was Aḥmad's nephew brought up in Aden though born in Sanaa, emerged in the 1950s as leader of the ATUC, "employed as a clerk by that most characteristic institution of the twentieth century in South Arabia – Aden Airways".[37] Colonial officials disliked him (he resembled them too much for comfort), and his politics were hard to deal with. He spoke often of unity. But unity with Imam Aḥmad's domain, where no politics of labour existed, was implausible; broader Arab unity presented no detailed programme. His rhetoric both obscured and expressed divisions among groups in Aden, which were deeply complex. Old Aden families, new class, and Lower Yemeni migrants, meanwhile, felt equally distant from the hinterland, which they all saw as filled with savages.[38]

The hinterland Rulers distrusted Aden, nor were they inclined to co-operate with each other. State systems, however, continued growing. A corps of locally-recruited political officers emerged (eleven already by 1947), and local functionaries in other fields: by 1955 there were fourteen local agricultural officers, for instance, besides a staff of clerks and drivers. Soldiers, mechanics, teachers and medical orderlies all appeared in the South in the 1950s, and in places development changed the social structure. Many of Abyan's new farmers, for example, had been non-tribal share-croppers, and two-thirds of the project staff were local, most of them, like trades-unionists in Aden, being newly educated men unattached to local governance. The pattern of education was itself specific. Aden put more children through school than the Protectorates, and in the Western Protectorate (by the end of the 1950s there were 56 primary schools, five intermediate) the schools were in small towns: "most pupils come from the non-tribal classes living nearby, the number of tribal boys in the schools being negligible".[39]

A later analyst, Volker Stanzel, speaks of a "provincial lower middle class". Qaḥṭān al-Shaʿbī, later to be President of South Yemen, was in the 1950s an agricultural officer; Anwar Khālid held a similar post later. Faḍl al-Salāmī and Sayf al-Ḍāliʿī (another famous name post-independence) were apparently political officers. ʿAbd al-Fattāḥ Ismāʿīl, from Ḥugariyyah in the Imam's domain, began his political life in the BP refinery at Aden and taught at a government school in Shaykh ʿUthmān. Through the 1950s a network of students, teachers and young functionaries comes gradually to link Aden with Yemen's regions through semi-clandestine parties, aided in part by the spread of village associations.[40] A small Communist party appeared in the 1940s. The Baʿth party's presence dates from about 1956, and George Habbash's Movement of Arab Nationalists (MAN) also later established cells. For the moment, however, party connections largely skipped the hinterland.

The border between North and South was permeable. Trucks trundled back and forth, and the line had small effect on older links. Tribes from north of the line, for instance, attended the festival of al-Muḥḍār in Yāfiʿ (south of the frontier) on the sixth day of ʿĪd al-Aḍḥā; tribes south of the line used to meet at the hot springs of al-Ḥajīlah, north of the frontier in al-Bayḍā', the latter festival on a solar calendar. Between the ʿAwlaqīs, south, and Āl Ḥumayqān, north, a famous exchange of poems is remembered, and disputes between Āl Ḥumayqān and Yāfiʿ over shared grazing took no account of the official border. But south of the line was a seething of influence between Aḥmad and the British (Map 3.1).

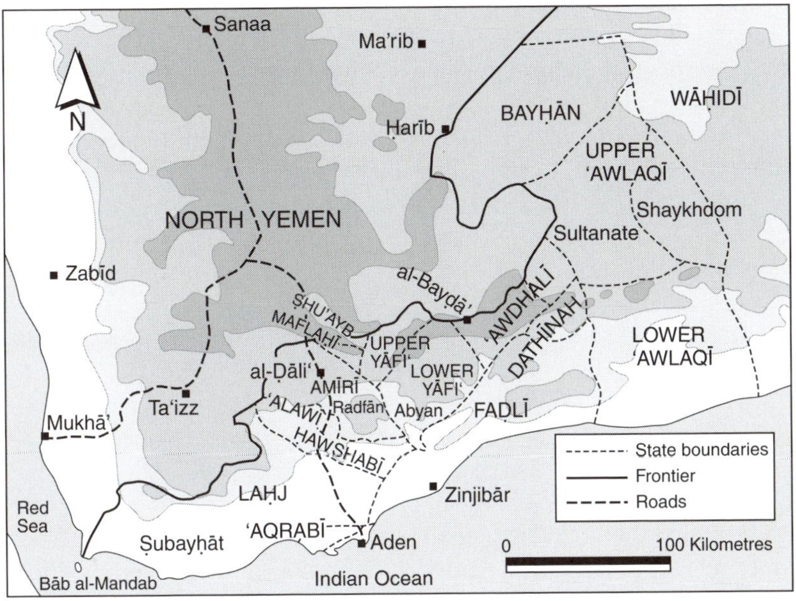

Map 3.1. Western Aden Protectorate, 1950s

The British tried to push a road through from Aden to Upper ʿAwlaqī: with Aḥmad's support, the Rabīzīs of Upper ʿAwlaqī (320 armed men) and Ḍammānīs of ʿAwdhalī (maybe 500 men) rose with effects far beyond their numbers. The ruling family of the Upper ʿAwlaqī Shaykhdom split. In 1954 assassination attempts were made on Europeans in Ḍāliʿ and Abyan; the Quṭaybīs through late 1956 were divided among themselves. Even Faḍlī, which borders the southern coast, received 3,000 rifles from the North in 1957–8 as some turned to one power, some the other, and Jaḥḥāf near al-Ḍāliʿ produced a "spectacular revolt". In the earlier part of this wave of troubles, what was meant to be the British instrument of order – the Aden Levies – proved largely useless. In summer 1954 there were 281 separate "incidents" in a two-week period, but the Levies deserted or failed to act, and having started to think in terms of development appropriate to such African territories of the 1950s as Nyasaland, officials found themselves back where their predecessors had been twenty years before: "Here we are," wrote Trevaskis, "spending the greater part of each day worrying about the reactions of this tribe or that section, . . . and . . . barely five minutes to devote to . . . administration . . ."[41]

Those states least administered seemed often to do best against Imam Aḥmad. The Sharīf of Bayḥān, for instance ("a robustly Tudor figure", one governor called him) pursued a private war: if the Imam subverted his tribes, he subverted the Imam's and was able to spread trouble a long way inside the Imam's territory, with the British often holding his coat-tails and asking him to stop. "Administration" around Ḍāliʿ or in Faḍlī, by contrast, upset more people than it pleased. Court-systems, taxes, organised budgets all trespassed on somebody's hopes or livelihood, and the colonial government lacked the means or will to push through a transformation.

In a few places south of the line, such as Ḍāliʿ, Aḥmad's "victory day" (defeat of the 1948 coup) was celebrated. He opened a school in Qaʿṭabah to children from Southern tribes, and plainly felt these were his people;[42] few of them felt so, but nor did most wish to be British "subjects" (*raʿiyyah*, a word also used of peasants and "weak" share-croppers). The British for their part, in support of the "agent Sultans", as Cairo Radio called them, and a general peace, used air control against "their" tribes; in the 1950s, however, unlike the 1920s, they were not willing to threaten the North with reprisals for running guns and ammunition across the border. The imperial certainties had disappeared, and exiled Liberals in Aden were constrained, if not expelled, for fear of offending the Imam. But the arbitrary divisions of the nineteenth century had caught up now with all involved.

The population of the Western Protectorate by the mid-1950s was about 400,000 and Ḥaḍramawt about 300,000. The population of the North was more than 4 million. Aden by itself was near 140,000 of whom less than a third were "Adenis", yet on this tiny foothold rested questions of global strategy in the face of both Russian policy (this, of course, was the period of the Cold War) and Arab Nationalism.[43] London's "defence white paper" of 1957 saw Aden as a major base and Britain as a global power still. To some, the way forward seemed to be to lease base-rights by treaty from an independent South comprising Aden and Protectorates together, but London, they complained, saw the port and its hinterland as separate issues.

The traditional link between Aden and the hinterland was Laḥj. Successive Sultans, with their palaces, turbans and Indian frock-coats, had been recognised as "premier chiefs". Sultan ʿAlī bin ʿAbd al-Karīm al-ʿAbdalī, however, from early in the 1950s declared himself an Arab Nationalist, supporting and supported by Muḥammad al-Jifrī of the *sayyid* family who had tried in the 1930s to help form a peace in ʿAwlaqī.

Al-Jifrī was president of the South Arabian League (SAL), formed in 1951, which demanded independence for Aden and Protectorates together.[44] They made much of Muḥammad ʿAydarūs's complaints against the Abyan Board; Shaykhān al-Ḥabshī, a Ḥaḍramī educated in Baghdad, was influential within Aden; and in Ḥaḍramawt, Aḥmad Bā Faqīh in Mukallā allied discontented tribes with young urban radicals against the Quʿayṭī Sultan. For a time the SAL seemed everywhere.

Rumours spread that the Sultan of Laḥj was about to join the Union of Syria and Egypt, declared in early 1958. Legally and in his own view Sultan ʿAlī remained a sovereign ruler. The Governor of Aden ordered the arrest of the Jifrī brothers, the Sultan complained in London, his little army left for the North, and the British had him formally deposed, congratulating themselves that no demonstration materialised in Laḥj. In 1959, however, Sultan ʿAlī broadcast from Cairo: "This time last year, the imperialists lost their temper and were betrayed by their tricks. The false mark of dignity was removed from their faces, revealing their premeditated intention and their malicious plan without shame or remorse. Their forces broke into peaceful Laḥj . . ."[45] The reason, he claimed, was the success of the Laḥj cotton scheme. Muḥammad ʿAydarūs of Yāfiʿ had made the Abyan scheme an issue because Laḥj received more for their cotton than did Abyan. Now the logic was reversed: "while the Abyan project, which was supervised by imperialism, was collapsing and deteriorating, the agricultural project of Laḥj, which is supervised by the people of Laḥj, was increasing in strength and prosperity; . . . we were achieving great deeds". These, so the argument ran, a jealous imperialism had to sabotage; and the fact the Laḥj scheme benefited largely the ruling family was not at this stage relevant.[46] At about the time of Sultan ʿAlī's overthrow, Qaḥṭān al-Shaʿbī of the agricultural department fled north as well and also soon appeared in Cairo.

CAIRO AND SANAA

The power of the Arab Nationalist "summons" turned on transistor radios. Imam Yaḥyā, quite successfully, had restricted wireless receivers, but Aḥmad, faced with pocket-sized devices, could not do the same and neither could the British. There is no doubt that northern tribesmen whom urbanites later mocked for ignorance were listening regularly to Cairo by the mid-1950s; so were tribesmen in both Protectorates.[47] But the effect was discounted by those higher up in British administration, where images of the "woolly badu" fit poorly with nationalism and unrest was attributed to such "traditional" causes as a prickly sense of honour or outright venality. Often this was right but never wholly so. Aḥmad was more realistic.

From before he was ever Imam, Aḥmad lived among talk of reform and of examples from other Arab states, the best of his advisers were in some sense reformers, and he himself was jealous of his Saudi neighbours' growing prosperity, not to speak of the apparent power at the time of such states as Syria and Egypt. He could sound very like his father: "It is a matter of choosing between liberty in poverty and dependence in luxury. I've chosen independence."[48] In practice, however, from the time he received the first American delegation in 1950 he sought help strategically and was thus trapped in contradiction. Having factions around him, provided he remained in charge, was integral to the way he ran his court and indeed the country.

Against the British in Aden, nationalist Egypt with its ambitions to dominate the region was a powerful ally; reformist Egypt with its modernist antipathy to "feudal" rulers was potentially a threat, but at first a muted one. Soon after Voice of the Arabs was first established by Egypt, Muḥammad al-Zubayrī, the most prominent Liberal to escape in 1948, was allowed to broadcast. A month later, in August 1953, Ismāʿīl al-Jirāfī of the Yemeni Legation in Cairo, got to broadcast in reply. About the time of Zubayrī's talk on radio, pamphlets from the United Yemeni Association, also partly based in Egypt, circulated in Taʿizz, Ḥudaydah and Sanaa. Zubayrī, however, also corresponded with the Imam directly.[49] One petitioned the Imam for change still or supported some rival claimant.

In 1955 a group of soldiers attacked villagers near Taʿizz, but then panicked from fear of retribution. They trapped the Imam in his Taʿizz palace and an *ad hoc* delegation of notables asked Aḥmad to step down in favour of ʿAbdullāh, to whom ʿAbbās telegraphed support from Sanaa. Al-Badr rallied help, however, and the Liberals, Nuʿmān and Zubayrī (one in Yemen, one in Cairo), supported al-Badr. The people of Taʿizz were soon as little keen on violent change.[50] The muddle collapsed, ʿAbbās was executed, supposedly in tears, and when ʿAbdullāh was beheaded a list of foreign bank accounts is said to have been found tied below his knee. Ḥasan, abroad at the time, was forbidden to return to Yemen; al-Badr gained influence, and among the Liberals who turned to him at this stage was Qadi ʿAbd al-Raḥmān al-Iryānī (later President of North Yemen), who had twice reached the execution ground before Imam Aḥmad changed his mind.

Al-Badr was sent on diplomatic missions to Britain, Eastern Europe, and not least to Egypt where he spoke of spending Imam Yaḥyā's vast inherited treasure (quite probably there was none) on development. Increasingly he was said to be impressed with the achievements of ʿAbd al-Nāṣir, as Trevaskis was told by a doubtful source:

> I came to know a Yemeni, who hovered on the fringe of Muḥammad al-Badr's household, and from him I would hear how eagerly the young man would read the Egyptian papers: his eyes shining as he looked at photographs of Nāṣir's triumphant progress, . . . of the thick khaki columns tramping past the saluting dais.
>
> 'We will make a new Yemen, just as they are making a new Egypt,' he would say excitedly . . .[51]

Egypt supported al-Badr strongly. At the time of the attempted coup, Cairo Radio supported Aḥmad. Nationalist Egypt for the moment outweighed reformist Egypt, and in 1956 Egypt, Saudi Arabia and Yemen agreed the Jiddah Pact, for Britain was the enemy of all. Saudi Arabia was at odds with London over oases that now belong to Oman and Abu Dhabi, and the Saudis used Sharūrah as a base to move weapons into both Protectorates; Egypt would pressure Britain where it could; and Aḥmad's claim to the South required allies. The interests of Yemeni Liberals in Cairo (Nuʿmān now joined Zubayrī there) were marginal to those of states.

In early 1956 Nuʿmān's and Zubayrī's names appeared on a pamphlet printed first in Aden, "The Demands of the People" (*maṭālib al-shaʿb*): "Poverty has driven hundreds of thousands abroad. The rulers of the country have been evil, false and ignorant . . . No-one is left in towns and villages. All live in fear of robbery, bloodshed and rebellion. Foreign powers hope to occupy, colonise and enslave the Yemen, seeing that the Yemenis have no government . . ."[52] The pamphlet may well have been the work of Muḥammad Nuʿmān, Aḥmad Nuʿmān's son. In Aden he allied the nationalist Yemeni Union with the United National Front, in effect a labour organisation, and by demanding an end to both "imperialism" and "reaction" drew his father's generation towards more radical politics. The Imam meanwhile attacked emigration by requiring that migrants guarantee a replacement on their fields.

The Tihāmah, where emigration rates seem not to have been so high, suffered worse than did the highlands. People there, after Aḥmad's campaigns of the 1920s, were like sheep with no shepherd, as ʿAbd al-Malik al-Ṭayyib was to phrase it later: "official control and military domination over them is greater and stronger than in any other area".[53]

Merchants in Ḥudaydah were able to organise a form of local co-operative and gain minor concessions from Aḥmad, though even here anti-Aḥmad slogans were appearing by now on walls; labourers in Ḥudaydah were miserably paid, and agricultural labourers beyond the town were paid still worse. In the Tihāmah and Lower Yemen alike, meanwhile, freelance northerners from the highlands imposed themselves as policemen and tax-gatherers, often chewing a silver riyāl's worth of *qāt* a day though army salaries were only eight riyāls a month.[54]

Aḥmad drew tax from a peasantry fragmented as in his father's day. Nor did soldiers form a coherent bloc. Whether regular or freelance, they were linked to those in power by *kafīl*s or personal guarantors. Shāfiʿī notables were often kept in place, as in Yaḥyā's time, for their influence was mainly local; great Zaydī figures among the tribes, whose influence might have reached much further, were not given governmental rank. Lesser shaykhs, with a following of six or ten men each, were instead made *ʿarāʾif*, people "recognised" by the Imam, and entrusted with petty tax-gathering. The resilience of this political system, where everything depended on personal ties and all decisions were referred to the Imam himself, was extraordinary. Economically the country rotted.

Peasants in many areas were by now losing over 70 per cent of their crop in tax and bribes, and it was said that 30,000 pilgrims to Mecca in 1956 elected simply not to return. Hādī Hayg, still a power in the Tihāmah as in Turkish days, reputedly charged those in his domain 25 riyāls (a fortune by farmers' standards) to have a marriage contract formed; in Sanaa an appeal judge acquired extensive real estate by way of dishonest judgements and a second notable sold passports at up to 100 riyāls a time.[55] Nor did "development" make progress. A French company hired in March 1953 to work at Mukhā' and Ḥudaydah achieved little. Some concessions were given to explore for oil and minerals, with no result. A textile factory was established with French help, at Bājil in 1957, but apparently produced nothing. And Aḥmad was effectively at war with Aden.

Qadi Aḥmad al-Sayāghī, governor of Ibb, arranged a meeting with the British at al-Ḍāliʿ under cover of discussing a border incident. There he suggested that no-one in court circles supported Aḥmad's dispute with British Aden, for all it was doing was giving the Egyptians and the Saudis influence. He claimed to be speaking for al-Badr. The British sometimes wondered if he did not have ambitions of his own, however, and his enemies whispered the same idea in the Imam's ear. Sayāghī was a leading figure. "His energy and sharpness . . . were such that a 'Sayāghī order' became proverbial. His renown increased and his repute grew higher, until his name was on people's lips in all the regions of Yemen, and Imam Aḥmad bin Yaḥyā bin Ḥamīd al-Dīn relied on him in many matters."[56] Such ability was frustrated constantly by intrigue and back-biting. When two Lower Yemeni shaykhs (ʿAlī Muḥsin Pāshā al-Jamāʿī and Muḥammad al-Ḥabūb) were at odds over tax farming, for instance, one denounced Sayāghī as the other's accomplice and had the Imam search Sayāghī's house for weapons. Sayāghī can scarcely have felt secure in any case. Two members of his family had been executed after the Taʿizz rising.

Everything turned on personal intrigue, and the Imam, as Aponte said of his father, had not a government but instead a court, where he decided even such tiny matters as whether a school could have ten ink-wells: had he not ruled like this, says Claudie Fayein, "he would have felt himself less a King". Muḥammad al-ʿAmrī, son of the ex-prime minister and grandson of the Turkish-era shaykh of shaykhs, was nominally deputy Foreign Minister but complained of "orders countermanding orders already countermanded" and of the Imam surrounding himself "with ignorant flatterers whose days were spent in agreeing with his opinions and filling his head with complete nonsense. . ." Years later a commission examined where Aḥmad lived: "In the private apartments of the women . . . were kept whole boxes of morphine. In the Taʿizz palace, the Imam's personal room where he gave himself over to drugs left members of the commission baffled: illuminated in green neon, it contained a huge quantity of toys."[57] The prominence of the morphine may be overstated but the nature of the rooms is not, and inefficiency beyond the palace struck many people:

> A lamp, costing over £100 and meant for the hospital operating theatre, was recently destroyed because the glass looked suitable for mending a broken window; four pianos – I do not know why they were ever bought – have been gutted because wire is always useful for other things; and a member of the French road-making company recently came across four unused bulldozers which had been lying, apparently forgotten, for so long that only one could be made serviceable.

By March 1956, with Egyptian encouragement, Aḥmad's delegates in Cairo were talking with the Russians. A shipment of arms arrived in October that year and further shipments followed, including a consignment of outdated aircraft which sat on the ground until their tyres perished. Tanks and self-propelled guns were bought. Egyptian instructors were provided, thus bringing the prospect of revolution very close to

Plate 3.4. Imam Aḥmad and relatives at an execution.

hand, and when Syria and Egypt united in 1958, Aḥmad joined them eager to take on the British: "The Arab giant will drive imperialism into the pit," said Sanaa Radio in the style of Cairo, "The claws of death have clutched at the imperialists." The Russians began work on Ḥudaydah port; the Chinese began work on the road from there to Sanaa. The Americans, alarmed, wondered how Aḥmad could afford a shipment of arms costing $3 million (it was not the only one) when the country's whole annual budget was only about $10 million. King Saʿūd was sanguine: "The Imam has enough money. He has been hoarding riyāls – he is very miserly. We have given him $3 million to build the Port of Ḥudaydah . . . we must take into account the way they do things . . ." When the Chinese requested payment, however, in January 1959, the Imam supposedly told al-Badr in despair, "You made up the dough, now bake the bread." There were no funds left. Aḥmad's commercial agent in Aden found his credit no longer good, and Aḥmad himself had been reduced already to selling gold abroad for silver riyāls to pay his soldiers.[58] People again were starving, for this was the third successive year of drought.

Baffled by Yemen's politics, a British diplomat quoted a comic novel: "*Je n'y comprends rien; j'en parle, j'en écris.*" Al-Badr was seen by some as inclined to the Eastern bloc, yet a story went around that he would marry a Saudi princess. Ḥasan, with land still near Ḥūth but exiled to New York, was supposed to favour the Saudis but was spoken of as a traditionalist Zaydī (relations between Wahhābīs and serious Zaydīs, one should mention, are seldom good); his distrust of foreign influence, made much of in the early 1950s, was meanwhile displaced by the assertion that he was somehow a friend of the Americans, and Zubayrī in Cairo decided al-Badr as well was an agent of the United States, which was "proved" by his appearance of support for Russia. The Egyptians would take over Yemen, or the Saudis would; the Saudis and Egyptians perhaps were hand in glove. A Yemeni told a Western diplomat, "the country is all petrol vapour but most of us are frightened to strike matches".

The North was not only affected by broad Arab rivalries but was linked both to Aden's politics (bombs exploded there in 1958, which the British blamed on the Imam and "Egyptian subversion"; mass demonstrations became extremely serious) and to a vast diaspora of Yemenis bemoaning oppression and their country's poverty. Muḥammad Ghālib's sad poem "The Stranger" remains well known,[59] and Muḥsin al-ʿAynī's *Battles and Conspiracies* (1957) laid out how far the country had fallen since antiquity: where once the Queen of Sheba reigned, now there was a "gang" who provided no schools, no roads, and only a handful of foreign doctors. Sent as a boy to study in Lebanon at the end of Imam Yaḥyā's reign, al-ʿAynī moved to Cairo and then to France. In Switzerland he wept, he says, for the mountains reminded him of Yemen yet the Swiss "in the eyes of the world are the most advanced of peoples: what has happened that Yemen's people should be the most backward and underdeveloped, poor, ignorant and miserable?"

Dissatisfaction at home was also widespread. In early 1958, certain networks of discontent around Taʿizz were co-ordinated by ʿAbd al-Ghanī Muṭahhar, a wealthy merchant newly returned from Ethiopia. Among the shaykhs one finds Ḥusayn al-Aḥmar, Qāsim Abū Raʾs, Muṭīʿ al-Dammāj and others; the army officers involved seem to come from everywhere; the merchants are a smaller group, but include such figures as Muḥammad al-Dumaynī (the family are from Baraṭ originally) and ʿAlī al-Wajīh as well as Aḥmad al-ʿUdaynī.[60] All were dissatisfied. The standard interpretations in terms of sect, class or métier, one might note in passing, render most of this unintelligible.

Aḥmad was deeply unwell by now. In April 1959 he went to Rome for treatment. Al-Badr was left in charge and early in May gave a speech at

Taʿizz: "We have decided to carry out extensive economic development projects. We have in fact begun to work on such projects. The duty of the UAR [Egyptian] mission which arrrived in Yemen recently is to implement these projects . . ."[61] A further speech followed on 20 May, addressing the emotive issue of the "occupied South": "Brothers, the current of Arab Nationalism is sweeping on. This current will wipe out every traitor and criminal . . ." The identity of the traitors was not specified but plainly they were close at hand and on 22 May al-Badr came to Sanaa to address the army, for soldiers who had gone unpaid were everywhere disobeying orders. In Sanaa they burned down the house of Yaḥyā al-ʿAmrī and destroyed his library; in Taʿizz they murdered a judge, Aḥmad al-Jabrī of Khawlān, and dragged the corpses of him and his brother around the town "Baghdad fashion". Both in Taʿizz and in Sanaa al-Badr called for help from northern tribesmen.

Ḥamīd al-Aḥmar, son of Ḥāshid's paramount shaykh, was as impressed by ʿAbd al-Nāṣir of Egypt as was al-Badr and pushed more strongly than many for a republican form of government, perhaps with al-Badr as president and himself as prime minister.[62] With Aḥmad on his death-bed, as people supposed, all things were possible – disorder and blood, the return of Ḥasan, or a republican future of progress and presumed prosperity. "The Taʿizz *sūq*," said a British report, "is cheerfully convinced that the Imam has gone for good." In August, however, Aḥmad returned hale and hearty:

> here I am, returned to you in good health [cheers]. Praise God and thank him for his unlimited bounties [cheers] . . .
>
> There have been some incidents involving deceived, discontented and conceited persons . . . But, praise be to God, their designs miscarried. God humiliated and routed them [jeers]. I am now going to apply the judgement of God to the leaders of the insurrection [cheers]. There will be some whose heads will be cut off . . . [cheers] and there will be others whose heads and legs will be cut off . . . [cheers][63]

Some fled at once. Al-Sayāghī was summoned to Ḥudaydah, where Aḥmad greeted him with his standard rough affability: "Oy, Qaḥṭānī, where have you been?" Fearing the Imam meant he was anti-*sayyid* (Qaḥṭānīs were native Yemenis, ʿAdnānīs the *sayyids*), Sayāghī arranged with friends in Nihm and Khawlān to flee to Bayḥān. For months, little further happened. But at the end of the year Aḥmad demanded his money back from tribesmen al-Badr had paid. Resistance among the tribes evaporated as always it had done since 1930, the Imam simply promising lesser shaykhs advancement against the greater. Houses in the al-Aḥmars' home area near Ḥūth were destroyed by soldiers and the granaries emptied; even Baraṭ was subdued. Early in 1960 the news spread that ʿAbd al-Laṭīf bin Qāyid al-Rājiḥ of Khawlān and Ḥamīd and Ḥusayn al-Aḥmar of Ḥāshid had been executed at Ḥajjah, and lesser tribal figures fled in scores.

CONSTITUTIONS AND REVOLUTION

A Federation of Amirates was now taking shape in Aden's hinterland. Laḥj, under a new sultan, joined in late 1959. Britain subsidised the Federation with £5 million and, with a sizeable budget to dispute at last, local problems intensified: old forms of corruption now seemed less bearable and reform cut out many tolls that tribesmen levied, with the result that "sound administration" clashed more bitterly than ever with local practice. The Ḥaḍramī states declined to involve themselves. They suspected they might soon find oil.[64] In the Kathīrī State a political officer reported still "no real opposition to the Sultan except from a few disgruntled members of his own family who wanted to be Sultan themselves", but the "Arab" families of Sayyūn did little work. That was done by black share-croppers.

> Among the Arab population . . . chronic unemployment and increasing penury now prevailed. I know of one noble blooded man whose date crop rotted on the trees because he could find nobody to pick it. His own family, several strong young men, loafed around Sayyūn seeking hopelessly for clean-fingered situations vacant . . .
>
> Among this distressed *jeunesse* the seeds of socialism and even republicanism were beginning to find fertile soil.[65]

Elsewhere, a development officer wrote of "terrific problems" of debt among Ḥaḍramī fishermen and farmers. Discontents of the very poor and complaints of the more privileged coincided only in anti-colonial rhetoric: schoolchildren in Sayyūn were "surfeited on radical politics" in the form simply of Arab Nationalism, and at Ghayl Bā Wazīr and Mukallā there already had been riots in 1958 around the subject of schools when the British opposed employment of Egyptian teachers. Quʿayṭī, like Kathīrī, politics retained an air of unreality, and mild dynastic intrigues in both states put the British in mind of comic opera.

Much of the Western Protectorate remained only loosely administered. Aden still stood aloof. But the Colonial Office option of a united South found favour at last with London, driven by larger strategy,[66] for in 1958 Aden became the headquarters of Britain's Middle East Command

and by late 1959 the service population had grown fourfold; in 1961 a further huge expansion was undertaken, bringing ever more jobs and money. The port was also booming, but prosperity "created more, not less trouble as the Colony's population was swollen with people new to the experience of contemporary wealth" – the total reached about 200,000, of whom perhaps 80,000 were Northern workers, still mainly unaccompanied men (Sanaa's whole population, by comparison, was 50,000 counting babes in arms). Not only was Aden part of Yemen in the view of most Yemenis, but it was "easily the most politically sophisticated territory in Arabia"[67] while the Imam's domain was denounced by nationalists as the most backward.

The only unifying view of specifically Yemeni affairs, as opposed to those of Arab Nationalism, was that beamed intermittently from Cairo by Zubayrī and Nuʿmān. The relation between Cairo and the Imam's regime itself remained ambiguous – both states were opposed to Britain – until the union of Syria and Egypt broke up in 1961 and Aḥmad rashly severed ties with ʿAbd al-Nāṣir of Egypt by means of a poem condemning Arab Socialism:

> Taking property by forbidden means
> On a pretext of "nationalisation", or of "justice"
> Between those who have wealth and those with none,
> Is a crime against Islamic law.

Aḥmad was now clearly Egypt's enemy and rhetoric from Cairo was stepped up. Even in the year before the split, however, Egyptian contempt for Yemenis was plain: ʿAbd al-Nāṣir's representative to Yemen boasted drunkenly to an American diplomat, "Everyone knows I run Sanaa", and there were Yemenis who feared he might prove right.

On the border, the Sharīf of Bayḥān was active. Resistance to the Imam in Khawlān (east of Sanaa) never quite died out, and the Sharīf enouraged it. Among Aḥmad's tribal opponents was Sinān Abū Laḥūm whose future brother-in-law Muḥsin al-ʿAynī was head of the Teacher's Union in Aden and a prominent figure in the ATUC until the British, alarmed by upsetting the Imam, expelled him. (Al-ʿAynī had joined the Baʿth Party as did younger members of the Abū Laḥūms and many young officers and functionaries now returning to the North from training elsewhere.) Al-Sayāghī remained in the South, writing home to the Imam that he could not come back for fear of an attempt on his life by al-Badr, "the biggest liar in the world", while at the end of 1961 a party of "Free Officers" formed within the North. The Sharīf of Bayḥān saw the main dispute as between Ḥasan and al-Badr, pro-Saudis and pro-Egyptians.

In the midst of the different plots, substantial changes occurred unnoticed. Most important was the arrival through 1959, from America and Russia, of wheat as famine aid:[68] there was no longer reason for mass starvation – perhaps for the first time in Yemen's history. The Chinese meanwhile pressed on with the Sanaa–Ḥudaydah road and the Americans started work on a road from Mukhāʾ to Taʿizz and thence to Sanaa. Around the American camp at Taʿizz formed the first organised left-wing movement in the North, a union established by the MAN, the Movement of Arab Nationalists. There were strikes in Taʿizz, and pamphlets circulated from the "Free Officers" while radio broadcasts from Cairo depicted Arab republics as everywhere the form of progress. Aḥmad "the Djinn" seemed the symbol of another age. The dynastic state, a radical innovation only decades before, appealed vainly to lost antiquity: "Yemen is a monarchy ruled by its lawful and spiritual leader, Imam al-Nāṣir Aḥmad bin Yaḥyā Ḥamīd al-Dīn the 66th, Imam of the Hāshemiyyah Dynasty which was founded 1101 years ago . . . The Kingdom of the Hāshemiyyah Dynasty is the oldest in the world with the exception of the Kingdom of the Japanese dynasty."[69]

Aḥmad died in his sleep in September 1962. Al-Badr succeeded unopposed to the Imamate. But on the night of 26 September the building where he was working in Sanaa was surrounded and shelled by tanks, and though al-Badr in fact slipped away, Sanaa radio announced his death. The Sharīf of Bayḥān was delighted: obviously the anti-Egyptian faction must at last have come out on top. By the end of the day it was clear that the opposite had happened and the Egyptians, who had seemed al-Badr's friends, had in fact backed the group who overthrew him. The Yemen Arab Republic was declared – the state later often described as North Yemen.

A Federation of South Arabia had been agreed just the day before, uniting Aden and the federated hinterland states at last, though still not the states of Ḥaḍramawt, under British auspices – the nucleus of a later South Yemen. This union of Aden and hinterland was to come into force in 1963. The agreement was railroaded through (only four out of twelve elected members of Aden State's government supported the decision: *ex officio* or appointed members made up the numbers), and even then a day's delay would have made it impossible. Serious rioting erupted: "Indeed we are one family", shouted ʿAbduh al-Adhal above the crowd, "one people, . . . all of us are brothers . . . we are gathered in one religion . . . our land is one", but the crowd attacked him.[70] The gap between Adeni unity and Arab unity remained unbridgeable. The following day the immediate issue was Yemen's unity, triggered by the Northern coup and expressed with a sense of destiny familiar from Europe a century before:

> The homeland will never surrender or submit.
> Spirit in revolt, she fills her breast with pure air.
> See how she lifts her head and moves forward,
> Trampling with disdain these foolish idols . . .
>
> What is North? And what the South?
> Two hearts whose joy and pain are joined
> Were united by hate and suffering,
> By history and by God.
> Shamsān will soon meet its brother Nuqum.[71]

Shamsān is the mountain beside Aden. Nuqum is the mountain beside Sanaa. As far off as Ḥuraydah in Wādī Ḥaḍramawt people clustered around transistor radios, swept up in "revolution fever", and from Aden migrants moved North by the thousand to help build a new Yemen.

CHAPTER FOUR

Revolutions and civil wars: the 1960s

Through the 1960s Yemen was trapped in overlapping wars. In the North a fight between royalists and republicans became a battle by proxy between Saudi Arabia and Egypt; in the South a fight against the British led to conflict among different nationalists. Only when Egyptians and British left at last were Yemeni disagreements that evolved through the war made explicit, and not until 1970 did politics take settled shape. When they did so, two Yemeni states were at odds across the 1905–1914 border.

REVOLUTION IN THE NORTH

Al-Badr was deposed by junior army officers. In the months before the coup they sought help from Egypt, whose own last feud with Imam Aḥmad involved broadcasts from Cairo not by Zubayrī and Nuʿmān (the established "Liberals" in exile) but by ʿAbd al-Raḥmān al-Bayḍānī, who knew little of Yemen, says one local author, not even "how to wear a turban". His broadcasts stressed conflict between Zaydīs and Shāfiʿīs, and again between Qaḥṭānīs and ʿAdnānīs, that is, "native" Yemenis and *sayyids*.[1] The new president, ʿAbdullāh al-Sallāl, for his part, was an army officer, not from a well-known family: he had studied in Iraq in the 1930s and now younger colleagues pushed him to the fore. Sallāl and Bayḍānī, unconnected with the detail of local demands or with locally known names, appeared to some as Egypt's puppets, to others as the country's saviours.

Just after the coup Bayḍānī and Zubayrī addressed Sanaani crowds in conflicting terms from different floors of the same building (Nuʿmān was forcibly detained in Cairo), while outside the "Republican Palace" in the following weeks

> a crowd of shouting, kilted tribesmen assembled every day. Petitions of loyalty fluttered in the brisk highland air; complaints about taxes, crops, camels and trade, appeals for more land and demands for better houses . . .

Only the Egyptian soldiers of the President's bodyguard and assorted visitors in Western suits were able to shoulder their way in and out . . .[2]

Egyptian soldiers arrived in the first few days – by early 1963 there were probably 15,000 in Yemen; six months later there were double that – and in every Yemeni office, as offices were set up, was an Egyptian adviser without whom nothing was allowed to happen. Sanaa radio, says ʿAbd al-Malik al-Ṭayyib, began to sound "as if it were not in Sanaa", and the impression formed in some quarters that "this was a revolution planned by ʿAbd al-Nāṣir, with ʿAbd al-Nāṣir's money and ʿAbd al-Nāṣir's ideas, . . . its present and its future for the benefit of ʿAbd al-Nāṣir".[3]

Having shelled al-Badr from Sanaa, the Yemeni army all but ceased to exist,[4] and volunteers were instead assembled for pushes east and south in support of the new republic. One expedition, towards Ḥarīb, collapsed because of rivalries within the tribe of al-Qayfah from which the column's leader came; a second, towards the Jawf, was destroyed; a third began negotiating with shaykhs in Khawlān, but Sanaa soon forbade such talks. Fighting went on also in the west around Ḥajjah, while in Sanaa a "National Guard" formed. Southern tribesmen came north from, for instance, Radfān and Yāfiʿ; far larger numbers of Shāfiʿīs from Lower Yemen arrived from Aden, where they were migrant workers, and Yemenis returned from Africa and the Middle East to support a new beginning to national life. Tens of thousands gathered in Taʿizz and Sanaa.

In parts of the countryside there was apprehension that soldiers had made the coup ("It was soldiers people feared," says a witness. "They didn't mind the Imam so much. What did they know about him?"). In a few areas there were peasant risings. But Sanaa's call for local officials to support the Republic meant usually that power-holders from the old regime took charge. The "sergeant" of the local prison in ʿAlī Zayd's novel, *The Coffee Flower*, declares: "A decree arrived this morning from the Supreme Command of the Army saying the highest military rank in each area should take charge in the Republic's name . . . Well, I'm the highest rank in the fortress here. I've taken charge . . ." Volunteers nonetheless came into Sanaa from peasant areas. They were sent to fight with no training and thousands, perhaps, were slaughtered:

He wrote each name in a broad, clear script and drew a line under it . . . Unfortunately nothing much, sometimes nothing at all, was known about most of the conscripts except the names. Lots of similar names – Muḥammad, Aḥmad, ʿAlī, Ḥamūd. . . . Sometimes, their own names forgotten, they were known by the names of their areas – al-ʿUdaynī, al-Radāʿī, al-ʿAbsī, . . . Some were just noted by distinctive features . . .[5]

The Saudis decided Egyptian-backed revolution on their borders was a mortal threat[6] and rapidly they armed the royalists, a term used by both sides from the start. The older pretensions of the Imamate had long gone. But as Deffarge and Troeller were to phrase it later, a fiery front dividing the whole Arab World now ran through Sanaa with on one side the Arab monarchies, most importantly Saudi Arabia, and on the other Egypt. From the South, meanwhile, help reached the royalists from the Sharīf of Bayḥān whose connections of amity and kinship extended through Ma'rib, the Jawf, where Bin Muʿaylī of ʿAbīdah was a friend, and Khawlān, the bloc of Bakīl tribes east of Sanaa. Britain helped supply the means.

The British (officially) were hesitant, with a Foreign Office inclination to recognise the new republic and a Colonial Office inclination the other way, but such Aden officials as Trevaskis shared the wish of right-wing politicians in London to "give ʿAbd al-Nāṣir a bloody nose" and the Colonial Office view prevailed. Aden looked to its defences. The Aden Levies, built up to 3,000 men, had been transferred in 1961 to the Federation as the Federal Regular Army; the Federal Guards were established at the same strength. In November 1962, although expenditure on the Guard alone was £1,000,000 per annum, expansion was recommended, and by October 1963, Trevaskis (who now became governor) was protesting they must implement the plan immediately or "take covert action to prevent a Republican victory . . ." In fact they were doing so already.[7]

In November 1962 (the same month a small British party was noticed in Arḥab, just north of Sanaa) the Egyptians had announced the formation of a National Liberation Army to free the South. This was headed by Qaḥṭān al-Shaʿbī, an ex-agricultural officer who had fled to Cairo in 1958. In February 1963, in Sanaa, the first conference was held of the Aden branch of the MAN (Movement of Arab Nationalists), and a second meeting, in June, announced the formation of the NLF (National Liberation Front) which also was headed by al-Shaʿbī. The Southern MAN was the nucleus. Around it coalesced such bodies as the Revolutionary Organisation of Youth, the Yāfiʿ Reform Front and the Mahrah Youth Organisation.[8] Southern tribesmen who had fought for the Republic in the North, as far off as Ḥajjah and Maḥābishah,[9] now returned to fight the British.

In Sanaa, which Egypt controlled directly, a police state emerged. An axis of long-established Liberals such as ʿAbd al-Salām Ṣabrah, ʿAbd al-Raḥmān al-Iryānī and Zubayrī, demanded a revised constitution and

Plate 4.1. Revolution in the North.

put together a delegation including tribal leaders – ʿAbdullāh al-Aḥmar of Ḥāshid, Amīn Abū Raʾs of Bakīl, most notably – to go to Cairo. A state of emergency was declared, however. Sallāl visited Syria, Iraq and Egypt, returning at last from Cairo "as the Imam [in 1959] returned from Italy", and arrests were made of such republicans as Aḥmad al-Sharjabī, ʿAlī al-Kuhhālī and ʿAlī Nāṣir Shawīṭ. Certain shaykhs were executed with Egypt's blessing.

In September 1963 the Liberals and their allies convened a conference north of Sanaa at ʿAmrān, beyond the immediate reach of government. This drew together royalist and republican shaykhs, most of whom would have walked for days to get there for trucks were all but a monopoly of the army still, and a peace council was proposed involving shaykhs from as far afield as Ḥumayqān near the North–South border and Ṣaʿdah near the Saudi frontier. A set of demands was composed to be submitted to Sallāl and ʿAbd al-Nāṣir, and a delegation went to Cairo, where Sallāl was again by now.[10] An answer came back by telegram. Days later, when Sallāl was to arrive in Sanaa, crowds marched to the airport but Sallāl eluded them, all public discussion was suppressed and politics at state level, much as under the Imams, disappeared into plot and counter-plot.

To Egyptians Yemen was a "primitive" country. They seemed convinced that Yemenis were incapable of conducting their own affairs and, as journalists noticed, spoke of them in the racist fashion the British once used of Egyptian peasants. An American official summarised ʿAbd al-Nāṣir's own position: "the UAR has to run the whole show".[11] Militarily they did so, and a series of Egyptian offensives pushed north and in a hook through Maʾrib to Ḥarīb to cut off royalist supply-lines, then into the Tihāmah and the western mountains also. As these spearheads moved on, there closed up behind them an indigenous world of alliance, dispute and shifting truces.

Many alignments as royalist or republican resulted almost from accident. Ḥusayn and Ḥamīd al-Aḥmar had been executed by Imam Aḥmad in 1960, and ʿAbdullāh bin Ḥusayn al-Aḥmar emerged as an implacable enemy of the Imam's family. Amīn Abū Raʾs of Dhū Muḥammad was as stout a republican. The al-Shāyif family and Dhū Ḥusayn, however, though they too had suffered under the Imams, were divided but mostly royalist. ʿAbd al-Laṭīf bin Qāyid of Khawlān had been executed with the al-Aḥmars, and Khawlān in 1960 never had quite submitted to Imam Aḥmad; but now, while Nuʿmān bin Qāyid (based mainly in Lower Yemen) was a noted republican, Khawlān was

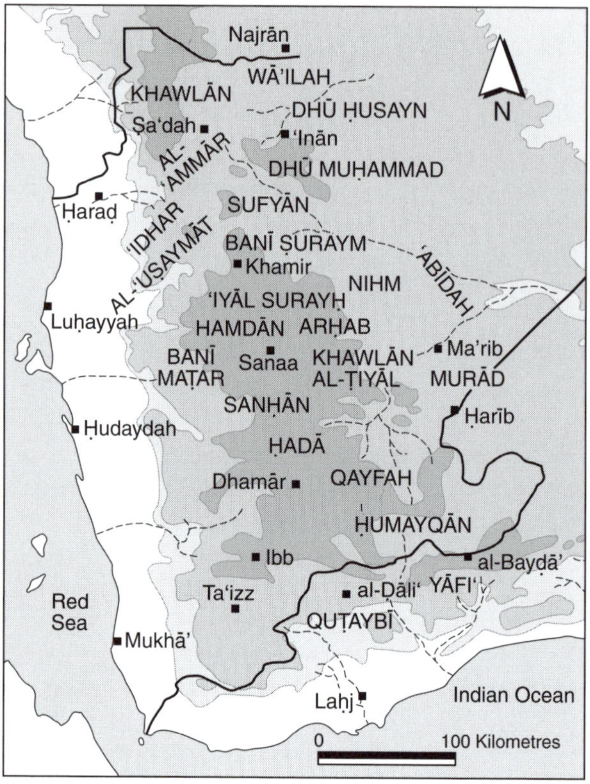

Map 4.1. Major tribes and the civil war

largely royalist and Shaykh Nājī al-Ghādir of Khawlān became one of the best known royalist commanders of the war.

One's impression is less of a royalist ideal than of widespread distrust of the Republic's government. Not only Khawlān, but Arḥab, 'Iyāl Yazīd, Sufyān and many other tribes would not accept the Egyptian presence or Sallāl as president.[12] Aḥmad al-Sayāghī, who had fled the North in Imam Aḥmad's time, hesitated to go back, for the republicans had shot his brother. He emerged as a "royalist" commander but as late as August 1963 met Zubayrī and Iryānī on the North–South border to seek a settlement (lured back to Khawlān, he later died in an ambush). The tribes, meanwhile, fought in their own terms. Here is Nājī al-Ghādir's challenge:

The high cliffs called and every notable in Yemen answered:
We'll never go republican, not if we are wiped off the earth,
Not if yesterday returns today and the sun rises in Aden,
Not if the earth catches fire and the sky rains lead.

The reply dismisses Khawlān and their allies as mercenaries bought with Saudi money from al-Badr and his uncle Ḥasan.

The Egyptian leader rules Yemen with his forces.
Migs and Ilyushins seek out your foxholes.
Bullets from M.1's and Lee-Enfields won't stop mortars.
Nājī, tell Ḥasan and Badr that maybe their silver is only brass.[13]

In Sanaa and Taʿizz the Imam's petty wealth was squandered and paper currency was printed. Wheat shipments established before the war continued (8–10,000 tons per year at first), and, apart from the flood of rifles and money from competing powers, the Egyptian presence transformed certain sectors of economic life. Merchants moved into Ibb, for instance, where they turned from exporting agricultural produce to importing foreign manufactures; small shopkeepers flourished, selling cloth and consumer goods to Egyptian soldiers. There was something of a building boom, and although most development projects came to little, several merchants (nearly all from Lower Yemen) invested in Tihāmah cotton and the wartime growth of Ḥudaydah port.[14]

A class of salaried urban bureaucrats emerged: about 4,000 in the first year. In parts of the North "co-operatives", based in part on the village-associations spun off by Aden labour, flourished in the 1960s. But areas far from trade routes simply dropped from view. Shaykhs around Maḥwīt in the western mountains, for instance, "did not overtly support the royalist campaigns . . ., nor did they resist the presence of a republican *ʿāmil* in al-Maḥwīt town. However, the *ʿāmil* made no demands which would have tested their loyalty one way or the other."[15] No class-like revolution happened, and such areas as al-Ahnūm (around Shahārah) and Ḥajjah, where extensive land was held by the Imam's family, largely stood with the Imam. Few places in Lower Yemen did so but nor were established shaykhs displaced.

Taʿizz is sometimes spoken of by Taʿizzis as "capital of two revolutions". It was here that the MAN established the first workers' union in the North, the year before Imam Aḥmad's death, and in June 1963 a General Union of Workers appeared there with lesser branches in Ḥudaydah and Sanaa.[16] A "Young Men's Club" was formed. A Popular

National Congress emerged by summer 1963. But a law of that year banning political associations was used against most such initiatives and tight Egyptian control left the two revolutions almost unconnected. Qaʿṭabah and Bayḍāʾ (with Taʿizz as the rear headquarters) were points from which Egypt encouraged war against the British in the South; Sanaa was the base for a quite different Northern fight against the Saudis. The major Yemeni ties between the two were clandestine parties, which spread like bindweed.

In most of the Tihāmah and Lower Yemen there was no fighting, and memories of the war among Lower Yemenis are seldom of military events. People were conscripted, but 25 of every 100 would disappear before ever reaching Sanaa: "When they get to the front there are 50. After two weeks half have absconded, and after a week the rest abscond. The front then asks for another lot, and so it goes." Equipment was poor, pay was in arrears, and men routinely sold their weapons. "The fighting was not as it had been in the first days of the war, a question of life or death. The big effort switched to the Egyptians or to war contractors (*muqāwilīn al-ḥarb*)" who gathered men for money,[17] and Yemen's war in the North became a war of tribesmen. It was not depicted greatly in economic terms, which war in the South was by some from the very start.

ARMED STRUGGLE IN THE SOUTH

In 1959, more than two years before the Sanaa coup, Qaḥṭān al-Shaʿbī had broadcast from Cairo:

> Could the iron screen which the British imperialists put around the Arab South prevent the spread of news about our struggling people? . . . Imperialism wants a very large military base in the area to protect its interests and . . . exploit the resources of our country and thus raise the standard of living of the British people, while our own live a miserable and abject life . . .[18]

Post-independence writers explain the war itself as class struggle against "feudal" rulers who with British support bled their people dry.[19] Economism poses difficult questions, however. Inequality of land tenure was striking in parts of Ḥaḍramawt, for instance; so it was in Laḥj where pump irrigation produced large holdings owned by the ruling family. Yet neither place was a focus of violent action. This developed in more ambiguous settings.

The start of fighting in Radfān, 14 October 1963, was accorded the same importance in the South as 26 September 1962 in the North –

revolution day. The Quṭaybīs of Radfān complained of oppression by the Amir of Ḍāliʿ, in whose domain the British always placed them and who, once the Federation was formed, controlled the purse-strings; the accession of Aden in January 1963 made the problem worse. By May 1963 many were going North for weapons, and at the start of October they submitted a petition which shows how British conceits of "sound administration" had miscarried.

> We submit to you this complaint from all Ahl Quteib Aqils [headmen] and Shaikhs against Naib [deputy; local governor] Mahmood Hasson . . . We have got nothing from him except oppression . . . He has changed the system of the Urfi [customary law] Court and Appeal Court . . . He has also made decisions and revoked the judgement of the Urfi Court . . . he has relinquished [sic] the Aqils and notables of Ahl Quteib from their responsibilities and deprived them of their stipends . . .
>
> The said Naib has separated the clans of the Ahl Quteib and placed one above the other.
>
> He deals with the affairs of the Treasury in a way unknown to all . . .[20]

The detailed demands concern state accounts and the farmers' association, whose treasurer had secured for himself a loan to buy a tractor. But the *nāʾib* was the focus of more general problems. The concern with new court procedure, depriving local leaders of their place in webs of arbitration, is indicative of the way that autonomy had been placed at issue – individuals and families, as much as clans, had been "placed one above the other".

In October 1963 a patrol was fired on. The Federal Army intervened, killing Rājiḥ Labūzah, a Quṭaybī shaykh who had been in the North. The British Army, not just local forces, then launched a major campaign in Spring 1964, leading much of the population to flee, and attempts to cut supply routes to the "dissidents" spread resistance. New "fronts" were opened by the NLF in Lower Yāfiʿ (the territory of Muḥammad ʿAydarūs, still active as he had been in the late 1950s but from the start at daggers drawn with Qaḥṭān al-Shaʿbī) and in Dathīnah, where a single camel-train was thought to have supplied 45 mines, 150 grenades, 200 rifles and a war-chest of 40,000 riyāls.[21] Radfān was subdued by the British, who were soon sinking wells there and encouraging agriculture, but guerrilla action recurred in many places.

The fighting was depicted at the time as war against colonialism, and later as class struggle. Such terms obscure the texture of events. In Shuʿayb in 1963, for instance, the Arab political officer, Aḥmad Faḍl Muḥsin of Faḍlī, was murdered by his radio operator, Ṣāliḥ Muqbil al-Maqdhūb, later prominent in the NLF.[22] Two years afterwards (1965), the new ruler of Shuʿayb, Nāshir ʿAbdullāh, was murdered in Aden. Both events appear part of the anti-imperialist struggle. But Aḥmad Faḍl on his deathbed blamed Yaḥyā Khalāqī, the Shuʿayb state treasurer, and cast Ṣāliḥ Maqdhūb as Khalāqī's catspaw. The relation of Khalāqī to Nāshir ʿAbdullāh, then an officer in the Federal Guard and present in the area on the day of the murder, was complex; the murderer himself meanwhile had a niece named Ṣāliḥah whose flashing eyes at the well, so people say, had met those of Aḥmad Faḍl. The stories extend in conflicting ripples. Nāshir's murder in Aden, claimed at once by the NLF as a blow against feudalism and colonialism, may as probably have been revenge by the "feudal" Faḍlīs, while suspicion that al-Maqdhūb's motivation was personal persists.

Institutions are no easier to write of. One of the organisations which made up the NLF was the Yāfiʿ Reform Front, which emerged in April 1963 near Labʿūs: a meeting was held at the ʿĪd when people from miles around traditionally gather at the tomb of Muḥḍār, and it was agreed that provocative *zāmil*s (tribal poems) not be answered but an effort be made to establish truces.[23] A later literature depicts the Front as part of a class struggle which culminates in well-theorised Marxism. Contemporary evidence is sparse. A political programme would only produce disagreement, it was thought, so the Yāfiʿ Front's constitution was pronounced to be the Holy Qurʾān: "For the Qurʾān is the Book of God and the reference point of all, and its judgements are a constitution to decide among people . . ."

Some idea of the period emerges from accounts by Egyptian journalists.[24] Local shaykhs are prominent as leaders, truce-making among tribes is as vital as combat against colonialists, and the everyday language reported is largely of Islam. One aspect of the region's volatility, however, is caught by Muthannā's story. The son of a minor shaykh, he had no schooling until, driving his father's pack-camels to Aden, "he saw another kind of life" and sold his rifle for a ticket to Kuwait where he worked at menial jobs and went to night school for a time, before "he set aside his great hope" again to return and fight. The Aden hinterland (like some parts of Lower Yemen) had many such figures, with a smattering of education, some experience of the wider world, and enormous hopes. For the moment the sheer recalcitrance of the area seemed to British eyes the result of "subversion" cross-cut with "tribalism".

What Egypt did to Britain in the South, the Saudis did to Egypt in the North without powerful ideology. The royalists never announced a programme, or even used terms, very different from those of their opponents. An early American assessment thus spoke of "Saudi gold and arms" keeping "the tribal pot bubbling".[25] Tribes themselves invoked such claims to autonomy as *al-nār qabla l-ʿār* ("rather fire than shame!", death before dishonour), many played all ends against the middle, and the Egyptians in the North, like the British in the South, identified tribalism with endemic treachery. What in fact was going on, of course, was that local concerns were more compelling than the aims of foreign governments.

ADEN AS POLITICAL FOCUS

If fighting in the countryside, North and South, could be taken for tribalism, events in Aden could not; and an attempt, in December 1963, to kill the Governor, Trevaskis, with a hand-grenade provoked a state of emergency which in varying forms was renewed thereafter. Those behind the attack were soon mostly freed. Indeed through the fight to follow, when bombings, murders and assassinations became common, few were ever held for long and none executed. Violence remained enmeshed in broader politics.[26] The political crux remained the franchise in Aden State, which excluded the ATUC's base of migrant workers, and a "pathological reluctance" among the British to deal with al-Aṣnaj of the ATUC in formal terms. They dealt instead with Aden State's government and with the Federation of South Arabia of which, from early 1963, Aden State was part. The workers' movement, most of whom were from the North, were excluded and relied on strikes, their frustrations aligning with Egypt's wish to drive the British out entirely.

At the time of Radfān, Cairo Radio menaced Aden too: "Tomorrow the revolution will extend to each of the 14 states which form the South Arabian Federation. Tomorrow the volcano will erupt in the heart of Aden; the free will destroy the base of colonialism; the revolutionaries will burn down the oil refineries."[27] Attempts to consolidate the Federation of port and hinterland threatened Egypt's interests, and Cairo Radio denounced not only the "agent Sultans" but anyone who might attend a conference: "Declare a relentless war that destroys everything. Do not give the agents a chance to travel to London. Dig graves for them and bury them . . ." In January 1964 an attempt was made to murder five Adeni politicians, two of them members of the ATUC's own political wing. A bomb went off at the Federal Legislature, denying the very chance of talks.

In June 1964 Federal rulers met in London: independence was now to be granted by late 1968 and rights to the base negotiated. The British, however, were no longer minded to give short-term responsibility for security to local forces, the authority of the Federal Government was thus limited and militants soon concluded it was not worth dealing with: "its dependence on ourselves [the British] is at times so humiliatingly intrusive that its claims to having a real potential for independence have no ring of truth and it is so obviously restricted by our controls that its behaviour does not even approximate to that of a real Arab Government".[28] Trevaskis, the author of this memorandum, thought no better of the Northern Republic ("a meaningless farce . . . propped up by 40,000 UAR troops") but admitted people did not see it that way. Yemenis hoped the Republic would become more fully Yemeni; meanwhile it was at least an Arab government and few people wished the Imamate back. As a tea-seller said to a journalist in Taʿizz, "Sallāl, very good! Imam fuggoff!" In the South the same was said of Britain.

Elections for Aden State were held on a narrow voter-base (10,000 Aden citizens who could pass a test in Arabic; the total population was now 220,000), which dissatisfied both militants and Federal rulers. The large turnout of this tiny electorate, despite al-Aṣnaj's call for a boycott, perhaps signifies how far Aden's politics stood from practicality. The man thought to have thrown the grenade at Trevaskis ("Grenadier Khalīfah" as the British called him) was elected, along with Hāshim ʿUmar, already with the NLF, and representatives of such old Aden families as Makāwī and Luqmān. No coherent policy emerged.

In Britain, at the same time as the Aden elections (October 1964), the Conservative government was replaced by Labour, who strongly favoured talks with the ATUC, not realising perhaps the difficulties of what in Aden passed as labour politics, and had as strong a distrust or incomprehension of the Federal rulers (all apparently "feudal" figures) as their predecessors had of Aṣnaj.[29] Trevaskis was replaced as governor. The Sharīf of Bayḥān, a key figure in the Federal Government, soon stopped attending meetings. Discussion of the constitution foundered, and at the end of 1964 the NLF began eliminating the Aden Special Branch. A grenade was then thrown into a teenagers' party; a second was thrown into a cinema used by British service families. At an Arab League meeting in March 1965 the group around al-Aṣnaj asked that funds be provided for schools and the NLF demanded they be spent on weapons.[30] Al-Aṣnaj was losing his hold on the ATUC itself, and by the time that emergency powers were invoked by Britain (June 1965) he had

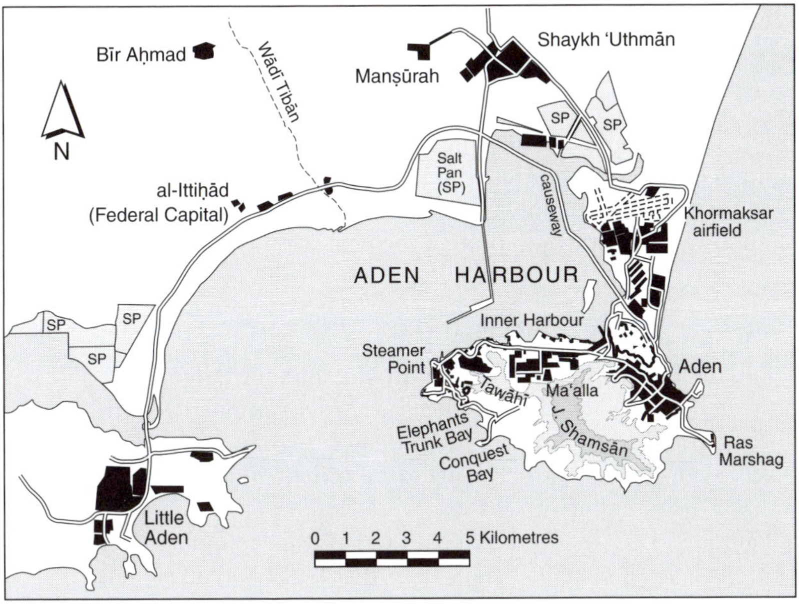

Map 4.2. Aden circa 1965

left for Cairo, where he was joined soon by ʿAbd al-Qawī Makāwī, Chief Minister of Aden's government.

As Yemeni nationalism became realistic politics with the coup of 1962 so the British for other reasons had raised the stakes, naming Aden's base as the major link between Britain and Singapore: it was elevated, says Pieragostini, "from colonial backwater to strategic necessity". An Iraqi threat to Kuwait (1961) provided one justification, troubles in Zanzibar (1964) another; through late 1965 the build-up and expenditure were enormous, adding ever more complexity and bitterness to what already was a large and sprawling city (Map 4.2). More and more soldiers were deployed to secure Aden, which itself was meant to secure the Indian Ocean and the oil-rich Gulf. The process went on until Aden, as a wit remarked, "consumed more security than it could ever produce".

Yemeni nationalists and Egyptians alike, says a British political officer thirty years later, "were living in an heroic age". All things seemed possible. The British felt themselves in an age of decline, by contrast, and their imperial pretensions rang deeply hollow. They were willing, as in the 1950s, to bomb and rocket their own side ("dissidents" in Federation territory), but bombing the Egyptians supplying the NLF was politically unacceptable; no Draconian measure of licensing or expelling Aden's migrant workers was considered either, and if authority be measured by the confidence with which power is used then the British had lost before they started. Their newer global pretensions proved as problematic, for the Treasury could not sustain the cost. With no warning to anyone, London declared in February 1966 that Aden was not vital after all, the British would leave by 1968, the base itself would be abandoned, and no defence agreement would protect the post-independence government.

ʿABD AL-NĀṢIR AND YEMEN

Before the British announced they would abandon Aden, the Egyptians in the North may have felt despair. Successive campaigns north and east of Sanaa had won them nothing, their casualties had been large, the drain on Egypt's treasury was vast, and by mid-1965, though the numbers fell off afterwards, there were close to 60,000 Egyptian troops in Yemen.[31] Despite their claim to defend the republic, they scarcely controlled more beyond Sanaa than the Turks had sixty years before. Beneath the plots and conspiracies, meanwhile, a certain sense of the Yemeni state took form.

The first book published under the Republic was probably *Ibn al-Amīr and His Age* (1964) by Qāsim Ghālib Aḥmad, who had once been a Shāfiʿī preacher in Aden and was several times Minister of Education. His subject, Ibn al-Amīr, was a Zaydī reformer of the eighteenth century. In Qāsim Ghālib's view he had been a radical whose insistence on using Sunni as well as Shiʿite sources meant "non-sectarian" rapprochement between Shāfiʿīs and Zaydīs and whose rhetoric was of impartial justice. Ibn al-Amīr had also been a *sayyid*, however. The anti-*sayyid* rhetoric which spread among *qāḍī* families in the 1950s (Chapter 3) was reinforced by Bayḍānī's broadcasts and grew as the war continued: baffled by Yemen's intractability, some Egyptians as well as Yemenis equated *sayyid*s as a class with feudalists. Qāsim Ghālib's second book (1968) thus shifted to Shawkānī, a "non-sectarian" *qāḍī* reformer. The irony went unremarked that Shawkānī in his day had been "judge of judges", the keystone in an autocratic type of government the Republic had overthrown.[32]

The second edition of Sharaf al-Dīn's *Yemen Throughout History*, continuing the nationalist approach first encouraged by Imam Yaḥyā, appeared at about the same time as Qāsim Ghālib's first book. In the same year (1964) ʿAbd al-Malik al-Ṭayyib, writing as ʿAbd al-Ilāh, published in Beirut his angry *Collapse of the Revolution in Yemen.* A Zaydī dismissed from government on the pretext of prejudice against Shāfiʿīs, he was soon to link himself with the Muslim Brothers and later also to be Minister of Education. Muḥammad al-Akwaʿ in 1966 published his edition of the second volume of Hamdānī's tenth-century *Diadem Book.* Imam Yaḥyā had encouraged historiography (Chapter 2), and the ancient past had become a reference point for young activists such as Muḥsin al-ʿAynī (Chapter 3) as much as for Imamic writers: Hamdānī, for all concerned, was a keystone of national heritage. More contemporary work included Muḥammad Nuʿmān's *The Interested Parties in Yemen* (1965).

Nuʿmān's work addresses the contrast between tribes and peasants (*qabāʾil* and *raʿiyyah*), which was largely, in his view, that between Zaydīs and Shāfiʿīs: the prominence of Zaydī tribesmen in national politics since the start of the war alarmed him. The same concern as with Qāsim Ghālib then recurs about *sayyid*s and non-*sayyid*s, although the *sayyid* aristocracy of the Imam's day was abetted, says Nuʿmān, by *qāḍī* families. But Yemen has always been "parties" in the sense of groups with different interests. That is the country's nature and has been so for millennia. The tragedy now, he argues, is that none can understand the other's viewpoint. Although, diplomatically, he downplays the question of rivalry on Yemeni terrain among Arab powers, his views emerged with the failure of successive attempts at peace between Egypt and the Saudis.

Iryānī, Zubayrī and Nuʿmān had all resigned in late 1964 in protest at "corrupt, incompetent and bankrupt government". Sallāl appointed a soldier, Ḥasan al-ʿAmrī, as prime minister. Despairing of politics in Sanaa, Zubayrī declared a "Party of God" and moved among the northern tribes in search of a general truce but was murdered on 1 April 1965 at Baraṭ in the far northeast, and under threat of massive tribal secession Sallāl appointed as prime minister Aḥmad Nuʿmān, who had been Zubayrī's colleague. The conference was convened that Zubayrī planned. Invitations were issued by ʿAbdullāh al-Aḥmar, paramount shaykh of Ḥāshid, who at that time was minister of the interior: from relative obscurity under the last Imams, tribal shaykhs had emerged since the start of the war as major governmental figures. The Khamir conference convened in early May 1965, and on 10 May Nuʿmān sent a telegram to King Fayṣal of Saudi Arabia inviting talks.[33]

Many authors see a split here, as at ʿAmrān, between "extreme" and "moderate" republicans, left and right, or indeed between social classes.[34] The sole distinction which carries through unambiguously in the record is that between soldiers attached to the Egyptian cause and others. On 27 June Sallāl announced a "supreme council of the armed forces", Nuʿmān resigned (some forty of his supporters were soon in prison), and in late July a large delegation of shaykhs left for the South by way of royalist territory. Some went on to Beirut, some to Saudi Arabia where talks were held at al-Ṭāʾif while in Yemen Egyptian military activity again increased until suddenly Nāṣir and King Fayṣal themselves met, to the great disquiet of Sallāl, the MAN and NLF. Again Nuʿmān, Iryānī and Muḥammad ʿAlī ʿUthmān were brought into government and preparations made for further talks.

A very different conference had been held at Taʿizz, in June 1965, where the NLF produced a "National Charter". This begins with a Qurʾānic quotation then invokes the pre-Islamic past as al-ʿAynī had done some years before: the civilisation (*ḥaḍārah*) of Yemen's ancient kingdoms "shows the collective efforts of our people and their vast, latent practical capacity". The analysis of Yemen's "backwardness" in modern times, so at odds with a noble past, unfolds in broadly Leninist terms from Europe's industrial revolution and the spread of imperialism to depict an alliance of colonialism and feudalism within the two parts of Yemen and between them whereby sultans in the South (by extension also shaykhs in the North) had seized the people's land. Revolution "must aim to replace exploitative social facts with progressive social facts . . . on the basis of revolutionary socialism".[35] To what extent other "interested parties" grasped the import at the time is unclear.

Lower Yemen was divided. Complaints were heard about the power of "merchants", Zaydīs complained of being squeezed from posts by Shāfiʿīs, and among the Shāfiʿīs themselves a group including Qāsim Ghālib complained of the Nuʿmāns: "We are not going to swear allegiance to an Imam named Aḥmad Nuʿmān", they said, after a difference over who controlled al-Rāhidah, a customs post involved with smuggling (not least of whisky and beer) from Aden. The NLF formed part of such disputes also, but the context was far from simple. Broad discontents, which raised the spectre of Shāfiʿī separatism, centred not only on Qāsim Ghālib but on such figures as ʿAbd al-Ghanī Muṭahhar and Muḥammad ʿAlī ʿUthmān who were centrally part of government. Nuʿmān, with certain shaykhs, was seeking an end to fighting in the North: demonstrations in Taʿizz against a meeting of sultans from the Aden hinterland in Spring 1965, may well have expressed concerns with the prospect of the Northern war being ended at Lower Yemeni expense as much as concerns about the Southern war, and if the NLF had reason to encourage such demonstrations, so too did Egypt. Shāfiʿī shaykhs who aligned themselves with al-Aḥmar (Zaydī) and Nuʿmān (Shāfiʿī) now found themselves attacked by troops from (Zaydī) Sanaa to the delight of the (Shāfiʿī) left. But if Nuʿmān was a focus of complex tensions, his picture was nonetheless seen on trucks and in shops throughout Lower Yemen.[36]

ʿAbd al-Nāṣir and King Fayṣal, for reasons of their own, agreed a cease-fire in August 1965, and Yemeni royalist and republican delegations met at Ḥaraḍ near the Saudi border in November, where Egypt pressured the republicans to accept the Saudi formulation of an "Islamic State". The republicans refused;[37] the talks failed. In early 1966, when Britain announced its intention to withdraw from Aden, Egypt consolidated its forces in the triangle of the main Northern cities, intent on waiting the British out, and the war quietened, but attempts to pursue independent Yemeni positions, whether by Nuʿmān and Iryānī or increasingly by Ḥasan al-ʿAmrī, were all frustrated by Egyptian policy. In the countryside, meanwhile, great names were made in the fighting, and such republican shaykhs as Mujāhid Abū Shawārib of Khārif in Ḥāshid became as widely known as their royalist opponents.

In August 1966 Sallāl returned to Yemen, having been in Cairo for the best part of a year. Al-ʿAmrī tried to prevent him landing. To protest against Sallāl's return the Presidential Council, along with eight ministers and many others, went to Cairo, where in effect the whole Yemeni government was detained by Egypt – "one is faced," said Muḥammad al-ʿAṭṭār, "with a phenomenon unprecedented in the history of international relations!" – and in Yemen a new administration was formed of such determinedly pro-Egyptian soldiers as ʿAbdullāh Juzaylān and Muḥammad al-Ahnūmī. Some were cynical about Ahnūmī himself, "who used to live in some hut in the Tihāmah where he didn't even own a mat and now lives in a great palace . . ."; his wedding had been so grand, they said, that 50,000 rounds had been fired off in celebration. Juzaylān, who grew up in Taʿizz though the family are originally from Baraṭ (his grandfather had been a cavalry trooper with the Turks), was very much Egypt's man: his wife was Egyptian and he himself saw Cairo as the model of progress and modernity. In October a State Security Court was established and several persons at odds with Egypt were shot by firing squad,[38] while the Egyptians again began bombing dissident tribal areas, sometimes using, as they had before, poisonous gas.

Eric Rouleau's account gives a vivid picture of the region east of Sanaa. Even royalist princes condemned Imam Aḥmad ("the 1962 revolution was ours and the Egyptians stole it from us!"), and many "royalists" seemed to feel a republic of some sort should be formed if Egypt left. People meanwhile slipped in and out of Sanaa. Prince ʿAbdullāh Ḥasan had fruit, meat, tinned chicken, Egyptian cigarettes and fuel for his generator from republican commerce, while sections of Khawlān took money and guns from both sides, but this was the third successive year of drought.

> The terraces which used to produce wheat and millet lie fallow . . . All along our route we saw hundreds of goats and sheep dead of hunger and thirst. With defeated expressions, men wander the plains and mountains begging for a piece of bread or sometimes for water to drink . . . rare were the mothers who had not lost at least one of their children in the past year.[39]

Shaykh Nājī al-Ghādir meanwhile, feasted his guests on meat and rice. From a vast pile of gold sovereigns he allotted two for a boy to receive medical attention in Najrān, where apparently his ills were attributed to malnutrition.

In January 1967, a little before Rouleau's visit, Sallāl formed a Popular Revolutionary Union. The meeting was attended by Makāwī (ex-head of Aden's government) and representatives of the Baʿth and of the MAN as well as more immediate allies. A counter-meeting was convened in Nihm during March by Sinān Abū Laḥūm, who had fought the Imam through 1959–62 and is counted in the literature as a major republican but at Khamir and Ḥaraḍ alike sat in fact with the royalist contingent. Al-Aḥmar of Ḥāshid demanded that the government detained in Cairo be returned and prisoners held since August 1966 be released.[40] The pro-Egyptian state security system maintained its grip, however, and thirty years later one of those who had studied abroad in Aḥmad's time remembers: "Many people co-operated with the Soviets. Some with the Americans. Some even with the British. But if they did so it was for the good of Yemen. We don't look down on them as we do on those who co-operated with the Egyptians."[41]

In the South the moral priorities were otherwise: to have talked with the British would rank as treachery, with the Egyptians as patriotism. But the South was no more amenable to foreign control than was the North, and part of Northern savagery in 1966–7 was for Southern reasons. At the same time as the "Khamir group" were hunted down by Egypt, so were the MAN and trades-unionists around Taʿizz: the "Young Men's

Association" was suppressed and demonstrations in Taʿizz (September 1966) were fired on by Egyptian troops.[42] On the one hand Egypt wished to play such figures as ʿAbd al-Ghanī Muṭahhar off against the Khamir axis; on the other it was increasingly wary of the MAN, of which ʿAbd al-Ghanī was a member, because the NLF (the National Liberation Front), which the MAN dominated, had split with Egyptian policy on Aden. The NLF itself soon split between "bourgeois" and "revolutionary" factions.

Al-Aṣnaj, the Aden trades union leader now in Cairo, had formed an alliance with such anti-colonial members of ruling families as Muḥammad ʿAydarūs of Yāfiʿ and with al-Jifrī's South Arabian League, themselves somewhat compromised in Yemeni affairs by Saudi connections which date to 1959. Setting aside some of the latter group, Egypt promoted an alliance with the NLF to form FLOSY (Front for the Liberation of Occupied South Yemen),[43] announced in January 1966. A second conference of the NLF met in June at Jiblah. The meeting was protected, it seems, by Muṭīʿ al-Dammāj, a shaykh from near Ibb who had fled to Aden in the 1940s to escape Imam Aḥmad (Chapter 2), seized Ibb for the republic in 1962, and gone on to espouse more radical ideals.[44] The conference rejected the Egyptian merger. They feared a compromise with the Saudis, they despised many of those in the South they were asked to work with, and their views had out-stripped Nāṣirism.

Three works, all translated to Arabic, recur in people's memories: Jack London's *The Iron Heel*, Maxim Gorky's *Mother* and Georges Politzer's *Principles of Philosophy*.[45] The last, which derived from lectures given to French workers in the 1930s, is classical Marxism of the Stalin period, informed by not only historical materialism but dialectical materialism, a whole philosophy of the universe which in Arabic might sometimes have seemed as obscure yet powerful as a tract of the Jewish kabbala. Such figures as Muthannā, whom we mentioned earlier returning from Kuwait with a little schooling, were open to such appeals quite as much as were the better read. Nor were practical connections lacking. Yāfiʿ tribesmen divided by a purely local quarrel had early in the war gone north to find which party to the feud were politically correct and which were the "henchmen of colonialism". Such questions would soon be posed in terms of feudalism, reaction and world imperialism.

Shaykhs and sultans in the South were becoming marginalised. Muḥammad ʿAydarūs, who had fought the British since 1957, would not join "Qaḥṭān al-Shaʿbī's Front" (disputes over precedence and money went back to 1963); al-Shaʿbī and al-Aṣnaj detested each other, and al-Aṣnaj's colleagues had negotiated with the "feudal" sultans; the MAN's dislike of al-Jifrī's League, with which the sultans were also in touch, was matched only by its loathing of the Baʿth, with whom al-Aṣnaj sympathised.[46] In November 1966, at a meeting in Ḥumar near the North–South border, the NLF made explicit the split with FLOSY.[47] Cairo Radio attributed to FLOSY all the NLF did, but in fact the Egyptian Intelligence Service had lost control.

Divisions among parties and states were not the whole reality. Aden was full of Northerners, of whom most were not closely involved with politics, and Yemenis, more surprisingly, worked in Saudi Arabia throughout the war: their numbers through the mid-1960s may have been in excess of 100,000. Although Sanaa's government portrayed itself often as Saudi Arabia's sworn enemy, depending on the shifts of Egyptian policy, not until 1967 did the Saudis block workers' remittances which, along with Egyptian subsidies, kept the North solvent. Most of the North's imports meanwhile still came through Aden, and for a period in 1966 the Federal Government closed the North–South border, with dire results for Northerners, but soon reopened it. Disputes between governments overlay, and only sometimes interrupted, an unwritten history of movement and migrant labour.

The border zone between North and South was from this viewpoint merely no-man's land. A local view might differ. Al-Ḥumayqān, for instance, had been represented at major conferences north of Sanaa (ʿAmrān and Khamir, notably), but also formed part of Yāfiʿ truce-making and thus of Southern politics, while Yāfiʿ themselves had people still fighting in the North. The "factional grouping", as some saw it, of ʿAbd al-Ghanī Muṭahhar, al-Ahnūmī and others was connected with Aden merchants such as al-Shumayrī and Shahāb, yet equally with rivalries and alliances north of Sanaa; Adenis involved with trades unions knew well such Northern figures as Nuʿmān and al-ʿAynī, and through al-ʿAynī the Abu Laḥūms of Nihm. Regardless of sect or party, everyone knew everyone else – or someone else who knew them. With the suppression of Taʿizz politics, all this was lost to view.[48] The NLF and MAN drew on different connections, owing more to the Yemeni disapora.

THE END OF THE BRITISH IN THE SOUTH

If ʿAbd al-Nāṣir's position was fast unravelling, so was that of the British, whose announcement of withdrawal seemed to gain them nothing, for the level of violence only rose the more. 9 June 1966 was a busy but not untypical day:

18.45 grenade incident in Crater
19.15 grenade incident in Crater (one local killed, several injured)
21.00 grenade incident in al-Manṣūrah
22.30 two grenades found near the Chartered Bank.

16 June was worse, with a land-mine going off at 18.30, a grenade at 19.15, and so on through the night.[49] In parts of the Aden hinterland the British had long since been drawn into dubious forms of "counter-insurgency" (planting mines surreptitiously, for instance, where others might be blamed for the results); in Aden itself they joined in what amounted to gang warfare, and more conventional operations within the town proved self-defeating. An enquiry into allegations of torture in late 1966 mentions that the way army raids and searches were carried out was "in no small measure responsible for the general ill-feeling towards the authorities . . ."[50]

The NLF, though still ill-defined internally, linked country and city now. In both domains the usual instrument of colonial control, a locally recruited police and army, proved a liability. The Federal Regular Army (FRA) to a large extent was de-tribalised and promotion depended on examinations; the Federal Guard (FG) on the other hand was more obviously laced with ties of kinship. Resentment in the FRA was widespread, and as Holden remarks more generally, the military was a "nursery of nationalism", for some 400 local officers had experience of command by now, a taste of solidarity beyond tribe or village, and every reason to replace the British. As early as January 1964 a joke military communiqué had gone around in British circles: "*Enemy* – consists of FRA and FG personnel on leave, armed with rifles on loan from their parent units . . . Occasionally they are reinforced by small numbers of tribesmen and they are normally commanded by an FRA or FG officer on leave of field rank . . ."[51] The joke wore thin as it became apparent that the police in Aden were as little committed to British aims as the Federal Army, and in the east, the small Quʿayṭī and Kathīrī State Forces and the Ḥaḍramī Bedouin Legion (HBL), although independent of Aden, showed the same processes as in the Federal Army. All are remembered from the 1950s as lecturing rural neighbours and relatives on correct Islamic practice; in the 1960s all were infiltrated by the NLF.

Certain Northerners had suggested early on that there was no need to fight in the South at all for the British were leaving anyway, and the

Plate 4.2. The Aden Emergency.

announcement of a date only strengthened that perception. Al-Aṣnaj, in Aden, had also rejected turning the South into "a second Congo" but ʿAbd al-Nāṣir, in his own polemic style and for reasons of Egyptian policy, had insisted on revolution: "Some may ask, why fight for independence when the British will grant it freely in 1968? Comrades, true independence is not given away but taken; . . . the people must wage armed revolution against the enemy, in which they must pay the highest price in life and blood."[52] Those who split from ʿAbd al-Nāṣir's camp took such rhetoric more seriously than did he and the NLF became committed to revolutionary violence in such a way that all talk of a relation between means and ends appeared treachery or cowardice.

In February 1966 ʿAbd al-Fattāḥ Ismāʿīl of the NLF murdered ʿAlī Ḥusayn al-Qāḍī, President of the ATUC (Aden Trades Union Congress).[53] ʿAlī Ḥusayn was himself a Baʿthist and very much a nationalist, but the ATUC was a key to controlling Aden, and although British Intelligence was blamed for the murder and an emotional general strike was called, the revolutionary factions were now fighting among themselves. Shaykh ʿAlī Bā Hāmish read a sermon on the radio: "As our Arab

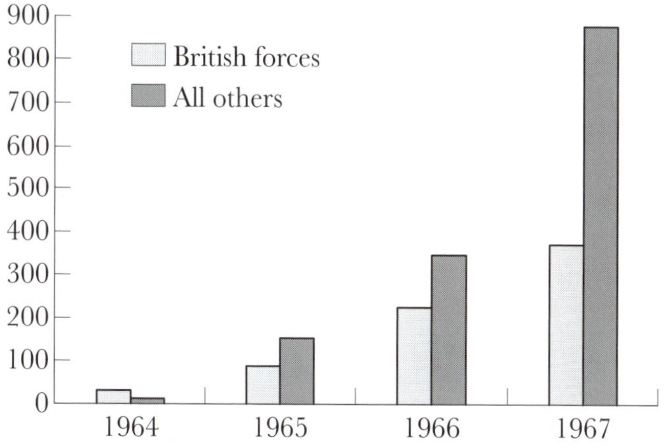

Figure 4.1. Aden casualties, 1960s

South approaches independence, we look for support from our brothers in Yemen [i.e. the North] . . . We appeal to our brothers in the name of God to cease interfering in our affairs . . . and allow us to solve our own problems."[54] In fact the core of the NLF was neither Northern nor Adeni, but precisely the "provincial lower middle class" which linked Aden to the towns of the rural South and to parts of the North such as Ḥugariyyah. Aden was their battleground. The murder of three of Makāwī's sons by the NLF in February 1967 led to a vast funeral at which supporters of al-Jifrī's South Arabian League were kicked to death, and in the months to follow, FLOSY and the NLF murdered each other in growing numbers as well as fighting the colonial power whose withdrawal had been announced already (Fig. 4.1).

The pace of events was not everywhere the same. A Kuwaiti magazine at the turn of 1965–6 published four illustrated pieces on Ḥaḍramawt.[55] Sickness and poverty are mentioned more than once, along with the troubles of the badu, lack of industry, double-taxation between Kathīrī and Quʿayṭī states, and insufficient funds for education. British hypocrisy and inefficiency are blamed. The dominant images, however, are of earnest little girls at school and of pumped wells being sunk in the major wadis. Revolution forms no part of the picture. British reports, also, suggest a world far removed from Aden. The South Arabian League remained a force in Wādī Duʿān and Wādī ʿAmd, while the coastal towns became dominated by the Arab Socialist Party, soon to be a stronghold of the NLF; but the Quʿayṭī government, under

Aḥmad al-ʿAṭṭās, had licensed both parties in late 1965, and politics still turned in large part on rivalries between the Āl al-ʿAṭṭās and their fellow *sayyids*.

In Ḥaḍramawt the first "terrorist incident" in British files was an attack in Mukallā in June 1966. The British deputy commander of the Bedouin Legion had been murdered in June the year before, and the commander himself was murdered in July 1966; neither was a "political" killing though both were claimed as such,[56] and conflict in most of Ḥaḍramawt remained low key. Mukallā, the scene of rioting in 1950, 1958 and again in 1964, became a dangerous place: there and in Sayyūn other factions, stimulated by new returnees from places such as Zanzibar, combined against the South Arabian League and drove them out in September 1966, but in the countryside revolution was hard to find. As late as July 1967 the assistant adviser visited Ghayl Bin Yumayn, in Ḥamūmī territory, for nothing more than a picnic. The women of the area, whose modesty is not that of tribes further west, danced all night while poetry was recited and Ḥamūmī songs were sung.

By the 1960s, Ḥaḍramī dependence on Indonesia and East Africa had given way to remittances from workers and business families in Saudi Arabia, some of the latter having been established there for twenty years. The South Arabian League, in Jiddah, suggested to such families as the Bin Lādins that the Ḥaḍramī Sultans be overthrown; but they also wanted FLOSY removed, preferably by the British, and the Ḥaḍramī business families themselves seemed to think in terms of Quʿayṭī ministerial intrigue. The Eastern states' chief aim, as of mid-1966,

> was to avoid becoming too closely involved in the struggle between feudalism and Arab socialism, and while both extremes are represented by minority groups which would like to come out firmly on one side or the other, the great majority hold no strong views . . . and are not much concerned which side comes out on top so long as they themselves do not suffer in the process.

The same writer goes on to say, however, that dreadful things were likely after independence. People were stockpiling arms and ammunition. It was the British who raised the issue of Ḥaḍramawt somehow combining with a non-Yemeni neighbour, perhaps Oman or more plausibly Saudi Arabia. The suggestion "was met with apathy".[57]

The arbiter among rival nationalists in both Eastern and Western Protectorates (as they had been not long before) proved often to be soldiers, and by the time the British left, at the end of 1967, there were 10,000 men in uniform, few of whom had interests parallel with British policy. In June 1967 four battalions of the Federal Guard were merged with the Federal Army; the rest of the Federal Guard were amalgamated with the Civil and Armed Police. The atmosphere could not have been less conducive to last-minute colonial manoeuvres, for in early June 1967, and with embarrassing ease, the Egyptian home army was destroyed by Israel. "The snake's head has been struck by a viper," said royalists in the North. FLOSY, the Egyptian-backed grouping in the South, was left exposed.

On 20 June 1967 a mass of plots and discontents exploded within the Federal Army when soldiers rioted north of Aden Town.[58] The police nearby killed eight British soldiers. The police in the Federal capital of al-Ittiḥād then panicked too and so did those in Crater, where looting broke out as the British for a time stood back. They still hoped the Federal Government might succeed them, but by now lacked the will to support that government, and as British troops withdrew from the countryside (a process well under way by the start of summer), the Federal Rulers and their little states fell one by one.

In August 1967 fighting broke out in Laḥj among FLOSY, the NLF and remnants of the South Arabian League. The Federal Army failed to restore order. They then declined to support the ruler of Shuʿayb, and al-Ḍāliʿ then fell to ʿAlī ʿAntar, who had fought in the area for years. In the early 1990s a dramatic mural in the Ḍāliʿ *sūq* still depicted nationalists in close-range combat with the British and storming the Amir's residence under fire; in practice, the two remaining British officers were simply told to leave as vast crowds gathered, and the Amir's brothers had their possessions looted as they later withdrew to Aden. FLOSY launched raids from the North, meanwhile, none of which secured lasting gains, while Dathīnah fell to the NLF, then so did ʿAwdhalī.

To unpick what the NLF was in each of these areas is difficult: a clandestine organisation of its nature keeps few records, a party flag might be hoist by anyone. But the flags appeared in strange places. Radfān, where the fighting had started four years earlier, Ḥawshabī, a thorn in British flesh since 1920, and Jabal Jaḥḥāf, enemies of the "feudal" Amir of Ḍāliʿ, all stood for the moment with FLOSY, as did the remaining rulers in what had once been the Western Protectorate – in Bayḥān, Upper ʿAwlaqī and Wāḥidī. At the end, the Sharīf of Bayḥān left for Saudi Arabia, pursuing some policy of his own; his state disappeared in his absence, most probably from family rivalry. The Sultans of Ḥaḍramawt returned from talks in Geneva in September 1967, only to find the Bedouin Legion and NLF had seized their capitals.[59]

FLOSY were more numerous perhaps within Aden, save among the oil workers and the dockers who were largely NLF. In Little Aden, around the refinery, the Federal Army had backed the NLF. In Shaykh ʿUthmān and al-Manṣūrah they gradually gained the upper hand, and in Aden Town itself the army arbitrated between the NLF and FLOSY until serious fighting erupted, then threw their weight behind the NLF who followed through their victory with a purge of FLOSY elements from the police and army and a settling of scores with civilians opposed to them. With the British behind wire and sandbags, no longer part of these events, hundreds of people were killed as if the revolution were merely starting. The last British troops were lifted off to an assault ship on 29 November 1967.

THE END OF THE EGYPTIANS IN THE NORTH

Defeat by Israel in June 1967 meant the end of Egypt's presence in Arabia. At Khartoum in August/September, Saudi Arabia and Egypt agreed a tripartite commission (Sudan, Iraq, Morocco) to arrange a compromise in Yemen. Sallāl rejected this, as did many others, and large demonstrations took place in Sanaa, where thirty Egyptians were killed by crowds. By mid-October, however, six weeks or so before the British left Aden, the last Egyptian troops had withdrawn from Sanaa to the coast: soon they were gone entirely. The Yemeni government held in Cairo was released, and in early November Sallāl left for Moscow, then retired to Iraq in the wake of a bloodless coup, being replaced as President by a council chaired by Iryānī, and at the start of December 1967 the royalists encircled Sanaa.

The "seventy days" became a national epic. As in 1962, Southerners came north to defend the revolution, and again, as at the start of the war, far larger numbers of volunteers flooded in from Shāfiʿī areas of the North. The National Guard of the early days was recreated as the Popular Resistance Forces. The NLF sent a contingent. Exiled FLOSY fighters from the South were in Sanaa too, however; and al-ʿAmrī stood his ground as well, while most leading Northern governmental and military figures fled. "It would be very difficult", admits ʿUmar al-Jāwī, "to say the republicans resisting the Saudi-Royalist threat had a coherent position . . ."[60] But many in the Popular Resistance, as a royalist commander said later, "were poor men, just returned from abroad . . . They had lost their roots, they didn't know their kin, they no longer had any family or clan with whom to take refuge if things went badly. They had nothing to lose . . . so they fought like lions." ʿAlī Muthannā Jibrān of Damt, for instance, who became artillery commander, grew up in Ethiopia. But the reference to family and clan runs deeper: many in the Popular Resistance felt, rightly, that "the tribes" could come to some accommodation with whomever won, whereas they, if they lost, would lose everything.

A strand of distrust had run through Lower Yemeni politics for years that negotiation with the Saudis might mean betrayal, and in Sanaa a "fifth column" was soon found to be trading with the royalists. Talks with royalists went on at higher level, not least in Beirut, while Algeria provided funds and Russia sent weapons: a dash to Moscow in search of guns and another to Beirut for talks were both made in December by the Foreign Minister, Ḥasan Makkī, who argued consistently, "better years of talks than a day of fighting". Talks and fighting, however, went on together. The Republican army was expanded hugely, from hundreds to thousands in two months, but the roads to Ḥudaydah and Taʿizz were reopened only in February 1968. Though "royalists" remained active in some northern areas until 1970, the war itself was won with the relief of Sanaa.

Many Shāfiʿīs attribute this final triumph to Aḥmad al-ʿAwāḍī, a shaykh from al-Bayḍāʾ who in many ways was larger than life: a fighter and a fierce man with a bottle, he was also a poet whose songs performed by Aḥmad Sanaydar of Sanaa remain famous.[61] Mujāhid Abū Shawārib of Ḥāshid had added to his own name as a fighter around Ḥajjah at the time of the Sanaa siege. Al-ʿAmrī was the Republic's "Napoleon". ʿAbd al-Raqīb bin ʿAbd al-Wahhāb, the young Shāfiʿī commander of the shock troops (*ṣāʿiqah*) made army chief of staff in the siege itself, was the hero of the hour, and the battles, which involved usually small numbers, were recounted "the way our history books described those of Tamburlane or Roland at Roncevalles".[62]

The MAN's distrust of shaykhs and tribes was intense, however; certain shaykhs and others feared the NLF; and rapid expansion of the army led to bitter rivalries, as for instance between ʿAbd al-Raqīb and ʿAlī Sayf al-Khawlānī over who should head newly raised units.[63] In March the MAN and al-ʿAmrī clashed over an arms shipment at Ḥudaydah, and in the forefront of those opposing the MAN was Sinān Abū Laḥūm of Nihm. Near Sanaa, ʿAbdullāh al-Aḥmar and Mujāhid Abū Shawārib of Ḥāshid allied with al-ʿAmrī. On 23 March 1968 a meeting of Bakīl shaykhs (many of them, presumably, had been royalist some months before) was held at Raydah. Their demands were very similar to those of the Popular Resistance.[64]

Plate 4.3. al-Iryānī and Nuʿmān.

In August the tensions erupted into serious fighting and ʿAbd al-Raqīb's supporters were crushed by force.[65] This was taken as a move against the left, which it surely was. It was also over who should control the army; others saw the conflict as primarily between Upper and Lower Yemen, marked by origins and accents, and Zaydī and Shāfiʿī officers were thus exiled to Algeria in equal numbers. When ʿAbd al-Raqīb returned in January 1969, by way of Aden and the NLF, however, he was murdered in Sanaa, quite possibly by adherents of FLOSY allied with al-ʿAmrī's people.

Those who knew him, remember ʿAbd al-Raqīb as a hero but scarcely a politician. In the course of the siege a committee had formed to lead the Popular Resistance: three Baʿthists, three MAN and three independent Marxists. When the Baʿthists conspired with al-ʿAmrī to exclude three others (the Popular Resistance Forces for a time in fact went on strike) all of them went to ʿAbd al-Raqīb, who told them to take no notice of political parties – quite unaware, apparently, that everyone present was a party member. The arbitrariness of events is caught by the story that before the confrontation in March 1968, al-ʿAmrī (symbol of a Zaydī right in much of the literature) intended marrying his sister to ʿAbd al-Raqīb (symbol of the Shāfiʿī left).

Deffarge and Troeller mention an effect that distorts most accounts of Yemen's politics. "As soon as you get away from Yemen, you tend to fall back into classificatory schemes: royalists and northern tribes (roughly the Zaydīs) on one side against mercantile republican trades-unionists (the Shāfiʿīs) on the other." They themselves showed that many Zaydī tribes were republican; one could add that certain royalist tribes were Shāfiʿī (Murād, ʿAbīdah, al-Qayfah, for example). To apply broader categories of left and right is no easier. When Sallāl was deposed in November 1967, crowds in Shāfiʿī Taʿizz had rioted, crying "We are your soldiers, Sallāl",[66] while those who ejected Sallāl had worried primarily about a counter-coup not from trades-unionists, merchants or the MAN, but from ʿAbd Rabbihi al-ʿAwāḍī, a Shāfiʿī shaykh of al-Bayḍāʾ. Among the crowds in Taʿizz fear of a deal with Saudi Arabia was prevalent; but Sallāl, a Zaydī soldier with a record of oppression south of Sanaa as much as north, had little in common, one would think, with any of the rival parties – Baʿthist, Nāṣirist or MAN – nor yet with most Shāfiʿīs be they workers or peasants, or even landlords.

Perhaps strangest of all is how naturally the country divided. The rhetoric throughout the war, as through the preceding decade, was of national unity yet Aden was declared a capital as the British left and six governorates were announced which between them formed a separate state (the People's Republic of South Yemen) on what had been British-protected territory. Little thought was given to making Taʿizz the capital as it had been in Aḥmad's time: a meeting there proved abortive, and ideology and practical connections alike soon drew apart two separate governments. The South was unified politically, for the first time including Ḥaḍramawt, and so was the North, as it had been since Imam Yaḥyā's day, but Yemen as a whole was not.

CONSOLIDATION OF TWO STATES

The South's economic situation at independence was grim. Aden port, now crippled by the closing of the Suez Canal in the Arab–Israeli war, had been the main source of income. The British base, now gone as well, had put perhaps £15,000,000 per annum into the local economy, and the Federal Government had depended on British subsidies. There is little reason to doubt the figure of 30,000 unemployed or of 80–100,000 people leaving Aden with the British withdrawal. Other people moved in: "The Adenis still speak . . . with horror of attacks on the Arab quarters of the city by 'bedouins', a term which for them is at best synonymous with 'savages'."[67] Depictions in the literature of a Maoist victory of countryside over city are misleading, however, for networks of the NLF had linked the two domains for years by now and much of the city population simply left as those from the hinterland arrived to claim the prize of revolution – which at the moment of victory turned out to be almost worthless.

As early as 1945, when accounts were still reckoned in sacks of 100,000 Indian rupees a time, the port had been the only source of wealth: "The Colony is extremely prosperous. It expects at the end of next year to have a surplus balance of Rs. 122 lakhs and a reserve fund of Rs. 69 lakhs, making a total of Rs. 191 lakhs, or nearly £1,500,000. . . . The Protectorate on the other hand produces no revenue whatsoever . . ."[68] Now all South Yemen stood where the erstwhile Protectorate once had. There were wealthy Ḥaḍramīs in Saudi Arabia, as we saw above, but the verdict of a British economist on Ḥaḍramawt in 1962 still held: "These states are not viable . . ." Even with appalling rates of infant mortality (400 per thousand births) the population had had to emigrate, and coldly the economist had minuted, "How is the future envisaged, if at all?" The same concerns had earlier been expressed for the Western Protectorate:

"it is wrong to think of [this] as an undeveloped territory, since the indications are that there is very little to develop".

Traditionally Aden's hinterland had supplied grain to Ḥaḍramawt in good years, and parts of the hinterland in bad years had imported grain from Bayḍāʾ and Qaʿṭabah in the North. Through the 1960s the export in return of sheep and goats to the North from Ḥaḍramawt had grown. The liaison of Aden port and Lower Yemen (Yemen's "eye" and its "green province") which had once made the country prosperous in the fourteenth century was even now not irrelevant. In a world of cheap wheat from Russia and America to cover the worst years, something might have been done. The traditional answer of emigration and remittances – being part not just of Greater Yemen but of global commerce – was not available on the scale it once had been, but it was still available, and estimates of Yemenis in the oil-producing states of Arabia ran as high as 300,000 even in 1970. South Yemen turned the other way, however. As hope of wider revolution faded, Aden's government attempted "socialism in one country".

CHAPTER FIVE

Two Yemeni states in the 1970s

Intermittently through twenty years, from about 1970 to 1990, each Yemen denounced the other in terms appropriate to the Cold War. Their disputes were in truth more intimate. "North Yemen was an internal problem for South Yemen and South Yemen was an internal problem for North Yemen, and the cause was not the connection of each republic to an international camp",[1] for while the South soon formed connections with the Eastern bloc, the North did not fit with either East or West. Each government meanwhile built a state apparatus in a period dominated by Gulf and Saudi oil wealth.

SOCIALISM IN HALF A COUNTRY

In Ḥaḍramawt, where the Quʿayṭī and Kathīrī "states" evaporated and Mahrah never had a state to speak of, there seemed little to resist change: "making the socialist revolution means transforming existing social relations", said the Mukallā NLF before the British left Aden, and an attempt to install "revolutionary relations" was made immediately. In the Aden hinterland two major figures to emerge were ʿAlī ʿAntar, who had fought around al-Ḍāliʿ, and "Sālmayn" (Sālim Rubayʿ ʿAlī) who, though often described as a fighter of Radfān, was most prominent now in his home area of Faḍlī. Qaḥṭān al-Shaʿbī, originally from the Ṣubayḥāt near Laḥj, was made President. The leading ideologist of revolution, however, was ʿAbd al-Fattāḥ Ismāʿīl, himself from Ḥugariyyah in the North, and the rhetoric he promoted of scientific socialism and a vanguard party soon displaced that of bourgeois nationalism.[2]

Great emphasis was placed on the "toiling masses" of workers and peasants to be led by revolutionary intellectuals. These components save the last were scarce. The proletariat of Aden had gone home now to North Yemen and the working class in the South numbered only a few thousand;[3] a peasantry, meanwhile, might be found in Ḥaḍramawt and in cotton-producing areas such as Laḥj and Abyan but elsewhere most farmers were tribespeople and supporters of Qaḥṭān al-Shaʿbī, himself from a family of tribal smallholders, complained that the left "passed lightly over realities and objective circumstances".

The Fourth NLF Congress, at Zinjibār just east of Aden in March 1968, was dominated by left progressives. The army arrested leaders of the left, only to face riots in Aden and in the Faḍlī cotton zone of Jaʿār, and Qaḥṭān al-Shaʿbī changed his line by proclaiming that property of deposed rulers would be redistributed to NLF guerrillas. This was not enough. Ḥaḍramawt in effect seceded; Jaʿār and Zinjibār – both cotton areas in Sālmayn's sphere of influence – erupted in "revolutionary" violence; while at the same time "counter-revolutionary" risings took place with exile support in ʿAwlaqī, Radfān and elsewhere. Qaḥṭān lacked a firm power base. He was forced to cede the office of prime minister in April 1969 (his brother-in-law Fayṣal held the post for a while) and in June was deposed as President in favour of Sālmayn.[4]

The "22 June corrective move" was part of a remarkable transformation. Tribal disputes had been suspended by decree in January 1968, and tribalism now collapsed from within as it once had further north in face of Imam Yaḥyā. The country was under attack from elsewhere. The Saudis had used Sharūrah as a base against the British in the 1950s (Chapter 3), but in November 1969 there was fighting at Wadīʿah, south of there, and an atmosphere of siege took hold throughout South Yemen. Minor shaykhs were expelled by local activists who condemned them as feudalists and agents of foreign powers; a more radical agrarian reform law was promulgated in November 1970, and in 1972, at the time of the Fifth Party Congress in Aden, the process of revolution was intense.

> Lorries packed with workers in overalls, badu with long curly black hair wearing indigo tunics, peasants with multicoloured *fūṭah*s wrapped around their waists . . . students in shirt-sleeves, soldiers in khaki, surge around the avenues and public squares, which are heavily decorated with posters and huge banners [condemning] . . . "reaction" and "imperialism" . . .[5]

At the Conference itself, we are told, discussion took place "in a comradely atmosphere within socialist parameters".

From the distance of Rouen a quarter century later, Habib Abdulrab looks back on Aden's suburb of Shaykh ʿUthmān in novel-form. The *rūfalāt* – the drinkers and wide-boys of colonial times – were cleared out and puritanism flourished:

> We don't want hippies or people wearing flared pants.
> We don't know if they're girls or boys.
> We don't want traitors or a reactionary line.
> Our people is entirely Marxist!

The "dunes" where couples had met and young men hung out to smoke or drink and discuss their dreams became an off-limits area patrolled by soldiers, while "kidnapped one night, South Yemeni prostitutes found themselves, come the dawn, as producers in a little tomato-sauce factory set up in an isolated place far from towns and men. Fishing was banned (it was theft of the State's property!). A law forbade talking to foreigners . . . Another made it illegal to go abroad."[6] The Adenis' mistrust and dislike of the countryside is caught in the figure of a "bedouin" simply drunk on the rhetoric of dialectical materialism, on the transformation of quantitative into qualitative change, the union of opposites, the resolution of thesis and antithesis, little of which made sense. "The absurd ranged the city, combed the streets and squatted everywhere . . ."

In the countryside change was uneven. Although the earliest attempts at radical reform (1967) had been in Ḥaḍramawt, visitors to Tarīm in 1972 found people still kissing the hands of *sayyids*; even Laḥj, where land tenure was grimly unequal, proved difficult to ignite, but on Jabal Jaḥḥāf at al-Ḍāliʿ "young girls with their faces decorated in fine black designs shout ultra-feminist slogans through microphones with great assurance and poets sing the glory of the President and agrarian reform".[7] Perhaps a quarter of the South's population simply fled the country. Feudalism was the enemy everywhere and rhetoric took small account of detail, for politics was in command as a Party official at al-Ḍāliʿ made clear years later: "What needed to be done was to establish new relations, to change the farmer's mentality . . . Although there were no feudal estates in the real meaning of the word, we had to use these methods in which the farmers took part with the encouragement of [State] authority."[8]

In the North no land reform took place. Sinān Abū Laḥūm, governor by self-appointment of Ḥudaydah Province, was as disturbed as were Aden's Marxists by long hair and flared trousers; but in other respects the two regimes differed. In 1968, as people returned from Aden or the army, peasant reform committees had appeared around Taʿizz, Radāʿ and Ibb, and in some places landlords were arrested.[9] Central Government set them free again. The North's achievement in the eyes of its rulers was simply to have expelled Bayt Ḥamīd al-Dīn, the Imam's family. The rhetoric of the time condemned personalised rule (*ḥukm fardī*, a slogan also applied to Sallāl's period) and contrasted republican progress, though in fact little changed at first, with the backwardness of "theocratic government". This extended to a prejudice against *sayyid*s, whose place in national affairs was filled by *qāḍī* families, while in the South, by contrast, the rhetoric of class replaced that of genealogy and Fayṣal al-ʿAṭṭās, from the well-known *sayyid* family, was a prominent revolutionary in Ḥaḍramawt.

Unmarked by official rhetoric, changes in class composition affected the North directly. Important merchants had shifted operations from Aden to Ḥudaydah soon after 1962; now, as socialist policies were applied in the South, lesser merchants also settled in Ḥudaydah, the North's only major port, where they were joined by returnees from Africa and by Adenis who had lost their property. Older Sanaani wholesalers were forced out of business. A Shāfiʿī commercial class took form, centred upon Taʿizz, and a certain practical alliance with shaykhs was evident, while the North also harboured large numbers of Southern refugees from tribal areas.[10] Although Sanaa's government was headed by cautious "Liberals" such as ʿAbd al-Raḥmān al-Iryānī, Muḥammad ʿAlī ʿUthmān and Aḥmad Nuʿmān, around them were constituencies that wished Aden's regime destroyed.

The phenomenon had its mirror image. Few people moved south after 1967, but such prominent figures in Southern politics as ʿAbd al-Fattāḥ Ismāʿīl and "Muḥsin" (Muḥammad Saʿīd ʿAbdullāh, for years head of state security) were Northerners. In Aden, lacking rural constituencies, they favoured a strong party-apparatus and demanded Yemen's integration more insistently than did colleagues from Faḍlī, Abyan or Ḥaḍramawt: "the borders and artificial separation which divide the Yemeni popular masses in two parts, the division between South Yemen and North Yemen which occurred during British occupation, should disappear . . ." The South accused the North of betraying the September Revolution (the coup of 1962), an accusation elaborated in terms not only of Saudi influence, which even those in the North who favoured the Saudis found clumsy and intrusive, but of global imperialism and the role of the United States. The North's claims were less dramatic. But already by 1969, before the 22 June corrective movement, the North's foreign minister could complain, "we are further from unity than we were a year ago".[11] In 1969, 52 per cent of the North's few exports went to the South and almost 30 per cent of its imports came from there: four years later the figures had dropped to less than 7 per cent and 6 per cent.

IRYĀNĪ, ḤAMDĪ AND SĀLMAYN

Resistance in the siege of Sanaa at the turn of 1967–8 had saved a republican government under the then prime minister, Ḥasan al-ʿAmrī. The left in the North was crushed. But al-ʿAmrī resigned in September 1971 after murdering a Sanaani photographer, and more prominence was given to the head of the Presidential Council (in effect the President), Qadi ʿAbd al-Raḥmān al-Iryānī, who had nominally been head of state since late 1967 and exemplified perfectly what Baraddūnī calls "the second republic". A republican but scarcely a radical, Iryānī retained the personal manners of the old regime. A brief biography by a fellow *qāḍī* describes him as "a learned and cultured man, a poet, a writer of letters, a great politician, pleasant in company, a raconteur and someone of great humility . . . He was able by his wise policy to hold the tiller of the ship amidst choppy waves and raging storms until peace was established for Yemen."[12] The absence of detail here is eloquent.

In 1970 the royalists, save the Imam's family, were integrated in the new republic; and in 1971 a Consultative Council was established with Shaykh ʿAbdullāh al-Aḥmar of Ḥāshid as its chairman (a suggested lower house, the People's Council, never met). In December 1970 the South changed its name to the People's Democratic Republic of Yemen, no longer simply "South" Yemen, while the North (the Yemen Arab Republic) gave a series of ministries to ʿAbdullāh al-Aṣnaj whose Aden associates in FLOSY had been crushed by the NLF; exile groups received support from Sanaa, and border incidents worsened until, in late 1972, a war was fought between the Yemens. There was widespread complaint within the North afterwards about "the influence of a foreign country". By this was meant Saudi Arabia.[13] The reconciliation of 1970 had brought a Saudi grant to Sanaa of $20 million, repeated intermittently thereafter, and many shaykhs received Saudi stipends, as did Southern exile leaders, independently of Sanaa's government.

The rains in these years were poor, which without foreign shipments of grain would have spelled famine, and the strain of South against Saudis was constant. Iryānī's most intransigent problem, however, was what passed as a state apparatus: "I see it as essential [he had said in 1969] that a complete administrative revolution be announced, aiming first to control administrative corruption and chaos and wanton misuse of the state's resources and powers." North Yemen at the time had an extraordinary 775 governmental figures with the salary and rank of minister. Subsidies paid to tribal shaykhs by Sanaa in 1971–2 were estimated at nearly YR 40 million, about three and a half times the total *zakāt* from farming, and shaykhs and officers often helped themselves to funds. The number of bureaucrats (4,000 in the first year of the revolution) had risen to over 13,000 by 1969 and continued rising to 30,000 by mid-decade.[14] Many lived from mild corruption. Nor was access to administration easy, as Messick describes for Ibb where new and old claims to prominence were apparent in people's clothing: "The simple attire of the peasants contrasts with the many-layered traditional garments of the *qāḍī* and *sayyid* functionaries, or the Western style dress of the townsmen in the office . . . People who attempt to deal with functionaries without having an acquaintance in the office or without an intermediary expect a difficult time." In the countryside near Ibb were intermittent cases of "banditry" or of "rebellion".

From 1970 the Organisation of Yemeni Revolutionary Resisters (*al-muqāwimīn al-thawriyyīn*) claimed to lead a struggle against "feudalist and reactionary forces" and "imperialist plans". The organisation contained members of the old MAN, now the Revolutionary Democratic Party. Their sincerity is not in doubt nor their courage (many died under torture), but their claims match unreliably with facts. At Raymah in 1972, for instance, the Resisters

> captured the lands of feudalist Shaykh Aḥmad bin Aḥmad al-Muntaṣir and distributed the lands to the masses of the poor peasants [despite heavy opposition from] the mercenaries of Shaykh (feudalist) Sinān Abū Laḥūm who is well known [for] his hiredom to Saudi reaction and link with the American central intelligence . . .[15]

The lands are still there, however. And Sinān is remembered locally as fighting not dispossessed peasants but a semi-independent government under Shaykh ʿAlī al-Fasīḥ, in schism since Sallāl's time. Shaykh Manṣūr Ḥasan, among the biggest of Raymah's feudalists, seems never to have been challenged by his tenantry or the left: he was challenged by a returning army officer, who wished to be shaykh and failed, but this was scarcely a rising of the poor against oppression.[16] The pattern recurs widely.

The struggle was in large part directed against Saudi influence and pursued in terms of grand theory. For example, a bomb was exploded in al-Jūbah "at the palace of puppet of Saudi Arabia Nāgī bin Manṣūr Nimrān", the Nimrāns being shaykhs in Murād, the tribe south of Ma'rib from which Imam Yaḥyā's assassin ʿAlī Nāṣir al-Qardaʿī had come a quarter century earlier. ("Comrade Muḥammad ʿAlī al-Qardaʿī" was "martyred" at Raymah, above; Ḥusayn Ḥusayn al-Qardaʿī was killed attacking the Sanaa house of "one of the heads of feudalism and hireling, reactionary Shaykh ʿAbdullāh al-Aḥmar". The Qardaʿīs, shaykhs or not, were active in the 1970s.) Nimrān's mud house was scarcely a palace, however. The shaykhs of the region were almost as poor as their tribesmen. In June 1972, near the Saudi border, the Resisters killed Qadi Yaḥyā al-ʿAnsī, a rather minor figure in local terms whom they refer to strangely as "the ruler of Baraṭ".[17]

Talk of feudalism meshed loosely at best with realities in rural Yemen, for people followed those they knew and the idea of class revolution failed to displace such patterns. A meeting as early as 1970 had to recognise "a lack of widespread objective conditions for armed struggle", but in 1972 Taʿizz "saw another face of sorrow . . . with the tragedy of the assassination of Shaykh Saʿīd bin Saʿīd al-Mikhlāfī at the western front corner of the Muẓaffar mosque beside the Maqṣūrah gate before the afternoon prayers during the excellent month of Ramaḍān. He was devoting himself to reading the bountiful Qur'ān . . ."[18] In May 1973, Muḥammad ʿAlī ʿUthmān, in government since 1962, was murdered in Taʿizz after dawn prayers, denounced by the Resisters as an "agent of Saudi feudalism and reaction". ʿAbdullāh al-Ḥajrī, as prime minister, secured a large Saudi loan and a reputation for severity in Lower Yemen, where executions and widespread arrests were carried out against Iryānī's wishes. Prime ministers changed frequently, supposedly under Saudi pressure,[19] and in July 1974 Iryānī was deposed as president in favour of Ibrāhīm al-Ḥamdī.

Ḥamdī had been a protégé of Ḥasan al-ʿAmrī and had occupied important posts in the expanding army.[20] His most interesting connection, however, was with co-operatives, and when a Confederation of these movements formed in 1973 Ḥamdī had been elected chief. Co-operatives (*taʿāwuniyyāt*), as Carapico notes, had no set form, for *taʿāwun ahlī* (local, almost "folk" co-operation) might centre on a village, a shaykh, family links or a few enthusiasts; a Development Association (*hay'at taṭwīr*) seemed more formal, and the latter idea gained ground with Ḥugariyyah claiming to set the trend: "After security and peace were established at the end of a destructive civil war . . . the Yemenis began to perceive a new path to escape from backwardness (*takhalluf*) and a rapid means to join the procession of nations who had preceded them on the path of civilisation (*ḥaḍārah*, culture) and of progress."[21]

This was broadly the rhetoric around Ḥamdī's accession. The Consultative Council was replaced by a Constituent Assembly and a

Plate 5.1. Ibrāhīm al-Ḥamdī.

Command Council established which included ten members, besides the President, all with army rank.[22] The "corrective movement of 13 June" won wide support, and the greatest of northern shaykhs, ʿAbdullāh al-Aḥmar, convened a meeting in Hamdān just north of Sanaa, which "joined together the tribes of Bayḍāʾ governorate and Ma'rib, of Ṣaʿdah, Dhamār and Ḥudaydah, Taʿizz and Sanaa, Ibb, Maḥwīt and Ḥajjah".[23] The meaning of "tribe" differs greatly among these regions (Chapter 1). In reality the shaykhs of all Yemen gathered, and their aim was to establish a tribal council independent of state control. Their support for Ḥamdī was clear, however, as was that of progressives of many persuasions, not least those from south of Sanaa, of officers and young administrators. "Ibrāhīm" stood for modern Yemen.

In the South, where shaykhs had been swept away, "Sālmayn" was as prominent. After June 1969 Sālmayn became President, with ʿAbd al-Fattāḥ Ismāʿīl as Party Secretary. ʿAbd al-Fattāḥ, the Northerner, favoured a centralised party on the Russian model, while Sālmayn, who visited China and was impressed by the cultural revolution, favoured "spontaneous" mass action, and he more than anyone encouraged peasant *intifāḍah*s. In late November 1973 he visited Shibām in Ḥaḍramawt: the crowds, lined up to dance and sing, saw something being dragged behind cars in the approaching retinue, which turned out to be the naked bodies of "feudalists".[24] Sālmayn's radicalism (not to mention his brutality) at home, however, was matched by caution abroad, where he approached Yemen's unity less impatiently than did ʿAbd al-Fattāḥ.

Within a year of Ḥamdī taking power, strains in the North were showing and the Abū Laḥūms of Nihm were ousted from their posts: Dirham Abū Laḥūm, for instance, was replaced as commander at Taʿizz by Major ʿAlī ʿAbdullāh Ṣāliḥ, a future president of Yemen who until then had commanded the post at al-Mafraq on the whisky road from Mukhāʾ to Taʿizz. Mujāhid Abū Shawārib of Khārif in Ḥāshid, who near the end of the civil war had made himself governor of Ḥajjah, was relieved of his post in Sanaa. In October 1975 the Constituent Assembly itself was suspended, which left ʿAbdullāh al-Aḥmar, Ḥāshid's paramount shaykh, outside the government, and a "second Khamir conference" was held to resist Ḥamdī. Little came of it, but many areas in the north refused access to soldiers and officials.

The Command Council still included, besides the technocratic prime minister ʿAbd al-ʿAzīz ʿAbd al-Ghanī, both Aḥmad al-Ghashmī and ʿAbdullāh ʿAbd al-ʿĀlim. Al-Ghashmī was a tank officer and brother of the Shaykh of Hamdān, a minor Ḥāshid tribe. Beyond this, for every tribe at odds with government was another receiving government's favour (the Bakīl tribes of ʿIyāl Surayḥ, ʿIyāl Yazīd and Arḥab, mainly royalist a decade earlier, became more prominent; Dhū Muḥammad were heavily involved with army politics). ʿAbd al-ʿĀlim, meanwhile, from an originally Ḥaḍramī family long settled in Lower Yemen, commanded the (Shāfiʿī) paratroops and had close links with Nāṣirists but in 1973 he had ordered the execution of ten Shāfiʿī officers sympathetic to the Resisters. Lower Yemen was as divided as Upper Yemen along other than class lines or lines of "modernity". The National Democratic Front (NDF), which took up broadly the cause of the Resisters, was formed there in February 1976, three months after the quite different "second Khamir conference" but as much distrustful of central government.[25]

Intrigues among those pursuing power in Sanaa concerned few North Yemenis, for outside major towns there was little administration. Even Ḥamdī's attempt to mobilise co-operatives as a political base proved unsuccessful. Some resented the imposition of shaykhs at the expense of village organisations; others, often shaykhs themselves, resented government co-opting them; most, of widely differing views, preferred autonomy to state involvement, and in the co-operative elections of 1975 – the first national elections ever held in the North – Ḥamdī supporters did badly.

The co-operatives are so important that a case is worth describing.[26] Ḥugariyyah had been the site of the earliest village associations in the 1940s, but in May 1970 "the shaykhs and notables of al-Shamātayn, al-Mawāsaṭ and al-Maqāṭirah" had answered ʿAbd al-Raḥmān Nuʿmān's summons. Ḥugariyyah, it was said, comprised 10,000 square kilometres and 300,000 people. A tax was agreed of 5 *buqshah*s (an eighth of a riyāl) for each riyāl paid the government as *zakāt*, and foreign donors were approached for help as well as ministries. Roads and schools were built, but the show-piece was a drinking-water project:

> The citizens of Ḥugariyyah living in al-Turbah and people going there, whether sons of Ḥugariyyah or elsewhere – these people before the water project was set up had never known clean, healthy water . . . now, because of this Association's efforts, they have pure, healthy water in their homes . . . The people benefiting . . . are not from China or America, or Africa or India, but are sons of beloved Yemen. . . .

A grand public meeting in May 1973 was disrupted by those who said only al-Turbah benefited or the Association was lining its own pockets.

In the following years younger activists demanded accounts for income and expenditure (Ḥugariyyah's *zakāt*, they thought, came to YR 2 million per annum; where the money went was unclear) and some of them seem to have supported other shaykhs against Nuʿmān, whose attention had shifted by then to Sanaa. Shaykh Aḥmad al-Kabāb and ʿAbduh ʿAṭā gained control.[27] "No active work took place worth mentioning except a well in ʿAṭā's own village" but sums of 3,000 to 5,000 riyāls were being given to local shaykhs, supposedly for development, and some said Kabāb paid this to his friends "because he was their Shaykh and their representative on the Consultative Council and a minister in the State". Such assumptions about the natural role of shaykhs and the State were common. Governmental rhetoric offered a different vision.

"Ibrāhīm" was the first of Yemen's leaders to master mass politics. His military uniform was set aside before long in favour of a short-sleeved suit, and he spoke in persuasive terms of progress; he welcomed home expatriates from the Horn of Africa (then slipping into long-term warfare) and from as far afield as Vietnam, and offered Yemen's help internationally in mediating, for instance, between Ethiopia and Eritrea, thus presenting his country as one to be taken seriously. His promise of administrative reform served rather to display than to alleviate the public distress, for in practice almost nothing changed, but "Ibrāhīm" was vastly popular. There was money in people's pockets, as we shall see below, the years 1974–7 were years of excellent rain, and part of Ḥamdī's message was Yemen's unity. From early 1975 he encouraged work on joint problems, and somewhat isolated from local powers in the North, turned increasingly to talks with Aden: in early 1977 Ḥamdī and Sālmayn met near the North–South border. In August 1977 Sālmayn came to Sanaa. But the tension with the Saudis was irresolvable (socialism aside, they disliked the idea of a united Yemen) and Ḥamdī proved incapable of sharing power. The widespread, if somewhat abstract, popularity of the President seemed to others *ḥukm fardī*, "individualised (self-centred) rule" of a kind the Imams had practised.[28]

It is often said Ḥamdī wished to be Yemen's ʿAbd al-Nāṣir. He was also, to take a lesser parallel, Yemen's Bill Clinton, with an undisciplined taste for young women; his close associates, arranging clandestine girls and whisky, rose from obscurity to power through his patronage and in the end, when his enemies wished him dead, arranged his destruction easily. In October 1977 "Ibrāhīm" and his brother ʿAbdullāh were murdered in circumstances of contrived squalor.[29] He had been scheduled only two days later to visit Sālmayn in Aden and again discuss unifying Yemen.

TWO STATES IN A SEA OF MIGRANTS

Ḥamdī's rise and fall (1974–7) coincided with a boom in migrant labour. Provoked by the Arab–Israeli war of June 1973 the oil states to Yemen's north raised prices fourfold and a spree of expansion followed in which Yemenis did the manual work, sending home what in aggregate were enormous sums. Remittances to North Yemen, which had stood at some $40 million in 1969–70, rose to $800 million in 1976–7 and continued rising, to $1.3 billion in 1978–9, dwarfing the revenue of central government. Imports rose correspondingly. Apart from salt, hides and small amounts of coffee (all much as under Imam Aḥmad) there were no exports, and the formal trade deficit was therefore vast. Regardless of the government's insolvency, the riyāl held steady at 4.5 to the US dollar for about a decade.

There are no precise figures for the numbers of migrants who left the North at various times, but a census in 1975 reckoned that migrants made up 630,000 of the North's total population of 5.3 million[30] and by the end of the decade there was talk of 800,000 migrants. Probably less than 20 per cent of remittances ever passed through the banking system. The largest of Ibb's merchants, Ḥajj Ḥasan, had thus been an agent for ʿAbduh Shūlaq of Jiddah since the mid-1950s and now ran a remittance office in Ibb in addition to his retail outlet for tyres, radios and cookers; in the mid-1970s, though his was quite a small operation, he had some half million riyāls out in loans to townspeople. Such financial activity did not feel oppressive in a period of expansion, but the world seemed to some to have been turned upside down: "At night Ibb used to glow with the lights of evening *qāt* sessions at which books were read and questions of history and religion discussed. With two other men I read Jurjī Zaydān's multi-volumed history of the Arabs aloud, taking turns. Now evening *qāt* sessions are rare and I sit alone at night."[31] Few felt this sense of loss. The glowing lights of years ago had been oil or kerosene beyond most people's means. Now there was electric light. The rattle of generators became part of village life and *qāt*, which before 1962 had been a pleasure of the elite and soldiers or a seeming necessity among Aden workers, was now everyone's indulgence. The acreage of *qāt* in the North expanded hugely.

Already before the boom, some complained of inequality and consumerism. In the 1970s, however, "the *sūq*s came to know foreign black bread from West Germany, birthday cakes from Italy, fig rolls from Britain" and indeed much else. Tins of Abū Shaybah rolled-oats, named for the "old man" on the Quaker Oats label, of "tuna" (often pilchards in fact) and processed cheese were everywhere, while the standard measure of volume in small transactions was a foreign pineapple tin. Powdered milk – Abū Nūnū or Nido – became a staple which in retrospect gave its name to a generation, and little shops which before dealt in local spices sold cigarettes, batteries and ballpoint pens.[32] Some commodities arrived in ship-sized batches: the whole country, to take a minor case, filled suddenly with identical green wheel-barrows.

The ebullience of the period was expressed in the pick-up trucks and taxis that appeared throughout the North, decorated often with nylon fur around the doors and brightly coloured fake feather-dusters upright on the front bumpers. Cassette recorders were among the first things bought. Under Yaḥyā, and to a large extent under Aḥmad too, music had been suspect and suppressed, and musicians from Kawkabān and Sanaa as well as Taʿizz moved to Aden. The "Sanaani" style of intricate melodic lute-runs, which some attribute to mediaeval Andalusia, had since spread as far afield as the Gulf.[33] Now it was everywhere, and Ayyūb Ṭārish's *Bilādī, Bilādī* became a popular anthem: "My homeland, my homeland, the land of Yemen, . . . Victory is ours, and death to the dark powers which oppressed our land!"

Skirt, shirt and turban, with a Western-style jacket, was the usual men's dress, the ensemble completed by a large dagger, usually in a "tribal" sheath. There were urban men in suits and wide ties and men in the towns with traditional learned robes, but the dominant image of the time was of farmers coming into the cities dressed often in skirts and shirts of surprising pastel colours. Women's fashion spread from town to countryside. Young Sanaani women during the civil war had set aside the coloured Indian prints their mothers wore over house clothes as outer veils in favour of *sharshaf*s, rather elegant black sets of overskirt, cape and veil, beneath which one could wear all kinds of frivolity. Now the fashion spread elsewhere. In the major cities, young women dressed in *sharshaf* and *lithmah* (a tightly wound scarf pulled up over the nose in company) found work in offices;[34] clothes shops, jewellers, even shops selling foreign perfumes, appeared in the major towns. Countrywomen claimed to despise all this, stressing their own strength and toughness as much as their good looks, but few farm girls were dressed any more in simple black and in the smallest rural markets there were bolts of tinselled cloth for sale.

Wage rates rose.[35] As Yemeni men streamed abroad to work, therefore, foreigners filled their places – by the end of the decade perhaps

50,000 of them – and the effects were sometimes strange. One Labour Day – "the feast of the workers", the first day of May – in Ḥajjah, for instance, the workers of the world, preceded by a brass band, marched past the provincial governor: Chinese road workers, Egyptian school-teachers, Sudanese hospital staff, American Peace Corps volunteers, and many others, while the Yemenis sat in the bleachers and applauded. Every hole in the ground, it seemed at this time, was named a *mashrūʿ* or "project". All things seemed possible and the future was being built at family or village level.

Political scientists speak bluntly of states as "capturing" economic surplus. The beginnings of the process were soon apparent. "With Ḥamdī the interest in national security increased . . ." but more importantly a certain vision held by technocrats found expression. A Central Planning Organisation (CPO) was established which in 1972 produced a three-year plan, and this was followed by a five-year plan (for 1976–81) that stressed, in ways faintly echoing the Imams, the necessity of self-reliance. By 1977 some 40 per cent of food for domestic consumption was imported, and ʿAbd al-Salām speaks of *laissez-faire* economics as "a killing blow to agriculture";[36] but wheat cost twice as much to produce locally as it did to import. Involvement with the wider world was depicted in graphs of wage rates, wheat prices and labour patterns. First in the imagination, then in practice, an economy took form,[37] and statistical yearbooks expressed what Peterson calls "the search for a modern state", a project as important and as little debated as establishing a Kingdom fifty years before.

Bilateral and international agencies promoted the common sense of planners. They stressed "institution building", which in effect meant "state building", and what the state was required to do that could not be done otherwise was seldom argued. Large ministries were erected; the number of clerks and officials multiplied, although with government wages low, many came from elsewhere in the Arab World. The army grew. More work passed through government hands, and in the course of the 1970s capital expenditure by government rose from almost nothing to about half North Yemen's total. Little was raised internally, almost none from direct taxation of remittance wealth, and most came from foreign aid and debt, a system of relations among banks and governments which attached only loosely to local needs.

The South ran parallel. A three-year plan, which events overtook, covered 1971–4, and then a five-year plan treated the period through 1978. Like the North, the Southern government in 1969 had joined the

IMF and sought advice from the World Bank. A strategic relationship was built with Russia also from 1969 onwards, but Russia contributed no more than a quarter of the PDRY's aid and even that in the form of projects, usually, not as budgetary support,[38] and the South's major funders in fact differed little from the North's: Kuwait from 1971, the World Bank from 1975, then Abu Dhabi. Like the North, the Southern government depended heavily on aid and loans.

In the South, state control of property (1969–73) discouraged remittances at first, and at the Aden refinery everyone sent abroad for training between 1967 and 1974 simply stayed abroad.[39] Faced now with a huge drain of manpower from a tiny workforce, Aden's government tried to ban emigration. This proved impossible. In 1975 about 125,000 Southerners were thought to be migrant workers, and by the end of the decade perhaps 200,000. Remittances by then accounted for 40 per cent of GDP and food imports for 30 per cent, very much as in the North, although the South assimilated remittance wealth to state expenditure far more efficiently, and the paradox developed of massive dependence on economies which the South's revolution was, in theory, committed to overthrow.

The dream of self-sufficiency was vigorously pursued. Less than 1 per cent of South Yemen's area was arable, and inputs of chemical fertiliser rose to twice the Northern figure while enormous efforts were made somehow to expand the acreage. Some 40 per cent of construction work in the PDRY remained in private hands, 50 per cent of transport, and 90 per cent of livestock; but the focus of progressive aims was always crop production, and land redistributed in the early 1970s – about two-thirds of total farmland – was organised in co-operatives. In some cases collective expenses were shared and production left in family hands, but ideology pushed strongly towards establishing state farms and even sympathetic witnesses speak of "the precipitate formation of such farms from lower-level co-operatives where the necessary political and social consciousness has yet to emerge among the peasantry".[40] Optimistically, the state required co-operatives to collect taxes also. Between 1975 and 1980 official wheat yields dropped from 1.8 to 0.63 tons per *feddān* (a *feddān* is about an acre), almost certainly because farmers were selling produce illegally. As population rose, agricultural production per capita decreased. "Democratic centralism" was itself centred heavily on Aden, and 70–75 per cent of the South's workforce was employed in what Vitali Naumkin calls the "non-productive sphere".

In rural areas of the South, prosperity spread less rapidly than in the

North. But at the end of the decade remittances allowed Yāfiʿ to build splendid stone houses in traditional style yet decorated with large red stars above the door. Criticism from visiting officials was rejected:

> Delegation, look at these honest men.
> No-one tells you off, so eyes off these towers here.
> We built them with the blood of our livers.
> We don't sing and dance like some folk.[41]

The autonomy of households was maintained in the South by law (one could not buy another's land), in the North by the fact that remittances were in private hands, and one's impression is of household life being rather similar in both Yemens. The worlds beyond the household differed. As Carapico says, a contrast was often drawn between South and North: *qānūn* and *niẓām* (law, order, "system") in the one and *fawḍā* (corruption or "chaos") in the other.[42]

SĀLMAYN AND GHASHMĪ

When Ḥamdī was murdered (October 1977), Aḥmad al-Ghashmī became President but he lacked "Ibrāhīm's" charisma and his announcements on hoardings around the capital, even when they were Ibrāhīm's with the name changed, had always a forlorn look; nor did he establish a firm grip on politics. A group of Nāṣirists and of paratroop officers sympathetic to ʿAbdullāh ʿAbd al-ʿĀlim, infuriated by Ḥamdī's murder and threatened by Ghashmī's Saudi sympathies, attempted to foment a tribal war north of Sanaa. Almost before the civil war ended (Chapter 4) tribes and shaykhs attached to the royalists had switched allegiance to the socialist South (Qāsim Munaṣṣir of Khawlān was a famous case), and the attachments of such figures as Mujāhid al-Quhālī of ʿIyāl Yazīd were now to trace a path with the NDF that makes sense in terms of local history and personal loyalty but none in terms that most political science recognises. Fighting broke out at Jabal Aswad on the border between Sufyān of Bakīl and al-ʿUṣaymāt of Ḥāshid.[43]

The fight at Jabal Aswad was emblematic. In the lulls of shooting, trucks crept north towards Saudi Arabia in a procession of winking fairy-lights and others moved south piled high with the goods of returning migrants until the cease-fire broke and the truck lights in the dark were replaced by tracer bullets; the cycle was repeated several times, for this was not, so to speak, total war. Finally a truce was arranged in traditional form. The two sides marched away, each singing their *zāmil*s or tribal ditties, and an intensely "political" clash was rewritten in tribal terms. Here is one of Sufyān's versions:

> Mountain of Sufyān, greetings and news
> Of how Ḥāshid fell back from you shattered.
> Al-Ghuzzī says go tell the Colonel
> It's Bakīl that advances everywhere.[44]

The "colonel" is Mujāhid Abū Shawārib. In fact, in such tribal affairs no-one advances anywhere. One adds to a fund of dramatic stories and the borders remain unchanged.

As revealing of the time are anonymous women's rhymes. In many places a quarter of the adult males were away in the Gulf or Saudi Arabia (in some cases it was far more), and in tribal areas of the north and east there grew up besides this a vast trucking business bringing petrol and consumer goods in overland. Women were left to run the household:

> O Muslims, we all sleep alone,
> On account of the petrol and the big trucks.[45]

Or again:

> God, it's your job you Jiddah traffic police:
> Tell my sweetheart hello and send him home.[46]

If women became more prominent in the fields, as in parts of the North they did, marriage became a tournament of value fuelled by new money and bridewealth in parts of Ḥāshid exceeded YR 100,000. In the South, on a smaller scale, the same occurred. The "family law" of 1974 set bridewealth in the South at YD 100 or 2,000 dirhams "but there are people", admitted ʿAbd al-Fattāḥ, ". . . who still outsmart the law and secretly agree to pay a bigger dowry of 10,000 or 15,000 dirhams".[47] Actually, it was often three or four times that. Brides themselves took pride in the amounts paid.

The loneliness of migrant work in the Imam's day was assimilated to the new prosperity in novels and short stories, and in several works, most by men but a few by women, the strains of divided families and of family politics became a theme.[48] Most people, however, glad to be richer than they were, simply got by. The following rhyme was sung in front of the house after a woman's husband came home from the Saudi run after driving day and night from near Riyāḍ, switched off the ignition at last and passed out across the steering wheel:

> The dawn breaks, may God bear witness.
> The bed was for two and came to be just for one.[49]

Cash and the need to earn it became part of everyone's lives. A farmer in Ḥugariyyah explains how families used to judge a potential bridegroom: "he had to have a bit of land, even just a small bit, to keep the girl and her family happy. That's all changed now. People are interested in how much money the husband has, not land."

Cynthia Myntti's friends in a village of Ta'izz governorate were typical. The grandfather, who had worked as a ship's stoker out of Aden in his youth, farmed with his wife while their daughter-in-law, 'Azīzah, ran the household. Their son, Muṣṭafā, worked in Saudi Arabia at several jobs at once (construction worker, cook, clerk), living with fellow migrants to keep down costs and remitting small amounts monthly until, at the end of four years, he returned with a lump sum and presents: "a fake fur coat for 'Azīzah, a color television, new and fashionable ready-made clothes for the children, imitation Persian carpets, a washing machine, a butagaz-fueled stove with oven, a blender and other household appliances".[50] By the late 1970s a surprising number of places in the North had generator electricity and water from pipes or from bowsers and donkey-carts (twin-tub washers and flush-toilets began to undermine the foundations of Sanaa houses). In most places water was carried on women's heads, but even there life was felt by the women themselves to be better, for thermos-flasks, biscuits, fresh bread every day, were things that few people ever had before.

As a good son, Muṣṭafā not only took his parents on the Mecca pilgrimage, but put his savings into building a house for his wife and children. His counterparts did the same everywhere and the price of building land rose, particularly in Sanaa where on some streets it reached that of European cities. The cost of living there rose fivefold in the 1970s, the cost of housing about ninefold.[51] The population of Ta'izz by the mid-1970s had grown to 81,000, Ḥudaydah to almost 83,000, even Ḥajjah to over 40,000, but Sanaa grew from perhaps 90,000 to 200,000 in the course of a decade. During the civil war a few streets had acquired cement buildings of Egyptian form, the space near the Imam's old palace ("Liberation Square") acquired tea-shops and such fun for small boys as hired bicycles and air-rifles; but the shape of the city had remained as in Turkish times. Now what once were fields around the town became building sites, with men chipping stone and pouring concrete (Map 5.1).

Even beyond Sanaa, land-fever blocked capitalist development and merchants bought land as a safe investment instead of ploughing profits back into trade: few factories appeared and no large-scale joint

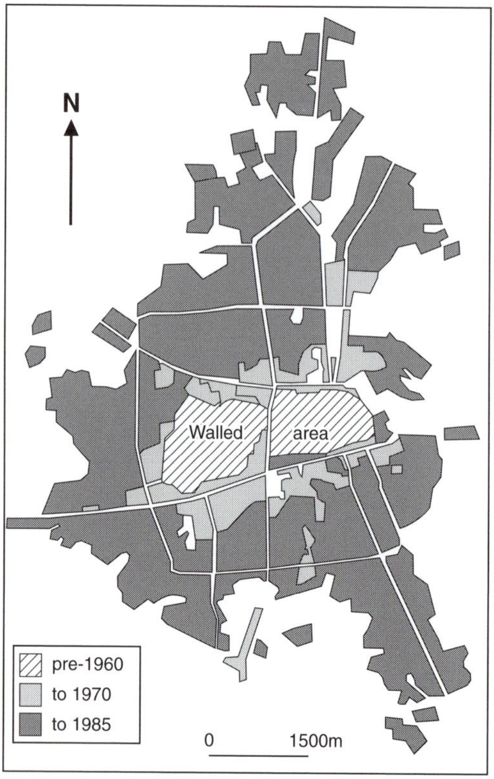

Map 5.1. The expansion of Sanaa, 1970–85

investments. The price of agricultural land as well as building land rose; the returns from agricultural land declined, for the huge inequalities of landed wealth on which the Resisters and NDF dwelt were no longer the whole of life (cash from wage-labour changed everything) and share-cropping agreements were often renegotiated or land ceased being worked. In the Tihāmah, however, production was susceptible to cash investment. Many Northern technocrats had made their start in Tihāmah projects with roots in the Egyptian period, or indeed in the Imamic era when large contiguous holdings were already a feature of the coastal lowlands. Development of both spate-fed and pump-fed schemes now marginalised traditional land-rights, leaving farmers (far poorer than in most highland regions) clinging to the land through subsidies from kin abroad and unpaid family help at home.[52]

Rain-fed land in the highlands was more labour intensive, and much

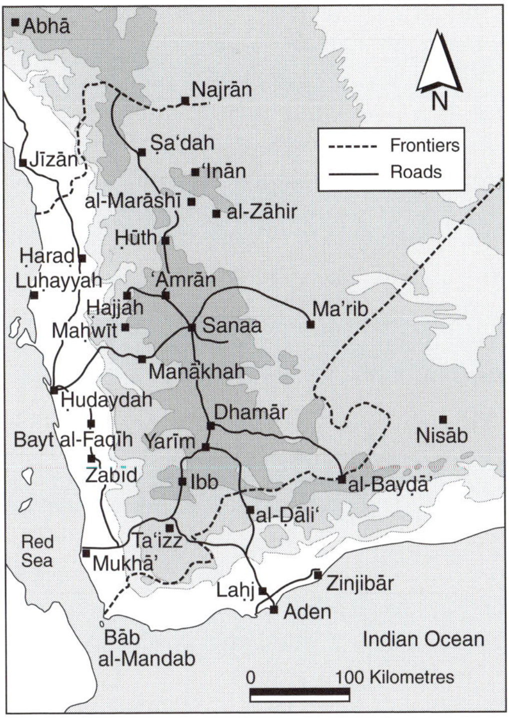

Map 5.2. North Yemen, late 1970s

was simply left fallow (grain production in the North as a whole dropped by 45 per cent); but *qāt*, although fortunes were made by a few big owners, was potentially a "democratic" crop giving many with smaller plots access to the new wealth and helping keep people in the countryside. As late as 1979, the North's population, now close to 6 million people, was reckoned to be 90 per cent rural. The energy displayed in rural areas matched that in the expanding cities, and by Carapico's reckoning, rural co-operatives built some 5,000 kilometres of feeder roads between 1973 and 1976, 6,550 kilometres in 1977–8, and over 17,000 kilometres in the period 1979–81. To walk the 80-kilometre length of Maḥwīt province still took locals four days (six or seven for "flatlanders"); but even near Maḥwīt one could now reach a road within a couple of hours, thus by truck a market, and thus the capital within a day or so instead of a week or two weeks.[53]

In the South far more of the infrastructural work was controlled centrally, but there was less of it overall. The Chinese built a road from Aden to Ḥaḍramawt; more than 90 new wells per annum were sunk in the 1970s, and fisheries and canning were expanded along the coast. The percentage of total population in the capital was far higher than in the North, however, and of almost 1,400 new dwellings envisaged in the South's first five-year plan, 74 per cent were in Aden. Aden's population in 1977 was thought to be somewhat over 270,000, dwarfing Yemen's other cities and dominating the Southern countryside; by 1980 it was somewhere near 300,000. The suburbs of British times grew further, but unlike the case in Sanaa, rents were at first brought down and then held steady.[54] Income distribution in the South was among the most equal in the world. In the North no-one knew quite what the pattern was.

THE CULTURE OF TWO STATES

Expansion of schooling was vigorous on both sides of the border, and through the 1970s the South led the way. While the North could claim about 30 per cent of ten-year-olds in school by 1976–7, the South claimed double that, and while the South could claim a 40 per cent literacy rate towards the decade's end, the North claimed only 20 per cent overall with literate women in a tiny minority. The substance was hard to judge.[55] Official Southern pronouncements, however, spoke particularly of producing a new type of person, an aim enshrined not only in education but for instance in the 1974 family law: "Building a new culture will be the basis of creating a new awareness, a new mentality, . . . burnishing in people's awareness and sentiment new spiritual values and the project of building the new person."[56] Southern schoolchildren, at least in some places, acquired uniforms of shorts or skirts, white shirts and coloured neckerchiefs of East European style. A rather Adeni view became standard in the South that Northerners were disorderly savages sunk in "backwardness" (*takhalluf*).

Northerners, with money in their pockets and secure in their possession of a vast cultural history, often revelled in the image, quoting Sallāl's line from the civil war that he was "ruler of five million lunatics". A certain rough familiarity had been the style of Imam Aḥmad and had not disappeared in the 1960s; now the manner was reinforced by so many people having money of their own and everyone of roughly equal age, and of any rank, was referred to or addressed as "brother" or "sister". An old *qāḍī* in Ibb complained of morality's collapse since pre-Revolutionary times: "Then there was knowledge, religion and

Plate 5.2. Spreading socialist enlightenment.

upbringing, all of which no longer exists. The young have no idea about the Book, the Sunnah of the Prophet, or religion. They are going toward communism, but they don't know what that is."[57] In a riot over education in Taʿizz in 1974 a Qur'ān was supposedly ripped up, though the story may have been wild rumour. The case of Islamic morality was in fact not desperate, any more than was that of daily manners.

Although no judges were being trained, a *muftī* of the Republic had been appointed under Iryānī's government thus continuing the process of revisionist theology begun under Yaḥyā and developed through the civil war. Viewed politically, "official" Islam now preached only the pious hope that rulers behave honestly; but freed by circumstance from practical concerns with conformity and power, Yemenis in everyday life got on with simply being Muslims. Traditional forms of piety remained in place at local level and in no way were conceived of as at odds with what people thought was progress. But a third term was evident by then. From early in the 1970s one finds mentions in the North of "Wahhābī" groups.

The Muslim Brothers, from the distance of Cairo in the 1940s, had been fascinated by Yemen as a Muslim country untouched by Western influence (Chapter 3). They won few converts. Young men dispatched to

Cairo in the 1950s and 1960s to become Sunni *ʿulamāʾ* had usually returned as leftists, and when enthusiasts for the Brothers' views were themselves expelled from Cairo they found little support in their homeland of Taʿizz province.[58] In the 1970s, however, they were seized on as a counterweight to the NDF by Sanaa's government. At national level, Ḥamdī appointed ʿAbd al-Majīd al-Zindānī, a man of deeply Wahhābī tendencies, as "Guide" or *murshid*,[59] and with funds from the Saudis, "Institutes" began to appear in North Yemen, spreading a generic Sunnism whose function was to block the socialists.

Within the South, Islamic practice had been brutally attacked in the early 1970s, when for instance the tombs of saints in Ḥaḍramawt were desecrated and many preachers and scholars murdered. In the later 1970s state officials would be seen to pray on major holidays, but religion was treated by the Party as something that would one day disappear and Islam viewed in instrumental terms as at best a primitive form of socialism. As early as 1974 ʿAbd al-Fattāḥ invoked names from the distant past, which "shone in movements of rebellion throughout history. Since the Khārijite, Muʿtazilī and Qarmatian movements of rebellion and others, Yemeni names have continued to glow in the firmament of thought, philosophy, dialectics and history."[60] A minor intellectual industry turned on the Qarmatians. Traditionally to Zaydī scholars, the "Qarāmiṭah" were heretics who abused the Islamic message and practised amorality in lurid forms; to official Southern writers they were primitive socialists who held land in common.[61] Most of this passed above people's heads, however, and the Qarāmiṭah remained for most rural Yemenis a mythic people who long ago had built walls or castles that no-one could otherwise explain.

In his 1974 address ʿAbd al-Fattāḥ continued with a list of later figures: "Hamdānī, Nashwān al-Ḥimyarī, ʿUmārah the Yemeni, al-Maqbalī, Ibn al-Amīr and al-Warīth were merely leading Yemeni scholars, a few slight cases from a vast caravan of revolutionary thinkers through the history of Yemen across the last twelve centuries." In what sense ʿUmārah (d. 1174/5) was a revolutionary thinker is unclear. But the list of names is canonical. These are historical writers on whom almost everyone agreed as distinctively part of Yemen's heritage, and foremost was Hamdānī, "the tongue of Yemen" who had lived in the tenth century, a contemporary and opponent of the first Imams. The Ministry of Culture in Sanaa announced a project of publishing 100 classics. Not all saw print, but Yemen at least began near the decade's end to acquire a literature in more accessible form than manuscript. Literacy rates were low. Enormous amounts of poetry were published, however, as well as circulating on cassette, and primary schools North and South saw issued a set of shared standard history texts which a preface signed by Ḥamdī and Sālmayn called "the first practical step on the road to unity . . ." (The presidents' names were later quietly removed but the wording remained unchanged.)

In the North in the early 1970s contemporary work, often published elsewhere, dealt with the civil war or transition to post-war politics. Zayd al-Wazīr's *Attempt to Understand the Yemeni Problem* (1971) is a famous case, providing a sophisticated structural view of the country's political and intellectual life; al-Shamāḥī's *Yemen: the people and the culture* (1972) took a different tack, giving a brief summary of Yemen's history in chronicle form as a prologue to discussing the people he knew personally and their struggle against the last Imams, while Baraddūnī's radio and magazine pieces (collected as Baraddūnī 1978) played off early Islam and the recent revolutionary past in reflections made acceptable to all through citation of the country's vast fund of poetry.

In 1977 ʿAbdullāh Juzaylān, whose close association with Egyptian state security led to his exile when Sallāl resigned, published an account of September 1962, the events around the revolution. He presented himself as a key figure, as indeed he was. A "committee of free officers" then published their own version, *Secrets and Documents of the Yemeni Revolution*, for there were arguments to be had over who was a "Septembrist", that is, rightly an inheritor of the nationalist revolution. In print there was no discussion of who in practice was a Baʿthist, for instance, or who a Nāṣirist, but often one had to know the details to grasp who was writing and reading what. To read more traditional-seeming works required a similar awareness of what was left unsaid. Muḥammad Zabārah, for instance, the best "official" historian under Imam Aḥmad, had been working at the time of his death (1961) on *The Excursion of Perusal*, a compendium of biographies of learned and influential Yemenis in Islam's fourteenth century (that is, from AD 1881). His son Aḥmad, the Republic's *muftī*, completed the work in 1979. Which author is which is usually hard to tell, though they were living in different worlds, and the final layer of ambiguity was added by an enthusiast at the newly formed Yemen Centre for Research and Studies, who, fired with republican zeal, razored out biographies of the last Imams and had colleagues scribble over doubtful passages. Those passages one could usually read by holding the pages to the light. The excised biographies circulated among those interested.

The "Revolution", both in popular and official discourse, marked a transition from darkness into light. In the North, the phrase "before the revolution" often really meant before the remittance boom and the years of the civil war were little focused on, but triumphal arches made reference on every public occasion to "the immortal revolution of 26 September". In the South, where revolution day was 14 October, streets in Sayyūn carried such names as Freedom Street and Democracy Street, and above the main road at the end of the 1970s ran signs and arches saying, "Let us struggle to defend the revolution, carry out the five-year plan, and build the vanguard party". Behind the banners in Sayyūn and Tarīm, poetry and literature seem to have continued in broadly pre-revolutionary form; so they did in Taʿizz and Sanaa. In the North, village festivals on Yawm al-Nushūr (much confused with Yawm al-Ghadīr) died away in most places as too much associated with the Imams, replaced by republican festivals which took their inspiration from the cities. In 1970 the official parade in Sanaa to celebrate 26 September included a float depicting women's work, on which sat young women "their outlines entirely shrouded in black, in front of sewing machines or with books in their laps". This was felt too adventurous, however, and in later years parades consisted mainly of marching soldiers.[62]

In the South at Shiḥr, on the Ḥaḍramī coast, a museum was opened in 1977 to commemorate seven martyrs killed in a Portuguese raid of the sixteenth century: interestingly, this was the site of what before the revolution was openly a saint's pilgrimage.[63] The second edition of Bā Maṭraf's book on the subject of the martyrs appeared in 1973; al-Shāṭirī's *Eras in Ḥaḍramī History* was published in Mukallā the year before, and in publishing terms Ḥaḍramawt bore a charmed life. Elsewhere in the South, particularly Yāfiʿ, distinctive local traditions persisted sometimes as official "folklore", but public events were everywhere grist to the mill of progress. "We have tried to enumerate [sic, *nuḥṣī*] the popular dances present in the republic so as to preserve our popular dance heritage and develop what is best in it . . . particularly dances which glorify work and defence of the homeland . . ."[64] Much of this was embarrassing to watch. In the North dance was something that simply happened: on revolution day, 26 September, men would dance with their daggers in Sanaa's "Liberation Square" for the sheer fun of it. A certain standardisation of dance and song was encouraged on both sides of the border by state-run television, which in Aden goes back to the colonial period but spread rather slowly through the countryside; Sanaa began transmitting in 1975. In both Yemens, radio was more important until the decade's end.

A survey in 1973 suggested large numbers of Northern farmers listening to Cairo as well as Sanaa, and students, intellectuals and functionaries also listening habitually to London. The Northern radio series "Pictures from Real Life" (1975), however, caught the texture of everyday Sanaa. A man takes a government job elsewhere, for instance, and his father-in-law says,

> Go and may God open the way for you. But as for my daughter, I say you are not to take her one step . . .
>
> But, Uncle, why? She's my wife, the mother of my children . . .[65]

Payment of the bridewealth turns out, as so often, to have been the opening move in endless family debates and conflicts. The failings of bureaucracy were touched on also; so was the opacity of legal procedure, where one was as likely to be ruined as ever get a fair judgement. But the detail of family life is what holds the attention. "Praise be to God you've returned safe and sound", says the husband sarcastically when his wife has only been around the corner to the Turkish bath or *ḥammām.*

> You're sure? Four hours to go to the ḥammām? If you'd gone ḥammāming on the Red Sea at Ḥudaydah, you'd have been back by now . . .

> Hah! If you'd seen the situation at the ḥammām! . . . If I weren't a resourceful woman I'd have been stuck there until nightfall . . .

Reading over these texts twenty-five years later is to recapture a group of good-humoured, sturdy people grappling with an odd world.

Several later series had the same effect of weaving character and family imagery – all in familiar dialect – into public issues, but "politics" was presented in less detail. In the North, television and radio adopted a style common elsewhere in the Arab World and the news began with a jaunty brass-band march (tubas were prominent) then went on to say almost nothing: "The President, Brother Colonel Aḥmad al-Ghashmī, Head of the Republican Council and Commander of the Armed Forces, today met in his office at the Republican Palace with the ambassadors of sister neighbouring Arab states and discussed with them regional developments. Agreement was expressed on a range of topics . . ."

POLITICS AND ECONOMICS

In Lower Yemen warfare between government and NDF went in cycles, which most people tried simply to avoid. There and in Upper Yemen one heard increasingly of "Nāṣirists", by which were meant primarily people furious at Ḥamdī's murder: some had once been supporters of Sallāl, others were from areas once mainly royalist, and others still were a younger generation caught by the ideal of Arab unity. In Lower Yemen landowners and power-brokers from further north remained prominent, as if little had changed since Imam Aḥmad's time, and in Upper Yemen such tribes as Arḥab, ʿIyāl Yazīd and Sufyān proclaimed sympathy with the NDF and Aden. Beyond the major cities government in the North was sparse, and wealth came from either remittances or political subventions by other states. Saudi stipends to shaykhs in Upper Yemen were large; on occasion, funds and weapons reached their rivals from Southern sources. Outside the ring-road around the capital disputes were elaborated, contained and managed almost wholly in tribal terms or in terms familiar to the non-tribal peasantry.

Competition for power within Sanaa appeared a matter of personal connections.[66] In Aden it seemed a matter of factions, one of which was made up of Northerners such as ʿAbd al-Fattāḥ and "Muḥsin", the latter forming links with political powers in Yāfiʿ; on the other hand, ʿAlī Nāṣir Muḥammad of Dathīnah, prime minister from 1971, was said often to be allied with neighbours from ʿAwlaqī. Others felt excluded and simply victims in faction-fights: "Every Southern family lost at least one of its members, particularly if they were Adenis, but not until 13 January 1986 did we hear of a Northern family losing one of its members, including the sons of al-Ḍāliʿ who held power in the South on a tribal basis."[67] In fact what emerged in Southern politics were groupings reminiscent of *khvosts* in Stalin's Russia,[68] whose leaders were seen from the start as contending patrons.

Aden was the centre of events and wealth; the countryside produced almost nothing. To have mimicked the North's *laissez-faire* approach would have meant as stateless a world as the British found in the 1930s, and the State in the South had thus to be run either tightly or not at all.

> The citizen in South Yemen lived under police surveillance all day, from the moment he left the house until he came back, and under surveillance from several organisations: the organs of State Security, those of the Presidency of the Republic, units of the army, gangs from the political organisation attached directly to the president of the ruling party, local committees . . .[69]

Tensions that might have dissipated in rural disputes or urban disobedience became focused within the party structure. While the North was characterised by mild but endemic "chaos", the "system" of the South was rent by spasms of violence at the centre.

Despite the South's alliance with Russia, both Yemens lived in the shadow of the Saudi state. Many Southerners, albeit some on Northern passports, now worked in the Kingdom and the Saudis themselves soon ceased treating seriously the South's claims to revolution. In parallel with attempting to "manage" Northern politics during Ḥamdī's time and then funding Ghashmī generously ($570 million was given in immediate aid), the Saudis from the mid-1970s reduced support for Southern exile groups and cautiously accepted overtures from Sālmayn in Aden, a process complicated by disputes about the war between Somalia and Ethiopia and by the Saudis' habitual indecision in matters of grand policy.[70] Sālmayn, however, was concentrating power too much in his own hands for the comfort of ʿAbd al-Fattāḥ, ʿAlī ʿAntar and ʿAlī Nāṣir.

In June 1978 matters came to a head. In perhaps the most convoluted even of Southern plots, the Northern president, Ghashmī, was blown up by a briefcase bomb in the hands of an emissary from Sālmayn. *Qāt* was officially frowned on in the South at the time, though not wholly banned, and the Southern president had supposedly received a shipment from his Northern counterpart, repaying him through an emissary. It proved embarrassing when the emissary was searched. On a second occasion, it would seem, Ghashmī waived the search, expecting a briefcase of cash, and was blown to pieces. Sālmayn was then executed by his colleagues who had sent the bomb. His popularity was in part his downfall:

> At every moment we see him descending unexpectedly on people in some organisation or some governorate, coming up to them in his Landrover. Sometimes he behaves like long-ago kings who pretended to be lowly people and came down among the folk. He asks people how they are and makes a point of kissing some old lady in the street or gives some poor person ten dinars . . .[71]

As with Ḥamdī in the North the year before, what to some was unstructured popularity seemed to others *ḥukm fardī*, individualised and arbitrary rule. The Saudis, said Sālmayn's enemies, had intended to dominate the South through "family rule by the tribe of Faḍlī". ʿAbd al-Fattāḥ, ʿAlī ʿAntar and ʿAlī Nāṣir claimed by contrast to support democratic centralism and thus collective rule.

In the North, Ghashmī's murder left a vacuum. Qadi ʿAbd al-Karīm al-ʿArashī, appointed caretaker head of state, considered taking the presidency until his female relatives, so the story goes, presented him with his winding-sheet and told him not to be so foolish, and an army officer then stepped forward. Major ʿAlī ʿAbdullāh Ṣāliḥ, who had once been a close associate of Ḥamdī and a colleague of Ghashmī, took

Plate 5.3. Northern optimism, late 1970s.

control and in July 1978 was declared President. His most conspicuous act before this, as commander at Taʿizz, had been to drive ʿAbdullāh ʿAbd al-ʿĀlim across the border into South Yemen at the time of the Jabal Aswad fighting. His stepfather had been a soldier with the Imam, as had he for a short while, and the President spent part of the civil war as tank crew with the rank of corporal.[72] ʿAlī ʿAbdullāh was a self-made man. At the time of writing, more than twenty years later, he still rules Yemen.

In some analyses the army is contrasted with the tribes as a source of power, in others a combination of tribal and army roles explains events, but distinctions need drawing among tribes. Sanḥān, ʿAlī ʿAbdullāh's tribe which abuts the south side of Sanaa, is part of Ḥāshid, just as is Hamdān the tribe of the former president Aḥmad al-Ghashmī, which abuts Sanaa's north side. Neither had been conspicuous in tribal affairs. Rather, both had been a source of soldiers for the Imam's army, which was not a prestigious role (Imam Aḥmad used scathingly to call ʿAbd al-Nāṣir of Egypt "al-ʿUkfī", the grunt or squaddy). The growth of a republican military late in the civil war brought Hamdān and Sanḥān to prominence, and both Ghashmī and ʿAlī ʿAbdullāh rose to prominence themselves through the army, as did Ḥamdī before them, not through connections of a broader kind.

The president's position was insecure, for Lower Yemen was at times a war-zone, in Upper Yemen tribal leaders all had their conflicting aims, and subterranean party rivalries connected both these domains with Sanaa and with each other. In October 1978 a Nāṣirist coup attempt was put down.[73] ʿAlī ʿAbdullāh relied from the start on those he knew. He had grown up with his stepfather Ṣāliḥ (full-brother of his deceased father) and placed his trust first of all in his own half-brother, ʿAlī Ṣāliḥ, whom he posted to Ḥizyaz, "the gate of Sanḥān". Muḥammad Ṣāliḥ also became prominent. The president's full-brother, Muḥammad ʿAbdullāh Ṣāliḥ, emerged as chief of Central Security, and other obvious relatives, such as ʿAlī Muḥsin al-Aḥmar, soon appeared on the lists of senior officers, as did members of families such as Bayt Ismāʿīl and Bayt al-Qāḍī related to the president's family by marriage.

In the South, where "family rule" was an affront to ideologies of modernity as much as of equality, the Yemeni Socialist Party (YSP) was established in October 1978 and a revised constitution granted it control of state and people: "The YSP, armed with the theory of Scientific Socialism, is the leader and guide of society and the state . . . [in] the struggle of the people and their mass organisations towards the absolute victory of the Yemeni revolution's strategy."[74] Yemen's history was "dialectically correlated with the struggle of the Arab and other peoples", and revolutionary struggle in the country's two parts was "dialectically correlated in its unity". The preamble states the aim of a united Yemen under the YSP. Part of the impetus was doubtless practical: "A united Yemen would be economically viable in a way that the South on its own is not . . . All other policies – relating to the Gulf, the Horn [of Africa] or the major world powers – are comprehensible only within the perspective of the uncompleted and ongoing Yemeni revolution."[75] Also, ʿAbd al-Fattāḥ, the champion of a central party, was himself a Northerner. The NDF in Lower Yemen had meanwhile become a factor in Southern (Adeni) politics and in the North had widespread allies north of Sanaa as well as south. As early as October 1978 a large contingent of northern tribesmen appeared in Aden, supporting revolution. The North responded with renewed support for exile groups. In January 1979 war broke out between the Yemens, and the Southerners took a number of towns beyond the border.

President Carter of the United States was under attack at the time as "soft on communism", someone in Washington gained a name by knowing where Yemen was, and suddenly Yemen was in the world press: huge aircraft shuttled in and out of Sanaa bringing tanks to see off the communist threat, such extravagant weapons as wire-guided anti-tank missiles were shipped to North Yemen (about 18 months was needed to learn to use these; one may wonder at the logic, but most in fact stayed in Saudi hands), and an American aircraft carrier was stationed off South Arabia. The North was said for a while to be in "the American camp". Some months later, however, Sanaa's government did a deal with the Eastern bloc for hundreds of tanks and forty fighter-planes, leaving analysts to write of a "politics of balance".

The dispute was brought under control, in fact, before the end of March 1979, by Arab states. Iraq and Syria were both concerned at the time to exclude Egypt from broader Arab affairs, for Egypt had recently signed a peace with Israel; the Saudis, much alarmed at the South's incursions, were willing to join a mainly Iraqi initiative to constrain the YSP; and Kuwait played, as often it did, the role of honest broker. The only dissenting voice, for a time, was Libya's. The division between "international camps" was less important, for Russia showed no wish to spoil its relations with the North and the North had never plausibly seemed a "Western ally". It had often seemed, to the fury of some Northerners, a Saudi client, and 1979 was the first time since the civil war that a broader Arab context became prominent in which the State, as opposed to individuals and clandestine parties, gained room for political manoeuvre.

The presidents of the two states (*shaṭrayn*, or "two parts", was the official formula) promised, as their predecessors had in 1972, to work towards Yemen's "unity". Few people thought the prospect imminent. But state-level politics is not the whole of life. At the end of the 1970s Sanaa television began broadcasting Muḥsin al-Jabrī's "Pictures of my Country" – still running, I believe, at the time of writing – which visited different parts of Yemen, North and South, interviewing local personalities, showing "customs and traditions" and, to the accompaniment of rippling lute music, panning across the mountains, fields and townscapes of what seemed obviously, at a great many levels now and to citizens on both sides, one country with two governments.

CHAPTER SIX

Yemen in a wider world: politics and economics through the 1980s

The oil boom reached its peak so far as Yemen was concerned before 1980 but the effects of declining oil prices in later years were uneven. The state apparatus in the North grew faster, with the aid from 1984 of locally produced oil and gas, while the South reached an impasse politically. The context was far beyond Yemeni control. Much as rainfall had determined affairs in decades earlier so now world commodity-prices affected whole areas at once, and at the end of the decade the structure of global politics fractured as dramatically as after World War II.

RIVALRY ACROSS THE CENTRAL AREA

In the North the result of the 1979 fighting was to stimulate interest in a stronger army (conscription was introduced that year), while in the South, where the army was strong already, the result was to seek an opening to the rest of the Peninsula. In part because of ʿAbd al-Fattāḥ's policies, South Yemen remained poor while Arabia as a whole seemed awash with money. The alternative strand within Southern policy was developed by ʿAlī Nāṣir Muḥammad, whose relations with ʿAlī ʿAbdullāh in the North replayed many problems of the Sālmayn and Ḥamdī era.

Despite the example of Sālmayn – deposed and shot in 1978 for concentrating power at his colleagues' expense – ʿAlī Nāṣir by late 1980 had amassed in his own hands all three key positions in the Southern state: president, prime minister, and secretary-general of the YSP. ʿAbd al-Fattāḥ was retired to Moscow. Muḥammad Ṣāliḥ Muṭīʿ, who supported ʿAlī Nāṣir in this manoeuvre, was arrested in August 1980 and "shot while trying to escape" in March 1981. In May 1981 ʿAlī ʿAntar, who had also opposed ʿAbd al-Fattāḥ, was replaced as minister of defence by Ṣāliḥ Muṣliḥ Qāsim (a supporter of the Northern NDF in a way that ʿAlī Nāṣir was not), while hundreds of party officials were displaced by ʿAlī

Nāṣir's men.[1] "Dialogue" between the Yemens developed within dangerous tensions, for manoeuvring in and around Sanaa was almost as intense as that in Aden.

The death of ʿAbd al-Salām al-Dumaynī in the North, in August 1980, was symptomatic. The family is originally from Baraṭ, in the far northeast, but he himself grew up near Ibb, joined the Baʿth Party as a young man and studied economics in Russia. He had joined the NDF and gone to Aden. The Northern negotiators were mainly old Baʿthists too and Dumaynī returned to the North with them to continue semi-clandestine negotiations. But when he went on his own to Arḥab, a disaffected Bakīl tribe near Sanaa, he somehow overstepped the mark, and he and his two apolitical brothers were picked up in Sanaa by "the Apparatus" (the secret police), strangled, and dumped in their car off the Yislaḥ pass.

The left, however broadly conceived, were not the only victims, and events were often hard to read. For example, Muḥammad Khamīs, the pro-Saudi head until recently of the North's "Apparatus" was assassinated in 1981, which seemed to illustrate the "ability of the radical opposition to destabilise the government".[2] In fact it was the government who got rid of him: the organiser of the operation later spoke too freely and was lucky to escape with a transfer to the criminal investigation branch.

The NDF claimed that sixty-five of its members were murdered in the period January to August 1980 despite Sanaa's promise of a government of national unity. But "dialogue" continued. In November 1981 yet another agreement was concluded,[3] and ʿAlī Nāṣir visited the North, the two presidents then met in Kuwait, and ʿAlī ʿAbdullāh went in turn to Aden. It was not until June 1982, however, that fighting with the NDF ended. The twists and turns of the process depended on divisions within the governments of North and South, but also on complexities of Arab politics, where Syria and Libya for a period supported elements of the NDF independently of Aden's government and Iraq emerged as a helper of the North, to which they promised $300 million of aid in 1979, and intermittently an enemy of the South. Western commentary stressed often the division between Cold War blocs, which obscured far more than it revealed.

The border zone of Damt and Qaʿṭabah, for instance, was deeply singular. Indeed, Damt more than once declared independence. These centres of Marxist revolution, as they seemed in Sanaa's rhetoric and occasionally in that of Western states, were heavily populated in fact by men who worked in the car factories of Detroit and drew American insurance benefits, while the army sent by Sanaa to confront them (in Cold War terms, the instrument of "imperialist" policy) was officered largely by men trained in Russia and Eastern Europe. There were Yemenis everywhere. The dominant experience, however, was migrant work in the Gulf states and Saudi Arabia, which by now was an important part of the country's unwritten history.

Such connections reach back to the 1940s. The numbers had grown in the 1950s, and migrant labour had continued through the wars of the 1960s. Although the majority of migrants must surely have been Shāfiʿī, the Saudis (or the Najdīs, at least) had referred dismissively to Yemenis in general as "Zuyūd" and accorded them such low status that Yemeni men were employed in the women's quarters of great families.[4] In the 1970s Yemenis had worked in construction. A change in the law in 1975 threatened to dispossess many who had been there longest, but others later opened little businesses, ran restaurants, or repaired machinery, as well as doing manual labour: whole quarters of Jiddah and Riyāḍ were Yemeni, full of people making money yet having no part at all in politics. By the mid-1980s millions of men had been subject to this experience. Not all disagreed with the Saudi mode of running things, but work in the oil states reinforced a common sense of identity.

The trace of earlier migration had not disappeared, and in many cases there were still family ties between North and South: indeed, ʿAlī ʿAbdullāh, the North's president, was later to claim that 65 per cent of Adenis were from the North originally, which was likely true. More commonly, experience somewhere abroad – everyone knew that Sanaa to Jiddah was one hour's flying time, while the rest of the world was guessed at by multiplying up – was the complement of quite parochial experience of village life, particularly in such regions as Ḥugariyyah, where little practical hope was placed in government. People spoke simply of a wish for *amn wa-istiqrār*, "security and stability", while around them swirled not only the problems of peasant life but rivalries among powerful factions.

From the time of the civil war, many Yemenis referred to "the Central Area", *al-minṭaqah al-wusṭā*. Parts of the region were a battle-ground, however, and existing literature understates the brutalising effect on Yemen's politics. The hideous death of "Qabūl al-Ward", a pregnant woman burned to death by soldiers for supporting the left, is still remembered in Lower Yemen. The fights among tribes further north and east, though they produced a superficial picture of instability, were not like this: an offence against women or children, or indeed against the house, was "disgrace". To discount such rhetoric is easy for those who have not lived with it, but very clear rules in tribal disputes expressed understandings of morality common to much of Yemen and in Lower Yemen such rules had often not applied. Here is a poem by Southern fighters:

> Greetings to you girls, and four hundred back from you.
> Whoever turns up, you can give him a screw.
> We'll give you a squeeze, treat you like women, and
> The money we leave you can stick in your pockets.[5]

"Dialogue" was pursued in different terms. Muḥammad al-Ṣūfī of Khawlān, for instance, went to mediate with the NDF and was greeted by Muḥammad al-Ḥaddī of Damt, near the North–South border. Interestingly, in view of revolutionary class rhetoric which was common around Damt, these polite forms of interaction were handled as from shaykh to shaykh. Al-Ḥaddī, a noted poet, thus declaims a *zāmil*:

> Black mountains, greet al-Ṣūfī,
> Leader of this first delegation. Let him prosper.
> Whether or not we find an answer, he counts as my guest.
> I have said there must be no quarrel from our side or from others like him.[6]

Al-Ṣūfī in reply reproduces al-Ḥaddī's rhyme scheme (one cannot mimic the effect in English) and politely defers to his host's sense of honour and of justice.

> You who welcome us, we trust in your judgement.
> We must answer though your words be weighty.
> I come to you from the state. My mission is what you requested,
> And the choice is entirely yours.[7]

The outcome of dialogue at higher levels was the promise of a National Charter (*mīthāq waṭanī*). The phrase had been used by those who overthrew Imam Yaḥyā in 1948, by the NLF in 1965, and indeed more widely. The charter was to be arrived at by wide consultation through convening a "general people's congress" (GPC, *mu'tamar sha'bī 'āmm*), again an almost standard phrase which Ḥaḍramīs had used in the 1960s and Ḥamdī had used in his day.[8] The document (first draft, February 1980) was itself composed of generalities. The process of discussion continued beyond truce-making north of the capital as well as south, however, so that shaykhs such as ʿAbduh Ḥubaysh (Sufyān) and Abū Nashtān (Arḥab) were brought within the fold of Sanaa's patronage just as much as were guerrillas in Lower Yemen. ʿAlī ʿAbdullāh's chances of survival as president had not been thought high when he first

Plate 6.1. ʿAlī ʿAbdullāh Ṣāliḥ.

took office but his ability to make friends of recent enemies impressed a wide range of Yemenis – more of them as time went on.

Building on the new-found peace in Lower Yemen, the GPC was convened in August 1982 with 700 elected delegates and 300 nominated by the President. It proved to be a permanent institution. An "institute" was established to comment on the text of the National Charter, "seminars" were convened which absorbed the energies of intellectuals, and compulsory "readings" were held in government offices as a ritual of state through the 1980s. The Charter's very generality made it hard to criticise:

> The revolution of 26 September 1962 was not a revolution against simply arbitrary and corrupt government or imported colonialism but rather a human revolution against the stagnation of life on Yemen's territory . . .
>
> The revolution transported all the Yemeni people from the dark ages to the advanced (*mutaṭawwarah*, developed) life of the twentieth century, and affirmed its intellectual release from a world of darkness and political deception . . . into a world of light and truth, changing all of life for the better.[9]

The text contained much scriptural quotation with which few could differ and many passages whose precise sense is indeterminate. The section on administration was clear, however. "Building an enlightened, powerful, democratic, central state" was the first step sought, and "realising the principle of participation at local level" came second. The 1980s in the North were dominated by the intersection of this urge to centralise with changes in the world economy.

THE NORTHERN STATE

After the oil-price rises of 1973–4, the OECD countries – North America, Japan, Western Europe – had gained control of "recycling" OPEC revenues (OPEC's trade balance went from a $67 billion surplus to a $2 billion deficit in the first four years) and Yemen was peripherally part of this. Toyota and Datsun pick-up trucks bought by Yemenis with money earned at few removes from oil were an aspect of the global phenomenon; power-stations, sewage systems and telephone networks built in Yemen by foreign companies through the 1970s were equally "recycling". But oil prices were high at the start of the 1980s. Partly because of this, OECD states went into recession, which had its effect on Yemen. Aid was not given on the scale it had been. Remittances from the oil states themselves levelled off, and the government, dependent on loans and indirect taxation, saw its foreign currency reserves evaporate.

The state in the North had commitments it would not relinquish: a Yemeni author estimates that of nearly YR 6 billion spent by government in 1983, over half went to the army and police, although many on the payroll turned up rarely.[10] In Khamir, to take a minor instance, an acquaintance received a salary from the old 1st Infantry Brigade, whose roots go back to the civil war, another small stipend from the Republican Guard, and a third from the Tribal Affairs Department while all the time running a grocery in New York.[11] Reconciliation with the NDF expanded such demands south of Sanaa as well as north, and the President's style was always to encourage loyalty through patronage in jobs and pay. One's assumption is that aspects of expenditure kept rising.

In 1983 a serious attempt was made to ban imports of fruit and vegetables, and Yemen now has grapes, melons, pomegranates, bananas, all locally produced where before they came in cardboard boxes from abroad. But austerity measures were not popular.[12] Small shopkeepers in Ḥudaydah and Taʿizz, and truckers further north, suffered as controls were imposed on trade and currency, the exception being trade with the South, where customs dues were removed by both sides. As Sanaa imposed restrictions, Aden's government was loosening others. State farms were allowed to move towards less stringent forms of co-operative and planners in the South placed more emphasis on the private sector, whose share of the economy rose from 66 per cent to 72 per cent between 1980 and 1985. Transport, building and internal commerce became dominated by what some condemned as a "parasitic bourgeoisie"[13] and Yemen's two economies converged, much of which, as Carapico argues, was due to the priorities of foreign donors.

The difference between state structures did not reduce to economics. The financial positions of Yemen's two governments, however, were very similar. Both depended for their country's viability on massive remittances from migrant labour, and both depended for the solvency of their state apparatus on grants and loans from elsewhere, not all of which appeared in published budgets; North and South Yemeni governments alike spent enormous amounts on the police and military, and both amassed huge external debts they had scant hope of paying off. They now faced in parallel a collapse of oil prices.

As of late 1981 the price of crude oil stood at $34 per barrel; by late 1985 Gulf crudes could be had for $7. An agreement was formed by OPEC to hold the price at $15, but the boom was over and construction projects in the oil states were wound down. The scale of these events was

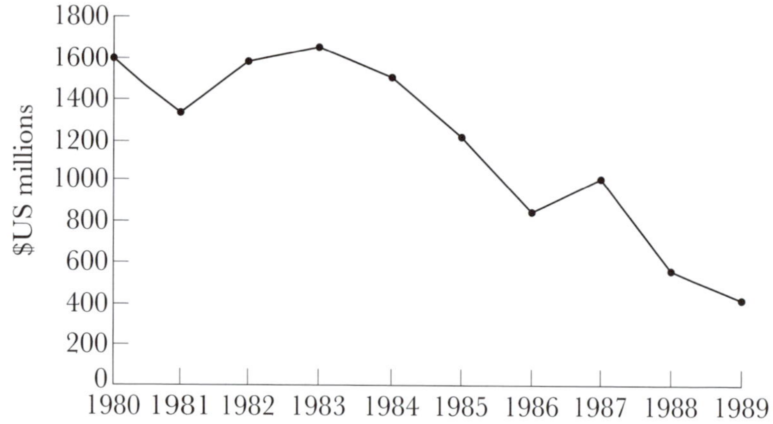

Figure 6.1. Yemen migrant remittances, 1980s

massive. Saudi revenue from oil dropped from $120 billion in 1981 to $17 billion only four years later (all the Gulf states suffered similar cut-backs), and Yemen had been dependent on activity such revenue supported.[14] North Yemen's remittances from workers halved (Fig. 6.1), the financial system of the 1970s unravelled and the Yemeni riyāl lost value. The official exchange rate against the $US went from near 4.5 to 6.5 within a matter of months in 1985 (black market rates were higher), budgetary support from richer governments shrank, and in 1986 a ban was pronounced in the North on private imports.[15]

To ban imports altogether was not possible. Machinery had become part of everyday life and Yemen produced none or even spare parts; the very clothes on people's backs were manufactured elsewhere; the North had imported grain on a large scale since at least Imam Aḥmad's time, and self-sufficiency on that score was impossible even in farming villages. A farmer from Ḥugariyyah was better off than some, for he owned a small plot of land and share-cropped as much again, but depended financially on his sons who worked as builders:

> We grow sorghum, millet . . . like in the old days . . . They're things that suit the land here . . .
>
> But what we produce ourselves isn't enough for more than two months [of the year]. The rest we buy from market in Turbah or Taʿizz, like wheat, flour, rice, sugar, [cooking] oil . . . Long ago most of what we ate was from our farming . . . It wasn't enough at all.[16]

Debt and starvation were a common memory of the period before large-scale remittances, and since Imam Yaḥyā's time the population of the

North had doubled. Grain imports, more recently, had risen from about 160,000 tons per annum in the mid-1970s to more than 650,000 tons. The question was how to manage imports.

Amidst the *laissez-faire* economics of the 1970s, the state apparatus had grown enormously with support from foreign governments and institutions. The Military Economic Corporation, or MECO, originally prominent in supplying boots and uniforms, bread and canned goods to soldiers, had recently expanded into other fields (its outlet on Zubayrī Street in Sanaa was a cut-price warehouse) and already was known for land deals and importing such unmilitary items as shower curtains and bathroom fittings.[17] Placed under the Ministry of Supply (the "*tamwīn*"), MECO was now allotted part of the import quota. With the Grain Corporation and Foreign Trade Corporation it had 60 per cent, while permissions for the rest were largely put out to tender, producing in effect monopolies of the kind sold by Europe's kings in the seventeenth and eighteenth centuries.

The great Shāfiʿī merchants did well. So did Zaydī notables of such families as al-Aḥmar, Abū Laḥūm and Ruwayshān. All might be seen as adapting existing prestige to circumstance; but certain others, like the president himself, were "new men" whose prominence depended on careers in the army and whose importance defies an economist's distinction between public and private sectors. ʿAlī Muḥammad Hāshim, an old Baʿthist colleague of the president, appeared in the Foreign Trade Corporation, for instance.[18] He was later to move to MECO and become extremely rich. ʿAbdullāh al-Ḥaḍramī of Sanḥān, who emerged as the head of MECO, became a by-word for ostentatious wealth and his house in Sanaa – four large towers in a private compound, linked supposedly by tunnels – was pointed out to visitors. With the promise, which emerged at this stage, of its own small oil revenues (the first find of oil and gas was in March 1984), North Yemen saw the structures of its internal politics turned inside out.

The GPC, in 1982, had built in part on co-operatives and promised means for local voices to be heard at national level. It began from 1984, however, to work top-down and use the co-operatives for purposes of central government; in 1985, indeed, they were merged with the GPC apparatus to form "local co-operative development councils" answerable to the Ministry of Local Administration. These "councils" were given the task of collecting tax, much as had happened with the otherwise different co-operatives of the South a decade earlier. More *zakāt* was collected. Back payments were secured widely. The immediate effect on the government's budget was gratifying; but the enormous energy apparent until then in so many co-operatives withered into disillusion as state control expanded.

The literature deals often in terms of state against tribe, in particular, as if these were separate entities and the advance of one geographically meant the other's retreat. Each in practice is a set of relations and ideas. As the NDF dissolved in Lower Yemen so in Upper Yemen, where tribes are more prominent, key relations were reordered and as early as 1983 army units were invited to garrison unruly parts of al-ʿUṣaymāt by ʿAbdullāh al-Aḥmar, himself an ʿUṣaymī as well as paramount shaykh of all Ḥāshid and widely spoken of at the time as more powerful than the president. Key points such as Ḥūth and Khamir were garrisoned: the men were all Ḥāshidīs and those in charge of them chosen by the Shaykh, but they wore uniform. Major shaykhs already owned important tracts of Sanaa real estate, they had a prominent place in the newly integrated system of local and regional councils, and we have mentioned their involvement with imports. In the countryside of Upper Yemen men complained of the greatest shaykhs becoming "distant", as usually they were in Lower Yemen.

The confrontation between North and South had given reason to build a large military. Now parochial concerns gave reason for imposing them on rural provinces, a process which concluded in the GPC elections of late 1988: district administrators, forming part of the GPC structure and controlling what had once been autonomous co-operatives, were all now army men and had almost absolute authority over local administration.[19] Such formal administration was not the whole of life. With changing economic circumstance, however, and with changes of scale in trade, key sources of funding and development were centred in Sanaa. If the catchword of the 1970s was *mashrūʿ* or "project" (Chapter 5), that of the 1980s was *barāmij*, "programmes" – of which the National Charter was perhaps the prototype.

OIL AND GAS

In a note on al-Ḥabashī's *L'évolution politique* (1966), Stookey said pointedly in 1982: "Its extended 'advice to princes' discussion of how best to manage South Yemen's oil resources has been rendered pointless by the failure to discover any."[20] A note of impatience is understandable, for in the North and the South alike oil had been an article of faith with Yemenis and was spoken of as people spoke of buried treasure. The centrality of Yemen in ancient history made the fact that in modern times only Yemen in all Arabia lacked petroleum wealth seem at best a paradox, and the fact no oil had been discovered was attributed widely to foreign plots.

In reality, oil surveys in both Yemens were encouraged by foreign donors, and World Bank funds, for instance, paid for a large effort in the South (1977–80). A Russian group found encouraging signs near Shabwah, an Italian firm made a small off-shore find near Mukallā in 1982; an American company, Hunt Oil, had signed an agreement for work in the North, near Maʾrib, in 1981, and at the end of 1983 a border clash occurred between Northerners and Saudis which some attributed to the sniff of oil, though smuggling is more likely to have been the issue. In March 1984, about 60 kilometres east of Maʾrib, Hunt struck oil and gas in commercial quantities.[21] In January 1985, Northerners and Saudis were at odds again (the North moved troops in to suppress the tribes; the Saudis committed troops nearby, though by most understandings this is well within Yemen's territory) and the South then became involved, provoking not only the Saudis but Northern shaykhs who rallied their men to defend "our" oil.[22]

This was the first time since 1934 that borders had been at issue between the Saudis and the North. (The Southerners saw Wadīʿah lost in 1969; troubles in the North, however, had usually been minor and carefully downplayed by all except the Southern government who sometimes raised the question of ʿAsīr and Najrān, both lost by Imam Yaḥyā.) For the first time since the late 1960s, North and South Yemen were potentially on the same side. An agreement was concluded, though never acted on, between Sanaa and Aden in the hope that oil and gas fields spanned the whole Shabwah-Maʾrib basin – the deceptively empty-looking space that ʿAlī Nāṣir al-Qardaʿī (Chapter 2) had contested with the British in the 1930s. By early 1986 plans were well advanced for a small refinery within the North. The South, however, made little progress.

The income per annum soon projected for the North was of the order of recently lost remittances (perhaps $600–700 million), and concessions produced income before oil and gas began flowing.[23] Such calculations take no account of declining aid, however, nor does an overall balance sheet suggest the structural effect, for where previously central government had depended on the kindness of strangers and wealth in hard currency came largely through private hands, now wealth came direct to the central government. State patronage expanded, and in preparation for the 1985 local elections, it was said (at a time when the country supposedly faced insolvency) that large numbers of private cars were shipped in by the President's office to serve as sweeteners for local notables.

The range of patronage widened. So did the state's effective reach. In 1982, before oil and gas were found, Shaykh Zāyid of Abu Dhabi had given funds to develop a dam at Ma'rib, thus reviving in a huge civil engineering project an image from the Holy Qur'ān: "two gardens to the right and to the left; eat from the sustenance given by your Lord . . ." (Qur'ān 34:15). The dam was inaugurated in 1986. Agriculture was established. But the tribes soon complained of losing their land to those with presidential connections (yet again, MECO was prominent; it eventually acquired about 20,000 hectares around Ma'rib and the Jawf, dwarfing most land-holdings of Imamic times), nor did local people benefit directly from oil in their own region. Questions were asked about where the money went.

Political scientists, as we noted in Chapter 5, speak of states as "capturing" resources. The aim in development theory, meanwhile, is to accumulate investment capital so that national wealth can be increased, which had not really happened in the North: roads had been built with foreign aid or by local co-operatives, the major cities acquired power stations and sewage systems, but "industry" remained largely a matter of family workshops. Most of commerce was consumption and exchange. The three money-changers in the old Sanaa market of 1971 had multiplied to twenty by 1985; in Sanaa as a whole between 1983 and 1987, the number of retail money-changers went from twenty to 260, and other large towns were similar.[24] These offices were repeatedly closed in the 1980s and the smaller traders jailed and beaten, but people with the right connections smuggled dollars and riyāls in huge amounts.

The most famous of Yemen's "merchants", Ḥayl Saʿīd Anʿam, deserves mention. Under Imam Aḥmad he had secured the right to 60 per cent of North Yemen's trade with Russia; after 1962 his base of operations shifted to Ḥudaydah from Aden, and later he suffered losses from Southern nationalisation. Aden governments, however, were content to deal with him. Not only did he export home-produced soap, vegetable oil, plastics and biscuits to the South but retained sufficient contacts to import from there such goods as dates and cigarettes,[25] while in the North he was major shareholder in the United Insurance Company and his show-rooms for tractors and bulldozers were a sight of the modern age. He also built factories, however. His industrial operations were capital intensive and technically efficient by any standard. Here was Yemeni wealth producing wealth in Yemen.

To reproduce the phenomenon required a climate conducive to sustained investment. The opposite in fact emerged, and "merchants" involved in money-changing who looked to place funds in other business complained that bribes to officials and army officers came to 15 per cent of likely profit before a project started. Not surprisingly, they moved capital abroad if possible. Western oil companies meanwhile invested in Yemen, and companies providing oil-related services followed them. Foreign writers were optimistic:

> the exploitation of even modest oil reserves means that the YAR [North Yemen] will be able to meet its own domestic energy needs and to finance the development of greater prosperity of Yemen out of its own resources. The leaders of the YAR will have to an unprecedented degree the freedom to take the destiny of Yemen into their own hands.[26]

The last of these statements, at least, proved true. A Yemeni author, at about the same time, wrote that oil was not corrupting "the noble badu" but rather "the badu" were corrupting oil revenue.

INTELLECTUALS, ECONOMISTS AND SOLDIERS

Intellectuals such as Muḥammad al-ʿAṭṭār in the 1960s had dreamed of rational development, and in the 1970s an apparatus to attempt this emerged in the form of the Central Planning Organisation under ʿAbd al-Karīm al-Iryānī. The romance of modernity swept up foreign writers as well as Yemenis, and an image arose of "development" as ineluctably the form of history, much of which, as ʿAbd al-Salām suggests, was wishful thinking.[27] Technocrats had no power base. They could advise the Prince (Machiavelli's image is not irrelevant: someone was teaching the book at Sanaa University and references to "*al-amīr*" were heard at *qāt* chews), but constraints on princes, not to mention their wishes, are seldom those only of planners' models.

There emerged by the mid-1980s a military–commercial complex. Production was not the basis of wealth and power, nor yet was aggression against outsiders. Rather, personal wealth accrued from control of the import business and of currency transactions linking Yemen to the wider world, and many of those who exercised such control were army officers. A young shaykh from one of the Bakīl tribes explained the phenomenon in his own terms. What Europe had once known, and so had Yemen, he argued, was a feudal agricultural system (*niẓām iqṭāʿī zirāʿī*);

this had been displaced in Europe by a feudal industrial system (*iqṭāʿī ṣanāʿī*) and the communist and capitalist versions, he thought, were variations on a single theme. What Yemen now had, like many third world states, was an administrative feudal system (*iqṭāʿī sulṭāwī* or *idārī*) where power depended on ownership of the state itself. All the analyst need add is that the value of the state derives from its place in a wider system.

In Lower Yemen the intellectual response was predictable, for Shāfiʿīs there had long blamed their troubles on Zaydīs to the point of forgetting the Imams ever had Shāfiʿī soldiers or tax-collectors. *Zakāt* in the republican age, once the Zaydī Imams were gone, was supposed to be paid voluntarily but in Lower Yemen was still collected by force or tax-farming, and ample cases could be found in the 1980s of Shāfiʿīs being robbed, beaten up or swindled (even murdered on occasion) and finding no redress.

> The citizen knows the limits of his aspirations and the ceiling of his practical hopes in the unwritten constitution. He is limited in advance by his sect and area. The army and national security are open before one person and closed in another's face. The limits of power do not derive from one's job or its importance but from membership in a sect or tribe or region.[28]

Since Ḥamdī's time the proportion of Zaydīs in key governmental posts had risen; now the military was extremely prominent and important officers were mainly from around Sanaa. A quarter of a century after the revolution, says the writer bitterly, people were asking whether this was the imamate without the Imam, for the State was in effect a Zaydī state.

The prejudice was reciprocated. The commerce for which Shāfiʿīs are famous in the standard accounts embraced Zaydīs also, but now free trade had given way to permissions and licences, all thought of as *wikālah* (an "agency", as one might have the agency to sell a brand of chocolate). Such "agencies" were bought and sold at higher levels than most men had access to. All they saw was that papers were needed and the bureaucrats who administered these were mostly from Lower Yemen, where education had outstripped other parts of the country when the British were still in Aden. Independent importers using trucks overland had been clamped down on also, to the benefit of large-scale merchants who shipped through Ḥudaydah port – again all Shāfiʿīs so far as men further north could see.

Remittances were still of basic importance (in 1987 they amounted to roughly $430 million), but the old pretence of independence was gone.

Al-Sharjabī's informants in Ḥugariyyah during 1984 had all depended on cash incomes, but the cash was in private hands and the local implications were deeply complex. Two families between them owned half the village land; 23 per cent share-cropped but owned nothing, and of those who did own land, 54 per cent held less than 6,000 *ṭīn* (1/8 ha). A middle-aged farmer had share-cropping rights on 4,000 *ṭīn*, and owned just 2,000 (about 4,000 square metres; almost nothing) yet he still had other people work for him: "There's not much income at all from land . . . Some of the time we work ourselves, even ploughing with our bull ourselves. Sometimes we hire labour . . . And labourers, some of them, ask 100 riyāls and some of them 70 or 80. And we give them enough to eat twice a day – breakfast and lunch – and *qāt* if we've got it . . ."[29] These arrangements, sustained by wealth from elsewhere, did not reduce to economics; nor did they centre on the State.

Destremau's account of the western mountains a few years later (admittedly in a larger settlement) places far less emphasis on land. The people getting by in the late 1980s were "those who had planted *qāt*, built shops to rent, opened a workshop or a pharmacy . . .". In most ethnographic accounts until then one heard of household economies somehow attached to farming. Here, by contrast, the husband of the family is earning YR 1,200 from a government job, which just pays for the firewood his wife uses baking bread, and the bread is then sold, not least to prisoners in the local jail.[30] Political connections, on whatever scale, gave access to the cash economy.

Most farmland was not a great source of income – the changes of the 1960s and 1970s proved irreversible – but continuity of ownership remained striking. Muḥsin Pāshā of al-ʿUdayn had carried through from Turkish to Imamic times (Chapter 2), and ʿAlī Muḥsin lasted through the revolution (Chapters 3 and 4); Ṣādiq ʿAlī Muḥsin continued through the 1980s, emerging as a staunch GPC man like his son in turn, ʿAbd al-Raqīb. The overlap of northern families with land south of Sanaa remained also: Muḥammad ʿAlī Abū Laḥūm, for instance, was a GPC deputy in the Jiblah area. Growing grain provided little wealth or power (Bayt Dammāj, near Ibb, remain substantial landowners but are not prosperous), while integration in the Sanaa-centred web of patronage now provided both.

The degree to which economics, in the sense dwelt upon by planners, could be separated from political economy was not great. The ban on imports of fruit and vegetables stimulated pump-irrigation in the Tihāmah, a region largely unrepresented in national government, where

Plate 6.2. Highland Yemen.

a fairly prosperous family in the period 1985–7 had household expenses of YR 4,000, not to mention the costs of fuelling irrigation-pumps (over YR 40,000 per annum) and marketing the produce.[31] Farming of this sort was capital intensive. Inequalities were built among neighbours and immediate kin, while larger-scale projects sponsored by government (a set of dams was being built in Wādī Mawr, for instance) encouraged more anonymous forms of exploitation. In an area politically neutralised by Aḥmad's campaigns of the 1920s (Chapter 2), market economics was feasible, and the only "inelasticity", so to speak, was in apportionment to favourites of state land.

In the very different setting of Ṣaʿdah new starts on irrigation wells went from 84 in 1983 to more than triple that number the next year as grapes, apples, even citrus fruits, were tried: the economic effects of banning imports were predictable and to planners gratifying. But some 190 wells had been sunk in 1982, the year the GPC formed, for different reasons. Briefly, communal rights that depend on run-off were being given up by some in favour of individualised rights to land on which farming could be expanded or which could be simply sold: large areas were acquired, often through the local *waqf* administration and increasingly as time went on through MECO, by people with government connections.[32] To establish ownership as much as turn a profit, wells were drilled. The water table sank rapidly. So it did around ʿAmrān where land-tenure was less disputed and cash-crops of tomatoes and alfalfa long preceded the ban on imports. Bore wells of 100 or 200 metres required ever larger pumps and ever greater cash-flow to purchase fuel.

The crop of choice in many highland areas was *qāt*, which produced more revenue than the rest of agriculture combined and nearly as much as did remittances, though, oddly, it was never listed in statistical yearbooks. Near Ḥūth, a friend was still expanding *qāt* fields at the decade's end: even after pumping water from a bore well, he reckoned *qāt* produced the cash equivalent of 25 sacks of wheat from land that otherwise would give three sacks,[33] and there seemed no limit to the amount of *qāt* one could sell. In Sanaa for a time *qāt*-selling was restricted to a market at Bīr ʿAbīd where retailers were charged for space. The owner, himself a big *qāt* farmer, must have made a fortune from these government-enforced charges, and as others were quick to note, he came from Sanḥān, the tribe to which the President belongs.

A suburb of the *nouveaux riches* emerged near Ḥaddah, just south of Sanaa. A certain symbolic transition had been made, perhaps, when the traditional meeting point between Sanaa and the tribes of Banī Maṭar became the site of a Kentucky Fried Chicken outlet; now the inner ring-road was well within the built-up area, and building began along an outer ring-road which linked major truck-routes west and south. Ḥaddah to the south and Rawḍah to the north became suburbs, while the way in which the whole city functioned changed. At the time of the 1967–8 siege "every house in Sanaa was a self-contained economic unit, and the original inhabitants depended on what was in their store rooms . . . and on their own wells".[34] Now most depended on supermarkets. By the early 1980s hand-dug wells of 20–30 metres depth had been replaced by bore wells to 120 metres; by late in the decade Sanaa was drawing from an aquifer 300–900 metres down and the water table was dropping five or six metres yearly.

Ecology, so to speak, was displaced by economics; and the urban boom led to new forms of architecture. The old tower-houses and new apartment blocks were complemented by walled suburban villas of the kind common in the Gulf, isolated from their neighbours and accessible by car, and along the Ḥaddah Road were palaces of new private money as well as a new hotel and the offices of several oil-related companies. Ḥaddah itself had been a picnic spot. There were trees there, perhaps bigger than anywhere in Yemen, and at some times of year it seemed almost a patch of Europe's woodland. Now the water was gone. All the trees died, and their leafless branches stood out against the sky like the remnants of a forest fire as Sanaa displaced Aden as by far Yemen's largest city.

THE SOUTHERN STATE

With the exile of ʿAbd al-Fattāḥ in 1980, an attempt had been made in the South to encourage the simpler forms of wealth. Migrant workers were praised, restrictions on domestic building were loosened, and remittances duly rose. Contraction of the Saudi economy cut short what opening there may have been, however,[35] and prosperity through other than state initiatives seemed a zero-sum game to some, a betrayal of the revolution. Sālim Ṣāliḥ Muḥammad, for instance, later scoffed at suggestions that agricultural investment be liberalised:

> Buying a tractor in Yemen represents the beginning of capitalism. The cost of a tractor is 100,000 dīnārs, and by the standards of the country that's a sum that makes its owner a capitalist . . . There are parts of our country where there is no drinking water. How can you talk about buying tractors in the private sector for 100,000 dīnārs?[36]

Openings to the oil-rich states and to the capitalist world were pursued by ʿAlī Nāṣir. They benefited some, not others: many Adenis, for instance, thought well of such policies but shanty towns appeared around the capital, and even beggars. Complaints were heard of consumerism, encouraged it was said by the arrival in 1983 of Palestinian fighters whom Israel had driven from Beirut. With oil exploration, commerce was encouraged further and tensions in the South soon focused on the image of a state within the state, where money, cars and buildings seemed all in the hands of ʿAlī Nāṣir's friends. The governor of Abyan, an ally of ʿAlī Nāṣir, is said by his enemies to have built no less than a palace, with gardens, swimming pool and satellite television: "As for the rooms for *qāt*-chewing, he had imported furnishings from the markets of the world . . . having covered the floors with the most splendid rugs; and attached to every *qāt*-chewing room was a sitting room with splendid furniture for drinking sessions after the chew . . ."[37]

The South, like the North, faced a balance of payments crisis, particularly acute in 1985, and "factional" disputes sharpened. ʿAlī ʿAntar, we might remember, had supported moves to depose ʿAbd al-Fattāḥ Ismāʿīl in 1980; early in 1984 he asked that ʿAbd al-Fattāḥ be allowed back. There were serious shifts in governmental posts, and ʿAlī ʿAntar now visited rural areas, denouncing ʿAlī Nāṣir's "excesses": ʿAlī Nāṣir had built a hotel costing millions of dollars in Aden, he said, and turned it into a fortress of capitalism; ʿAlī Nāṣir was pouring water away in the streets of Aden (a pond and fountain had been built in public gardens) while the countryside lived in drought and poverty.[38] When the Party Congress convened in October 1985 it was clear to Southerners how serious the divisions were.

In the last two months of the year agreements worth $50 million were signed with foreign companies (Russian, Chinese, British) for development work, much of it concentrated in ʿAlī Nāṣir's home area of Abyan and adjacent Shabwah. There was little for Laḥj or Ḥaḍramawt. In Aden each faction plotted against the other, stock-piling arms at home and buying abroad both weapons and equipment, and at a meeting on 13 January 1986 a large part of the Politbureau was slaughtered by ʿAlī Nāṣir's men, who themselves feared a coup from the other faction. Violence erupted in Aden and beyond, and in ten days of street-fighting, and grotesque forms of vengeance afterwards, thousands died. ʿAlī ʿNāṣir fled North with perhaps 30,000 followers.

The Director of the CIA in Washington depicted these events as an episode in the Cold War: "a sudden and dramatic display of Gorbachev's application of the Brezhnev Doctrine . . . Recently ʿAlī Nāṣir, president of South Yemen, began to draw away a little from the Soviets and seek help elsewhere . . .; hardline pro-Soviet elements in his government initiated a coup . . ."[39] This was utter nonsense, and the January events plainly baffled and appalled the Russians as much as anyone. The official South Yemeni version was fantastical in a different genre:

> The triumph of the Yemeni Socialist Party over this bloody treasonable conspiracy proves the organisational and ideological strength of the party as a militant vanguard of the workers, farmers and all toilers during the stage of the national democratic revolution with its socialist horizons, and its being the guarantee for preserving the revolution from . . . opportunist right and left deviations . . .[40]

Sadly, however, the right opportunist tendency had been supported by "elements of toiling class origin who stood with this stream as a result of regional and tribal influence . . . and the influence of mischievous demagogic postulations". The exasperation of would-be allies was expressed to ʿAlī Sālim al-Bīḍ, now leader of the YSP, by Fidel Castro: "When are you people going to stop killing each other?"

Plate 6.3. Workers, peasants and intellectuals.

Government, when the fighting subsided, was in the hands of Ḥaḍramīs: ʿAlī Sālim al-Bīḍ as General Secretary of the YSP, Ṣāliḥ Munaṣṣir al-Siyaylī as Minister of the Interior, and Ḥaydar Abū Bakr al-ʿAṭṭās as President. Adenis were not much represented, and there were said to be tensions between a "Southern" contingent under Sālim Ṣāliḥ of Yāfiʿ and a "Northern" contingent under Muḥsin. In practice ʿAlī Nāṣir's general policies were continued, though with far greater care to avoid antagonism and with a gloss of older rhetoric to sustain the appearance of rectitude, while throughout the South pictures of "the four martyrs" were put up: ʿAbd al-Fattāḥ, Ṣāliḥ Muṣliḥ, ʿAlī ʿAntar, and

ʿAlī Shāyiʿ (all Politbureau members killed in the coup) became part of state iconography.

The damage in Aden was repaired in some degree and public art refurbished. In a square at Tawāhī where Queen Victoria once glowered in bronze, a modernist statue of the revolution and her martyred son had been done in concrete in 1982 (at a time, apparently, of acute cement shortages): this survived unscathed. Hoardings and the sides of public buildings showed wheat-fields, combine harvesters, vast factories, and electricity pylons in the Russian manner – none of which existed – and the toiling masses were depicted similarly. Stern, mustachioed soldiers and workers waved flags and rifles; sturdy, large-breasted, blonde-haired matrons of a kind perhaps common in Ukraine but not in Yemen held sickles or wrenches on the march of progress.[41] The trace of the past remained, however, and shop-fronts at Steamer Point still looked as they had in colonial times twenty years before, though the steamers had long gone: Hajji Abdullah Thompson's, The Red Sea Store, The United Services Store, none of them, it seemed, repainted since the British left.

A West German diplomat reported "disillusioned cynicism". Adenis said sourly that where once there had been twenty sultans (in British times) now there were nine (the Politbureau), and that was all there was of progress in twenty years.[42] The Adenis were never strong supporters of the Party. It was true, however, that the system as a whole had stalled, and ʿAlī Sālim al-Bīḍ himself spoke of paralysis in what there was of industry (its share of the national budget almost halved over three years) in part on account of overmanning: at the same time there was "false unemployment" in that people with relatives abroad who could send them remittances preferred simply not to work. Whether false or real, the number of unemployed in Aden at the end of 1987 was reckoned at 25,000, and the German diplomat speaks of mass organisations working mindlessly like "Marxist prayer wheels".

The virtues of the Southern system had not wholly disappeared. Foodstuffs and basics such as washing powder were subsidised, "security and stability" were guaranteed, and basic education was widely available. To some, Aden's state still seemed, at least potentially, a model of equality and order, but increasingly one heard of *fawḍā* or "chaos" of a kind the South had attributed to Northerners: soldiers simply not turning up if they did not feel like it, payments being made outside official channels, deals being done that made sense at local level but not in terms of socialism. The period 1986–9 was empty in the South.

School reading-primers showing workers, peasants and intellectuals before a stylised sunrise no longer rang true, and Jārullāh ʿUmar wrote a lengthy memorandum to the Party Secretary in Spring 1989. A measure of pluralism was needed, he said, for "the working class here is quantitatively and qualitatively weak" (in truth, there hardly was any); bureaucracy had everywhere congealed, and if Yemen was to be discussed, not merely a reflection of East Germany, then education should address local history in local terms and political terminology should all be Arabised.[43] These reflections he attached to events in Russia.

Russia had never "controlled" the South. It did have an important strategic interest in Aden's port and airfield, and had that interest been threatened until now, steps might well have been taken, but the Soviet system itself was changing. Gorbachev's famous address to the Party Congress, on "openness" and "reform" (*glasnost* and *perestroika*) came six weeks after the Aden fighting: it might have meant almost anything at the time or nothing, but the Russians' overseas commitments were soon to prove unsustainable and their empire fell apart as completely as had that of the British a generation earlier. "It is no longer anticipated," wrote ʿUmar in April 1989, "that the Soviets will send their armies to defend their other allies once they face domestic turmoil . . ."

MODERN YEMEN

The Americans pursued the Cold War with vigour. Most importantly, they helped the Saudis support a *jihād* in Afghanistan, where the Russians had been trapped since 1979 (only at the start of 1989 did the Russians extricate themselves), and the literature of that struggle was now everywhere in the Muslim World, not least in Yemen.[44] In rural houses in the North by the decade's end one found magazines, often printed in Pakistan, with such articles as "Towards a jurisprudence of killing", a discussion of conditions in which murder and assassination were justified in support of an Islamic cause.

The state in the South had treated Islam as a feeble, rather distant case of socialist reform and turned it solely to the ends of nationalism. A textbook on religious education for the fourth year of secondary schools, for instance, begins with "general conscription and defence of the homeland", for "love of country", according to a Tradition quoted, "is part of godliness". Islam had aimed to free humanity from slavery, says the text, and the chapters jump directly from the conquest of Mecca (seventh century AD) to the nineteenth century: "Egypt, like all the Arab World, was in a severe state of backwardness . . ." and Muḥammad ʿAbduh in his studies of the Qurʾān had therefore adopted a "new method of interpretation" compatible with progress. Little clue is given how positions might be argued in Islamic terms.

This official view was insufficient. As early as 1985, Aden University tried to ban neo-Islamic dress which had recently appeared among female students. Everywhere within the region Islamist ideas and groups were spreading, and migrant work in the Gulf and in Saudi Arabia exposed Yemenis in particular to examples where godliness and worldly wealth seemed natural allies. By 1989, Jārullāh ʿUmar could say, "The religious groups have, within a decade and a half, been transformed into a major power centre exercising extensive political and ideological influence and undertaking active propaganda work, while in the past they had neither existence nor even any historic roots in the area."[45] This was true in a narrow sense, but Islamist and socialist puritanism were close relatives and had in the past been equally hostile to such easy-going local practice as the visiting of saints. In the South, however, as ʿUmar argues, socialist fervour had decayed into mere bureaucracy.

In the North, with Saudi encouragement and funding, Islamists had been used to oppose the left. A formal "Islamic Front", supported by Shaykh ʿAbdullāh of Ḥāshid, had emerged in 1979 (this was active in fighting against the NDF but continued in existence afterwards); and amidst the manoeuvring among Arab powers and local constituencies, ʿAbd al-Majīd al-Zindānī, whom we mentioned in Ḥamdī's day, was appointed Minister of Education in late 1983. He did not stay long in the post (he upset so many people, in fact, that he left the country). The "Institutes" he supported continued multiplying, however, with large subventions from the education budget as well as with Saudi funds: by 1986–7 there were reckoned to be 1,126 "religious schools", and by the following year they claimed 118,000 students of whom more than 4,600 were trainee teachers to continue the work.[46] Enthusiasts from Saudi Arabia, Sudan and not least Egypt became prominent. Many of them, disillusioned with their governments at home, quoted a Tradition of the Prophet: "If disorder threatens, take refuge in Yemen" (*in hājat al-fitan fa-ʿalayak al-yaman*).[47]

The new Islam of the 1980s was a generic Sunnism which claimed to be non-sectarian. Somewhat Qāsimī views of state and religion (Chapters 1 and 2) had recurred and been developed in the thought of, for instance, Qāsim Ghālib (Chapter 4), a man of his time for whom Nāṣirism and the views of the Muslim Brothers were ideally compatible:[48]

an authoritarian, nationalist state seemed a better path to justice than personal decision or insistence that the ruler himself be pious. Shawkānī, whom Qāsim Ghālib had praised, and those who built the Imam's dynastic state had praised before him, was now claimed as ancestor by many groups – by the State and by those with radical pretensions. In a world contracting economically, however, the wish for clear religious authority was very likely to result in mere conflicting claims of absolute right and wrong. Everywhere the terms of debate had shifted. With the fall of the Imamate what remained of Zaydī learning had been marginalised by Zaydī notables (not least by Shaykh ʿAbdullāh of Ḥāshid), and generic schooling meant boys around Sanaa and northward prayed usually in Sunni style. Their fathers' style of prayer simply seemed old-fashioned.[49]

The State in the North encouraged Islamist movements as compatible with the National Charter. Presidential Decree No. 61 of 1986 reads,

> 1) The national slogan of the Yemen Arab Republic shall be as follows: God, The Nation, The Revolution . . .
> 2) The text and spirit of this slogan must be adhered to in the order and arrangement mentioned, to deepen faith in God and strengthen loyalty to the nation and revolution.
> 3) All units of the armed forces and security forces . . . shall repeat the national slogan in their salutes. Also, all schools and educational colleges, at all levels, shall repeat the national slogan at the start of the school day . . .[50]

Such rituals doubtless had some effect. But the rhetoric sustaining them led nowhere. A book in 1987 by the Deputy Head of Sanaa University's Department of Education – also "President of the Department of Theoretical Enablement (*ta'hīl naẓarī*) of the Institute for the Study of the National Charter" – was typical:

> The National Charter provided clarification of a general philosophy . . . in light of which the young people of Yemeni society will be educated to escape the indecision in which the Third World [as a whole] lives . . .
>
> Arab youth and Yemeni youth faces certain economic and political problems . . . economic backwardness, high costs of living, lack of unity in the Islamic Arab nation, and the fact that Palestine has not been liberated . . .

What was to be done about this remained obscure.

Other imagery came from elsewhere. Destremau's account describes how television soap operas were now a fixture for women in the North: tales of romance, crossed loved and family intrigue in Jordan or in urban Egypt were avidly watched and then discussed.[51] The same had happened in the South, where Lackner takes a stern view: "What can these ridiculous stories tell a rural Yemeni woman who spends two hours a day collecting water, and the rest of her waking hours cooking, cleaning and bringing up many children . . . ? For her evening entertainment she seems happy to watch ladies of leisure with numerous servants gossip over silver tea sets . . ." With a broader grasp of what counts as "politics"(and more human sympathy), Destremau points to women's place in the conduct and imagery of continuity. In a world contracting economically, yet bombarded with imagined alternatives, male–female relations were almost certain to be marked – as sometimes they had been in the Imams' time – and very likely to be linked with mass education. Islamic girls' schools in the North had some 25,000 pupils enrolled already by 1984, of whom 5,000 were apparently in Sanaa.

A census in 1981 had reckoned that half North Yemen's population were less than fifteen years old.[52] Young populations tend to become still younger as their cohorts come to marriageable age, but the effect goes beyond statistics: the estimated 1989 population figures for all Yemen suggest that 62 per cent were below the age of twenty and thus were not even born when the wars of the 1960s ended let alone when the formative events of revolution took place. The expulsion of the Imam from Sanaa and the British from Aden were now merely paragraphs in school books, and very distant from those teaching – many of whom were not Yemeni.[53] The numbers enrolled in schools in the North rose steadily from 567,000 at the decade's start to over 1 million by 1985/6 and to 1,300,000 for 1986/7. Of 46,000 who reached secondary level in the last of those years, less than one-tenth were girls.

Segregation of the sexes was an issue much promoted by Islamists, and at Sanaa University an attempt was made not to ban Islamic dress, as in Aden, but impose it. A compromise of head-scarf and belted overcoat flourished briefly but activists soon controlled all the student unions. Student movements had their parallels in certain army units; preachers of radical tendency were encouraged by some among the President's relatives and not opposed by the President himself, while Islamists identified with the Muslim Brothers were permitted to launch a distinctive newspaper (*al-Ṣaḥwah*, "The Awakening") in 1985. The editor, Muḥammad al-Yadūmī, was widely held to have worked with National Security. More generally the prominence of the movement depended on overlaps between Islamists and the State, not on formal alliances. Soon intolerance made news, and in 1986 Ḥamūd al-ʿAwḍī, a writer on development and popular culture, was hounded out of Sanaa University for supposedly denying the Prophet's infallibility.[54]

In the 1988 Consultative Council elections Islamist candidates swept

Sanaa, winning six out of seven constituencies.[55] The President's apparatus, the GPC, more concerned with a politics of notables (including those of the Brotherhood), was taken quite unawares. Elsewhere in the country those elected were seldom members of the older assembly which the Council replaced – scarcely more than a dozen among 128 – and it was clear, even in the muddled conditions of no explicit parties or party platforms and of large numbers of candidates, that people wished for a change. In Sanaa the Islamists seemed those who might promote such change.

Authors differ as to how fast the capital had grown, but from something of the order of 200,000 people at the end of the 1970s, Sanaa's population had doubled by 1986 (a census that year gave 427,000) and continued growing to perhaps 780,000 by the decade's end.[56] What even ten years before had been a Zaydī city became cosmopolitan. Africans, Europeans, Arabs from elsewhere, were all highly visible, and shopkeepers, taxi-drivers and day-labourers had moved in from both Upper and Lower Yemen in enormous numbers. Bright lights, traffic, modern shopfronts gave an impression of extraordinary energy. But there was now, as there had not been before, a noticeable population of under-employed day-labourers, many of whom were poorer Shāfiʿīs living south of Bāb al-Yaman. On the other hand, the panoply of State was prominent.

The Republican Palace, taken over from the Imam at the start of the revolution, was supplemented by Presidential Palaces, not least in Sanaa;[57] government limousines multiplied, and the grandeur of the State increased. Muḥammad al-Akwaʿ in his old age makes no explicit criticism but expresses surprise at how the world has changed:

> If we compare the condition of the Imam [Imam Yaḥyā] with that of the revolution's great ones and the heads of the Yemen Republic we find a huge difference. On the one hand, parsimony, stinginess, a [certain] greediness and yet sticking to one sort of food; on the other hand, luxury and expenditure, a profusion of variety, any number of kitchens and cooks, so there is no end to it. It's as if you were in a dream or at a feast of the ʿAbbāsids or Barmecides. So it was with the Kings of Ḥimyar and the sons of Ḥimyaritic nobles, God spare them and help them![58]

Other practices had changed less but suffered monetary inflation. Under Yaḥyā and Aḥmad, policemen and soldiers charged people for the privilege of arrest and imprisonment. They still did so, but where it used to be two riyāls at worst, says al-Akwaʿ, now one was charged 50 or 100 riyāls to be arrested in the simplest circumstance and up to 1,000 riyāls if the soldiers had to stir from town: they could not any longer be bothered walking anywhere and the person arrested was expected, on top of everything else, to pay for car-hire.

The old system of *kufalāʾ* or "guarantors" remained (compare Chapters 2 and 3). In court procedure and dispute settlement, in commercial transactions, in employment by the State, one found endless personal connections of responsibility just as there were in the Imams' time. Despite the efforts of the Islamists, and despite mass schooling, people did not often act as solidary blocs. Nor did ʿAlī ʿAbdullāh require they do so. A case in point would be al-Ḥadā. Yaḥyā Muṣliḥ, an army officer from Raymah then governor of Dhamār, was appalled by disorder in the countryside and what seemed to him "rebellion". Having lost a number of his soldiers, he demanded that Ḥadā be crushed by the army, but the President told him simply to let it go: so long as personal relations with notables were managed and the centres of the State not threatened, feuds and squabbles were of small concern. ʿAbd al-Salām writes of a "neotribal" style.

Eruptions of such squabbles within the major cities were to those from other regions or classes an offence against modernist ideals but also something of a joke. More serious was the conduct of those in power who were claimed to be "eating" other people's wealth, and many people found it difficult to ignore inequality which did not take "traditional" forms of learning or genealogy but simply of consumption and self-advancement. In America and Europe the late 1980s were proverbial for greed, and the symbol of the age was the mobile phone: in Yemen the symbol was a make of car, a four-wheel drive up-market Toyota, which on account of its attractive roundedness Yemenis named for the Egyptian film starlet Layla ʿAlawī. At the end of the decade these were prominent among rural notables and in Sanaa jammed the better streets at *qāt*-time.

Ordinary people had faced a strain with the slowing and decline of remittance wealth. The decline in value of the riyāl against the US dollar (in late 1986 it had touched 18:1) increased that strain, for staple goods such as sugar and tea were all imported. The key division now was between those with access, directly or at few removes, to hard currency and those without such access. The order of life had shifted drastically for the third or fourth time in living memory. The Imamate had produced a nation-state but then collapsed in war and revolution, and a greater revolution had followed with the spread of trade and cash from migrant labour, which in turn seemed to be collapsing.

Sheila Carapico's Sanaani friends provide an insight. A minor *sayyid*

Plate 6.4. *Qāt* farming.

family, they had lived in a traditional house of the Old City, sustaining family attachments and an old-fashioned piety through the 1970s: the young male head of the family, who worked first as a government clerk, had gone into painting scriptural quotations on coloured glass, and the women socialised among neighbours and kin they had known all their lives. The real head of house, the painter's mother, arranged sound marriages; the house filled with children, and the family, pooling what they had, built a new house outside the Old City in the early 1980s. By summer 1989, however, they were not doing well at all. Painted quotations brought in half what they had, and the cost of materials rose as the riyāl lost value. The new world of government connections was not one the family could master, and the women, now surrounded by strangers, regretted ever leaving their old home.

Cynthia Myntti's friends in Taʿizz province, whom we mentioned in Chapter 5, are again a touchstone for Lower Yemen.[59] Late in the 1970s ʿAzīzah had run the house, while her parents-in-law farmed and her husband gained money from migrant labour. ʿAzīzah's eldest son, in the late 1980s, was now grown up (three children of his own to worry about) and her daughters were in their teens. ʿAzīzah wants them to marry close by, "but views the pool of desirable bridegrooms as distressingly small". The rise of fundamentalism did not impress her favourably, for the activists seemed insincere, and her son meanwhile spent more on *qāt* and cigarettes than he earned from his government job. But that was the shape of the modern world: everything seemed to rest not on work and saving but on having the right contacts.

A friend in a village as far north of Sanaa as ʿAzīzah was south (among "the tribes", indeed, whom others supposed now owned the country) was in a worse state. His immediate family were never prosperous. In a village unusual in that part of Yemen for its literacy he never got far beyond spelling his name, but as a young man he had fought through the civil war, he had worked as a migrant in the Saudi oil-fields far earlier than most, and had tales to tell. Now he got by on painting and odd construction jobs. Farming had collapsed, and several houses in the village, although they retained a full complement of women, were treated by their men as somewhere simply to relax. One had a son in the Grain Corporation. Another drew a handsome stipend from the Republican Guard in Sanaa: he scarcely went there once a month, but at home he had *qāt*, tobacco, meat for lunch, and his television. The part-time painter had none of this. Even batteries for his radio were unaffordable. He would look at his neighbour's house in despair and say, "Who *are* these people?"

REGIONAL AND WIDER POLITICS

If large-scale geopolitics helped Islamists (above), so they did the Northern government. Through the 1980s Iraq was at war with Iran, and North Yemeni volunteers went to support Iraq (they were used, it seems, on lines of communications), while South Yemen took a more neutral stance. Though Iraq had little cash to spare beyond the $300 million committed to the North in 1979, many scholarships were given. The Saudis and the Gulf states, partly bank-rolling Iraq, found some aid to spare for Yemen also. An obvious potential source of conflict between the Yemens, and thus among their allies, was the tens of thousands of ʿAlī Nāṣir supporters who moved North after January 1986. This was carefully downplayed: the Gulf states in particular provided funds for support of ʿAlī Nāṣir's men on condition they not make trouble, and such funds went through central government.

Yemen's financial crisis of 1986 had been alleviated partly by a grant from the Saudis, whose policy no doubt was to promote "stable and peaceful relations between Sanaa and Aden, but not so cooperative as to risk real unity . . ."[60] This style of political management was very different from that of the NDF period. Whatever unannounced funds were given, Saudi money formed part now of a far more complex system. Some $200 million, for instance, was lent by Europe in 1986, and a $200 million loan was secured from Arab banks in 1987 to finance oil imports while Yemen's own oil production was developed. Enmeshed in financial links, both commercial and governmental, the North became a more conventional part than previously of relations among states. Only rarely did rural disputes draw attention elsewhere and remind one how complex are the local histories omitted from narratives of finance.

In January 1988 Nāṣir Aḥmad al-Dhahab of Qayfah was killed, having been in Saudi Arabia recently.[61] Perhaps two years before, al-Qayfah and ʿAwāḍ, near Bayḍāʾ, had been at odds and the problem had spread from Dhamār eastward as ʿAwāḍ appealed to Khawlān for help and al-Qayfah sought help from other Madhḥij tribes such as ʿAns, al-Ḥadā and Murād. The government had intervened between Khawlān and Murād (across Khawlān ran a massive new pipeline to export oil). Nāṣir al-Dhahab sought to arbitrate in the dispute. His attempt to do so coincided with something of a Madhḥij revival, which promised to span the border between North and South and in which the Saudis must surely have shown interest. His death was assumed to have been sought by Sanaa.

These disputes entangled Khawlān and Murād with tribes as far east as ʿAbīdah, around the oilfields, and Sanaa and the army intervened, setting tribes, so the tribes felt, against each other. (ʿAlī Muḥsin, from the President's village and commander of the 1st Armoured Brigade, was widely blamed; his relation by marriage, Muḥammad Ismāʿīl, commander of the eastern region, was scarcely more popular with the eastern tribes.) In 1989 soldiers injured a woman of Bayt Qaʿlān of Nihm, and a separate dispute broke out. Bin Muʿaylī and Bin Jalāl of ʿAbīdah were among the arbitrators. They were shot at by soldiers, again under the command of a Sanḥānī officer, and the Jawf erupted. Full-scale battles were fought. The senior figures on the army side could all be found on the President's family tree. Arbitration was provided by the greatest of shaykhs not involved in the dispute, and some tribes at least accepted payment; others said still years later that "blood remains" (*ʿād al-dam*) between themselves and government.

Such things did not happen in the South. Enfeebled as it was after

1986, the Southern state contrived to act as a unit – not least towards the North. Despite the care with which relations were usually handled now, troops massed each side of the border as late as March 1988. A succession of summit meetings led in May that year to revivifying the 1985 agreement on the border area and setting up a joint development company to handle oil matters in a zone shared between the Yemens; a scheme to link the two electricity grids was taken up; it was agreed to facilitate movement of Yemen's nationals between the two "sister states", which soon led to Southerners buying luxuries in the North and to Northerners buying subsidised sugar and tea in Aden.[62] The North seemed plainly in the healthier position. This was true economically, but also diplomatically.

With the end of the Iraq–Iran war (July 1988), a realignment of Arab politics was sought by the Iraqis, who revived talk of Arab Unity and asked for the first time since the Nāṣirist age of the 1960s why the lines between Arab states should be as they are and why "Arab" wealth should be distributed as in fact it is. Egypt wished to regain what Egyptians saw as their proper place at the head of the Arab League, lost in the aftermath of agreement with Israel a decade earlier. In February 1989 an Arab Co-operation Council was established, comprising Egypt, Iraq, Jordan and North Yemen. The Saudis, whose influence in the North until now had been widespread, were appalled.

Yemen, it seemed, was at the top table. The President of the North was seated with the region's power-brokers and was granted a palace in Iraq by Ṣaddām Ḥusayn (as too was King Ḥusayn of Jordan but not, it seems, Egypt's Ḥusnī Mubārak). A summit of the Co-operation Council was held in Sanaa, 25–6 September 1989, with the banners on the main roads proclaiming "God, the Nation, the Revolution". Yemen's own concerns moved forward in parallel with major shifts both in Arab and global politics, and in November 1989 (the same month the Berlin Wall fell) ʿAlī ʿAbdullāh and ʿAlī Sālim al-Bīḍ announced in Aden that a draft unity agreement dating back to 1981 would be the subject of a nationwide referendum in November 1990. Islamists rioted in Mukallā in March, whether for or against or for quite other reasons is unclear. Zindānī in April, in the North, called for a boycott. Suddenly the whole process – without any referendum – came forward six months.

Only two years earlier (October 1987), a North Yemeni official had voiced what until then was common sense: "Except by some historic [or historical] accident, unity will only come about over a long period of time."[63] In fact several accidents combined. The pattern of Arab politics was shifting; the Russian empire was dissolving at the same period; presumably the Saudi preference for a divided Yemen was thwarted by the change of schedule. If the rulers of both Yemens could agree a deal among themselves then, other than tactically, there was suddenly little in their way, and the rulers of the South faced otherwise the prospect of losing power entirely.

CHAPTER SEVEN

Yemen as a single state

A certain distance is needed to pick out the structure of events. Also, the nearer one comes to the present, the more difficult become problems of discretion, not to mention those of secrecy and contrived illusion in political affairs – and to write of the 1990s in the spirit with which one approaches the reign of Imam Yaḥyā is open to misunderstanding. But let us try. At last there is a single Yemeni state, and that state seems to dominate life in ways not seen before.

YEMEN AND THE GULF CRISIS

Most Yemenis were little prepared for unity. In the past (1972 and 1979) talk of merger between the Yemens had been associated with bitter conflict, and friends in one of the Ḥāshid tribes thus spent Unification Day – 22 May 1990 – picketing the hills around their villages or squatting on the roof-tops with binoculars and rifles. Late in the afternoon they sent people down to Sanaa. Crowds were celebrating in the streets, as indeed they were in all Yemen's major towns. The concrete-filled barrels at check-points on the border between North and South had been rolled away and crowds chanted *baʿd al-yawm mā ʿād barāmīl*, "after today, no more barrels!"

Public media depicted first the spectacle. Northern television, for instance, showed Southern tribes performing greeting rituals on a scale not seen since British days, with long snake-like lines of men dancing with rifles and daggers; Southern television showed Sanaa and the mountains of the North. Private enterprise took up the theme, and T-shirts appeared with pictures of Shamsān and Nuqum, the mountains beside Aden and Sanaa, crowned with the slogan "Long live United Yemen". The flag was changed. Long ago in the Nāṣirist age, the common red, white and black of Arab state-flags had been differentiated and by a quirk of diplomatic history North Yemen had inherited one green star in the centre, while Syria had two and Iraq three. South Yemen had no green star but a triangle of light blue at the hoist. Removing the distinguishing marks left a newly unified Yemen Republic with unadorned red, white and black as if it were the first-formed republic of the Arab World. To the north, of course, the solid green Saudi flag, with its appropriation of the confession of Islamic faith almost as a family slogan, suggested a very different idea of what a state might be. Indeed, the Saudi adoption some years before of the title "Servant of the Holy Places" suggested republicanism had been irrelevant.

In early July, perhaps partly to set minds at rest after a crowd accident at Mecca, Sanaa television interviewed Yemeni pilgrims for nights on end. Scores of them each came in turn to the microphone in the Saudi desert and said a few words to neighbours and friends at home. The camera cut back and forth to a Yemeni flag, rather tatty in the breeze. Perhaps a quarter of those interviewed made reference, formulaically but often with enthusiasm, to "the President, General ʿAlī ʿAbdullāh Ṣāliḥ, and his Deputy ʿAlī Sālim al-Bīḍ" and many greeted not only their kin but also some regional or village notable. All of those speaking were plainly Yemenis – very different as a group from other Peninsula Arabs – yet each had their distinctive accent and their village names. The effect was a homely image of a naturally united country.

Domestic events made reference to a new age. On Yawm al-Nushūr, just after the pilgrimage season, tribes near Raydah gather at the tomb of al-Ḥusayn bin al-Qāsim al-ʿIyānī (died AD 1013). The groups which meet there each year all figure in accounts of Ḥusayn's death, and if the meetings indeed have roots in a lost mediaeval world it would come as no surprise. In 1990 Yawm al-Nushūr fell on 11 July. A delegation from al-Birār of ʿIyāl Surayḥ delivered a poem:

> Praise God who sends rain clouds . . .
> We return here each year at every festival.
> Now there is a new festival, through fresh effort (*ijtihād*) and
> accomplishment
> Of union complete from the South to the North.
> We ask God for success and the return of greatness (*jalāl*) . . .[1]

In other words, for a return to the prominence which Yemen enjoyed in early history. The next line complains that prices have gone up but rejoices that "oppression has ended" (the speaker means the Northern government will be constrained; ʿIyāl Yazīd and ʿIyāl Surayḥ had for years been at odds with Sanaa, just an hour's drive away, and both rather favoured Aden). Raydah's reply avoids controversy:

. . . Praise God all is well.
May God who brings rain preserve Yemen's president,
Make victorious each year the revolution in Palestine,
Make the Arabs victorious in each age of history.

Within weeks, however, Yemen was swept up in Arab events it could not manage.

On 2 August 1990 Ṣaddām Ḥusayn invaded Kuwait. Soon it became apparent that America might fight over this, in part to protect the Saudi realm, and gradually a coalition was built to do the fighting. The most dramatic intersection of Western and Arab politics since Suez (1956) unfolded and as it did so Yemen had the great misfortune to be on the UN Security Council – the only Arab state among fifteen members. When Iraq's invasion of Kuwait was formally condemned, Yemen's was the one abstention. Silence was not an option, however, and as a coalition formed whose Arab elements accepted the presence of Western troops in Arabia, those around Yemen's president moved the other way. Soon there were crowds in Sanaa, much encouraged by the Iraqi embassy, pelting the Saudi and American embassies with rocks and chanting *baʿd al-yawm mā ʿād amrīkā*, "after today no more America".

The importance of "events" in history was very clear. Heated debates in parliament expressed every possible view, while the President was away during crucial early days (at one point in Cairo) and King Ḥusayn of Jordan's policy at the time seemed to be to remain airborne. Yemen was soon trapped. Two Iraqi oil-tankers were at sea and late in August turned for Aden. The Americans, concerned in those weeks to retain Russian diplomatic support, let them go despite a UN resolution supporting a trade embargo against Iraq and the tankers docked. An official of the British consulate was arrested for photographing them; the Yemenis tried to split the difference by unloading one ship and not the other, which solved nothing.[2] In the Security Council Yemen spoke still for an (unspecified) "Arab solution" to the crisis, which in the circumstances implied support for Iraq, and on 19 September 1990 the Saudi government revoked the special status of Yemenis within the Kingdom. Hundreds of thousands, obliged often to sell at derisory prices whatever they could not take by truck, were forced home.

The conflict itself passed quietly in Yemen, and in the capital two years later the only visible remnant of the Gulf War, apart from jobless Iraqis, was a Yemeni enthusiast, supposedly financed by the Ministry of Culture, who danced all over Sanaa with his dagger and a flag-belt in the socket of which was set a pole with a "boom-box" cassette-player, national flags and portraits of ʿAlī ʿAbdullāh Ṣāliḥ and of Ṣaddām. There were also some wry jokes.[3] Yemen, however, had something of the order of 800,000 returnees to consider (many Gulf states had followed the Saudi lead in expelling Yemenis) and a collapse of both remittance and foreign aid income. Diplomatically the country was isolated. Kuwait, having for years helped Yemen with few strings attached, had reason to feel aggrieved; Saudi Arabia, already discontented if not alarmed by unification before the war, turned more fiercely than any against Yemen's government and the dislike of Saudi rulers for Yemen's president gained the colouring of feud.

To blame Yemen's subsequent problems on the Gulf War would be easy and largely false. The Yemeni riyāl had fallen in the 1980s from 4.5 against the US dollar to 12 or so, and in 1990–1 it dropped to 30. It has since then, without international crisis, dropped to near 160 (as of mid-1999) and on occasion it has sunk still lower. The effects are monstrous. Twenty years ago the North, although the government was often bankrupt and statistical indicators such as infant mortality were grim, was not in most ways a poor country: people had enough to eat, and usually more. The South, far poorer, always subsidised basic foodstuffs. South or North, the pride of Yemenis in what they had achieved by their own efforts was almost tangible, and despite the economic contraction of the late 1980s, the image of prosperity a decade earlier remained and unity seemed to promise a return to better times.

THE "TRANSITIONAL PERIOD"

The North's population of about 11 million far outnumbered the South's (perhaps 2.5 million), but the unity accords of 1990 divided most governmental posts equally.[4] A transitional period was specified in which integration would be achieved, and within this, "democracy" was given rein. The press, freed to a small degree before unification, flourished, while committees, councils and conventions of all sorts appeared and the freedom of speech long common in the Northern countryside emerged within cities also and more hesitantly throughout the South. The erstwhile governments remained in place as parties: the GPC (General Popular Congress), which had ruled the North, and the YSP (Yemeni Socialist Party) which had ruled the South. ʿAlī ʿAbdullāh Ṣāliḥ, general secretary of the GPC, was President and ʿAlī Sālim al-Bīḍ, general secretary of the YSP, was Vice-President.

The third major party, based very much within the North, was Iṣlāḥ (*al-Tajammuʿ al-yamanī li-l-iṣlāḥ*, the Yemeni Reform Grouping), which was often described as a tribal-Islamist force.[5] In fact, the tribes were not the strongest of the Islamists' supporters, nor were Islamists impressed with tribal custom. If the party had a centre of gravity, numerically, it was in regions once contested by the NDF – from Raymah through Taʿizz towards al-Bayḍāʾ – and three tendencies were widely recognised within Iṣlāḥ, each denoted by a leading figure: the tribalists (Shaykh ʿAbdullāh of Ḥāshid), the Muslim Brothers of traditional stamp (Yāsīn al-Qubāṭī, from near Taʿizz) and the Brothers of more radical inclination (ʿAbd al-Majīd al-Zindānī). ʿAbd al-Wahhāb al-Ānisī, whose relations with the President were always good, played the role of party secretary. Muḥammad al-Yadūmī, whom we mentioned in Chapter 5, remained editor of *Ṣaḥwah*, which formally was now a party paper.[6]

The strength of Iṣlāḥ lay in two very different spheres. Shaykh ʿAbdullāh had enormous influence north of Sanaa, and from there down through Taʿizz, Iṣlāḥ was often hard to distinguish from the GPC. In the South, by contrast, the Islamists spoke for the dispossessed who in turn differed greatly among themselves. The poor around Aden and Mukallā formed part of this constituency; such figures as Ṭāriq al-Faḍlī (son of Faḍlī's ex-ruler from British times and himself a veteran of the Afghan wars, newly returned from exile) formed quite another. Al-Faḍlī and Ṣāliḥ al-Hindī were identified by the socialist press as leaders of *Jamāʿat al-jihād*, which itself was depicted as an organised group with connections to those Islamist elements around the world whom Western media identified with chaos.

Within the South, land tenure was a major problem, for the anti-feudalist reforms of the early 1970s had expelled great landowners and often, where no plausible feudalists could be found, "peasant risings" meant small parcels of land were swapped among families. Much land was sequestered. In Aden, meanwhile, each change in Party leadership resulted in redistributing rights to housing. Many properties bore plaques saying they were granted to a "martyr", but claims which preceded the grant were now revived, the grant's beneficiaries themselves had often moved on but still collected rent, and claims were made also by those now living there. In countryside and town alike there were commonly three or four claimants to a house or to farmland, many bringing with them the bitterness of years in exile.[7] Aligning itself conspicuously with the poor, Iṣlāḥ built on Southern disputes while basing itself within the North.

The YSP also straddled the border. In parts of the South it had been

Plate 7.1. ʿAbd al-Majīd al-Zindānī.

on the point of collapse: at Jabal Tharwah in the Yāfiʿī highlands, for instance, a huge slogan laid out in white stones, "Glory to the Party and immortality to the martyrs", had been changed before May 1990 to "Glory to the people", and elsewhere opposition in the last months of socialism was violent. As the difficulties of new forms of life unsettled Southerners, however, many turned to the powers they knew. In Bayḍāʾ, by contrast, where Iṣlāḥ was also active, many Northerners felt the socialists were a new path to job security, cheap housing and a ceiling on bride-price. Nearer Sanaa the Party attracted interest among tribes, some of whom looked simply for a counterweight to the President, others of whom hoped the Party had become, as it claimed, less authoritarian and might change the whole style of politics, while at national level the YSP stressed unity and modernity and an end to tribal divisiveness.

The GPC was as difficult as ever to pin down. The poet and political commentator ʿAbdullāh al-Baraddūnī characterised it as "the party of government employees. These were drafted to membership, and I wonder about their degree of commitment."[8] Had the GPC been a party like others these doubts might have been justified, but in fact it was the tissue of the Northern state and indirect election procedures meant that everywhere officials, shaykhs or officers dispensed benefits which the GPC controlled. These webs of patronage centred on the military, which in turn centred heavily on a handful of Sanḥānī villages. The YSP paper, *Ṣawt al-ʿummāl* ("Voice of the Workers") later published a list of thirty-three names: not only the President's full-brother Muḥammad, head of Central Security, and their half-brother ʿAlī Ṣāliḥ, head of the Republican Guard, but such lesser figures as Muḥammad Aḥmad Ismāʿīl (8th Shock Brigade), Ḥusayn al-Akwaʿ (1st Infantry Brigade), ʿAlī Aḥmad al-Sayyānī (General Intelligence), and ʿAlī ʿAlī al-Sayyānī (1st Rocket Brigade). Aḥmad Ḥusayn Shumaylah, also of Sanḥān, ran the passport office while ʿAlī Ḥusayn Shumaylah served as chief of staff of the Republican Guard.[9]

The GPC faced little problem with pluralism, for it acquired the habit of simply duplicating groups that claimed an independent view: a "National Conference" which emerged in 1992, for instance, was promptly matched by a "Conference of Parties" and a counterfeit Nāṣirist party was established also. Less conspicuously, at local level, people often hedged their bets and acquired several party cards. This in no sense disqualified them from acting within the previous form of politics, and the style was nicely caught by a newspaper cartoon where the first man asks the other which party he belongs to: "I've told you twenty times," replies the second, "I belong to the GPC." "Yes, yes," says the first impatiently, "but which *party*!"[10]

No shortage existed of other parties (at one point there were more than forty) and it seemed that every grouping in recent history had reappeared. The SAL of the 1950s – literally translated, the "League of the Sons of the Arab South" – was represented by the "League of the Sons of Yemen", and ʿAbd al-Raḥmān al-Jifrī, long resident in Saudi Arabia until 1990, headed this as Muḥammad al-Jifrī once headed the League which allied with Sultan ʿAlī of Laḥj against the British. A "Union of Popular Forces" was headed by Ibrāhīm al-Wazīr, also until now an exile. The family's history includes the coup of 1948 against Imam Yaḥyā, and during the civil war (1962–7) they played a shadowy role as a "third force": they were not a plausible electoral power, but the al-Wazīrs produce admirable books and pamphlets and they gained positions on committees of several kinds. Three different "Nāṣirist" parties emerged. A tiny "Party of Truth", promoting a tolerant and learned Zaydīsm, was headed by Sayyid Aḥmad al-Shāmī who reputedly had turned down the presidency of the appeal court as too close to the dishonesties of government. The Baʿth, though secretly divided, took public form. Certain smaller parties were hardly more than a few friends with an office and a telephone, but each had its newspaper and many had more than one.

The literacy rate was not high. More importantly, many people distrusted parties: often they were felt to divide the otherwise natural unity of villages, regions, tribes or even the community of Muslims.[11] Tribal conferences, secular discussion groups and Islamist organisations, though they differed enormously in their aims and methods, all claimed on occasion not to be "parties" (*aḥzāb*, pl. of *ḥizb*) and somehow not to be "political" (*siyāsī*), the exception being the YSP. None of the parties, including the YSP, ever quite lost the mark of clandestinity, and locally, in towns and countryside, there was talk of who "really" belonged to which and what really their aims might be. Pronouncements of party literature attracted interest from foreign readers. Many Yemenis looked cautiously at local detail.

On Northern television a popular serial featured a character named Daḥbāsh, an uncivilised thug with a Northern accent. Given he was safely on the screen and not next door, his violence, stupidity and dishonesty were found hilarious, and Southerners (particularly Adenis) made a plural of his name, calling Northerners all *daḥābishah*.[12] The President was reportedly displeased. Some effort was given to finding a suitable reply, but nothing useful came to mind. An image of modernity and order, based largely on an imagined West, had often been used by Shāfiʿī intellectuals against Zaydīs; now the style of the South was pitted against the North's by modernists of whatever region and a presumed lack of "civilisation" was equated widely with tribalism. But the tribes of the north and east complained that their own world was invaded by urban forces. Banditry occurred of a kind not seen before. Cars and trucks were stolen (sometimes the owners were killed anonymously), and when tribespeople traced where the vehicles had gone they found often the police or army. Assassinations of a kind once common in Lower Yemen were attempted in Upper Yemen. Party feuds were blamed for this by some, foreign intervention by others, but the governance of disputes by custom was breaking down and conflicts once left in the countryside were pursued in towns. Sanaa had been known as *makhzan al-ruʾūs*, the place where people's "heads" were safe; now it was best avoided.

The socialists soon complained that their people were being killed, as indeed they were. Iṣlāḥ and the GPC both blamed this on feuds within the YSP; the socialists blamed Islamists in the South and, increasingly, the President's security apparatus within the North. Ḥasan al-Ḥuraybī of the YSP was killed in Sanaa itself in September 1991 (ʿUmar al-Jāwī may have been the target) and a Sanaa traffic policeman who stopped "someone close to the army and the GPC" was murdered on the street in what seems to have been an episode of pure impatience and brutality. In October 1991 there were large demonstrations, fuelled not only by dislike of thuggery but by economic troubles: "The people are fed up with the widening disparity among economic classes in the country, especially as the poor feel the rich have not earned their way up, but they stole the money they are playing with."[13]

Remittances had all but disappeared with the Gulf War, the riyāl fell against the US dollar, and the effect was particularly marked in the South where subsidies for staple goods had been withdrawn: a medium-sized tin of powdered milk thus went from YD 1 (=YR 26) to YD 7 or 8 in the space of two years. In early 1992 the President visited Aden and was met by hostile crowds throwing old *shib-shib*s (the cheap rubber sandals that some call flip-flops) and chanting, "Go home, Zaydīs! Come back ʿAlī Nāṣir!"[14] ʿAlī Nāṣir, the president of the PDRY until 1986, had left North Yemen as one of the YSP's conditions for unification, and the chance of him returning was never great. But while Adenis called for ʿAlī Nāṣir against the President, ʿAlī ʿAbdullāh, so ʿAlī ʿAbdullāh himself used the name of ʿAlī Nāṣir to frighten supporters of ʿAlī Sālim al-Bīḍ within the YSP, and speculation came to centre on the foreign connections of noted figures. Very early it was said by those close to the detail of politics that the Saudis would support ʿAlī Sālim al-Bīḍ if the chance arose.

Both major parties claimed to favour a state based on system and law, *dawlat al-niẓām wa-l-qānūn*, which cynics at street level turned to *dawlat al-niẓām wa-l-sālūn*, a state more interested in fancy cars. Large elements of YSP bureaucracy moved to Sanaa where many seemed to live as extravagantly as their counterparts in the GPC, and in December 1992, when the riyāl slipped from 30 to 42 against the US dollar, riots broke out not least at Taʿizz where the crowds turned often on expensive cars. Such events had been prefigured in Sanaa some months before this. A car was crashed on the ring road late at night by one of the President's nephews and his friends. When people came out to help, they found a group of plainly drunk young men and unrelated young women: the car was set fire to not by "fundamentalists" or the like but by angry householders.

The feeling that something was deeply wrong with the polity was widespread, fuelled by the riyāl's decline. By late 1992 new bank-notes were appearing which many feared were backed by nothing and the prime minister of the time, Ḥaydar al-ʿAṭṭās (a Southerner from Ḥaḍramawt), threatened to resign, for with the two major parties at odds no decisions were possible and the State seemed to be disintegrating. Nor was "democracy" the only model invoked. Unity and order were called for by several groups, and the President himself declared ambiguously to an army audience, "the armed forces are the party of all the parties" (*ḥizb kulli l-aḥzāb*).[15] Other forms of organisation, unattached to the State, became prominent.

The first of the large tribal meetings was the Solidarity Conference (*Muʾtamar al-taḍāmun*) of October 1990, news of which was suppressed because it took a less than pro-Iraqi line. A National Cohesion Conference (*Muʾtamar al-talāḥum*), emerging from troubles in the North that predated Unification, declared itself in 1991, and in late 1992 the Saba' conference – named for Yemen's great pre-Islamic state, the very image of past national unity – drew together mainly Bakīl and Madhḥij tribes. This was opposed not only by the President, who claimed it was a tool of the YSP, but also by such tribal figures as Shaykh ʿAbdullāh of Ḥāshid and Sinān Abū Laḥūm. The meeting convened anyway, and al-Ḥadā in a *zāmil* denounced concentration of power in Sanḥānī hands, "a hundred officials from only one house and family . . ." Murād replied:

al-Ḥadā's voice is a lion's roar, making clear to me how things are.
There's no-one atop the world but these hundred that you've mentioned.
. . .
We won't be a family legacy like Saudi or Kuwait.[16]

Besides objections to "family rule", such conferences produced announcements and programmes which concentrated on rural development, access to education, the conduct of governmental administration and the state of the national budget.

At about the same time as the Saba' conference a "National Conference" was convened in Sanaa. This was chaired by ʿUmar al-Jāwī, an independent socialist who headed the Unionist Gathering (*Tajammuʿ waḥdawī*; "the party of the intellectuals" in ʿAbdullāh al-Baraddūnī's judgement), and it drew in an enormous number of minor parties. Its resolutions called for pluralism and restraint, while admitting that hopes for order rested mainly with "the political forces" (*quwā siyāsiyyah*). The YSP, however, showed no sign of joining a broad-based opposition. Rather, stories went around of an impending merger between YSP and GPC, the "political forces" against the rest. ʿAlī Sālim al-Bīḍ had withdrawn to Aden in August 1992. When he returned, no-one knew what deal had been struck with the GPC and among northern tribes at least – doubtless more generally – hopes of real change in the YSP foundered.

The elections promised for November 1992 were postponed at the eleventh hour. The "National Conference" called for a general strike and it seemed for a moment plausible that urban intellectuals and rural shaykhs might combine to force a change in the style of politics. But until the President and Vice-President both condemned the strike, many in Sanaa knew little of it. "Politicians" in minor parties of usually secular bent did not feel it part of their job to deal with ordinary people. Iṣlāḥ, by contrast, did; but its main interventions at the time were to swamp or disrupt attempts to discuss such issues as human rights. The two erstwhile governments (GPC and YSP), meanwhile, retained troops of their own and sources of state funds.

The South gained significant oil and gas resources only after unification, and oil-related commerce fell largely into Northern hands. The Palestinian entrepreneurs Ḥasīb al-Ṣabbāgh and Saʿīd Khūrī established a huge contracting firm to work on a pipeline from Masīlah (the big new oilfield in Ḥaḍramawt) to the coast and their commercial agent was said to be Shaykh ʿAbdullāh of Ḥāshid; the French company, Elf, began large-scale work and their agent was Aḥmad Shumaylah, a relative of the President's by marriage and himself from Sanḥān; ʿAbdullāh al-Ḥaḍramī, head of MECO, acted as agent for a US-based gas operation.[17] Oil and gas revenue itself was a bone of contention. Quite how Northern revenues were paid was unclear and the YSP claimed often that not all the money reached government accounts in Sanaa, while Southern revenues for a time (the actual product began flowing in late 1993) were paid directly to Aden. If the pattern of oil exploration had helped pull two governments together in 1989–90, it was now to encourage Southern separatism.

Parliamentary elections took place in April 1993. There were certainly irregularities (famously, Ḥamīd al-Aḥmar in Ḥajjah removed the ballot boxes at gunpoint; the YSP office there was destroyed by bazooka fire) but generally the polling was conducted fairly.[18] The subtleties preceding the poll were complex. In several places GPC and Iṣlāḥ ceded place one to the other, and vast numbers of independent candidates coalesced, realigned and suddenly withdrew in patterns specific to each constituency but producing a result in which GPC managers had confidence before the process started.[19] The surprises of the North's 1988 elections (Chapter 6) were avoided. The results only sharpened the major problem.

The YSP gained few seats in the North and lost some in the South to Iṣlāḥ, but with 56 of 301 seats (as against 62 for Iṣlāḥ, 123 for the GPC) the socialists' claims to a half-share in power were weak. A vote was later cast in parliament for the five-member Presidential Council. The YSP's Sālim Ṣāliḥ Muḥammad failed to gain sufficient support, which implied a council of two GPC, two Iṣlāḥ and only one YSP member. Shaykh ʿAbdullāh, now Speaker of the parliament, called for Sālim Ṣāliḥ to be appointed anyway but the YSP walked out and again ʿAlī Sālim al-Bīḍ withdrew to Aden and then to Ḥaḍramawt. This latter move to Shiḥr, on the Indian Ocean coast, caused serious alarm in Northern circles. The socialists in the 1970s had often feared Saudi influence in Ḥaḍramawt, mediated perhaps by great business families; now the GPC feared Saudi alliance with the socialists themselves and Ḥaḍramawt contained a large oilfield. Talk of decentralisation and of federalism was replaced among Northerners by sterner terms of unity (*waḥdah*) against secession (*infiṣāl*). Among the sternest of Northern speakers was ʿAbd al-Karīm al-Iryānī.

CONTROL OF YEMEN

As early as March 1992 there were troop movements by the President's people, which perhaps were intended to place the YSP in pawn; if so, they failed. Gradually through 1993, however, the pieces were put in place. The 1st Armoured Division, commanded by ʿAlī Muḥsin al-Aḥmar, from the President's home village, embraced widely scattered units – from ʿAlī Nāṣir's 5th Infantry at Ḥarf Sufyān through the 1st and 3rd Armoured Brigades (one Northern, one Southern) at ʿAmrān, to the 2nd Armoured Brigade in Radfān.[20] Unstated realignments of troops were made. The (Northern) ʿAmāliqah Brigade in Abyan swelled far beyond its normal size, while the Republican Guard, some 20–30,000 men mostly around Sanaa, absorbed much divisional artillery and two great blocs of Northern troops formed, one around Sanaa and the other in Abyan set to sever the Aden hinterland from Ḥaḍramawt.

A "Dialogue Committee" was set up under largely civilian pressure. The YSP had submitted eighteen points to be met, the GPC submitted nineteen, and the Dialogue Committee produced in the end a list of many points with what appeared to be almost a fresh constitution. The practical requirements included real integration of the armed forces, control of Islamist groups, and return of financial and administrative autonomy to what had once been the local co-operatives. The President and Vice-President met in Oman, then finally in Jordan where ʿAlī ʿAbdullāh and ʿAlī Sālim al-Bīḍ shook hands before the cameras with what was plainly bad grace.[21]

At the time of the Jordan meeting (February 1994) there was trouble in Abyan. The Southern brigade at Ḥarf Sufyān, well north of Sanaa, was broken up also. Some twenty to thirty people died in the latter process, but this was not just a "military" event: ʿAbdullāh Shalīl, an old ʿAlī Nāṣir loyalist from before 1986, would seem to have supported al-Bīḍ, who in 1986 had overthrown ʿAlī Nāṣir, and Shalīl had now misjudged the balance of likely power. The categories of the time (for instance, "the ʿAlī Nāṣir bloc") proved, as often they do, misleading. In Sufyān and Abyan alike large sums of money changed hands. Several mediators gave up the struggle, and on 3 March 1994 Sinān Abū Laḥūm and Mujāhid Abū Shawārib published an open letter:

> We were hoping that reason must prevail . . . and the rights of 14 million citizens would again be put before the personal benefit of rulers . . . We have made continuously every effort we can to reach agreement with those driving the country towards ruin and destruction, but unfortunately, bitterly, sadly all we

have found are lies. We have run up against the solid rocks of those who care for nothing but individual benefit . . .[22]

Fighting started on 27 April 1994 at ʿAmrān[23] and the President's forces elsewhere slowly ground down the YSP's troops, who proved thin on the ground in many regions.[24] Some were not willing to fight in the first place, others were bought off. In a few cases Islamist auxiliaries were important and a Southern commander at Shabwah spoke of them "advancing like ants as if blind in the face of heavy fire". But the highest estimate by either side of their numbers was 5,000. The bulk of the fighting was done by Northern conscripts, mostly from south of Sanaa, and it was they who suffered heavy casualties. On at least two occasions they were caught in the open by the Southern airforce, and the President's kinsman ʿAlī Ṣāliḥ (never a stable person) suffered a nervous breakdown. He has not since formed part of the ruling circle.

Several Islamists claimed that fighting the socialists was *jihād* or holy war. Shaykh ʿAbdullāh was firm against the YSP. Perhaps more strikingly, al-Iryānī, who from even before the unity agreement of 1990 was central to the GPC's negotiations, attacked the YSP in uncompromising terms and rejected all chance of mediation: best known in Western literature on modern Yemen as a technocrat and patient diplomatist, he now appeared far more the party man. The tribes, on whom ʿAlī Sālim seems to have placed weight, largely refused to become involved and in areas such as Yāfiʿ they simply let pass the army.

Saudi support for ʿAlī Sālim al-Bīḍ became blatant. Apart from diplomatic moves and control of much Arab media, large shipments of arms were evident, and on 21 May the YSP leader announced secession. Al-Bīḍ is reported to have said later that this was al-Jifrī's doing.[25] Their alliance, perhaps formed under Saudi auspices, set aside all considerations of ideology and around them clustered also such figures from the Adeni past as ʿAbd al-Qawī Makāwī and ʿAbdullāh al-Aṣnaj (Chapter 4). They attracted only scant support: "the vast majority of Yemenis were for unity but against the war at the start, in the first two weeks. However, the announcement of secession changed public opinion . . ."[26] A key YSP unit, composed of ex-members of the Northern NDF, refused to defend Mukallā, and al-Bīḍ and his supporters left for prosperous exile. Aden itself fell on 7 July 1994. Ṣāliḥ Munaṣṣir al-Siyaylī, scourge of "feudalists" and radical governor of Ḥaḍramawt twenty years before, disappeared and with him, by some accounts, there disappeared $15 million.

Aden was sacked. Not only weapons and money, but electrical and bathroom fittings, window frames, even door knobs, were carried off; large garbage trucks given Aden municipality by foreign donors were driven away northwards. Some houses were protected, others looted, and Northern army units, tribal groups and ex-ʿAlī Nāṣir people took control of this part or that of Aden city while young Adeni Islamists enrolled themselves as auxiliaries who claimed to uphold order. Many at the time drew parallels with the 1948 sack of Sanaa (Chapter 2). The new deputy prime minister, ʿAbd al-Qādir Bā Jamāl – a Ḥaḍramī who had once been an ʿAlī Nāṣir man – said at last that the looting had been stopped on the orders of the President, to which ʿUmar al-Jāwī replied, "There is nothing else left to loot."

Although the war was not North versus South but rather between parties, the effect was felt by Southerners to be a Northern invasion: "from hurried unity to internal colonialism" runs the title of a famous pamphlet.[27] In certain areas Southern governors were appointed, usually men connected with what once had been ʿAlī Nāṣir's faction. The dominant presence, however, was the Northern-controlled military. Ḥaḍramawt was controlled by Muḥammad Ismāʿīl of Sanḥān, for instance, the governor in this case was a Northerner also (ʿAbbād al-Khawlānī), and the head of political security was from Nihm, northeast of Sanaa. Abyan was controlled by the President's son Aḥmad. A story in 1995 was not untypical in which a soldier refused to pay for *qāt* in a Southern market and came back with four truck-loads of his colleagues to beat up the *qāt* seller.[28] In early 1996 a rape case, again involving security forces, led to riots in Mukallā. After the fighting of 1994, as indeed before it, soldiers often seemed beyond control, and a survey of the press suggests appalling misconduct by the military in parts of Lower Yemen as well as in the South and a widespread feeling of oppression among civilians everywhere. The feeling was most intense in Aden, however: "through 130 years of British rule and thirty years of socialist rule, we learned the forms of a developed state. We can't accept going back to tribal rule."

Almost from the moment of unification (May 1990) Southerners complained of "retribalisation". YSP ideology and local memory combined in an image of primitive disorder to which modernity and "culture" (*ḥaḍārah*) were both opposed. By 1994 such areas as Yāfiʿ had reacquired certain tribal forms; conferences broadly similar to those in the North were held in Ḥaḍramawt. But the style of politics complained of by Southerners as a return of tribalism was complained of by others, within the North, as tribalism's negation, and most of Yemen's population makes no claim to be tribal in any sense. A false exoticism is all too easy. Rather than great solidary blocs of persons, aligned with each other on "traditional" grounds, one was dealing in day-to-day politics with networks of individuals who controlled both trade and real estate.

Immediately after the fighting of 1994, a son of perhaps the most famous of Northern shaykhs asserted rights over property on the Aden waterfront: having built a rough breakwater he trucked in sand and gravel from elsewhere to extend this seaward, a curious example of what diplomats or lawyers in other contexts might speak of as "creating facts". In the years to follow, there were endless cases of those with good connections seizing property; on occasion, property granted by the powerful was seized by lesser predators.[29] The promise was that Aden would be developed again as a major port and that real estate there would be as valuable as in Sanaa and thus part of transnational wealth.

POLITICAL ECONOMY

The debt inherited by the Yemen Republic in 1990 was approximately twice the whole country's GNP, and in the years between 1990 and 1994, when the YSP and GPC were deadlocked, deficits in the published accounts of government kept rising as the two contending parties tried to buy support. With the fighting concluded, the complexities of finance were addressed at last, the IMF was consulted and in 1995 a process of "structural adjustment" was agreed which tied Yemen into global forms of political discussion as well as of economics. To depict the world of the 1990s as "uni-polar", as if America were responsible for all that happened, would be too simple. The imagery to be managed, however, is surely different from that of the Cold War.

The Islamist mountain described in YSP rhetoric before the fighting brought forth a mouse. Ṭāriq al-Faḍlī, the "Afghan" warrior, whose sister married ʿAlī Muḥsin al-Aḥmar of Sanḥān, became the GPC's man in his home area: asked in an interview did he support Iṣlāḥ or the GPC, he replied, "There's no difference."[30] A difference did exist, however, between the core of Iṣlāḥ and other Islamists, most of whom defined themselves as Salafīs, that is, as people concerned to follow the ancestral practice of the Prophet and his companions. Immediately after the fighting of 1994 a group of them descended on Aden and attacked the tombs of saints there. The same happened later in Ḥaḍramawt, and alarm was expressed by other governments at the seeming pan-Islamic

Plate 7.2. Shaykh ʿAbdullāh bin Ḥusayn al-Aḥmar.

connections of Yemen's Salafīs. Those of broadly similar persuasion further north were not taken seriously by Shaykh ʿAbdullāh of Ḥāshid, however: "They have a guide (*murshid*) in Ṣaʿdah called Muqbil al-Wādaʿī. What he does is declare people infidels and write books against everyone else." A lack of interest is almost audible.

The religious "institutes" continued growing. By 1996 there were close to 400 in Yemen at secondary level alone, and they claimed overall to have 330,000 pupils of whom 12,600 were training as teachers to instruct the next generation (governmental teacher training institutes, meanwhile, had a quarter that number).[31] Their ability to shape public discourse was important. In the period 1990–4 Islamists had become notorious for opposing the right of women to act in politics, for example, and it was often female members of such groups who did so: "In many civic fora in Sanaa, ironically, proponents of women's restrictions to private space tended to dominate public discussion of women's rights."[32] Carapico presents the memorable image of a veiled young figure shouting down a woman member of parliament with "You're a communist and I speak for God." This continued, though often in more nuanced form.

In areas of impoverished small-scale farming – at Raymah, Wuṣāb, al-ʿUdayn and elsewhere – Islamists continued to agitate for land and funds to build schools, and Salafīs and Iṣlāḥīs remained entangled. The Islamist mainstream, however, lay elsewhere. From at least 1990 – in some cases earlier – Islamic charities were evident whose affiliations to activist groups were various but whose sponsors were extremely wealthy. The returnees of the Gulf crisis provided a large field of action (returnees from the Tihāmah were often not reintegrated easily; those from the highlands went largely to swell the number of city-dwellers)[33] and increased poverty more generally encouraged charity. The style of pious care for those less fortunate is familiar from the record of Imam Yaḥyā's reign, but the setting in which such piety may thrive is different.

From 1995, when the programme of "structural adjustment" began, Islamic banks became prominent.[34] To generate a more active financial system, central government withdrew state accounts from commercial banks, raised base interest rates, and allowed commercial banks to set their own rates. Money-changers were again cracked down on. The smaller operators were ruined; the larger, who combined exchange with commerce, so dominated the market, however, that their withdrawals threatened to leave commercial banks insolvent, and among these large-scale investors and speculators were those who now committed capital to Islamic banks. The major shareholders make up a list of Yemen's financial powers: al-Aḥmar, Ruwayshān, Ḥayl Saʿīd, al-Aswadī and others.

A potentially large deposit base for Islamic banks was available in the form of those who trusted ʿAbd al-Majīd al-Zindānī, the rhetorician of Iṣlāḥ. Opportunities for small investors were offered in a scheme to expand Yemen's fisheries; a chain of Islamic groceries existed; and Detalle speaks of the Islamists' "attempt to set up their own economic network which would coexist with that of the President's friends", a pattern which had also been looked for in 1990 when Ḥaḍramī traders first encountered Sanaa's economy. Scriptural pieties do not change the major sources of income and expenditure, however. The mere form of the country's balance sheet, together with the overlap long evident between Iṣlāḥ and the GPC, might lead one to suspect that existing patterns of wealth will largely be reproduced.[35]

A consolidation of interests has taken place. Through the literature on modern Yemen run such categories as merchant, shaykh, officer, modernist, all of which derive from local rhetoric but were never quite mutually exclusive (shaykhs of Bayt Ruwayshān from Khawlān, for instance, have been "merchants" since the 1960s) and reading back through Yemen's history these categories provide a shadow-theatre of how the country works. In the 1970s, with trade providing income of one kind and Saudi payments to shaykhs providing quite another (Chapter 5), the categories acquired for a while some substance. In the 1990s, in elite circles, they finally collapsed, however, and in late 1997 the President himself – the army man par excellence – became a partner in Ḥayl Saʿīd Enterprises, the best known of Yemen's industrial and commercial companies. His kin have also moved into commerce: Tawfīq, son of the President's deceased full-brother Ṣāliḥ and brother of the wife of the President's eldest son, emerged more recently as head of Yemen's tobacco and matches company; ʿAbdullāh al-Qāḍī, the President's maternal cousin (*ibn khāl*), took over the pharmaceutical company; ʿAbd al-Khāliq al-Qāḍī, husband of the President's daughter Fawziyyah, became head of the national airline.

The ruling family are not the only ones involved in commerce. Two sons of ʿAbdullāh al-Aḥmar, the paramount shaykh of Ḥāshid, threw themselves into lives of multinational money-making, and a succession of quiet scandals unfolded in Sanaa as property that was *waqf* (gifted for religion) fell under their control. Yemenis suppose the more active of these young men runs no less than 300 companies. Sons of other great shaykhs have emerged as businessmen and one cannot see them ever being shaykhs themselves. Their interests lie instead in real estate, commerce and a life based in part on Paris, London or New York. People outside such circles point often to links of marriage and of shared descent in an effort to explain who deals with whom.

Political commentary is coloured also by kinship.[36] At the centre of the imagined web is the President's eldest daughter, Bilqīs, as important as "Amat Karīm" once was to Imam Aḥmad (Chapter 3) – perhaps more so, indeed, for Bilqīs knows foreign capitals as well as the detail of Yemen's families. She married her cousin, Yaḥyā Muḥammad ʿAbdullāh, who could not take the strain of life at the political centre and quietly moved out to marry a second wife;[37] Bilqīs herself remained *en poste*, however. The President's son, Aḥmad, as we saw, is married to a daughter of Ṣāliḥ ʿAbdullāh, the President's deceased full-brother. To pursue the links of marriage with such families as Bayt al-Qāḍī is to list a great many notables. The more explicit links of shared male descent are important too. Muḥammad ʿAbdullāh and Muḥammad Ṣāliḥ (the latter married to the President's sister) remain prominent.[38] The Office of the Presidency, meanwhile, has come to play second string to the Presidential Palace, where the secretariat is run by the President's sons-in-law: Muḥammad Duwayd, of a famous shaykhly family in Khawlān, most notably, is married to the President's daughter Sabaʾ. The Office of the Presidency, under ʿAlī al-ʿAnsī of Sanaa, seems now (late 1999) to deal with mere routine.

At *qāt* chews in the evenings of Ramaḍān in the late 1990s, the President had always two empty spaces each side of him, which Yemenis took often to mean a claim to status.[39] On visits to rural areas he was mobbed by crowds trying usually to present a mass of personal petitions and requests, and often would announce as largesse to the region some governmental project not previously planned or declared officially. The mode of rule is in most respects as personal as forty or even sixty years before. The family, however, live mainly in the presidential palaces, which Yemenis unaccustomed to modern forms of state equate sometimes with massive army camps, and those beyond ruling circles now speculate about family affairs – about how relations might develop for instance between the President's son, Aḥmad ʿAlī, and the President's elder kinsman, ʿAlī Muḥsin al-Aḥmar. In November 1999, Aḥmad ʿAli ʿAbdullāh was named head of a 20,000-strong special forces division, while his cousin Ṭāriq Muḥammad ʿAbdullāh gained control of a special guard unit and Muḥammad ʿAlī Muḥsin al-Aḥmar was named commander of the eastern region. Rumours swirl around them as once they did around the brothers of Imam Aḥmad, and as once people far from power assumed Imam Yaḥyā had treasure chests of silver and gold in the fortress of Shahārah, so now they talk of foreign bank accounts. The reality to be addressed is complex.

The freedom with which the Yemeni riyāl responds to political news suggests a great deal of liquid capital, much of which lies with a large, ill-defined diaspora or is kept abroad by traders within Yemen. The management of domestic finance is sophisticated. While the riyāl was let float against the US dollar only in June 1996, treasury bills had been issued six months earlier and behaved as one would expect of financial markets elsewhere: the rates paid at first were very high (close to 30 per cent per annum) and then dropped in the course of a year to 14 per cent as the deficit in the government's budget came down and liquidity was absorbed into state accounts. The change of method is striking in a country that twenty years earlier had dealt in a mix of silver riyāls and foreign currencies. How much liquidity there is locally one cannot guess, but many people by now had already spent key savings (women's gold, for instance); the fall of the riyāl's value against the US dollar had led to wealth becoming concentrated in fewer hands. The aim of repatriating emigrant capital or drawing large-scale investment from foreign sources made less progress than domestic finance, for security still depended, or appeared to, on connections with a very few power-brokers. Economic and fiscal reform of a standardised global kind coexists with far rougher domestic facts.

The architect of much reform was ʿAbd al-Karīm al-Iryānī, perhaps the best known of Yemen's "technocrats", who in 1995 was named secretary general of the GPC. This used to be one of the President's titles, and for more than a decade, newspapers and television had rolled out the sequence of posts as inseparable: "Brother General [or Colonel earlier] ʿAlī ʿAbdullāh Ṣāliḥ, President of the Republic, Commander in Chief of the Armed Forces, and Secretary General of the General Popular Congress . . ." Management of the Congress, one might think, had now become a technical matter comparable to, and closely entangled with, the conduct of foreign policy and finance. The state acquired a certain quality of routine management, while the Presidency stood above the fray.

Embezzlement remained widespread, however. So did intimidation. Nabīl al-Khāmirī, a famous merchant whose family is from Ḥugariyyah and who himself owns, among much else, the Ḥaddah Hotel, is married to a daughter of Shaykh ʿAbdullāh of Ḥāshid; but he was still held up in his Sanaa office, in early 1998, by tribesmen from Khawlān. The President expressed concern and sent troops, whose presence al-Khāmirī found himself paying for. Talk of "family rule" misrepresents the problem. Far from restricting illicit wealth to small circles of kin or colleagues, the government proved ecumenical, and a man caught simply plundering the petrol company at home (on a massive scale) was not jailed or even forced to pay back his gains but appointed ambassador to a European capital. Ordinary Yemenis, with their fields and their little shops, simply do not have access to much of the national wealth.

THE WIDER WORLD

Late in Qāsimī times, around 1820, a single elephant sent to the Imam as a present from the Ottoman Sultan was given away again for lack of fodder (it was given, in fact, to Muḥammad ʿAlī of Egypt with whom we started the present book). Throughout the country's history one finds accounts of famine, and in the twentieth century migrant labour funded ordinary people's lives, as first the Ḥaḍramīs, then Lower Yemenis, then Upper Yemenis all worked elsewhere. Changes in global trade and labour are integral to Yemen's history. As talk of transnationalism, globalisation and the like became prominent in Western print, through the 1990s, however, the world was shrinking again for those Yemenis who lacked high-level contacts.

The estimated population for the year 2000 is of the order of 18 million – four times or more what it was in 1900 – and a growth rate of 3.7 per cent per annum suggests a doubling every twenty years. Grain shipments of 10,000 tons had been significant less than forty years ago. Now Yemen consumes perhaps 80,000 tons a month, of which only 15–20,000 tons is produced locally. On the latter score, room for development is limited. Talk of increased self-sufficiency takes little note of the poverty one would need to force on farmers or the sheer lack of water, where the country's problems are reckoned by United Nations experts to be as serious as anywhere on earth. Yemen by the mid-1990s was running out of space, save perhaps in the imagination.

In Summer 1997, two Yemenis laid claim to the planet Mars. The government released a statement that the pair were "abnormal",[40] but the reasoning perhaps was not unsound. The Americans had been seen, many years before, planting flags on the moon; more recently they had landed a space-craft on Mars, and the plaintiffs now demanded they cease and desist until written permission had been negotiated. The British once planted a flag at Aden and stayed there 129 years to what profit one could not be certain. The most determined rationalist might think Mars worth filing papers. Unfortunately we are not told what detailed argument made Mars the particular property of Muṣṭafā Khalīl and ʿAbdullāh al-ʿUmarī, but there doubtless was one, for Hamdānī, a millennium ago, began his *Description of the Arabian Peninsula* with an outline of the world's regions and their relation to celestial bodies and famously, in volume eight of his *Diadem Book*, he attributed the fate of Sanaa to the combined effects of Mars and Venus. If the people of specific regions are governed in their natures by different planets, doubtless some relation of ownership might run the other way.

The cosmology with which Hamdānī worked was broadly that of ancient Greek geographers, but the human value given to places he knew was distinctively his own and Yemeni. The Arabian Peninsula, he argued, was "the best of the world's lands" and Yemen was particularly favoured within Arabia. The vision he presented, repeated endlessly since then, was of a vast genealogy spread across the Islamic World but centred on his homeland, which itself showed a certain symmetry: Sanaa "is the mother of Yemen and its axis", Hamdānī said, "for it is at the centre. The distance between there and Aden is the same as between there and Yemen's borders with Najd and Ḥijāz." A thousand years later, political Yemen is smaller. Talks with Saudi Arabia on a formal border had stalled, however, and one could not specify Yemen's exact extent.

The hopes of a decade earlier that massive oil reserves spanned the southern desert have proved ill-founded. There is little to dispute but sand, and a ruler could be laid on the map with almost the freedom that the British and Turks enjoyed at the century's beginning (Chapter 1). The Omanis drew a line with the Yemenis, and the Saudis with the Omanis, but the Saudis had not decided yet, as of late 1999, how to handle a united Yemen whose population far exceeds their own and whose traditions are very different (the layout of Saudi roads suggests strategic worries; see Map 7.1), and for the moment the Yemenis had more to lose from uncertainty than did their neighbours. Geography, economics and politics had become inseparable. The border issue month by month connected with claims by each party that the other harboured hostile Islamists or exiles and with attempts to sell or resell the oil and gas concessions which fund Yemen's government. Oil revenue accounts for 60 per cent of the state budget. Production of some 400,000 barrels per day does not go far among 17 million people (Saudi Arabia,

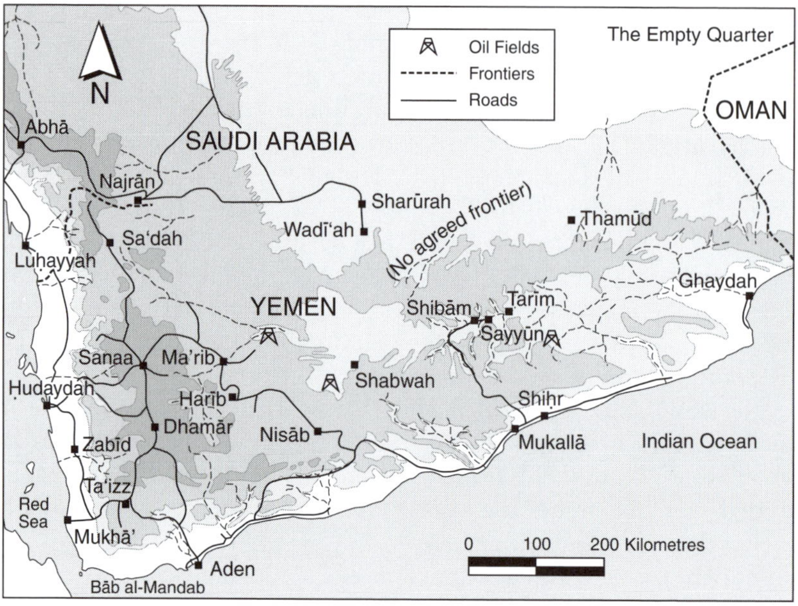

Map 7.1. The Yemen Republic, late 1990s

with a smaller national population pumps 8,000,000 barrels per day) but revenue is needed for "structural adjustment" and to service debt – the logic of which is as singular as that of influence by planets.

To live a quietly middle-class life in Sanaa at the end of the decade (to run a car, clothe the children decently and send them to school, though not to a private school which secularists and Islamists were both opening) cost about $1,000 a month. The official salary of a minister was about $US 200 per month. A junior civil servant who held a degree was reckoned to earn YR 8,000: rent alone took YR 5,000, utilities another 1,500, and food for the family about 15,000, for a monthly total of four times his official salary.[41] Two-income families, where wife and husband both hold paid jobs, have become common in the capital and elsewhere. Increasingly, in the towns, nuclear families have seemed important, although the networks of what were once co-resident extended families remain and the strategies pursued by families are extremely various. But all live within what was earlier described (Chapter 6) as "the feudal administrative system": "a whole category of the population can live comfortably if it has good connections with the administration. Opposed to these privileged citizens are the growing mass of country people who have some of the region's highest levels of [for instance] infant mortality . . ."[42] It is not only country people. Despite the way the *qāt* economy maintains rural life (Yemen's population at the end of the century is still more than 70 per cent rural), cities and towns keep growing and contain an ever larger population of the poor and the unemployed. The capital itself, a fairy-tale "Islamic city" only decades ago in the eyes of many, has a population in excess of 1 million.

Most people in towns maintain links with their rural *bilād* or territory. But in very few cases does the countryside support the city and Sharjabī's informants in the mid-1980s seemed already by the early 1990s to be speaking of a lost world: "I'd like to buy land and make a modern farm, because land makes a person's life secure . . .; but where's the money to come from? As for selling land, I'd never think of it. Land's about the one thing that makes a person connected to his country, makes him stay there." The object of migrant labour, so prominent through the twentieth century and so extraordinary a feature of Yemeni experience, was nearly always to bring money home, to pay off one's debts and secure a landholding. "I'd love to buy some land. Who wouldn't? I want to buy some for those after me [my children and grandchildren]. But what can I do . . . when there's no cash? I want to fix the land that the wash destroyed, but where's the money to come from (*min ayn al-fulūs*)?" Another man, better off and able to recite in its entirety the Holy Qur'ān, echoed the same idea: "If I had any money I'd buy land for my children because it's security for their future."

The dream of independent people to live off their own land is now as difficult to realise in Yemen as it is anywhere – food, clothes, machinery all require money, and more than that, hard currency. If in recent years some Yemenis have re-established access to the Gulf states and Saudi Arabia (all must now have a local "guarantor" just like other migrants), the numbers are insufficient to displace the importance of central government. "The economy" is an issue as it never was before and in certain respects accords more directly with the world system than with the needs of local farmers or small shopkeepers.

Technocrats early in the civil war of the 1960s were seen as "the 'modern magicians' who transform paper into legal tender or negotiate international loans to purchase modern goods . . ."[43] At that date they had no great impact: the Egyptian-dominated war economy swamped all else (Chapter 4). In the 1990s, however, they were indispensable. In early 1996 a stand-by credit of $US 190 million was secured from the IMF, and in the following month $US 80 million from the World Bank:

both were in support of "structural readjustment". Close to $70 million followed from Europe and as much from the Arab Monetary Fund, and another $60 million followed from the World Bank in January 1997 specifically to help establish a financial market. Adjustment to the world financial system has itself become a source of governmental finance.

In 1997 it was said that of 700,000 public employees – this included both civil and military, yet was still an enormous number – 30,000 were to be laid off. A survey at the time suggested 40 per cent of civil servants never turned up to work; the bureaucrats of the old Southern regime were in any case not allowed to act (after 1994, electricity in many Southern offices was simply not reconnected) and they seemed expendable. Where the victims of such cuts would go was unclear, but the government itself was "adjusting without pain", as Renaud Detalle puts it: "As for soldiers, policemen and the defence budget, these remain carefully spared, even increased perhaps, for, contrary to what certain foreign experts feel able to believe, the oil revenues which allow them to be paid for are not all included in the [published] budget."[44]

MECO, meanwhile – the very substance of the military–commercial complex – remains huge and, renamed the Yemeni Economic Corporation, has expanded from farming and retailing to packing and canning, transport and refrigeration, even running a well-known dairy business. "Privatisation", much favoured by international agencies, means commercialisation, and doubtless MECO could be redefined in such a way that what now appears on government accounts would instead be listed in the private sector. "Structural readjustment" is primarily an adjustment of balance sheets. To adjust the more substantial structures underlying these would, in Yemen's case, mean dismantling the state itself, which is not sought by international agencies or by other governments. Quite the opposite, indeed. The maintenance of Yemen's state within a system of stronger states means that Yemen is no longer historically unique, as it was even twenty years ago, but instead is now a Third World country.

Favourable terms in negotiating aid depend in part on approval of the political system. Such organisations as the National Democratic Institute, funded in effect by the US government, have emerged in the post-Cold War world as bodies that "validate" other countries' politics, and along with European agencies they promote what Carapico calls "elections tourism", monitoring polling and the like without reference to, or seeming interest in, local context. The counters to be swapped by Yemen's rulers at meetings with foreign institutions are "democracy", "pluralism", and "civil society". The last of these, with its concrete form of "non-governmental organisations" or NGOs, is popular with foreign donors; the "local councils", which might play the role of NGOs, are meanwhile defined in Yemen's constitutional amendments of 1994 as an "inseparable part of the power of the state", which suggests a certain mismatch of expectation. But there are always funds for another conference.[45] To assume naiveté on either side of such transactions would itself perhaps be naive, and the game is played for substantial prizes. Successful completion of the 1997 parliamentary elections, for instance, produced loan facilities equivalent to Yemen's whole national debt and by mid-1997 aid commitments had been secured to the tune of $1.8 billion for the next three years.

Locally the elections of 1997 stirred none of the excitement felt four years earlier. In 1993, elections had been thought to matter; in 1997, the outcome was assumed to be broadly known in advance and adjustments in parliamentary seats were judged to make little difference. The remnants of the YSP boycotted the process. So did three minor parties: al-Jifrī's "League", the Unionist Gathering, and the United Popular Front. Of 301 seats, the GPC took 188, compared with 123 four years earlier, and Iṣlāḥ's share dropped from 62 to 53. Where the parties (or those sections of their membership with real influence) overlapped so much and the GPC was so loosely defined to start with, refinements of psephology reveal little. In 1999, with presidential elections due and his party (the GPC) holding 226 of 301 parliamentary seats, the President offered formally to step down. To no-one's surprise, the GPC insisted by acclamation that he again run for office. Iṣlāḥ, the main "opposition" party, also nominated ʿAlī ʿAbdullāh Ṣāliḥ. Though opinions differ as to how large the turnout was, the President could claim by the end of the exercise 96.3 per cent of all the votes cast and thus to be Yemen's unquestioned ruler.

SOMEONE ELSE'S MILLENNIUM

When Imam Yaḥyā claimed dominion over Yemen, near the start of the fourteenth Muslim century (AD 1906, AH 1324), he invoked the fact that Zaydī Imams had ruled "all or part of it" for a thousand years. That claim was opposed, as we saw, by those who felt historical identity and political unity bore no simple relation. Through the twentieth (Christian) century, however, the idea was pursued by fits and starts of a Yemeni national state, and in the century's last decade the idea became fact at last. The state turns out to be much like other states. The country remains singular.

Plate 7.3. Modern Sanaa: supporters of the president in the run-up to elections.

A government advertising supplement in *Newsweek* (19 October 1998) is entitled "Poised for growth into the next millennium" and consigns the specificities of Yemeni life to the visual domain of landscape and architecture. The generalities of the age cover little of how the country works, however. Yemen remains a "soft" state in more than the technical sense of political scientists; people express their views more freely than in most Arab countries. More importantly, the expectations and structures of everyday life permeate all that happens and political events are often hard to read. The 1997 elections passed quietly, for instance, but arrests and harassments in August that year (fairly mild by the standards of most Arab countries) were primarily among parties which had boycotted the event. None was a serious rival to the GPC. A refusal to endorse the appearance of pluralism, however, seems not to have been welcome, for fear perhaps that such refusal might compromise relations with the world's bankers, and the style of political management continued to be that of often charming illusion, much discussed by Yemenis and unremarked by casual visitors. Yemenis in fact came up with a new term – "cloning" or *istinsākh* – to describe the way groups are neutralised politically by the government inventing groups that look very like them. To tell one from the other, the real from the false, requires almost a knowledge of everyone's family history.

In that year, as in later years, bombs went off here and there in Yemen, most particularly in what are now "the southern governorates". The government blamed foreign intervention, and a veritable obsession developed with an exile group run by ʿAbd al-Raḥmān al-Jifrī and named MAWJ (an Arabic reverse acronym for National Association of Opposition Groupings): presumably a fear of Saudi influence in, for instance, Ḥaḍramawt coincided with distrust of the group's great fluency with international terms that might influence the world's administrators. Socialists were meanwhile blamed for events that many might attach to Islamists, and Islamists for events that some would attach to socialists. Islamists were the more alarming for a foreign (mainly Western) audience. The Saudis and Egyptians in particular depicted Yemen itself as a hotbed of radicalism connected with global intrigues, but to pursue these links, some real and some imagined, is to enter a world of such fragmented conspiracy that many Yemenis long ago lost interest in the subject.

"Retribalisation" is more the bugbear of modernists. But while confrontations in the cities are submitted to tribal law, in the countryside tribal divisions are cross-cut and infested with state intrigue which seems to many the symptom of tribalism's weakness. As al-ʿUṣaymāt in the heyday of Shaykh ʿAbdullāh's influence through the mid-1980s was a very poor place indeed, though Shaykh ʿAbdullāh himself is of al-ʿUṣaymāt, so now Sanḥān, the President's tribe, is far from prosperous and tribal blocs on the map coincide only partially with the personal and family networks that structure politics. The key pipeline from Maʾrib to the Red Sea is regularly attacked with explosives. The President has a daughter married into Khawlān, through whose territory the pipeline passes, and if Khawlān and Sanḥān themselves are constantly at odds (Khawlān at one point carried off ʿAlī Shumaylah, former chief of staff of the Republican Guard) that seems not to alarm those in power. Throughout the 1990s tribes have also been carrying off foreigners, an easy way to bring pressure on the government. Yet even this on occasion has the appearance of pantomime.[46] The generalities of the age are meanwhile applied at international level to structures and events in Yemen that properly make sense only in local terms, and this overlap of contradictory imagery seems almost to define the most recent of "modern" periods – that following the Cold War.

In June 1999 an international conference on "emerging democracies" was held in Sanaa, sponsored in part by the (US) National Democratic Institute. The IMF, at about the same date, released a further $50 million from an agreed line of credit, and the conference closed with a resolution, in approved international form, to "encourage the role of women and minorities".[47] What minorities Yemen had, save perhaps its 1,500 or so remaining Jews, was unclear. The transition to modernity and pluralism required funds, however, and the prime minister – again ʿAbd al-Karīm al-Iryānī at this date – stressed Yemen's need for support financially as well as otherwise to "ensure the continuation of democracy", as if poverty of its nature might preclude civility. The aviation press meanwhile discussed a deal to buy fighters from the Czechs; months earlier a squadron of Sukhoyev 27s had been set to cost the government $500 million.[48] The country is extremely poor, but how poor the government may be is hard to judge and those attached to government seem extremely prosperous.

In late 1998, when a 50 kilogram sack of wheat cost YR 1,800 (more than twice the salary of an educated junior civil servant), extravagant "shopping centres" were opening in Sanaa to sell international brands of clothes and shoes, perfume and make-up, even Baskin-Robbins' many flavours of ice-cream. The Sanaa Sheraton ran a "Layālī al-Ḥilmiyyah" tent during Ramaḍān. Layālī al-Ḥilmiyyah is the name of a famous Egyptian television serial depicting an earlier age of Cairene history, and Ramaḍān tents are a feature of life among regional elites from Cairo through Damascus to the oil states of the Gulf. One can show off one's clothes and jewellery while nibbling pistachios, smoking ornamental water-pipes, and enjoying in the round the "theme" of a generic Arab culture which nowhere ever quite existed.

That Yemen now has cultural facsimiles of the kind enjoyed by more rootless oil states may seem peculiar, for Yemen has, if anything, an excess of culture and one could study for a lifetime and still miss the significance of half what one has read or heard. But "Ramaḍān tents" are no different in essence from, for instance, film or radio. For years now, young women in Yemen have been acquiring fragments of Egyptian and Levantine speech from television; generations ago, fragments of Turkish strayed into Sanaani usage, while Aden gave part of the population, mainly male, such English derivatives as *mukartasīn* (merchants, people who put things in cartons) and the verb *damfala* (to act as a damned fool). The vocabulary of trucks and engines spread through Yemen as it did through all Arabia. What difference imported imagery through cassettes, films and foreign television will make (if much at all) one must wait and see.

Yemeni television itself established a satellite channel. All over the world – or, most easily, from within the Arab World – one could flip through the stations and find Yemen. The most striking feature was still the parliament. On adjacent channels one might catch the Saudi "Consultative Council", who for all their individual virtues present a most sombre picture: serried ranks of overweight men at expensive desks, all dressed almost identically and saying such uniform things that public life seems hardly worth the bother. The Yemeni channel differed. Though the "Council" lacked the powers some wished and women members were not in evidence as they had been in 1990, there was no lack of debate. And the members seemed a pleasant variety, some in suits, most in skirts and jackets, not a few with their decorated belts and daggers, many wearing old sweaters or deeply casual arrangements of cloths and scarves. They gave the appearance of people very much at home in their own country.

These are not the power-brokers – by their own estimation they achieve fairly little, although they do enjoy a certain status. Their apparent ease with being Yemeni is typical, however. Yemen has its modernist men in suits and its men in neo-Islamic beards, its women in old Sanaani dress and its modern "veiled ones" (*muḥajjabāt*), but the desperate unease that afflicts much of the Arab World in the face of the West afflicts rather few of them deeply, and arguments about global affairs return constantly even now to local detail. The country has been there continuously for some millennia, whatever foreigners may have come and gone, and doubtless it will be there a long time yet.

In local perspective, events often seem familiar from the literature of centuries before, yet the Yemeni world is itself intensely "modern". The meeting around the tomb of al-Ḥusayn at Raydah, which we mentioned at the chapter's start, may be ancient but the poems change year by year. Islamic charities have recently promoted mass weddings, on the model of those found in Egypt and in the Gulf states alike: the aim in part is to avoid expensive rivalries over bride-price and to demonstrate an ideal solidarity. The socialists in the South, however, once used very different terms and methods to broadly the same ends, with small success, and Imam Yaḥyā, we remember, used to order on occasion that everyone get married, a programme that appears in retrospect to tell us more of the Imam's views on moral order than it does about the practical history of most Yemenis. Several authors now point to a revival of tradition – of Zaydīsm, for instance, though without an Imam, to forms of regional identity (a literature has emerged on Ibn ʿAlwān, the lost saint of Lower Yemen), and to local readings of what otherwise pass as global events. To disentangle real from apparent continuity is as complex as it would be for France, say, or for Italy. Only the dramas are political. "The whole period is misleading," says a Yemeni friend: "All the people we thought were dangerous (*khaṭīr*; perceptive, they saw to the centre of things) are poor, simple farmers. They are nothing special. They are all simple people (*insān basīṭ*). They seemed complicated (*muʿaqqad*) because of our circumstances." The knowledge and assumptions brought to such circumstance by Yemenis are far from simple.

As this book went to print, in July 2000, a settlement of the Saudi–Yemeni border was announced.

APPENDIX I

Major tribal groupings of the North

Ḥāshid: al-ʿUṣaymāt, ʿIdhar, Banī Ṣuraym, Khārif, Hamdān, Sanḥān, Bilād al-Rūs.

Bakīl: Khawlān Ṣaʿdah, Āl ʿAmmār, Āl Sālim, al-ʿAmālisah, Dhū Muḥammad, Dhū Ḥusayn, Banī Nawf (the last five form part of Dahm), Wāʾilah, Sufyān, Arḥab, Murhibah, Nihm, ʿIyāl Yazīd, ʿIyāl Surayḥ, Banī Ḥushaysh, Khawlān al-Ṭiyāl.

Madhḥij: Murād, ʿAns, al-Ḥadā, Qayfah, but the category seems still to be re-forming.

APPENDIX 2

A different history

Asked to summarise the modern history of Yemen, a friend from Ḥugariyyah began with a list of villages and their specialities in migrant labour; for example, al-ʿAbūs, photographers; al-Maqāṭirah, construction work; Banī Ghazī, gold and silver jewellery; al-ʿArūq, commerce (Hayl Saʿīd Anʿam and Abd al-Ghanī Muṭahhar were both from near here); al-Maʿāmirah, restaurants and hotels.

He then went on to list the major party figures and where they came from; for example, al-ʿAbūs, Sulṭān ʿUmar (MAN); al-Aghābirah, ʿAbd al-Fattāḥ Ismāʿīl (NLF) and ʿAbd al-Qādir Saʿīd (MAN); al-ʿArūq, ʿAbd al-ʿAzīz ʿAbd al-Ghanī; al-Sharjab, Qāsim Salām (Baʿth).

That he never in two hours' discussion named a tribe will come as no surprise to those who know Lower Yemen; the centrality to his account of Cardiff and Sheffield, Dearborn and Asmara requires a quite different form of history than I have written here.

Glossary

ʿāmil	a local governor, in charge of anything from a village or town to a whole province
amīr	"prince" or "commander". Used *inter alia* of provincial governors under the last Imams.
badu	tribesmen far from towns: in the extreme case, nomads
Baʿth	an Arab nationalist political party, influential in Yemen from the 1960s onward
bayt	a house, both literally and in the sense of a family
dawlah	a state or dynasty
dīwān	royal court
faḍl	preference, as for instance of God for a given claimant to the Imamate
fatwā	a formal opinion on a point of Islamic law
ḥadīth	a Tradition of the Prophet
ḥākim	a judge
ʿīd	a festival
Imam	leader of the Muslim community. In Shāfiʿī theory akin to a king and responsible for temporal order. In Zaydī theory the most perfect man available at a given time, *a fortiori* of the Prophet's house
intifāḍah	an uprising or upheaval. Here used of peasant risings against landowners
jabal	a mountain
jihād	holy war
kafīl	a personal guarantor in tribal truces or in state employment such as being a soldier in the army
khurūj	"coming out" against oppression; a key Zaydī tenet
kufalāʾ	plural of *kafīl*
libnah	a measure of land, about 8 metres by 8 metres
mashāyikh	plural of *shaykh*, but in South Yemen used of non-*sayyid* religious specialists
muftī	one who issues *fatwā*s
qāḍī	"judge". In North Yemen usually an inherited title held by non-*sayyid* families with some history of learning

Qarāmiṭah the Qarmatians or Carmartians, an early movement in Islam, probably akin to the Khārijites and later Ibāḍīs but whose history is almost impossible to trace

qāt a mildly narcotic shrub which, when chewed in company, stimulates conversation

Salafīs those in pursuit of the Prophet's "ancestral" practice. Nowadays rather fragmented groups holding scripture and abstract ideals in common but little else

sanjak Turkish administrative division below *vilayet*

sayyid a descendant of the Prophet. A female (*sayyidah*) is usually called a *sharīfah*

sharīʿah the totality of Islamic law and custom, adherence to which is God's command

sharīf a descendant of the Prophet

shaykh a senior man, usually in Yemen the leader of a tribe, tribal section or village

sulṭān "authority", one who rules

sunnah the totality of what is known of the Prophet's speech and practice, a model ideally guiding Muslims

sūq market

ṭīn a measure of land, about 2 square metres

ʿulamāʾ persons learned in religion (plural of *ʿālim*)

vilayet a province of the Ottoman empire

wādī a valley or wash

Wahhābī term applied by others to followers of Muḥammad ʿAbd al-Wahhāb's teachings. An intolerant sect, originally from Najd

waqf property gifted for religious ends and thus "stopped" from inheritance and normal sale

zakāt canonical taxes whose payment by Muslims is prescribed by scripture as one of the pillars of the faith

zāmil a rhyming ditty or marching song

Zuyūd plural of Zaydī

Brief chronology

1831	Excellent rains but "afflictions were many". Rival claimants to the Imamate warring.
1837	Muḥammad ʿAlī acquires nominal allegiance of Taʿizz.
1839	British occupy Aden.
1845	Large meteorite crosses Yemen from West to East. The Faqīh Saʿīd marches against Aden.
1849	Ottomans establish themselves on the Red Sea coast.
1869	Suez Canal opens.
1872	Ottomans occupy Sanaa.
1904	Yaḥyā Muḥammad Ḥamīd al-Dīn becomes Imam.
1905	Border established between North and South.
1911	Treaty between Imam Yaḥyā and the Ottomans.
1914–18	World War I.
1918–19	Ottomans withdraw from Yemen.
1918–20	Imam Yaḥyā conquers Lower Yemen.
1920	Idrīsī pact with Ibn Saʿūd.
1923	The end of the Ottoman caliphate.
1924	Petition for Yaḥyā's son Aḥmad to be made Crown Prince.
1926	Yaḥyā's treaty with Italy. First use of the title "King of Yemen".
1927–9	Aḥmad conquers the Tihāmah.
1928	Al-Wasiʿī's *History of Yemen* published.
1934	Treaty of Sanaa: Britain and Yaḥyā agree an administrative frontier.
	Saudi–Yemen war.
	Treaty of Ṭāyif: the Saudis and Yaḥyā agree a frontier.
1935	First organised "modernist" groupings in the North.
1935–6	Al-Bakrī's *Political History of Ḥaḍramawt* published.
1936–7	Ingrams pacifies Ḥaḍramawt.
1938	Yaḥyā attempts to gain control of Shabwah.

1939–45 World War II.
1948 Assassination of Imam Yaḥyā. Aḥmad becomes Imam.

1950 American delegation visits Imam Aḥmad.
1952 Egypt's revolution.
1953 Turkish salt works at Ṣalīf revived.
1955 Attempted coup against Imam Aḥmad.
1956 British invade Suez.
The Jiddah Pact unites Egypt, Yemen and Saudi Arabia against Britain.
Publication of *Demands of the People.*
1957 Publication of al-ʿAynī's *Battles and Conspiracies.*
1958 North Yemen joins Syria and Egypt in the Union of Arab States.
Sultan ʿAlī of Laḥj deposed by the British.
1959 Federation of Arab Amirates in Aden's hinterland.
1960 Tribal rising against Imam Aḥmad.
1961 Organisation of "Free Officers" noticed in the North.
1962 26 September Revolution drives out Imam al-Badr and establishes the Yemen Arab Republic.

1962 Formation of "National Guard" to defend the new republic.
1963 Federation of South Arabia, uniting Aden and several hinterland states.
ʿAmrān conference.
14 October, the beginning of fighting in Radfān.
1964 Publication of *Ibn al-Amīr and his Age* and *The Collapse of the Revolution in Yemen.*
1965 The murder of Zubayrī.
Khamir conference.
NLF conference at Jiblah.
1966 Britain announces the intention of leaving Aden by late 1968.
Ḥumar conference: split in the NLF.
1967 June, Egypt is defeated by Israel in Sinai.
5 November, Sallāl overthrown in Sanaa.
29 November, British leave Aden.
The siege of Sanaa.

1968 22 June, corrective movement in the South deposes Qaḥṭān al-Shaʿbī.

1969 Saudis attack Wadīʿah.
1970 National Reconciliation between royalists and republicans within the North.
Publication of Sulṭān ʿUmar's *A Perspective on Development in Yemen's Society.*
1972 War between the Yemens.
1974 Oil prices go up.
Beginning of the great remittance boom.
13 June, al-Ḥamdī becomes President of YAR.
1975 First nationwide elections in the North.
1976 National Democratic Front (NDF) established in Lower Yemen.
1977 al-Ḥamdī murdered. Aḥmad al-Ghashmī becomes President of YAR.
1978 al-Ghashmī murdered. ʿAlī ʿAbdullāh Ṣāliḥ becomes President of YAR.
Sālmayn murdered in the PDRY.
1979 Second war between the Yemens.
Islamic Front established in Lower Yemen.
Beginning of the fifteenth Muslim millennium; little notice taken.

1981 "National Dialogue" begun within the North.
1982 Establishment in the North of the General Popular Congress (GPC).
1983 Balance of payments crisis.
1984 Oil strike in North Yemen.
1985 Balance of payments crisis.
1986 Coup and civil war within the South.
1987 Publication of al-Akwa's *Life of a Scholar and of a Prince.*
1988 GPC assumes control of Northern co-operatives.
Publication of ʿAbd al-Salām's *The Republic between Authority and Tribe.*
1989 Establishment of Arab Co-operation Council (Iraq, Egypt, Jordan and North Yemen).
Berlin Wall comes down.

1990 22 May, union of South and North to form the Yemen Republic.
2 August, Ṣaddām Ḥusayn invades Kuwait.
Yemenis expelled from Saudi Arabia.

1992	Urban and tribal conferences.
1993	National elections.
1994	War between the ruling parties.
1995	New relation formed with the IMF.
1997	National elections.
	Yemenis claim possession of the planet Mars.
1999	ʿAlī ʿAbdullāh Ṣāliḥ re-elected President of Yemen Republic.
	Text of "The Trotting Camel" finished.
2000	The Muslim year 1420–1.

Notes

1 TURKEY, BRITAIN AND IMAM YAḤYĀ: THE YEARS AROUND 1900

1 Wahb bin Munabbih (d. 732) is an important early source. Works of history thereafter routinely define themselves in local terms, e.g. al-Hamdānī's *Diadem Book of Information about Yemen and the People of Ḥimyar*, circa 920, and Yaḥyā al-Ḥusayn's *The Goal of Desires on Information about the Yemeni Region*, circa 1765. The list is long.

2 Mackintosh-Smith's travel book (1997) catches this feeling of historical density very well.

3 For the story behind Aden's occupation, see the excellent first chapter of Gavin 1975. Also Playfair 1859; Jacob 1923; Waterfield 1968.

4 For the "time of corruption", Ḥarāzī 1986; al-ʿAmrī 1988; Dresch 1989: 212 ff. For the broader history, al-Wāsiʿī 1928.

5 Ḥarāzī, whom we quoted earlier (1986: 80), uses *dawlah* or "state" unreflectively, and an anonymous chronicler who takes the story down to 1898 sees the great days of the Qāsimīs as a golden age, for "all of Yemen was in the hands of the state" (quoted Dresch 1989: 208).

6 For Yaḥyā's father, al-Manṣūr Muḥammad, see Zabārah 1956, I and Kruse 1984 which discusses Zaydī arguments against the Turks. Father and son disagreed on several matters of theology (Haykel 1997: 249, 257); Zaydi objections to Turkish rule, however, were much what they had been around 1600 (Blukacz 1993).

7 For conflicting poems in the far north, Dresch 1989: 411–14. For divisions further south, al-Akwaʿ 1980: 105–8; 1987. The Turkish period remains seriously understudied. For a sketch of Ottoman hopes for reform, Mandaville 1984. For a start to new work, Kuhn 1996, forthcoming.

8 For detail until 1900, Zabārah 1956, I; al-Jirāfī 1992. Also Baldry 1976, 1977a, and Abāẓah 1979. Al-Akwaʿ (1987) gives an excellent picture of Lower Yemen.

9 al-Wāsiʿī 1928: 203. Famine had killed a great many people elsewhere too, but the tribes besieging Sanaa were given grain from the Imam's treasury. What this treasury comprised, where the grain was stored, and how Yaḥyā controlled its distribution is obscure.

10 Compare, for instance, Dresch 1989 with Messick 1978, 1993 and al-Akwaʿ 1987. The number of rural chiefs granted Ottoman rank in Upper Yemen

could be counted on the fingers of one hand; by contrast, in Lower Yemen a great many families retained Turkish titles for decades afterwards and some still retain them as family names.

11 al-Wāsiʿī 1928: 213.

12 For a colourful account of the siege, Wavell 1912. For a description of Ottoman Yemen a few years later, Bury 1915.

13 Gavin 1975: 240–1. For the text of the agreement, Zabārah 1956, II: 213–15; Sālim 1971: 516–18; ʿAfīf 1982: 207–9.

14 For the biography of Ḥusayn bin ʿAlī al-ʿAmrī, see Zabārah 1979: 265 ff; al-Akwaʿ 1995, III: 1459. For other appointments at the time and thus the roots of a "civil service", see Zabārah 1956, II: 242.

15 Sālim 1982: 257–75. A *qadaḥ* is about a bushel. The riyāls in question were silver coins of a pattern first struck in Austria in the eighteenth century, "showing the big bust of her Imperial Majesty Queen Maria Theresa . . ." (Luqmān 1970: 91). They weighed about 28 grams.

16 Dresch 1996: 64–6; cf. Zabārah 1956, II: 253. For a proclamation from the Idrīsī, Bang 1996: Appendix B.

17 "Infidel British". Western students of the Middle East often content themselves with thinking Christians are "people of the book". Yemeni correspondence condemns them usually as *kuffār*, infidels. And where most schools of Islamic law allow marriage between a Muslim man and a Christian or Jewish woman, Zaydism insisted she convert.

18 Jacob 1923: 114, 145; al-Akwaʿ 1987: 243 ff; Mujāhid 1997: 189–98.

19 Sālim 1971, the standard account of Yaḥyā's reign.

20 Hunter and Sealey 1909: 154 ff.

21 To what extent these were really tribes we shall see later. In early British material one finds the term "cantons" and the usual term in Arabic is *nāḥiyah*, not *qabīlah*. Treaties of protection kept being signed until 1954. The last was with "the Buʾsi Shaykh of Upper Yāfiʿ" and took precisely the form of those signed with his neighbours fifty years before (CO 1015/985).

22 The irrelevance of what they were doing for those in the immediate area comes across from British writing. See Bury 1911: 20 and *passim*.

23 The great geographers such as al-Muqaddasī (circa 990) are one obvious locus of tradition. See also the quotation from Ibn Khaldūn in Baldry 1976 and the discussion in Bashear 1989.

24 Wilkinson 1991: 3–4.

25 Mecca was ruled by Sharīfs for instance (descendants of the Prophet, one of whom now rules Jordan). For the demise of the Sharīfs at Mecca and an interesting side-light on the Ottomans in Yemen circa 1900, see Stitt 1948.

26 The same phenomenon recurs on a smaller scale. When Upper ʿAwlaqī, south of the later line, said "Yemen" they meant places south again from them – ʿAwdhalī and Faḍlī on the Indian Ocean coast (Hunter and Sealey 1909: 56).

27 Before the British seized it, Aden was in decline. Ḥudaydah, on the Red Sea, became important under the Turks. Before that, in the days of the coffee trade, Mukhāʾ had been the main port. For the reasons, Gavin 1975.

28 Ingrams 1937: 141–66. For a later appreciation of economic problems, CO 1055/157. Several papers in Freitag and Clarence-Smith 1997 survey Ḥaḍramī migration. For African connections in particular, Martin 1971.

29 Scholars in Lower Yemen went to Zabīd for learning, not to Ḥaḍramawt. The Imam al-Shāfiʿī himself (d. 819) visited Yemen and left important students there. Probably, however, the dominance of the Shāfiʿī school around Taʿizz comes later, in Ayyūbid and Rasūlid times, from the twelfth to the fourteenth centuries.

30 Forms of prayer were sometimes an issue among Zaydīs themselves, who fought over doctrine. But the imposition of Zaydī practice on Shāfiʿī areas (the call to prayer, for instance: "Come to the best of works . . .") is rare. When the British in Aden raised the 1st Yemen Infantry at the end of World War I they were surprised to find Shāfiʿī and Zaydī soldiers would happily pray together, which Sunnis and Shiʿites in India never would (Jacob 1923: 273).

31 The most important modern politician associated with the Tihāmah is Ḥasan Makkī, who grew up in Ḥudaydah. He is not in any sense (*pace* Chaudhry 1997: 126) a "southern economist". His family came, in fact, from ʿAsīr, further north, at the time of the Saudi–Yemeni war in 1934.

32 For the Tihāmah, Bury 1915: 106, 135–42; Bonnenfant 1995a; and, in recent times, for Zabīd, Meneley 1996.

33 al-Akwaʿ 1980: 31. For the point made below see Mundy's splendid article on dress (Mundy 1983). For the practical implications of women's silence, Mundy 1979.

34 al-Akwaʿ 1980: 114.

35 For a *hijrah*-agreement taken over by Imam Yaḥyā in 1913, see Sālim 1982: 209–22; Puin 1984. Compare Dresch 1990; Weir 1991; Bédoucha and Albergoni 1991; Dostal 1996.

36 Balfour-Paul 1991: 51.

37 Gavin 1975: 126–8. For the story below, concerning Abū ʿArīsh, ibid. 73.

38 Poem collected by Ṣalāḥ al-Bakrī, cited al-ʿAbdalī 1931: 112. The significance of the citation will appear in Chapter 2. For poetry's importance, Caton 1990; Rodionov 1996; Taminian 1999.

39 Messick 1978: 56–7. Interestingly, Messick's friends in Ibb thought of Faqīh Saʿīd as having formed a *dawlah*. Sufi "brotherhoods" were important but in Lower Yemen they seem not to have acted as political units in the manner reported from, for example, Morocco.

40 For ʿAsīr, al-Wishalī 1982 and particularly Bang 1996, which takes the story of the Idrīsī state to its end in the 1930s. For an ethnographic sketch of areas now on Yemen's frontier with the Saudis, Gingrich 1987, 1988. For detailed history still further north, Zulfah 1995, 1997.

41 Control of the Upper Tihāmah was lost at the time of the first Wahhābī movement (Playfair 1859: 127 ff), then taken by the Egyptians briefly and then the Turks. Under Ottoman administration ʿAsīr was part of the *vilayet* of Yemen, the other *sanjaks* being Sanaa, Taʿizz and Ḥudaydah (Abāẓah 1979).

42 Ingrams 1937: 27–34. Bakrī (1935–6) goes into detail. For Ḥaḍramawt in the late nineteenth century, Van den Berg 1886. People paid nominal allegiance to the Ottoman Caliph and for some reason were fascinated by Russia (ibid. 177). For British involvement, Bakrī 1949; Collins 1969. For a traveller's account of the Wādī and the Aden hinterland, Bent and Bent 1900.

43 al-Mahrī 1994. Also Dostal 1967: 123–35 for badu there.

44 For a sketch of economic history, Wenner 1988. There is no good Western source yet on the history of learning, but biographical dictionaries show constant exchanges with North Africa and India as well as with the great Arab capitals.

45 Bury 1911: 296. For continuation of the theme half a century later, Johnston 1964: 197.

46 In the North in the 1980s several new weapons appeared, not least Vulcan anti-aircraft guns which, at 5,000 rounds per minute, flatten houses with a squirt: tribes promptly agreed they should not be used in squabbles. Long before that, in the matchlock age, one finds elaborate rules about who can shoot at what in which circumstance.

47 Mujāhid 1997: 173. For the survival of Ottoman lamb's-wool caps decades later, Scott 1942: 117; Aponte 1948: 65.

48 Glaser 1884, 1993. He visited Arḥab and part of Ḥāshid at a difficult time, and his romancing is sometimes tedious; but the picture that emerges (also Glaser 1913 for the Jawf) is persuasive and the detail impeccable. See Dostal 1990. Ḥayyim Ḥabshūsh (1941, 1995) provides a famous account of the North a few years earlier.

49 Trevaskis 1968: 6.

50 al-Akwaʿ 1980: 23, 28, 30, 65, 96 ff.

51 al-Akwaʿ 1980: 115; and below, ibid. 106. Locusts, he reminds us, remained a menace until the 1950s.

52 For an excellent analysis of the relation between power and land, from fieldwork in the 1970s, see Swagman 1988. His account is of adjoining areas: Raymah (Shāfiʿī as it happens) and Ānis (Zaydī as it happens). For dynasties and tribes near Aden, Gavin 1975: 63–4, 142, 201–3; Admiralty 1946; Dresch forthcoming. For Upper Yemen, Tutwiler 1987; Dresch 1989; Mundy 1995.

53 Messick 1978, 1983 describes the town of Ibb, but the death of Ron Hart robbed us of any detailed ethnography of Lower Yemen's peasantry. Sharjabī 1990 goes some way to fill the gap. For the distinction between peasants and tribesmen, Nuʿmān 1965; ʿUmar 1970; ʿAbd al-Salām 1988. The term should properly be *raʿāyā*, but *rāʿyā* seems common.

54 Bury 1915: 82. For Sanaa, see Kopp and Wirth 1994; Mermier 1997a. Also Serjeant and Lewcock 1983 for an extraordinary range of detail and fine pictures, and Bonnenfant 1995b.

55 Bury 1915: 135.
56 The literature on Yemen's Jews is large. For outlines, Klein-Franke 1988; Nini 1991.

2 YAḤYĀ AND THE BRITISH: 1918–1948

1 Nājī 1979: 78–80; Zabārah 1956, III: 8–9, 15–16, 63–5; al-Wazīr 1987: 89, 127; al-Akwaʿ 1987: 343–8; Dawlah 1988. For the abortive meeting at al-ʿAmāqī, which discussed Shāfiʿī independence, al-Akwaʿ 1987: 274 ff; Mujāhid 1997: 203–5.
2 al-ʿInān 1983: 7; al-Akwaʿ 1987: 407–14; al-Wazīr 1987: 175–87.
3 al-ʿInān 1983: 7, 75; Mundy 1995: 28. How much the shaykh was appealing to "the principle of direct representation" (ibid.) and how much to the will of God, which is more what ʿInān suggests, is open to question.
4 Zabārah 1956, III: 13. Also Nājī 1979, part 4; al-ʿInān 1983: 8–18.
5 Jacob 1923: 232; al-Akwaʿ 1987: 344.
6 Fear of losing the Tihāmah ports weighed heavily with Yaḥyā. Among highland tribes, the story goes, Yaḥyā was *imām al-madhhab* (Imam of our sect, in other words) but the Idrīsī was *imām al-dhahab* (the Imam with money).
7 In fact the British had ceased arming the Idrīsī. When they found that Italy was arming Yaḥyā (July 1926) they again allowed guns through commercial channels (CO 537/656). For the broader story of imperial rivalry, Baldry 1977b.
8 al-Wāsiʿī 1928: 276–7.
9 For accounts of the al-Wazīrs, see al-Akwaʿ 1995, I: 176 ff. (under Bayt al-Sayyid); al-Wazīr A. 1987.
10 al-Akwaʿ 1995, II: 817–54 for Aḥmad's biography. Something of his character emerges also from Aponte 1948: 112–13; Shamāḥī 1972.
11 For Yaḥyā's disdain for the Ḥāshid shaykhs, al-Akwaʿ 1987: 291 ff, and for shaykhs in general, ibid. 321. For certain Shāfiʿī notables, below, ibid. 489. Chaudhry (1997: 106) insists Ḥāshid and Bakīl were highly centralised, autonomous units. They were not. From 1930 to 1960 there is no sign at all of them acting that way.
12 Shamāḥī 1972: 172–4; al-Akwaʿ 1995, II: 819–20. For a sketch of events in the Tihāmah, below, al-ʿAzm 1937, I: 51, 66 ff.
13 Zabārah 1956, III: 195. It goes without saying that the term Wahhābī, above, was not used in self-description; in so far as Ibn Saʿūd's followers thought of themselves as warriors of God, however, the status of negotiations and treaties with the Zaydīs must surely have been problematic.
14 ʿAbd al-Salām (1988: 180) assumes a sinister connection with oil. In fact Standard Oil's interest was in eastern Arabia. A concession for Ḥijāz and ʿAsīr was given only in 1936, and then to IPC. Charles Crane (a great forgotten benefactor of Arabia) and Karl Twitchell were involved with both Yemen and the Saudis, but little is at issue, it seems, save the link between the Middle East and Indio, California, "home of the date-shake".

15 For useful summaries of the period, Wenner 1967; Bidwell 1983; and Gavin 1975. For parts of Yaḥyā's correspondence with for instance Laḥj, see al-ʿAbdalī 1931; al-Thaʿālabī 1997.

16 Bakrī 1936: 35–6.

17 quoted al-Jirāfī 1951: 239. When the British bombed Taʿizz local people abandoned the Imam's currency and demanded Zaydī troops be withdrawn (al-Wazīr 1987: 269–70). See also Mujāhid 1997: 216–17.

18 Rossi 1939: 111–12 for soldiers' songs on Najrān and Aden that remain widely known. Also Aponte 1948: 76 ff, 93 ff.

19 Aircraft had been used against the Turks in World War I. Indeed one was shot down and the wreckage carried off through Yemen (al-Akwaʿ 1987: 261 ff). By the late 1920s, however, airmen in the Western World were everywhere talking of deep penetration, strategic threats and the mystical powers of bombing (Townshend 1986).

20 Reilly's ambitions for reform developed with the transfer of responsibility for the Protectorate from the India Office to the Colonial Office, in 1921. Aden itself was under Bombay until 1932, Delhi until 1937 and then the Colonial Office as a Crown Colony.

21 The quotation (Ingrams D. 1949: 25) is out of sequence but represents the attitude of Reilly's young protégés towards the WAP from the start. See also Trevaskis 1968: 12; Gavin 1975: 277 ff; 308–9; Dresch forthcoming.

22 Ingrams 1966 (intro.): 25. For accounts of Ḥaḍramawt around this period, Ingrams 1936; Van der Meulen 1932, 1947; Stark 1936. Also van der Kroef 1953. For retrospective analysis, Freitag and Clarence-Smith 1997. Much depended on the Ḥaḍramī diaspora, whose influence was apparent architecturally: "In Tarīm and Sayyūn the interested traveller can see reproductions of Rangoon railway stations, of Batavia banking houses, of Penang public libraries . . ." (Allfree 1967: 147).

23 Ingrams D. 1949: 26. On the sociology of these southern areas, Hamilton 1943; Admiralty 1946; Gavin 1975: 201–3; Dresch forthcoming.

24 Hamilton 1955: 136. He goes on to provide a vivid picture of how the Amir, told by the British to seize Quṭaybī hostages, burst into tears. The hostages were more a threat to him than he to them, and he fled to Aden.

25 Hamilton 1949: 74. Yet much of Hamilton's time was spent enforcing this imaginary rule by having recalcitrant tribes bombed into submission. His books (1949, 1955) provide a detailed account. See also Luqmān 1985: 125–7, 143–9.

26 Dresch 1990. For guaranty of individuals, below, see Messick 1978: 203–9; Nājī 1979: 109; Tutwiler 1987: 247.

27 Zabārah quoted Dresch 1989: 229. For the political significance of listing *ḥadd* punishments, Obermeyer 1981: 181–2. For a tribesman's fascination with the Imam's "strong rule", al-ʿAzm 1937, I: 87–8.

28 Gavin 1975: 265–8; Zabārah 1956, II: 260; Ingrams 1966; Freitag and Clarence-Smith 1997. The original ʿAlawī-Irshādī dispute is covered by Ho

(forthcoming); Bakrī (1936) gives much of the correspondence. For biographies of al-Saqqāf (al-ʿAlawī) and Bin ʿAqīl, see Zabārah 1979: 244, 557. Bin ʿAqīl, who encouraged Yaḥyā's dynastic ambitions, visited *inter alia* Java, Singapore, India, China, Japan, Persia, France, Germany and Egypt, besides making the *ḥajj* more than once. He died in Ḥudaydah in 1930 and Yaḥyā closed the law-courts to mark his passing.

29 Zabārah 1956, III: 98–9; Gavin 1975: 265–6.

30 Bakrī 1936: 56–7, 83.

31 Colonial Office 1946: 73; Ingrams 1966; Bujra 1967, 1971. Ingrams' views rather dominate the literature (he was known to colleagues, indeed, as "Headline Harold"); for a blistering view of Ingrams from the man he deposed, Muḥḍār 1983.

32 The Sharīfs of Bayḥān are Awlād Muqbil, those of Ma'rib are Awlād Khālid, Ḥarīb are Awlād Aḥmad, and the Jawf Awlād Ṣāliḥ. The Āl Ḥusayn at Baraṭ are sometimes said to be kin; other "tribal" families of Dhū Ḥusayn have often married daughters to the Ashrāf.

33 trans. Dresch 1995b: 245, 251. For eastern Yemen and the Jawf before this, al-ʿAzm 1937, II; al-ʿAmrī 1996. After 1934 Ibn Saʿūd never contested Yemen's territory with Yaḥyā. He did, however, have an argument with Britain over borders, for which see Wilkinson 1991: chs. 7, 9.

34 *al-Ḥikmah* quoted Nājī 1984: 245. For political links among North, South and Ḥaḍramawt in the mid-1920s (two decades before most accounts would stress them), Thaʿālabī 1997. Meanwhile in ʿAlī Nāṣir's poems one notes a certain "Shiʿite" imagery from a Sunni tribe.

35 al-Wāsiʿī 1928: 279. Al-Wazīr A. (1987: 211–12, 341) names Sayyid ʿAlī al-Shāmī as one of many who objected to the royal title, for "majesty" is an attribute of God.

36 The very first Imam (al-Hādī, d. 911) was succeeded by his son, and so was his brother after him. But semi-institutionalised succession characterised the Qāsimī period (1620 to al-Mahdī ʿAbdullāh's succession in 1816), and the next father-son succession was Yaḥyā's own in 1904. The title Crown Prince (*walī al-ʿahd*) was new.

37 For the petition, Zabārah 1956, III: 106–10; for the theology, Haykel 1997: 270.

38 See al-Akwaʿ 1995, III: 1756–9, not least the charming photograph. For the family and court personalities, Ingrams 1963: 22–6; al-ʿAzm 1937, I: 226–31.

39 Ingrams (1963: 67) refers to Bin ʿAqīl in this connection as "an eminent Zaydī leader". Actually he was a Ḥaḍramī and a Shāfiʿī by upbringing. His theology was Shiʿite and was complex but not Zaydī.

40 Rīḥānī 1930: 222; also Aponte 1948: 65–9, 102 ff; al-Akwaʿ 1987: 324–38.

41 Rīḥānī 1930: 220–4. Also al-Wāsiʿī 1928: 295–6; al-ʿAzm 1937, I: 180–2. Messick (1993: 172–3) notes the "openness" of the Imam's style. One has to be careful here. A "closed" style (described with the same vocabulary) is as typical of Imams. Two different dramas of power turn equally on *haybah*, the dread inspired by the ruler's person.

42 Zabārah 1956, III: 332–3. For Coon as a witness, Messick 1993: 242. For a better account from the late 1930s, Scott 1942: 163–77.

43 *Records* 10: 33–4.

44 Zabārah 1956, III: 256–8, where the connection with military expenditure is made explicit. Chaudhry (1997: 101, 133) suggests the Imam had no standing army. In fact by the late 1930s there were probably 30,000 men under arms – an expression of a new form of state-craft (Messick 1993) and a vast financial burden.

45 Maqbalī 1986: 16. Rouaud 1984 provides a brief overview of migration. For Yemeni communities in America and Britain, Friedlander 1988 and Halliday 1992.

46 Aḥmad al-Sayāghī, of a *qāḍī* family, married a *sayyid* lady; most *sayyids* were not pleased (al-Akwaʿ 1995, III: 1537). Rajab is when Islam is supposed first to have come to Yemen; al-Ghadīr commemorates the Prophet granting ʿAlī the Caliphate (Haykel 1997: 262, 268). For the call to prayer, below, al-Akwaʿ 1987: 383–5.

47 Rīḥānī 1930: 68; Aponte 1948: 47. For the quote below (1946), Rashid 1984: 5. For regional accents, Juzaylān 1984: 12, 19. For the prominence of Shāfiʿī soldiers, ibid. 16–17.

48 Aḥmad al-Muṭāʿ is said to have formed *Hay'at al-niḍāl* in 1934. Muḥammad al-Akwa's *Jamʿiyyat al-iṣlāḥ* dates to the 1940s. *Pace* Chaudhry (1997: 121) neither was formed in Aden. The first centred on Sanaa and the second on Ibb.

49 The title goes back to the seventeenth century, but in recent times had not simply been hereditary: Aḥmad Qāsim Ḥamīd al-Dīn, Yaḥyā's cousin, for instance, had held it as a warrior in God's cause (al-Akwaʿ 1995, II: 1083, III: 1650 and *passim*).

50 *Records* 8: 313. One cannot help liking al-Ḥusayn. Instead of fleeing Sanaa when the coup broke in 1948, he went to see his mother. He was shot, unfortunately.

51 al-Akwaʿ, M. 1987: 329–31; al-Akwaʿ, I. 1995, III: 1730; Maqbalī 1986: 16, 65. The national finances are hard to guess at. Some tax figures are given by Lambardi (1947), reproduced by Heyworth-Dunne (1952).

52 al-Wazīr A. 1987: 435. Ingrams (1963: 21–2, 26) reports Sanaa as quite prosperous in 1941. Clark in 1945 describes conditions there as "poor" and in southern areas "appalling" (Stookey 1978: 173). A drought had intervened. For the political effects of drought in rural areas, Tutwiler 1987: 251–7.

53 Stookey 1978: 194; Juzaylān 1984: 81.

54 Stookey 1978: 181. For the text, Markaz 1982b: 561–3, where the signatories are listed. Al-Daylamī had been among those who suggested making Aḥmad Crown Prince in 1924.

55 Douglas 1987: 118. Several Yemenis contest the truth of this tale, but only to substitute other noted figures for Zayd al-Daylamī.

56 Dresch 1989: 237; Messick 1993: 123–9. Messick's discussion is recommended highly.

57 al-Jirāfī 1951 (preface) trans. Messick 1993: 124.
58 *The Gift of the Age; Chronicles of the Kings of Lahj and Aden* (al-ʿAbdalī 1931).
59 Bakrī 1935–6, 1949; Serjeant 1962. For a sketch of Ḥaḍramī schooling and self-help associations at the period, Carapico 1998: 79–80.
60 Nuʿmān 1965: 50–3. Compare Messick 1993: 107–9; Carapico 1998: 70–1. For printing at the time, Rossi 1938. A fashionable Western view would have the advent of print transform society; political awareness in Taʿizz and Sanaa seems in fact to have turned on poems in manuscript.
61 al-ʿAzm 1937, I: 183–4, also 245, 307–8. Douglas (1987: 11) quotes Stookey (1978: 189) quoting Sālim (1971: 441). The sentiment may be Yaḥyā's. The wording almost certainly is not. The term *shaʿb*, which now meant "people" in the solidary nationalist sense, was current in writings by certain Yemeni historians and jurists; but Yaḥyā himself said usually *ahl*, suggesting an older, more dispersed identity.
62 For the standard Yemeni account, Douglas 1987: 30. Messick (1993: 107) prefers to stress in the manner of Foucault's disciples "the cumulative importance of detailed shifts" since Turkish times. This is surely right. More mundanely, also, the more one reads, the more Yemenis one finds who travelled and corresponded widely before 1935. For the prominence of Yemen in the wider press, al-ʿAmrī 1987. For Shakīb Arslān's activities, Cleveland 1985.
63 Maqbalī 1986: 19.
64 al-Akwaʿ 1995, II: 695; Douglas 1987: 41–2. In Sanaa also there were fervid debates over "the whirlwinds of Western civilisation" (al-Wāsiʿī 1948: 245). For older forms of schooling, al-Akwaʿ 1980: 32–54; Juzaylān 1984: 25 ff; Maqbalī 1986: 17–18. For the quote at the end of the paragraph, Rashid 1984: 7.
65 The best account of the "liberal" movement as a whole is still that of the late Leigh Douglas (1987). "Liberal" is not the ideal word. Douglas himself uses the term "Free Yemenis", but this refers at times to a specific organisation.
66 Quoted Douglas 1987: 66. Compare also the views of an American-employed Ḥijāzī (Rashid 1984: 1–9) and of the Muslim Brothers' Algerian emissary, al-Wartalānī (al-Wāsiʿī 1948: 357–60).
67 al-ʿInān 1983: 5; Rossi 1939: 108–9; Aponte 1948: 63; Zabārah 1956, III: 145–8, 196, 200. Al-Akwaʿ (1995, III: 1711) says al-Wishalī, not Sarājī, was the second victim. Still, al-ʿInān provides a picture of al-Kibsī in his high-collared Italian airforce uniform and very dashing he looks too.
68 Hickinbotham 1958: 20, quoted Nājī 1984: 243. The speaker was Khān Bahādur Sir Muḥammad Makāwī, a figure interestingly specific to the period: after World War II such Anglo-Indian-Arab identities were simply no longer possible.
69 Nājī 1984: 245; al-Wazīr A. 1987; Douglas 1987: 46–53 and *passim*. Farago (1939) gives a picture of Aden's intellectual life. Again see Thaʿālabī 1997 for how far back the links go among activists in different parts of Yemen.

70 Bakrī 1955: 124–7.
71 For the text, Douglas 1987, appendix 2. For the place of Yemen in the Muslim Brothers' strategy, al-ʿUbaydī 1993.
72 al-Akwaʿ 1995, II: 838–9; ibid., I: 196–209 and *passim* for further detail.
73 For 1948 see Shamāḥī 1972; Markaz 1982b; Maqbalī 1986; and al-Wazīr A. 1987. It is noticeable that the last of these, which documents the al-Wazīrs over a half century, makes no mention at all of Ḥāshid – save Dhū Fāriʿ of al-ʿUṣaymāt who supposedly was offered money to kill Yaḥyā. Wenner (1967: 97–108) is recommended.
74 al-Shāmī 1975: 46. For the longer quotation following, Mujāhid 1997: 241.

3 A NEW FORM OF POLITICS: THE 1950S

1 Trevaskis 1968. Several governors wrote memoirs (Hickinbotham 1958, Johnston 1964, Trevelyan 1970). But Trevaskis, who began as a senior political officer, had a keen analytic eye and repays close reading.
2 al-Adhal 1993: 80. For loathing of immigrants, ibid. 79, 121 ff, 184. While Indians remained in Aden, Yemenis were forced home from India (CO 1015/322, 325), and as Bujra (1970: 196) and Gavin (1975: 351) both point out, it was Indians threatening jobs of the new middle class who attracted prejudice, not Somalis who competed for jobs with labourers. For the quote below, Holden 1966: 25.
3 Colonial Office 1946: 73–4.
4 Colonial Office 1946: 72. Bin ʿAbdāt gets a poor press in British writing (not least from Ingrams, whom he once locked up) as a "mediaeval" figure. The family's money came largely from Indonesia. Their dispute with the Kathīrī sultans was of long standing, and the Foreign Office admitted Bin ʿAbdāt's claim to be an "Independent Rajah" had much truth to it. For Bin ʿAbdāt as proto-nationalist, Hādī 1978: 269, Daʾūd 1989.
5 Gavin 1975: 311; al-Janāḥī 1992: 109; Jibrīl 1962: 42–4; ʿAbd al-Fattāḥ 1974: 29. For changes in the form of rural politics, Bujra 1967, 1971: 115 ff. For relations with Indonesia, Van der Kroef 1953.
6 Ingrams 1966: (intro.) 36. In fact, minor dissent continued, often over loss of income to government-protected motor traffic, and in the late 1950s became connected with town-based nationalism (CO 1015/1081; Jibrīl 1962; Kostiner 1984; al-Khanbashī 1989; ʿAlī and Malāḥī 1989).
7 A scheme for debt-relief would not work, it was claimed, "without a measure of direct intervention by the British Agent which would be incompatible with his proper functions as Adviser" (*Records* 10: 660–3).
8 *Records* 10: 524. Compare Kipling "The Widow's Party", last verse. ʿIzz al-Dīn (1989) provides a sketch of the Western Protectorate in the early 1940s, when he himself was a political officer and the process of reform first gathered pace.
9 *Records* 10: 468–70.

10 Townshend 1986; *Records* 10: 451–62. More than 87 tons of bombs and rockets, and 3,400 cannon rounds, were expended. The Bal Ḥārith numbered only 250 arms-bearing men. None was killed, but their camels and thorn trees were destroyed.

11 Balfour-Paul 1991: 66, 148. For Treasury penny-pinching, ibid. 163. For the 1954 application, above, CO 1015/1041. The whole Western Protectorate budget for 1953–4, including Government Guards, was less than £ 300,000 (Trevaskis 1956: 13). Some idea of how poorly Aden fitted in wider British schemes is given by the fact the Colonial Office placed it under the Central Africa department.

12 Trevaskis 1968: 26 ff, 84–7.

13 Trevaskis 1968: 15, 105–6, 138. For detail, *Records* 12: 348 ff. "Dissident" was used by the British among themselves; in Arabic they condemned their opponents as *mufsidīn*, people of corruption and disorder.

14 For the Abyan scheme, successive Colonial Office *Annual Reports* particularly Appendix 1 for 1953–4. Also al-Ḥabashī 1968. Lackner (1985: 172) is scathing. The South Yemeni government after independence, however, gave several Russian visitors the impression that what the British built through the 1950s was built by themselves in the 1970s.

15 CO 1015/1041. There is little doubt that local notables bought into new cotton land quite heavily (Hickinbotham 1958: 122). Unfortunately no proper survey work was ever done and analyses through political economy rest on weak foundations.

16 Trevaskis 1956: 114; 1959: 50.

17 *Records* 11: 488–90 for such pamphlets. That this one is from Aḥmad is suggested by hostile mention of ʿAbdullāh al-Ḥakīmī, a Free Yemeni based first in Cardiff.

18 Slavery was formally abolished under the Republic in 1962. Again and again in talking with ex-slaves, however, one finds their manumission precedes that by several years.

19 al-Janāḥī 1992: 155 ff. For details on the Liberals' relations with the Imam and his relatives, Nuʿmān 1965: 66–71; Shamāḥī 1972; Shāmī 1984: 414 ff.

20 *Records* 10: 285. Nuʿmān was then attached to al-Badr's retinue (Douglas 1987: 161). This speech continued a long tradition of poetic persuasion reaching back through Imam Yaḥyā's time. See particularly Taminian 1999.

21 Shāmī 1965: 8–9, 12–13, 102–3, 119. Republishing this when he and Nuʿmān were on opposite sides in a civil war is typical of al-Shāmī's sense of humour. But for 1953 note the breadth of reference.

22 *Records* 10: 285, 11: 17, 261. When Yaḥyā was murdered, said Aḥmad in the 1953 version of Victory Day, "people lost security as if the garment which had protected them had suddenly been snatched from them. Meanwhile, the roads were cut, fortunes were robbed and many were slain, while the enemies of Islam looked covetously at this dear country . . ." (Rashid 1985: 96).

23 *Foreign Relations* 5: 1360, 12: 801–3, 13: 748–9, 757–9, and *passim*; Mujāhid 1997: 254; ʿAfīf 1982: 286 ff.

24 Fayein 1955: 45. For the quote below, Ingrams 1963: 14. Compare ʿAṭṭār 1964: 73; Holden 1966: 84–7.

25 vom Bruck forthcoming, p. 27, where the practice of important women using male names is discussed. Apparently the practice still continues. See Mujāhid 1997: 273. For the Taʿizz "palaces", ibid. 293 and *passim*. Fayein (1955) gives some insight into court life.

26 al-Akwaʿ 1995, III: 1534. For an incident in 1953 of schoolboys arguing over *sayyid*s versus non-*sayyid*s, Rashid 1985: 137. Presumably such rhetoric was promoted by *qāḍī*s who were later, when the revolution broke, to take all the *sayyid*s' posts. There are two famous families called Bayt al-Shāmī, one *sayyid* and one *qāḍī*.

27 Rashid 1985: 60. For Ibn ʿAlwān's tomb, Juzaylān 1984: 85–6; al-Akwaʿ 1995, II: 750–1.

28 *Records* 11: 29. For the Iraqi quote below, *Records* 10: 35, and for the nature of the State, ʿAbd al-Salām 1988: 23; Mujāhid 1997: 246.

29 The title was used by al-Badr himself, though his uncles disliked it, from late 1949. "Al-Badr" means "the moon". Traditionally, people named Muḥammad were called Badr al-Dīn or ʿIzz al-Islām, Aḥmads were Shams al-Dīn, ʿAlīs were Jamāl al-Dīn and ʿAbdullāhs were Fakhr al-Dīn (Rossi 1939: 174). For ʿAlī's drunkenness, below, Rashid 1985: 113.

30 ʿAṭṭār 1964: 110. For the argument following, ibid. 143, ʿUmar 1970: 68–73. For Ibb, Messick 1978: 149–52, 155–6. For Ḥugariyyah, Sharjabī 1990: 199 ff, 275–82, 386, 402–7. For Maḥwīt, Tutwiler 1987: 129–32. Farouk-Sluglett (1993) suggests complexity of land-rights even in the coastal lowlands, which were generally extremely poor.

31 Douglas 1987: 198. For the "famous forty", Juzaylān 1984; for other students abroad, Maqbalī 1986. By the mid-1950s there were probably 200 Yemeni students in Cairo. Long before that there was a merchant community (Heyworth-Dunne 1952: 53).

32 Messick 1978: 280–1, 287–9; *Records* 11: 416–17; Chaudhry 1997: 115, 120–1. Chaudhry (1997: 111) says monopolies produced "a small but-powerful merchant class – drawn largely from the *sayyid* strata in the capital": unfortunately of the ten family names she gives few are *sayyid*s.

33 CO 537/656, CO 1015/814; *Records* 10: 287, 12: 433. For minor disturbances in the early 1950s, Rashid 1985: 63, 72, 84, 137.

34 For Aden at the time, Colonial Office 1958; Gavin 1975: 319–27; Trevaskis 1968: 97. Also al-Adhal 1993.

35 Colonial Office 1956: 8; Trevaskis 1968: 40; Gavin 1975: 312 ff. Watt 1962 is particularly useful. For an overview of groups and parties within Aden, Bujra 1970; Douglas 1987: ch. 7. Bernier (1958) places Aden in Protectorates context.

36 Gavin 1975: 328.

37 Holden 1966: 55. For the contrast with the preceding generation, Hickinbotham 1958: 20–1, 49, 182 ff. For his own account of the movement he helped lead, Aṣnaj 1991.

38 Trevaskis (1968: 94) catches Adenis' parochialism well: "having, with the rarest exceptions, never passed a day of their lives out of sight of Jabal Shamsān they had come to look on Aden not as the untidy municipal area it was, but as a country in its own right".

39 Trevaskis 1959: 154. The Quʿayṭī Sultanate in Ḥaḍramawt acquired 21 primary schools (Jibrīl 1962: 25). Both there and in Aden, governmental employment was important (ibid., 21; ʿAbd al-Fattāḥ 1974: 20–1). What Trevaskis rather excludes is the presence at schools of rulers' children but he is nearer right in summary than the later socialist version that only the privileged were educated: the newly educated, whatever their family background, were largely peripheral to existing forms of politics.

40 For village associations, Douglas 1987: 99–100; Dayyān and ʿAbd Rabbihi 1992: 63; Carapico 1998: 80–1, 94. For parties in the South, ʿAbd al-Fattāḥ 1974; Kostiner 1984. Janāḥī (1992: 723) lists members everywhere. Also al-Adhal 1993: 137–8, 199.

41 Trevaskis to Hobson 6.9.1954 (Trevaskis n.d., file 5/1). For detail on disputes and risings, Trevaskis 1959: 34–68; 1968: *passim*. Also Bidwell 1983: 99–100.

42 Rashid 1985: 50, 99.

43 For figures at the period, Colonial Office 1955–6; Luqmān 1970: 47.

44 "Separatism" is now much criticised. In fact the manifestos of the SAL and the ATUC – the latter judged correct, the former not – were near identical, and the ATUC itself later called for a Southern state before being told by Cairo not to (CO 1015/1499; *SWB* 27 April 1959; also *Records* 15: 588–9). Distaste for the SAL (e.g. Janāḥī 1992) derives not from their detailed strategy but from the fact that in 1959 they concluded an alliance with the Saudis.

45 Voice of the Arabs, 18 April 1959, *SWB*.

46 Ledger 1983: 159 on later control of irrigation pumps. Gavin 1975; Ḥabashī 1968; Maktari 1971: 11. Ḥawāṭmah (1968: 185) suggests three-fifths of the land belonged to the Sultans and their allies.

47 Bakrī 1955: 31–2, 39, 65. A widespread later image is of people not knowing what a *jumhūriyyah* or "republic" was and assuming it must be a girl's name (Deffarge and Troeller 1969: 147; Halliday 1974: 127; Messick 1978: 73). Not to have known what a republic was by late 1956 one would have had to be a hermit.

48 Quoted ʿAṭṭār 1964: 73. Compare Nuʿmān 1965: 74; Rashid 1985: 98.

49 *Records* 11: 99, 169–71.

50 For accounts of 1955, Nuʿmān 1965: 38; Shāmī 1984: 476 ff; Douglas 1987: 187–91; Janāḥī 1992: 118 ff. As a younger Shāfiʿī activist explained to me, "Nuʿmān did not like soldiers". One of those involved in the initial attack on the peasants was apparently Ṣāliḥ, stepfather of the later president, ʿAlī ʿAbdullāh Ṣāliḥ.

51 Trevaskis 1968: 68. One might prefer to see this as mere imagery. But it accords with the memory of people who knew al-Badr and with the tenor of recorded speeches.

52 *Records* 12: 73; Douglas 1987: 214–17.

53 al-Ṭayyib 1995: 393. For a summary of Ḥudaydah, below, Carapico 1998: 81–2.

54 ʿUmar 1970: 79–80, 131; ʿAṯṭār 1964: 117–18, 125; Carapico 1998: 82; *Records* 12: 453.

55 *Records* 12: 399, 481; ʿAṯṭār 1964: 80–1; Janāḥī 1992: 161–4.

56 al-Akwaʿ 1995, III: 1533. For the border meeting, Trevaskis 1968: 101–2; ʿIzz al-Dīn 1989: 128. Muḥammad al-Shāmī spread the same message, and ʿIzz al-Dīn misattributes the quotation.

57 ʿAṯṭār 1964: 73. For the court, Aponte 1948: 102; Fayein 1955: 47. For al-ʿAmrī, *Records* 11: 49–50. For the quotation below, *Records* 12: 482.

58 *Records* 14: 66, 15: 9; ʿAbd al-Salām 1988: 115. For the above quotation from King Saʿūd, *Foreign Relations* 13: 763.

59 Many educated Yemenis can recite parts of "The Stranger". The whole text, unfortunately, seems never to have been published. ʿAbd al-Walī's later novel (1989[1978]) gives an excellent feel for the period. For the quote below, al-ʿAynī 1999: 143. Also ibid. 51, 71–2, 145, 172.

60 We have only ʿAbd al-Ghanī's testimony (see Janāḥī 1992: 731–4) and there is reason for him to spread wide the net of memory. But the connections he depicts can be traced through the 1960s.

61 Middle East News Agency, 9 May 1959, *SWB*.

62 Ḥamīd al-Aḥmar had known many Liberals when a hostage, been taught at one time by Aḥmad Nuʿmān, and accompanied the 1956 delegation which concluded the Jiddah Pact with ʿAbd al-Nāṣir (al-Akwaʿ 1995, I: 435–6, II: 702–3, 850). Talk of tribal "isolation" and "conservatism" (Nuʿmān 1965: 78 ff; ʿUmar 1970: 203; Douglas 1987: 227) is not wholly realistic.

63 Sanaa Radio, 13 August 1959, *SWB*.

64 Jibrīl 1962: 53, 69 ff.

65 Allfree 1967: 141. For the comments following, *Records* 14: 751 ff. Two themes run through Jibrīl's account (1962): government administration of Ḥaḍramī migration and loathing of Indian migrants moving the other way.

66 Compare Johnston 1964 and Trevaskis 1968, the first by a Foreign Office appointee to the post of governor, the second by a Colonial Office official whose experience lay with the Federal rulers. Balfour-Paul (1991) provides a good summary.

67 Holden 1966: 25. For Aden's political press at the time, Luqmān 1972; Jāwī n.d. Aḥmad's poem, below, is taken from al-Akwaʿ 1995, II: 849. For the full text, ʿIzz al-Din 1990: 227–30. For the Egyptian quote, below again, *Records* 14: 59.

68 ʿUmar 1970: 129; *Records* 14: 67, 112. Janāḥī (1992: 162) mentions a sudden burst of proto-capitalism by the Imam at this period. Tracing the merchants involved has proved impossible.

69 Sharafaddin 1961: 12, 55.

70 Adhal (1993: 52), who attributes the crowd's lack of sympathy to them not being "cultured persons". For details of the vote, Bidwell 1983: 145.

71 al-Baraddūnī, cited Renaud and Fayein 1979: 19–20. For the quote above, al-Adhal 1993: 52. For revolution fever, below, Bujra 1967, II: 17. For migrants going North, ʿAbd al-Fattāḥ 1974: 48.

4 REVOLUTIONS AND CIVIL WARS: THE 1960S

1 Serjeant 1979; al-Shāmī 1984: 17–37. Bayḍānī proved a sad figure. By late 1963 he was in Aden promoting a separate Shāfiʿī state (Bayḍānī 1992) and was disowned by most Yemenis of both main sects. For brief accounts of him, Sarūrī 1987: 88; Janāḥī 1992: 231–2. For his own account of the revolution, Bayḍānī 1984.

2 Holden 1966: 96; Sarūrī 1987: 111. For detail on Sanaa in the first year, Deffarge and Troeller 1969. For petitioning later, Zayd 1998: 312–14.

3 ʿAbd al-Ilāh 1964: 53, 143.

4 On the night of the coup, ordinary soldiers had been locked in their barracks: see ʿAṭṭār 1964: 252; ʿAbd al-Ilāh 1964: 69. For much of what follows, ibid. 75–81. Also Ḍubbāṭ 1978; Sarūrī 1987: 123 ff; Juzaylān 1995; Aḥmad M. 1992; and the interviews in Markaz 1982a.

5 Zayd 1998: 311. For the quote above, ibid. 230–1. The novel uses literary devices: "here is the sword and here the field", says the sergeant of the prison, a line from Imam Aḥmad used later in the last of Zubayrī's poems. But much of the detail is historical. The area-names of the forgotten victims all refer to places much involved with migrant labour.

6 *Foreign Relations* 18: 160, 174. For Saudi views, Gause 1990, which is also extremely good on later Yemeni detail.

7 Trevaskis to Secretary of State for Colonies, 14 Oct. 1963, CO 1055/213. The 1962 plan is not in this file at the PRO, but a copy is in the Trevaskis papers at Rhodes House. There one also finds an unweeded message dated 5 Oct. 1962 (sic) already implicating British Intelligence in covert action against the North (Trevaskis n.d. file 6/10). For an account by the British chargé in Taʿizz, left quite in the dark, Gandy 1998: 249–50.

8 ʿAbd al-Fattāḥ 1974: 52 ff; Lackner 1985: 38. The Mahrah Youth Front perhaps rested on Mahrīs who had worked in Kuwait, where a tradition existed of placement in the Emiri Guard. The Yāfiʿ Front we shall come back to. For other connections, Riḍā 1969: 72–3; Kostiner 1984.

9 Ḥamdī 1964, I: 5; Luṭfī 1967: 24, 47; Hādī 1978: 49–50, 57. Southern tribesmen's losses fighting royalists were heavy.

10 ʿAbd al-Ilāh 1964: 146–60. For the ʿAmrān resolutions, ʿAfīf 1982: 339–45; Dresch 1989: 249. The spread of people involved is largely accounted for by connections dating to 1958 (Janāḥī 1992: 732).

11 *Foreign Relations* 18: 711. For a bibliography of Egyptian works, Aḥmad 1992. For Egyptian disdain for Yemenis, Holden 1966: 101; Schmidt 1968: 85, 87; Deffarge and Troeller 1969: 75 and *passim*.

12 Sarūrī 1987: 126–9. For Sayāghī, below, al-Akwaʿ 1995, III: 1542–3; O'Ballance 1971: 109–10, 114.

13 Dresch 1989: 246–7 (also Caton 1990: 151–2). For detail on the way tribes conducted their affairs through the war, Dresch 1989: 245, 254–61; Deffarge and Troeller 1969; Rouleau 1967; Schmidt 1968.

14 ʿAbd al-Ilāh 1964: 32–5; ʿAṭṭār 1964: 197–201; Deffarge and Troeller 1969: 237–8; ʿUmar 1970: 132, 135–6, 143, 147; Messick 1978: 276–7, 301–2.

15 Tutwiler 1987: 282–4. Maḥwīt is Zaydī. Its experiences run closely parallel to those of Shāfiʿī Raymah, for instance, whose social structure is much the same. For Banī ʿAwwām, near Ḥajjah, rather later, al-Ṭayyib 1995: 390–2.

16 ʿUmar 1970: 190–1, 201–2; Mujāhid 1997: 277–8; Deffarge and Troeller 1969: 227–9.

17 Zayd 1998: 297–8 and *passim*; Aḥmad 1992: 298 ff; O'Ballance 1971: 136, 145. ʿAbd al-Ilāh (1964) and Butūl (1994), discussing different periods, both mention how officer cadets were used in the fighting; there were seldom soldiers available. While Egypt was there, Yemen's regular army was scarcely more than 5,000 strong. Nājī (1979) lists the units, but most were vastly undermanned.

18 Voice of the Arabs, 9 May 1959, *SWB*.

19 e.g. Ḥawāṭmah 1968; Shahārī 1972, building on Jabhah 1965. Halliday 1974 reproduces the post-independence view. For closer-range analysis, Ḥabashī 1968; Bujra 1971; ʿUmar 1970; Maktari 1971.

20 CO 1055/277 contains the petition in translation. The tribes' disgust at subordination to Ḍāliʿ still rankled a year later (Ḥamdī 1964, I: 5). The *nāʾib* (Maḥmūd bin Ḥasan), whose appointment the British felt would soothe problems, was brother of the Quṭaybī shaykh (Sayf bin Ḥasan) who led the protest; the treasurer was the shaykh's brother-in-law. As ʿAbd al-Fattāḥ remarks (1974: 27), it is difficult to use the term "class" of tribal settings.

21 Dayyān and ʿAbd Rabbihi 1992: 206, 211, 213 and *passim*. Also Riḍā 1969: 43; CO 1055/195 and 196.

22 Strictly speaking, political officers were now called advisers. In popular usage, however, political officer (*ḍābiṭ siyāsī*) remained current until the British left. Governors, strictly speaking, were now high commissioners.

23 Dayyān and ʿAbd Rabbihi 1992; Traboulsi 1991: 133. For the salience of truce-making elsewhere, Ḥamdī 1964, III: 37, VII: 32.

24 Ḥamdī (1964) and Luṭfī (1967) provide vivid accounts. There is no doubt (not least because of misunderstood local stories) that this is serious first-hand reporting. For Muthannā, below, Ḥamdī 1964, V: 27.

25 *Foreign Relations* 18: 710 (Sept. 1963). The Americans tried to act as honest brokers. But the same official worried, "Fayṣal [the Saudi Crown Prince; later King] may even be conning us . . . Worse yet, the UK may be at least covertly encouraging the Saudis and the royalists." He was right on both scores.

26 For narratives, Bidwell 1983; Ledger 1983; Pieragostini 1991. The last, quoting excellent dispatches from the US Consul, explains the muddle of

British thinking. British global strategy, in so far as it existed, is beyond the scope of the present book, but see also Darby 1973; Balfour-Paul 1991.

27 3 May 1964 *SWB*. The broadcast cited below is 30 May 1964.

28 Trevaskis to Secretary of State for Colonies, 20 Apr. 1964, CO 1055/194.

29 The new Secretary of State for Colonies visited in December 1964. His discussions with the Sharīf of Bayḥān (CO 1055/84) suggest total incomprehension. The Sharīf was concerned about a place called Ḍabt Abū Ṭayf, which he said the Imam had taken from him, and was keen to attack the North; Mr Greenwood, for his part, was expecting something more conventional in the way of minutes and draft proposals.

30 Kostiner 1984, Pieragostini 1991 and Jawharī 1992 cover the period from published sources; Ledger 1983 gives a first-hand British account; al-Adhal 1993 and Muḥsin 1989 give conflicting Yemeni versions.

31 For estimates of Egyptian casualties and troop numbers, Schmidt 1968: 234–5; Aḥmad 1992: 286, 290, 591–7.

32 Haykel 1997: 282–3. Qāsim Ghālib played a hero's role in finding places abroad for Yemeni students, but his work on Ibn al-Amīr (Aḥmad 1964; for hostile comment, Serjeant 1979) scarcely ranks as sound history.

33 For detail on Zubayrī and his death, al-Ṭayyib 1990. For the Khamir resolutions, ʿAfīf 1982: 349–52. Also Gause 1990: 66. The sudden twists and turns of relations between Saudis and Egyptians are explained in Kerr 1971.

34 ʿAfīf 1982: 131–4; Janāḥī 1992: 294. The latter's attempt to deduce class relations is complex: one of its results is to cast Sallāl as a figure of the left, which is seldom the view of more distant analysts.

35 Jabhah 1965: 4–5, 9, 27, 92. I am indebted for a copy to Fred Halliday. For a summary, Riḍā 1969: 81–109; Lackner 1985: 40–2.

36 al-Ṭayyib 1995: 19, 47–8, 53–7, 102, 108–10. As so often, one is forced to read Shāfiʿī events mainly through Zaydī sources (none of the Shāfiʿīs involved seems to have published memoirs), but the shape of disputes is clear. Also Riḍā 1969: 150; Kostiner 1984: 112.

37 al-Akwaʿ 1995, I: 97; Janāḥī 1992: 288, 292. For the NLF and MAN's fears of betrayal through such talks, ibid., 297–9; Jāwī 1975: 50; Muḥsin 1989: 52.

38 Among them Hādī ʿĪsā, a "war contractor" who had gained a reputation for killing prisoners for fun when drunk. Others, however, included Ḥusayn al-Ahjarī, Ḥusayn al-ʿAwāḍī, ʿAlī Hārūn, and Muḥammad al-Ruʿaynī. Their geographical and social origins were extremely various. Al-Ahnūmī had loathed Ruʿaynī since at least 1962, when they disputed who should have charge of Ḥudaydah.

39 Rouleau 1967, II: 5.

40 Janāḥī 1992: 334–7. The meeting in Nihm was presumably that referred to by O'Ballance (1971: 176) as the Yemeni Revolutionary Front.

41 The speaker, a distinguished administrator, had best remain nameless. I am indebted to Kevin Rosser for the quotation. For the range of accusations, O'Ballance 1971: 161, 164–6. One of the oddest events was the expulsion of Americans on grounds of espionage in April 1967 (ʿUmar 1970: 174; Janāḥī

1992: 337). The CIA had been in Taʿizz for years by then. Why America was turned on now is unclear.

42 ʿUmar 1970: 173, 187. The key union organiser in Taʿizz was ʿAlī Sayf Muqbil (Deffarge and Troeller 1969: 227 ff). Communists tried to unionise labourers in Ḥudaydah, with little success; the MAN concentrated far more successfully, as they had in Aden, on clerks and drivers.

43 The two fronts are usually referred to in Arabic as *al-jabhat al-qawmiyyah* (NLF) and *jabhat al-taḥrīr* (FLOSY).

44 ʿUmar (1970: 182) describes a group of merchants and shaykhs as a "bourgeois" faction. There is little doubt, however, that Dammāj protected the Jiblah conference and helped fund the NLF in the South when Egypt turned against it. Two of his sons, Zayd and Aḥmad, were later well-known writers; his cousin Qāsim was a MAN theoretician.

45 Occasionally one finds references in print (Ismāʿīl 1986: 70; Muḥsin 1989: 48), but personal memories are consistent: these three titles recur constantly, with far more scattered recollections of Fanon, Debray and others. For developments in NLF/MAN thinking, ʿAbd al-Fattāḥ 1974: 61; for Yāfiʿ, below, Dayyān and ʿAbd Rabbihi 1992: 99.

46 Riḍā 1969: 70, 72; ʿAbd al-Fattāḥ 1974: 44; Dayyān and ʿAbd Rabbihi 1992: 97, 108, 170–2, 225. Concentrating on nationalist revolution obscures the fact that older structures in Ḥaḍramawt remained valid also: see Dostal 1984; Serjeant 1989.

47 Riḍā 1969: 184 ff. Muḥsin (1989: 146) reproduces the document. ʿAbd al-Fattāḥ Ismāʿīl, a famous NLF leader, was at this stage in a Sanaa prison.

48 al-Ṭayyib 1995: 215–16, 271, 358 ff; Dayyān and ʿAbd Rabbihi 1992: 111, 175, 217. Were there room for detail, one might examine the importance of customs concessions granted border tribes by Sanaa (ibid.: 167) and tribal manoeuvrings around FLOSY and the NLF (Riḍā 1969: 168–9; Kostiner 1984: 135–6). In most published sources the history of the period has been much simplified.

49 FO 371/185232 (BA 1016/1 and 4).

50 Bowen Report, Nov. 1966 (FO 371/185237). The files on torture (FO 371/185236, 237) make foul reading. Also Halliday 1974: 203–5; Crouch 1993: 195–6.

51 Crouch 1993: 155. From the Yemeni side the rhetoric is more intense but the facts not dissimilar (Ḥamdī 1964, II: 49, IV: 26–7, VI: 27; Luṭfī 1967: 22, 24–5, 35–6, 54 and *passim*).

52 18 January 1965, quoted Ledger 1983: 41. For the views cited just above, ʿAbd al-Ilāh 1964: 62–3; al-Adhal 1993: 198; Kostiner 1984: 109–10; Riḍā 1969: 57–9; ʿUmar 1970: 240; ʿAbd al-Fattāḥ 1974: 69.

53 Ledger 1983: 69; al-Adhal 1993: 203.

54 FO 371/185244 (BA 10112/29). The networks linking Aden and the countryside, below, are apparent in Muḥsin 1989, Janāḥī 1992, Dayyān and ʿAbd Rabbihi 1992. See also Kostiner 1984. Unfortunately, Muḥsin 1989 is the only source giving detail on the NLF in Aden. Few now admit they were

part of it, and leaders of the later socialist period when its history was written display a baffling cynicism: *kunnā shabāb* ("we were young"), says a famous figure.

55 Zabal 1965–6. I am indebted to John Shipman for copies. CO 1055/74, FO 371/185241, 185243, 185244 cover Ḥaḍramī affairs in detail. Also Crouch 1993; Kostiner 1984: 134–5; Ledger 1983: 98–100; Riḍā 1969: 187; Bā ʿAbbād 1989.

56 Both men died as a result of parochial discontents (Crouch 1993: 170, 186), though a minute of the time remarks that morale in the HBL generally was not good and if they killed yet another commander (!) they might have to be disbanded (FO 371/185241, BA 1019/25).

57 Turnbull 24 Sept. 1966, FO 371/185244, BA 10112/43. The Saudis themselves showed little interest in these schemes, but 371/185244 contains extraordinary fantasies on the part of wealthy Ḥaḍramīs in Riyāḍ and Jiddah.

58 Ledger 1983: 134 ff; Muḥsin 1989: 96–7. For the military more broadly, ibid.: 103–4; Riḍā 1969: 196.

59 Kostiner 1984: 157–60. The collapse was so rapid that many attribute it to British Intelligence (al-Adhal 1993: 213, 222–5, 232, 245 and *passim*). The British indeed betrayed their allies and brought the NLF to power; but FLOSY's canard that the NLF were a British invention persists in bizarre claims that the outcome was planned years earlier.

60 Jāwī 1975: 100. Also ibid.: 38–9, 44–5, 50, 81. Markaz 1989 provides a later official version. For the quote from Prince Muḥammad Ismāʿīl, below, Deffarge and Troeller 1969: 263.

61 al-ʿAwāḍī died as he lived. Years later a passing car flicked a stone at him and, thinking he was being attacked, he opened fire, killing a Zaydī officer. Mediation was arranged. Fearing betrayal, however, al-ʿAwāḍī and a few friends holed up in a house in Sanaa and fought against absurd odds until buried in the rubble: how many of his enemies he took with him depends on whom one asks.

62 Deffarge and Troeller 1969: 242.

63 Janāḥī 1992: 440, 479, 483, 490–2. Though written from a very different viewpoint, the account fits neatly on this score with that of Butūl (1994: 45 ff, 97, 100–3, 117).

64 Janāḥī 1992: 481–2.

65 al-ʿAmrī sent Shaykh ʿAbdullāh of Ḥāshid, Ḥasan Makkī and Muḥammad al-ʿAṭṭār to ʿAbd al-Raqīb, who had objected violently to the arrest of ʿAlī Muthannā Jibrān. ʿUmar al-Jāwī and his colleagues hoped to provoke a limited crisis and extract from it political advantage. They forgot to tell ʿAbd al-Raqīb, however, who arrested most of the delegation – tank units under the command of Zaydī officers then crushed al-Jāwī's followers.

66 Mujāhid 1997: 280. For the quote above, Deffarge and Troeller 1969: 264–5.

67 Lefort 1971: 3. Also Shuʿaybī 1973, whose account of Democratic Yemen's early years seems to have led to his murder in Beirut (al-Adhal 1993: 409; Bidwell 1983: 266).

68 CO 725/97/4. For the quotations below, CO 1055/157, Petrie Report (September 1959), cited Trevaskis n.d. file 5/13.

5 TWO YEMENI STATES IN THE 1970S

1 ʿAbd al-Salām 1988: 193; also ibid.: 57. ʿAbd al-Salām is widely assumed to be the pseudonym of Abū Bakr Saqqāf, an accomplished and well-known local sociologist.

2 The vanguard party emerged formally as the YSP (Yemeni Socialist Party) in 1978, but the Fifth NLF Congress of 1972 set the goals in detail, and the idea goes back at least to 1968 (Ḥawāṭmah 1968: 250–3). The NLF became the NF, then the UPONF, then the YSP. "The Party" applies to all.

3 Naʿnaʿ 1988: 39. Farmers outnumbered workers perhaps 100 to 1 (Lefort 1971: 3). For statistics on the 1970s, World Bank 1979a.

4 Fayṣal, by far the more dangerous figure politically, was executed. He is often written of as Qaḥṭān's cousin, but the connection through descent was distant: more important was that Qaḥṭān married Fayṣal's sister (ʿIzz al-Dīn 1989: 146).

5 Rouleau 1972, I: 1, 5. For the quotation following, Lackner 1985: 64, 67.

6 Abdulrab 1998: 14, 35, 136. Events are run together here (the formal ban on talking to foreigners, for instance, dates to 1975). For the section below, Abdulrab 1998: 11, 139–43. The jibe about prostitutes in the tomato-sauce factory is a little sharp, but it is true that factory work never gained respectability (Lackner 1985: 115).

7 Deffarge and Troeller 1972: 6. Also Lefort 1971; Rouleau 1972, II: 6–7; ibid., III. For a lyrical account of revolution, see Stork 1973 (from which comes the phrase "socialism in half a country").

8 Hādī 1978: 157. The quotation is of particular interest because the rhetoric of anti-feudalism remained current. For peasant "risings" elsewhere, ibid.: 117, 257–8. "Politics in command" is from al-Ashtal 1976.

9 ʿUmar 1970: 106, 193–4. Compare Tutwiler (1987: 292–9) for Maḥwīt. Radāʿ is an interesting case: lying almost due west of Dhamār, it was heavily involved in Aden labour and with for instance the MAN – "Zaydīs", says a one-time Shāfiʿī activist, "but very enlightened [sic]".

10 Southern political leaders sometimes cited the figure of a million emigrés, which is scarcely possible: the South's total population was less than 2 million. But even 500,000 (Halliday 1979: 5; Ismael and Ismael 1986: 65) is an amazing figure. On Ḥudaydah, Chaudhry 1997: 128.

11 Lefort 1971: 4 (from which also the ʿAbd al-Fattāḥ quote just above); Bidwell 1983: 256–7; Lackner 1985: 59. For figures on trade, below, Shamsuldin 1993: 109.

12 al-Akwaʿ 1995, I: 95–8. The account of Iryānī's selection is in traditionalising form: "There joined around him the wishes of the powerful and the learned of Yemen and of the heads of tribes and clans, and about him

twined different hearts that he be president . . ." (ibid.: 97). For a different view, Baraddūnī 1983: 582–91.

13 Gause 1990: 96–103.

14 Speech to the first session of the National Council, March 1969, quoted ʿUmar 1970: 154. For the details following, ibid.: 153; Stookey 1978: 262; Chaudhry 1997: 125, 200. Also Carapico 1984: 129; Tutwiler 1987: 308 for drought at the time; Burrowes 1987: 37, 45 for shaykhs and finance. For Ibb, below, Messick 1978: 188.

15 Revolutionary Resisters, military communiqué 163. Communiqué 211 (Feb. 1973) mentions attacks on the shaykhs of al-ʿArqab near Maḥwīt. Compare Tutwiler 1978: 341. For parties, ʿUmar 1970: 189; al-Janāḥī 1992: 514 ff. I am indebted to Fred Halliday for documents from the period.

16 Shaykh Manṣūr was known as "al-Mudīr", a title the family gained in Turkish times. He was so much the grand seigneur as to have someone grind his *qāt* to save the trouble of chewing it.

17 Yemeni Revolutionary Resisters, communiqués 20 Aug., 18 Nov. 1972, and military communiqué 163.

18 Mujāhid 1997: 281. The author misdates Muḥammad ʿAlī ʿUthmān's death (see below). For the lack of objective conditions for revolution, above, al-Janāḥī 1992: 514.

19 Peterson 1982: 112. Several figures such as Muḥsin al-ʿAynī were prime minister more than once, but between Sallāl's demise (November 1967) and Ḥamdī taking power (June 1974) there were at least eleven "governments". For al-Ḥajrī, Burrowes 1987: 44–7; Gause 1990: 105. He was murdered in London in 1977 and not greatly mourned south of Sanaa.

20 From a family of Zaydī *qāḍīs*, north of Sanaa, Ḥamdī grew up in Qaʿṭabah on the North–South border and his mother was Shāfiʿī. I have never heard it seriously argued by a Yemeni that his family background accounted for his rise to power or for his popularity.

21 Ḥugariyyah 1973: 28–30. The list as of 1973 (ibid.: 40) was Sanaa, Ḥudaydah, Ibb, Ānis, Wuṣābayn, Raymah, Ḥugariyyah and, suggesting Upper Yemen's marginality, "the Development Association of the Northwest Region". The Northeast was unrepresented. For the broader story, Carapico 1984, 1998.

22 ʿAbd al-ʿAzīz ʿAbd al-Ghanī, the governor of the Central Bank, was appointed in early 1975, replacing Muḥsin al-ʿAynī, appointed a few months earlier. At first, however, the Command Council was entirely military.

23 Qabā'il 1974: 5. This pamphlet and ʿAbd al-Raḥmān Nuʿmān's from Lower Yemen (Ḥugariyyah 1973) bear an identical slogan in the same typescript: "on the road to progress in Yemen". Nuʿmān was a delegate at Hamdān.

24 I am indebted to Engseng Ho for information from interviews. Witnesses remember people being ill for days after this, and some going mad. The moving force behind the murders was supposedly Ṣāliḥ Siyaylī, who later for a time was governor of Ḥaḍramawt.

25 Ḥamdī approached the left when he first took power, but they refused him help: the ex-MAN opposed him and the Baʿthists on the whole supported him. ʿAbd al-Salām's mother is said to have been ʿAbd al-Raqīb ʿAbd al-Wahhāb's sister, hence an immediate connection with the Sanaa events of 1968 (Chapter 4).
26 What follows is drawn from Ḥugariyyah 1973 and Yūsufī 1976. I am indebted to Sheila Carapico for material.
27 ʿAbduh ʿAṭā had been deputy minister for education in the early 1960s. Aḥmad Muḥammad Kabāb had briefly been minister for South Yemen and was now the Minister for Religious Endowments.
28 Burrowes (1987: 57–87) is good on the Ḥamdī period. For a complementary "development-oriented" view, Wenner 1991.
29 Butūl 1994: 151–3; Bidwell 1983: 275; Carapico 1984: 140, 154; Chaudhry 1997: 137; Peterson 1982: 121. Too often structure (army officers against shaykhs, conservatives against progressives, sect against sect) is read into events which at close range are merely gangsterism.
30 The original estimate was lower, and the Yemeni government figure much higher (Tutwiler 1987: 312). In Upper Yemen people often slipped into Saudi Arabia for short periods of work; in the Tihāmah, by contrast, many were permanent Saudi residents.
31 Messick 1978: 108. For a well informed view of both Yemens at the time, giving this sort of human detail, Rouaud 1979. Fayein 1975 depicts the Yemens some years earlier.
32 ʿUmar 1970: 143, 149; ʿAbd al-Salām 1988: 160; Messick 1978: 291.
33 For a sketch of music's history, al-Qāsimī 1988. For the Sanaani tradition in particular, Lambert 1997.
34 For history of the *sharshaf*, originally a Turkish fashion adopted by Imam Aḥmad's women, Mundy 1983. Around 1970 there were cases of zealots attacking unveiled women (Fayein 1975: 138), but the later spread of female office work passed smoothly. Panic about sexual roles, very common in Najd, has usually not been a feature of life in Yemen.
35 Tutwiler 1987: 120; Chaudhry 1997: 197.
36 ʿAbd al-Salām 1988: 116; ibid.: 62; Tutwiler 1987: 310, 315–18; Burrowes 1987: 48. For the background of those involved in state-building, ibid.: 38 ff. We might remind ourselves that even in Turkish times the North imported foodstuffs (Bury 1915: 116).
37 There is ample evidence of statecraft in early Yemen: the Rasūlids, for instance, systematically encouraged agriculture. But *al-iqtiṣād* (the economy) is no part of pre-modern thought. For *iqtiṣād* in Imam Yaḥyā's time, Obermeyer 1981: 187–8.
38 The Russians, like the British, wanted only the Aden base, from which they flew reconnaissance in support of their growing navy; Aden's hinterland they largely left alone. Several authors (e.g. Halliday 1984: 210, 222; Cigar 1985) note their seeming lack of generosity to Aden. For sources of finance, below, Lackner 1985: 75.

39 Halliday 1979: 7; Stookey 1982: 91.
40 Ismael and Ismael 1986: 96. Also ibid.: 86–7; Hādī 1978: 186–9; Carapico 1993a: 12. For the figures below, Lackner 1985: 179 and *passim*. The structure of the economy is reviewed in World Bank 1979a. Also Couland 1984; Naumkin 1985. For an overview, Stookey 1982: 82–91, and for Southern political structures, Halliday 1983.
41 Dresch forthcoming. Compare Traboulsi 1991: 138.
42 Lackner (1985: 111) internalises the Southern view: "In the small town in the YAR [the North] where I lived for six months, on a single day six people were killed over an argument about 2 riyāls (about $0.50), and this case was not unique." Nor was it entirely typical, or there would soon have been no-one left.
43 Dresch 1989: 365–7.
44 *yā jabal sufyān ʿilm-ak wa-khabar / kayfa ḥāshid yawm ḍalat min-ak kasīrah // balagh al-ghuzzī yuḥākī al-muqaddam / bakīl dhī hājamat kulli dayrah.* There is little point here adding Ḥāshid's versions.
45 *yā muslimīn kullan raqad li-ḥāl-hā / fī dhimmat al-batrūl wa-abū maḥālah.* (Abū Maḥālah is a late-model Mercedes truck, the *maḥālah* being a big rear-axle hub). By convention such verse is anonymous, but all those quoted here are from al-Sinnatayan near Khamir. For the trucking business, Dresch 1989: 308–12.
46 *billāh ʿalay-kum yā murūr jiddah / balagh ḥabībī bi-salām wa-ridd-hu.*
47 Ismāʿīl 1986: 33. Compare Lackner 1985: 117. "Tournament of value" is from Meneley 1996. The high rates of bridewealth (YR 100,000 or about $22,000) in parts of Ḥāshid were notorious. But by late in the decade $10,000 was not unusual in Sanaa, $4,500 in Zabīd and $6–7,000 even at Jabal Raymah (Myntti 1979: 27).
48 For a detailed overview of literature, with much translated poetry, Renaud 1982. Also Tuchscherer 1985.
49 *al-fajr lāḥ wallāh ʿalayik al-shāhid / kān al-firāsh li-thnyan wa-aṣbaḥ ilī wāḥid.* For the quote below, Sharjabī 1990: 387. Also ibid.: 393 and *passim.*
50 Carapico and Myntti 1991: 28. For changes in women's lives also Myntti 1979, 1984. Fayein (1990), using earlier material, underlines transformations since the revolution. For rural structures Mundy 1979, a classic of the analytic literature.
51 Kopp and Wirth 1994: 65. For an excellent map of Sanaa's growth, ibid.: 59. Also Grandguillaume et al. 1995. For urbanisation more generally, Prost-Tournier 1978.
52 For an incisive analysis near the time, Mundy 1985. Also, later, Farouk-Sluglett 1993. For highland agriculture, Carapico and Tutwiler 1981.
53 Carapico 1984: 258; Bury 1915: 35; Tutwiler 1987: 70. For the role of *qāt*, Weir 1985. For the Northern economy, Rodinson 1984.
54 For a summary of Aden's growth, Mercier 1997. For trade figures, below, Shamsuldin 1993.
55 Compare World Bank 1979a and 1979b; also Noban 1984, Iryani 1985. Deffarge and Troeller (1969: 69, 195) a decade earlier remarked how many

men seemed to have rudimentary literacy despite the figures. My own experience in the countryside north of Sanaa was that writing letters was reckoned something of an accomplishment in 1978; by 1983 it no longer was.

56 Ismāʿīl 1986: 64, also ibid.: 32; Hādī 1978: 158–60, 224 ff and *passim*. Molyneux (1991) reviews legal changes in the position of women but says little of real life. Lackner (1985: 110, 114–18) suggests practical change beyond the towns was limited, which is much what one gathers from Southern women.

57 Messick 1978: 110. For the Taʿizz story, following, Fayein 1975: 168.

58 Nāṣir executed Sayyid Quṭb, the Brothers' ideologue, in 1965 and certain Yemenis were expelled from Cairo: ʿAbduh Muḥammad al-Mikhlāfī, ʿAbd al-Salām Khālid and Yāsīn Qubāṭī, for instance, all from the same part of Lower Yemen. They refounded the Brotherhood in Yemen, which by then had effectively died out. For a summary, Janāḥī 1992: 516–17.

59 Zindānī remains a name in Yemen at the time of writing. As a young man he accompanied Zubayrī in his search for peace in the civil war, but after 1970 denounced Zubayrī's friend Iryānī (then president of North Yemen, beset by the Southern left) as a "communist agent". Many Yemenis of note think Zindānī a little disconnected from reality.

60 Ismāʿīl 1978: 66–7. "Dialectics" here is *ʿilm al-kalām*. In most Southern usage of the time "dialectic", in the Marxist sense, was the deeply un-Arabic looking *diyyalaktiyyah*.

61 Shahārī 1972: 196. Resistance at al-Maqāṭirah to the Ḥamīd al-Dīn Imams before World War II, led by a Sufi who himself claimed the name Ḥamīd al-Dīn, was glossed in similar style (Jāwī 1975: 41).

62 Fayein 1975: 126.

63 Hādī 1978: 176, 261, 266; Knysh 1993: 147–8.

64 Ismāʿīl 1986: 68. ʿAbd al-Fattāḥ was widely known as "the *faqīh*", a village preacher – a theoretician "aloof from . . . daily problems" (Lackner 1985: 89; also ibid.: 82, 152 and *passim*). His poetry I cannot judge. His prose, one has to say, was deathly: but the poet Adônis, from whose interview this quote is taken, declared him an Arab genius.

65 Renaud n.d. For radio programming and listening, al-Zayn 1985: 214, 218, 220. The patterns were to change rather little over the next decade (Nahārī n.d).

66 Most analyses stress tribal affiliation. The northern tribes were largely autonomous, and their leaders had vast influence; but who held which post in government depended on clandestine party links and brute ambition.

67 al-Adhal 1993: 187. The author, once in SAL circles, then with FLOSY, had a string of pharmacies nationalised in 1972. He remained an angry man. Needless to say, he is Adeni. For a similarly bitter exile view, Makāwī 1979.

68 Cigar 1989; Traboulsi 1991: 127, 136–7, 142.

69 al-Adhal 1993: 408. The degree to which ordinary citizens were terrorised was exaggerated by Western propaganda, and it was worse in the early 1970s than later (Lackner 1985: 74–5). But it was bad enough in all conscience. Amnesty International's reports make grim reading.

70 Gause 1990 and Halliday 1990 should be read in parallel.

71 Hādī 1978: 120. Also Naʿnaʿ 1988. Literature on state politics in the South gives an impression of simply poisonous intrigue and double-dealing.

72 As a tank driver earlier in his career, he is remembered as motoring along ʿAbd al-Mughnī Street in Sanaa, during the fighting of 1968, and shelling point-blank such symbols of leftist progress as the pharmacy and the Bilqīs cinema. That was before he entered politics.

73 Burrowes 1987: 95; Bidwell 1983: 282. Several Shāfiʿīs in prison at the time of the attempted coup (Sulṭān al-Qirshī, ʿAbd al-Warīth ʿAbd al-Karīm, ʿAbd al-Wahhāb Hizām) were executed. ʿAlī Muthannā Jibrān, the artillery commander in the siege of Sanaa who had taken no part in politics for ten years, was arrested at home and killed. Zaydī plotters from important tribes were quietly packed off abroad.

74 PDRY 1978, article two.

75 Halliday 1979: 14. For the arrival of 2,000 Northern tribesmen in Aden, below, Lackner 1985: 85; Gause 1990: 131.

6 YEMEN IN A WIDER WORLD: POLITICS AND ECONOMICS THROUGH THE 1980S

1 Naʿnaʿ 1988: 48–51; Qandīl 1986: 16–17. The documents Naʿnaʿ presents (1988: 133–65), in which ʿAlī ʿAntar denounces Muḥsin, Muḥsin denounces ʿAlī ʿAntar, and al-Siyaylī seeks Muḥammad al-Muṭī's execution, give an extraordinary impression of state politics.

2 Peterson 1982: 126. Exactly what lay behind Khamīs's demise remains unclear. But al-Aṣnaj, foreign minister in the North, was arrested in 1980 for plotting with the Saudis – "a conspiracy", says Lackner darkly (1985: 105), "for which there was both evidence and cause". Actually he was caught as it were passing notes in class: snide remarks about the President were his downfall, not global politics.

3 Burrowes 1987: 102–6, 119–20; Gause 1990: 138–9, 145–7. For divisions within the South and within the NDF, Bidwell 1983: 324–5; Halliday 1990: 35–6, 127–30.

4 Thanks are due to Madawi al-Rasheed for childhood memories. Far earlier, in the 1930s, Ibn Saʿūd's governor in Najrān had reported to his master that the place was full of *zuyūd wa-junūd wa-qurūd wa-yahūd*, "Zaydīs and soldiers and apes and Jews".

5 *ya ṣalāmī li-kinn wa-arbaʿ miʾat min-kinn / man waṣal ʿindi-kinn lāzim takhallin-hu // wa-nā ahdīnā li-kinn lāzim nakhannith-kinn / wa-l-biyas minanā wa-antin tujar-ran-hu*

6 *raḥabī yā l-jibāl al-sūd bi-ṣawfī / qāyid al-lajnat al-awwalah kuthar khayr-hu // in shayʾ ḥall wa-lā yuʿtabar ḍayfī / qad athart aqṭanaʿ min-nā wa-min ghayr-hu*

7 *yā muraḥḥib bi-nā fī sharʿ-kum mawfī / wājib al-radd wa-lā kalimat-ak jayrah // jiʾt-kum min qibal al-dawlah wa-maklawfī / mā ṭalabt-hu wa-ant la-k khayrah*

8 Burrowes 1987: 76, 124–5, 301 and *passim*. For earlier Ḥaḍramī usage, in the 1960s, Bā ʿAbbād 1989. A "popular congress" had been convened in Sanaa in 1967.

9 GPC 1982: 5, 17–18. For the quote on centralised government, below, ibid.: 62–3.

10 ʿAbd al-Salām 1988: 120, 160. Such figures are hard to track. A 1979 arms deal with the Eastern bloc, however, was reckoned at $600 million; in 1986 Sanaa's government was thought to be paying for the tribes and military something like $300 million per annum outside the formal budget (*Middle East Economic Digest* 20 Dec. 1986).

11 It would be useful, though difficult, to know the origins of officers and soldiers. *Pace* ʿAbd al-Salām (1988: 121) it was not the case, and is not now, that the army are all northerners: officers from around Sanaa controlled the tank and artillery units, but the soldiers in most units seemed to be from south of Sanaa.

12 In late 1983 al-Iryānī was dismissed as prime minister in favour of ʿAbd al-ʿAzīz ʿAbd al-Ghanī, whom we mentioned as a technocrat under Ḥamdī.

13 Sālim Ṣāliḥ Muḥammad, quoted Qandīl 1986: 53–4. For the point made below, Carapico 1993a: 12.

14 Chaudhry 1997: 8.

15 Destremau 1993: 131–2; Chaudhry 1997: 273, 276, 283. Official development aid to the North stood at about $1 billion per annum in 1980; by 1985 it had halved and by 1988 was a tenth of what it had been (Carapico 1998: 43). For a summary and analysis of exchange rate history, Maytamī 1997.

16 Sharjabī 1990: 397–8. For import figures, below, el-Daher and Geissler 1990: 532. For the Northern economy, Destremau 1991.

17 Both Chaudhry (1997: 276) and Carapico (1998: 46) mention MECO. It emerged in 1983 from an Army and Police Corporation, founded 1978; and the other main instruments of economic control date to the mid-1970s (Destremau 1991: 213). I cannot estimate what percentage of GDP it controlled, but it must have been very large.

18 Until the mid-1970s ʿAlī Muḥammad would have been ʿAlī ʿAbdullāh's superior in the Baʿth. He comes from Ḥugariyyah and is a useful reminder that the military elite, although largely from Upper Yemen, were never wholly so.

19 Carapico 1998: 38, 117. Elections to the Consultative Council were held in July: the GPC elections ended in December.

20 Stookey 1982: 110.

21 Barakāt 1991: 57, 59, 92–4, 98; Burrowes 1987: 134 ff, 1989: 441–2; ʿAbd al-Salām 1988: 179–84. For the romance of exploration and for later development of the Maʾrib project, *Oil and Gas Investor* Mar. 1988, *World Oil*, Apr. 1988.

22 ʿAbd al-Salām 1988: 179, 182–5, 195–6. Northern shaykhs from many tribes became caught up in national enthusiasm for the first oil strikes, but the oilfields (*pace* Chaudhry 1997: 302) are nowhere near Ḥāshid's territory.

23 BP took a licence to explore the northern Tihāmah in 1984, Total for the southern Tihāmah in 1986 and Exxon for the central highlands. The sums accruing to government at different stages of exploration are not clear.
24 Mermier 1991: 153; Destremau 1991; Chaudhry 1997: 247, 249, 283, 285.
25 Shamsuldin 1993: 119; Chaudhry 1997: 129. Among the few items whose production increased between 1980 and 1985 were cement (a governmental project) and soap and detergents, largely Ḥayl Saʿīd's doing (CPO 1985: 110–12).
26 Burrowes 1987: 141. For the contrary view, below, ʿAbd al-Salām 1988: 188. See also Wenner 1991.
27 ʿAbd al-Salām 1988: 201, referring to Burrowes' work. Burrowes (1987) provides an excellent account of development history but tends, if one may say so, to take what ʿAbd al-Karīm al-Iryānī says as gospel. Dr ʿAbd al-Karīm in turn is a man of great intelligence and charm; as a Minister of his country's government, however, his duty often lies elsewhere than scholarship.
28 ʿAbd al-Salām 1988: 82. He mentions the case of ʿAbd al-Qādir Hamrah's murder in 1984. Al-ʿAbbāsī (1990: 81 ff) gives a long list of other cases. This latter work is propaganda, written when relations among Egypt, Iraq and Yemen turned sour. It contains much tendentious material, but much that is true also. For taxation in Lower Yemen, Sharjabī 1990: 205, 365–70.
29 Sharjabī 1990: 281, 395.
30 Destremau 1990: 57, 64, 238–41. The settlement in question is given a pseudonym but sounds, one has to say, rather like Maḥwīt.
31 Farouk-Sluglett 1993. See also Meneley 1996: 62–4 on wealth owned by non-farming landlords near Zabīd.
32 Lichtenthaler 1999. The mechanisms in customary law had been agreed in the mid-1970s, but the process gathered pace in the mid-1980s and continued through the decade's end (Dresch 1995a: 47).
33 Some 50 *libnah* of *qāt* produced YR 40–50,000 a year, minus the cost of pump-fuel, which here came to YR 6–8,000. This was a small and not untypical operation; it was also not untypical that the farmer, in al-ʿUṣaymāt, drew about YR 3,500 from army sources. But he was far from wealthy.
34 Jāwī 1975: 19. Contrast Kopp and Wirth 1994: 65–7. For new forms of architecture, below, Arnaud 1995.
35 Private transfers rose from YD 112 million to YD 140 million between 1980 and 1985 (CSO 1987: 201), but no figures are given for intervening years; in 1986 they dropped back to YD 96 million (CSO 1988: 219).
36 quoted Naʿnaʿ 1988: 232. For a generally sympathetic view of the ʿAlī Nāṣir period, Lackner 1985.
37 Qandīl 1986: 46. For the Palestinians, above, ibid: 70–1. For the state of the economy around Aden, Cigar 1990: 202, n. 31.
38 Naʿnaʿ 1988: 42, 52. Also Halliday 1983, 1984, 1990: 39–48; Cigar 1985, 1989; Dresch forthcoming.

39 Quoted Halliday 1990: 95. The contrast with the quality of American policy-making in the area two decades earlier is deeply sobering.
40 YSP 1986: 5, 54–5.
41 Compare Lackner 1985: 124. I do not know of any published collections of Russian-style public art. After unification (1990) I photographed a range of examples, but someone by then must have seen their absurdity: my camera was popped open and the film removed.
42 Stanzel 1988: 269, and, below, ibid.: 270–1. For perceptions just after the coup see particularly Naʿnaʿ 1988.
43 ʿUmar 1989: 6, 13. He makes reference to an earlier intervention (1987), but I have failed to find a copy of his collected essays. For continuing "liberalisation" of the South's economy after the coup see, for example, *Middle East Economic Digest* 20 Dec. 1986 and 3 Jan. 1987.
44 American involvement with the Afghan *mujāhidīn* went back to President Carter's time; but in the mid-1980s annual subventions rose from about $60 million to $250 million, with matching funds from Saudi Arabia.
45 ʿUmar 1989: 14. For details on Islamists in the South, Cigar 1990: 191. Also Knysh 1993: 147.
46 ʿAbd al-Salām 1988: 135; Ghamess 1989: 152; Destremau 1990: 186–8; CPO 1988: 173. Janāḥī (1992: 517) gives slightly lower figures. The curriculum in other schools was a battle-ground. ʿAbd al-Karīm al-Iryānī had resigned as minister of education in 1978, having tried to hold the line against Zindānī's friends; Ḥusayn al-ʿAmrī was dismissed in turn in 1985.
47 Rouaud (1979, thus surprisingly early) uses this *ḥadīth* as the epigraph for his book. It is not in the standard or canonical collections, and most educated Yemenis seem to have noticed it only in the mid-1980s.
48 Qāsim Ghālib was never a Muslim Brother, but he sent abroad to those who sympathised with the Brothers many Yemeni students. Most returned as socialists. Qāsim Ghālib himself distrusted Aḥmad Nuʿmān (Chapter 4) not least because Nuʿmān seemed to him so secular as almost to be an unbeliever.
49 For the rise of the Islamists and sundry reactions to them, Grosgurin 1994, Haykel 1995, Weir 1997, vom Bruck 1999.
50 *al-Thawrah* (Sanaa) 25 Dec. 1986. The quotations below are from Bā ʿAbbād 1987: 16, 39, 61.
51 Destremau 1990: 214, 221–6. Also ibid.: 30. For the South, below, Lackner 1985: 123.
52 CPO 1985: 66. Average age at first marriage (ibid.: 70) was surprisingly high: 17.6 years for women, 22.2 for men. For figures below, CSO 1989: 17.
53 The South had trained its own teachers, the North had not. In 1989 there were said to be 102 Yemeni teachers in the capital and 147 non-Yemeni. In the rest of Sanaa governorate, the figures were 71 and 913. In Ṣaʿdah, only three local teachers were recorded and 128 foreigners (CSO 1989: 139).
54 For a good summary of the Islamists' history, Mermier 1997c. Already during campaigns against the NDF (1981–2) certain army units, such as the

6th and 7th Armoured Brigades, had gained a reputation with tribesmen for their adherence to Islamists and for their political cohesion.

55 Detalle 1995. Unlike the co-operative and GPC elections, those for the Consultative Council were by direct ballot. At the next such elections (1993) a great deal more care was taken to anticipate the outcome.

56 Kopp and Wirth (1994: 60) suggest 190,000 for 1980; Troin (1995: 17) says almost 278,000. The 1981 Co-operative Confederation census gave 211,150 (CPO 1985: 29). For Sanaa in the 1980s, Grandguillaume et al. 1995.

57 al-ʿAbbāsī (1990: 62 ff) cites speculations in the exile press: $450 million for the Presidential Palace in Sanaa (surely much too high a guess?), with lesser palaces in Ḥudaydah, Taʿizz and Ibb. One was also inaugurated in Maʾrib, apparently, at the time of Shaykh Zāyid's visit (*al-Thawrah* 22 Dec. 1986).

58 al-Akwaʿ 1987: 334. For the practice of soldiers and policemen charging for their services, ibid.: 354. Also Sharjabī 1990: 262, 387.

59 Both this case and that above are drawn from Carapico and Myntti 1991.

60 Gause 1990: 156.

61 ʿAbd al-Salām 1988: 91; Dresch 1995a: 45–6. Al-ʿAbbāsī's details on later troubles around Maʾrib (al-ʿAbbāsī 1990: 134 ff) are substantially correct.

62 Shamsuldin 1993: 122.

63 Cited Halliday 1990: 136. Compare Gause's discussion (1990: 156–7). Detalle (1997a: 23) mentions also a "wedding present of some tens of millions of dollars" from the Iraqi ruler.

7 YEMEN AS A SINGLE STATE

1 The details, I hope, will be published elsewhere. For a sketch of the Raydah festival some years later, Detalle 1997b.

2 The final irony was that having unloaded the oil at huge political cost, the Yemenis were sent a bill by the Iraqis. The initial drama can be followed in *The Economist* (4 and 25 Aug., 1 Sept. 1990).

3 A man in Wādaʿah, north of Khamir, watching the bombing of Iraq on television is supposed to have cried *laʿan allāh ʿalā būsh* ("God curse George Bush"), which his wife heard as *laʿan allāh ʿal abūsh* ("God curse your father") and dumped the dinner on his head.

4 A five-man presidential council divided 3:2, the parliament produced by merging those of two states was divided 159:111 with 31 appointees, and 40 ministerial posts were divided equally (Carapico 1998: 137).

5 Iṣlāḥ was founded in 1990 in the wake of unification, much as the Islamic Front formed after the 1979 peace-treaty between North and South. For the details following, Dresch and Haykel 1995.

6 For a recent picture of Yadūmī, *Yemen Times* 5 Oct. 1998. As many Yemenis remark, he looks in his suit and tie more like a prosperous Baʿthist than an Islamist. His education, I believe, was not at al-Azhar or the like but rather at the Cairo police college.

7 For Aden, Mercier 1997a, 1997b.

8 *Yemen Times* 19 Feb. 1992. With readers in mind who do not have Arabic I have tried to give references to the country's only English-language paper (now also on www.yementimes.com). For those who have Arabic, *Shūrā* and *al-Ayyām* are richer sources. For a survey of titles at the high point of press freedom, Bā Salīm 1992.
9 The list (which is not altogether accurate) was republished widely, e.g. in the Lebanese magazine *al-Shirā*ʿ and by Bakr 1995: 131–2. The socialists made play with the phrase "the Bayt al-Aḥmar gang". It deserves pointing out that Bayt al-Aḥmar as the name of the President's village has no known connection of descent with the famous family of Ḥāshid shaykhs named Bayt al-Aḥmar. Nor are the President's family and that of the shaykh intermarried.
10 *al-Ḥadath* 14 Feb. 1992, cited Dresch and Haykel 1995: 407.
11 One would not wish to depict Yemenis as naive on this score. Generally they were not. But many were alarmed at the number of parties, and the mere fact of explicit division in politics was thought by many to presage disorder. Existing Western literature dwells on an overlap of expectation between foreigners and modernists, discounting too much what ordinary people said.
12 *al-Mustaqbal* (87) 22 Mar., (89) 19 Apr. 1992; Saqqāf 1996: 33–4, 40. Daḥbāsh means a big, rough sheep.
13 Quoted *Yemen Times* 23–29 Oct. 1991. See also Carapico 1998: 172. For the economy at the time, Maytamī 1993.
14 *barāḥ, barāḥ, yā zuyūd; ʿalī nāṣir ba-yaʿūd.* ʿAlī Nāṣir at the time was living luxuriously in Damascus, largely at Emirati expense, and had recently married someone far younger than himself. He has since established an "Institute" in Damascus, again at largely Emirati expense, to consider in general terms the state of the Arab World.
15 See *22 May* (60) 19 Aug. 1992.
16 Dresch and Haykel 1995: 422. Also Dresch 1995a: 51 and *passim*. For the urban meetings of the time, see particularly Carapico 1998. A great deal of documentation from both spheres deserves to see print at some point.
17 Bakr 1995: 26.
18 Couland 1993; Detalle 1993a, 1993b, 1995.
19 Three months before the poll a senior GPC politician predicted the results to me within a couple of seats. He could not predict with confidence which seats. Quite how the plethora of local detail was mastered is mysterious.
20 The army's formal organisation ran *fasīlah*, *sariyyah* (roughly, a company; about 100 men), *katībah*, *liwāʾ* (regiment, brigade; usually 1,000–2,000 men), *firqah* (division). In certain key areas the labels and the numbers bore no relation to each other.
21 Detalle 1994; Carapico 1998: 180.
22 Quoted Bakr 1995: 36.
23 Shumayrī (1995: 88) gives the casualties at ʿAmrān as 73 killed, 113 wounded. If so, then given 130 or so tanks fought at point-blank range in a very confined space, this was close to a miracle. His estimate of 4,000 dead, 12,000 wounded for the whole war sounds very low.

24 Detailed accounts have each their own political axe to grind. The Saudi press took a strongly pro-YSP position (see the pieces collected as al-Sharq al-Awsaṭ 1994); for the opposite view, of the YSP as the source of all villainy, Shumayrī 1995. But these two and, for example, Bakr 1995, between them give a consistent picture of who was where.

25 Bakr (1995: 70) offers some support for this view. For the quote following, *Wasaṭ* (129) 18 July 1994. For Siyaylī's disappearance, below, *Wasaṭ* (191), 25 Sept. 1995. Although *Wasaṭ* is characterised on occasion as "Saudi owned", its coverage of Yemen has generally been excellent.

26 *Wasaṭ* (129) 18 July 1994.

27 Saqqāf 1996. The author, who taught philosophy at Sanaa University, joined the YSP government in the South as minister of education. As Carapico remarks (1998: 187) he was the only member of that government to stand his ground when Aden fell and to continue the argument within Yemen.

28 Saqqāf 1996: 26–7. For further cases *Yemen Times* 16 June, 22 Dec. 1997, 29 Nov. 1998. For the Adeni comment, below, *Wasaṭ* (129) 18 July 1994.

29 Mercier 1997b: 69–70; *Yemen Times* 19–24 Apr. 1999.

30 Cited Dresch and Haykel 1995: 425. For the Salafīs, below, *Wasaṭ* (193) 9 Oct. 1995.

31 CSO 1996: 134–77.

32 Carapico 1998: 162. For later developments of Islamist women's networks, Clark 1997.

33 Shanty towns grew up around Ḥudaydah, and never quite disappeared. Elsewhere a strain was put on land and housing. See Stevenson 1993, van Hear 1994, Lucet 1995. Yemen had already absorbed a great many Somali refugees from fighting in Africa, and received little help supporting them.

34 Saqqāf 1997. Maytamī 1997 should be read in parallel. See also Detalle 1997a and issues of the *Economist Intelligence Unit Quarterly Reports*, which at this date were compiled by an extremely knowledgeable student of Yemen's history and society.

35 Many Yemenis worry what will happen when Shaykh ʿAbdullāh leaves the scene (he is not at all well at the time of writing). Doubtless there will be some drama, but it is hard to imagine an Islamist opposition displacing present forms of politics.

36 One should make it clear that kinship is the outsider's explanation, seized on alike by peasants and professors. Within a family one can just as well squabble with a brother or sister as get along with them.

37 A widespread rumour among Yemenis is that Bilqīs cannot have children. Actually she has a son. The fact such rumours exist is symptomatic of how mysterious power seems.

38 What rivalries there may be within the family have usually been quietly handled. The only exception is that when ʿAlī Ṣāliḥ fell from favour in 1994, his son tried to force himself on the President's attention and was shot. But Sanaa is not Baghdad.

39 The President said in May 1999 he intends giving up *qāt*. For years, however, these Ramaḍān *qāt* chews, where the ruler could talk informally with the country's notables, were mentioned on television. For the details of army appointments, below, *al-Ḥayāt* (London) 7 Nov. 1999.
40 Reuters (Sanaa) 24 July 1997, cited Ho 1999.
41 *Yemen Times* 8 Dec. 1997, also 24 Aug. 1998. For family relations in modern Sanaa, Wurth 1995. For recent years more generally, Grandguillaume et al. (eds.) 1995 and the edition of *Maghreb-Machrek* edited by Mermier (1997b) are indispensable. For a still more recent overview, Leveau, Mermier and Steinbach 1999.
42 Detalle 1997a: 35. For the quotes on land, below, Sharjabī 1990: 384 ff.
43 Burrowes 1987: 31. For the figures below, *Economist Intelligence Unit Quarterly Report*, third quarter 1997, first quarter 1998.
44 Detalle 1997a: 27. To say the national accounts are not transparent is to understate matters. For civil servants at the time, and sundry forms of corruption, *Yemen Times* 8 Dec. and 22 Dec. 1997.
45 Detalle (1997a: 32) refers justly to "la fameuse société civile . . . souvent embrigadée par le gouvernment et les donateurs étrangers pour servir d'administration . . ." For the quote above, by an author less suspicious of the phrase, Carapico 1998: 195.
46 To take a recent case, a noted figure was photographed as the "mediator" who helped free British hostages. As any tribesman would tell you, he had kidnapped them himself (or his retainers had) to have the government free his nephew; his romantic role as desert shaykh, meanwhile, obscured the fact that he lives in an enormous house in North London.
47 Reuters (Sanaa) 30 June 1999.
48 See also *Yemen Times* 23 Nov. 1998, where a deal for 12 patrol boats and 600 trucks is discussed, besides a supposed further 4,000 cars for the use of government officials. Since that date there has been considerable, and acrimonious, debate about supposed re-exports of weapons from Yemen to other countries.

References

Abāẓah, Fārūq. 1979 *al-Ḥukm al-ʿuthmānī fī l-yaman*, Beirut: Dār al-ʿAwdah.

al-ʿAbbāsī, Muḥammad. 1990 *Shāwīsh al-bāʿth: ʿalī ʿabdullāh ṣāliḥ*, Cairo: al-Zahrāʾ li-l-Iʿlām.

ʿAbd al-Fattāḥ, Fatḥī. 1974 *Tajribat al-thawrah fī l-yaman al-dīmuqrāṭiyyah*, Beirut: Dār Ibn Khaldūn.

ʿAbd al-Ilāh, ʿAbdullāh (ʿAbd al-Malik al-Ṭayyib). 1964 *Naksat al-thawrah fī l-yaman*, Beirut: no publisher listed.

al-ʿAbdalī, Aḥmad Faḍl. 1931 *Hadiyyat al-zaman fī akhbār mulūk lahj wa-ʿadan* (reprinted 1980), Beirut: Dār al-ʿAwdah.

ʿAbd al-Salām, Muḥammad (Abū Bakr al-Saqqāf). 1988 *al-Jumhūriyyah bayn al-salṭanah wa-l-qabīlah fī l-yaman al-shimāliyyah*, Cairo: al-Amal li-l-Ṭibāʿah.

ʿAbd al-Walī, Muḥammad. 1989 *Sanaa, . . . ville ouverte: journal d'un yéménite dans les années 50* (trans. Luc Baldit), Paris and Beirut: Edifra.

Abdulrab, Habib. 1998 *La reine étripée*, Paris: L'Harmattan.

al-Adhal, Ḥusayn Sulaymān. 1993 *al-Istiqlāl al-ḍāʾiʿ: al-malaff al-mansī li-aḥdāth al-yaman al-janūbiyyah*. Cairo: Dār al-ʿAhd.

Admiralty (UK). 1946 *Western Arabia and the Red Sea*, Geographical Handbook series, London: Naval Intelligence Division.

ʿAfīf, Aḥmad Jābir. 1982 *al-Ḥarakat al-waṭaniyyah fī l-yaman*, Damascus: Dār al-Fikr.

ʿAfīf, Aḥmad Jābir and Aḥmad ʿAlī al-Wādaʿī, et al. 1992 *al-Mawsūʿat al-yamaniyyah* (2 vols.), Sanaa: Muʾassasat al-ʿAfīf, Beirut: Dār al-Fikr al-Muʿāṣir.

Aḥmad, Maḥmūd ʿĀdil. 1992 *Dhikrayāt ḥarb al-yaman, 1962–1967*, Cairo: Maṭbaʿat al-Ikhwah.

Aḥmad, Qāsim Ghālib, et al. 1964 *Ibn al-amīr wa-aṣru-hu* (2nd edition, Mashrūʿ al-Kitāb 3/13, 1983), Sanaa: Wizārat al-Iʿlām.

1969 *Min aʿlām al-yaman: shaykh al-islām al-mujtahid muḥammad ʿalī al-shawkānī*, Cairo: Maṭābiʿ al-Ahrām.

al-Akwaʿ, Ismāʿīl. 1995 *Hijar al-ʿilm wa-maʿāqil-hu fī l-yaman* (5 vols.), Beirut: Dār al-Fikr al-Muʿāṣir, Damascus: Dār al-Fikr.

al-Akwaʿ, Muḥammad ʿAlī. 1980 *Ṣafḥah min tārīkh al-yaman al-ijtimāʿī wa-qiṣṣat ḥayātī*, Damascus: Maṭbaʿat al-Kātib al-ʿArabī.

1987 *Ḥayāt ʿālim wa-amīr: yaḥyā bin muḥammad al-iryānī wa-ismāʿīl bin muḥammad bā salāmah wa-ṣafḥah majhūlah min tārīkh al-yaman*, Sanaa: Maktabat al-Jīl al-Jadīd.

ʿAlī, ʿAlī Ḥasan and ʿAbd al-Raḥmān al-Malāḥī. 1989 al-Ṣirāʿ al-ḥamūmī al-quʿayṭī wa-dawāfiʿ-hu 1867–1967, in Ṣāliḥ Bā Surrah and Muḥammad Daʾūd (eds.), *Wathāʾiq al-nadwah al-ʿilmiyyah al-tārīkhiyyah ḥawl al-muqāwamat al-shaʿbiyyah fī ḥadramawt*, Aden: Aden University Press.

Allfree, P. S. 1967 *Hawks of the Hadramaut*, London: Robert Hale.

al-ʿAmrī, Ḥusayn ʿAbdullāh. 1985 *The Yemen in the 18th and 19th Centuries: a political and intellectual history*, London: Ithaca Press.

1987 *al-Manār wa-l-yaman*, Damascus: Dār al-Fikr.

1988 *Miʾat ʿāmin min tārīkh al-yaman al-ḥadīth*, Beirut and Damascus: Dār al-Fikr.

1996 The correspondence of Imam Yaḥyā Ḥamīd al-Dīn with the tribes of Eastern and Southern Yemen, *New Arabian Studies* 3, 1–7.

Aponte, Salvatore. 1948 *Mamlakat al-imām yaḥyā: riḥlah fī l-bilād al-ʿarabiyyah al-saʿīdah* (trans. Ṭāhā Fawzī), Cairo: Maṭbaʿat al-Saʿādah.

Arnaud, J.-L. 1995 Formation de l'architecture contemporaine à Sanaa (1965–1990) in G. Grandguillaume et al. (eds). *Sanaa hors les murs: une ville arabe contemporaine*, Tours: URBAMA, Sanaa: Centre Français d'Etudes Yéménites.

al-Ashtal, A. 1976 PDRY: politics in command, *Race and Class* 17/3, 275–80.

al-Aṣnaj, ʿAbdullāh. 1991 *Dawr al-ḥarakat al-niqābiyyat al-yamaniyyah fī l-niḍāl al-waṭanī*, Cairo: Maktabat Madbūlī.

al-ʿAṭṭār, Mohamed Said. 1964 *Le sous-développement économique et sociale du Yémen: perspectives de la révolution yéménite*, Algiers: Editions Tiers-Monde.

Auchterlonie, P. 1998 *Yemen*, World Bibliographical Series 50, Oxford, Santa Barbara, Denver: Clio Press.

al-ʿAynī, Muḥsin. 1999 *Maʿārik wa-muʾāmarāt ḍidd qaḍiyyat al-yaman* (first published 1957), Cairo: Dār al-Shurūq.

al-ʿAẓm, Nazīh Muʾayyad. 1937 *Riḥlah fī l-bilād al-ʿarabiyyah al-saʿīdah* (reprinted in one vol., 1985), London: Fāḍī Press.

Bā ʿAbbād, ʿAlī. 1987 *Tarbiyat al-shabāb al-yamanī fī ḍawʾ mabādiʾ wa-ahdāf al-mīthāq al-waṭanī*, Sanaa: Maṭābiʿ al-Mufaḍḍal.

Bā ʿAbbād, ʿUmar. 1989 *Ḥaḍramawt wa-l-aḥdāth*, Damascus and Beirut: Dāniyah.

Bā Maṭraf, ʿAbd al-Qādir. 1973 *al-Shuhadāʾ al-sabʿah* (2nd edition), Aden: Dār al-Hamdānī.

Bā Salīm, Ḥusayn. 1992 *Dalīl al-ṣaḥāfat al-yamaniyyah*, Sanaa: Wizārat al-Iʿlām.

Bā Surrah, Ṣāliḥ. 1988 Intifāḍāt talāmīdh wa-ṭullāb madāris madīnat ghayl bā wazīr, 1958, *Sabaʾ* 4, 142–53.

1989 Lamaḥāt mūjazah nūshūʾ wa-niḍāl ḥarakat al-talāmīdh wa-l-ṭullāb fī Ḥaḍramawt, in Ṣāliḥ Bā Surrah and Muḥammad Daʾūd (eds)., *Wathāʾiq al-nadwah al-ʿilmiyyah al-tārīkhiyyah ḥawl al-muqāwamat al-shaʿbiyyah fī ḥaḍramawt*, Aden: Aden University Press.

Bā Surrah, Ṣāliḥ and Muḥammad Daʾūd (eds.) 1989 *Wathāʾiq al-nadwah al-ʿilmiyyah al-tārīkhiyyah ḥawl al-muqāwamat al-shaʿbiyyah fī ḥaḍramawt*, Aden: Aden University Press.

Bā Wazīr, Saʿīd. 1983 *Ṣafaḥāt min al-tārīkh al-ḥaḍramī* (2nd edition; first published 1957) Aden: Dār al-Hamdānī.

al-Bakr, Bashīr. 1995 *Ḥarb al-yaman: al-qabīlah tantaṣir ʿalā l-dawlah*, Beirut: al-Muʾassasat al-ʿArabiyyah li-l-Dirāsāt wa-l-Nashr.

al-Bakrī, Ṣalāḥ. 1935–6 *Tārīkh ḥadramawt al-siyāsī* (2 vols.), Cairo: Muṣṭafā al-Bābī al-Ḥalabī.

1949 *Fī janūb al-jazīrat al-ʿarabiyyah*, Cairo: Muṣṭafā al-Bābī al-Ḥalabī.

1955 *Fī sharq al-yaman*, Beirut: Dār al-Kashshāf.

Baldry, J. 1976 al-Yaman and the Turkish Occupation 1849–1914, *Arabica* 23/2, 156–96.

1977a Imam Yaḥyā and the Yemeni uprising of 1904–7, *ʿAbr al-Nahrain* 18, 33–73.

1977b The Anglo-Italian rivalry in Yemen and ʿAsīr, 1900–34, *Die Welt des Islams* 17 (104), 155–93.

Balfour-Paul, G. 1991 *The End of Empire in the Middle East*, Cambridge: Cambridge University Press.

Bang, A. K. 1996 *The Idrīsī State in ʿAsīr: politics, religion, and prestige in Arabia*, London: C. Hurst.

Baraddūnī, ʿAbdullāh. 1978 *Qaḍāyā yamaniyyah* (2nd edition), Beirut: Dār al-Andalūs.

1983 *al-Yaman al-jumhūrī*, Damascus: Maṭbaʿat al-Kātib al-ʿArabī.

Barakāt, Aḥmad Qāʾid. 1991 *al-Nafṭ fī l-yaman*, Sanaa: Muʾassasat al-ʿAfīf.

Bashear, S. 1989 Yemen in early Islam: an examination of non-tribal traditions, *Arabica* 36/3, 327–61.

al-Bayḍānī, ʿAbd al-Raḥmān. 1984 *Azmat al-ummat al-ʿarabiyyah wa-thawrat al-yaman*, Cairo: no publisher listed.

1992 *Shawāfiʿ al-yaman*, Cairo: Dār al-Maʿārif.

Bédoucha, G. and G. Albergoni. 1991 Hiérarchie, médiation et tribalisme en Arabie du sud: la *hijra* yéménite, *L'Homme* 118, 7–36.

Bent, J. T. and M. V. A. Bent. 1900 *Southern Arabia* (reprinted 1994), Reading (UK): Garnet Press.

Bernier, T. 1958 Naissance d'un nationalisme arabe à Aden, *L'Afrique et l'Asie* 44, 25–41.

Bidwell, R. 1983 *The Two Yemens*, Harlow and Boulder: Longmans, Westview.

Blukacz, F. 1993 Le Yémen sous l'autorité des imams zaidites au XVIIe siècle: une éphémère unité, *Revue du monde musulman et de la Mediterranée* 67/1, 39–51.

Bonnenfant, P. (ed.) 1982 *La peninsule arabique d'aujourd'hui* (2 vols.), Paris: CNRS.

1995a Zabīd: anti-développement et potentialités, *Peuples Mediterranéens* 72–3, 219–42.

1995b *Sanaa: architecture domestique et société*, Paris: CNRS.

Bonte, P., E. Conte and P. Dresch (eds.) forthcoming *Tribus, parentèle, état en pays d'islam*.

Bujra, A. S. 1967 Political conflict and stratification in Ḥaḍramawt (two parts), *Middle Eastern Studies* 4/3, 355–75; 4/4, 1–28.
1970 Urban elites and colonialism: the national elite of Aden and South Arabia, *Middle East Journal* 6, 189–211.
1971 *The Politics of Stratification: a study of political change in a South Arabian town.* Oxford: Clarendon Press.
Burrowes, R. D. 1987 *The Yemen Arab Republic: the politics of development 1962–86*, Boulder: Westview.
1989 Oil strikes and leadership struggle in South Yemen: 1986 and beyond, *Middle East Journal* 43/3, 437–53.
Bury, G. Wyman (ʿAbdullāh Mansour). 1911 *The Land of Uz*, London: Macmillan.
1915 *Arabia Infelix: or the Turks in Yemen*, London: Macmillan.
Butūl, Naṣr. 1994 *Mudhakkirāt ḍābiṭ mukhābarāt yamanī*, Nicosia: al-Dār al-Miṣriyyah.
Carapico, S. 1984 The political economy of self-help: development cooperatives in the Yemen Arab Republic. Unpublished Ph.D. thesis, SUNY Binghamton.
1993a The economic dimensions of Yemeni unity, *Merip* 184, 9–14.
1993b Elections and mass politics in Yemen, *Merip* 185, 2–6.
1998 *Civil Society in Yemen: the political economy of activism in modern Arabia*, Cambridge: Cambridge University Press.
Carapico, S. and C. Myntti. 1991 A tale of two families: change in North Yemen, 1977–89, *Merip* 170, 24–9.
Carapico, S. and R. Tutwiler. 1981 *Yemeni Agriculture and Economic Change: studies of two highland regions*, Sanaa: American Institute for Yemeni Studies.
Caton. S. 1990 *Peaks of Yemen I Summon: poetry as cultural performance in a North Yemeni tribe*, Berkeley: University of California Press.
Chaudhry, K. 1997 *The Price of Wealth: economies and institutions in the Middle East*, Ithaca and London: Cornell University Press.
Chelhod, J. 1984–85 *L'Arabie du sud* (3 vols.), Paris: G-P Maisonneuve et Larose.
Cigar, N. 1985 South Yemen and the USSR: prospects for a relationship, *Middle East Journal* 39/4, 775–95.
1989 Local and national loyalties in the People's Republic of Yemen, *Journal of Arab Affairs* 8, 136–40.
1990 Islam and the state in South Yemen: an uneasy coexistence, *Middle Eastern Studies* 26, 185–203.
Clark, J. 1997 Women and Islamic activism in Yemen, *Yemen Update* 39, reprinted *Yemen Times*, 3 and 10 November.
Cleveland, W. L. 1985 *Islam against the West: Shakīb Arslān and the campaign for Islamic nationalism*, London: Saqi Books.
Collins, B. 1969 Ḥaḍramawt: crisis and intervention, 1866–1881. Unpublished Ph.D. thesis, Princeton.
Colonial Office (UK). *Annual Report on Aden*, London: HMSO [cited by years covered, not year of publication].

Couland, J. 1984 Une économie qui se cherche: la voie nationale démocratique à perspectives socialistes au sud, in J. Chelhod (ed.), *L'Arabie du sud*, volume II, Paris: G-P Maisonneuve et Larose.
1993 Lendemains d'élections, *Cahiers du GREMAMO* 11, 163–73.
CPO (Central Planning Organisation, Sanaa). *Statistical Yearbooks*. From 1989, CSO.
Crouch, M. 1993 *An Element of Luck: to South Arabia and beyond*, London and New York: Radcliffe Press.
CSO (Central Statistical Organisation) various years, *Statistical Yearbooks*, Aden (and Sanaa, from 1989).
el-Daher, S. and C. Geissler. 1990 North Yemen: from farming to foreign funding, *Food Policy* 15/6, 531–5.
Darby, P. 1973 *British Defence Policy East of Suez 1947–68*, London: Oxford University Press.
Daʾūd, Muḥammad Saʿīd. 1989 Ḥarakat ibn ʿabdāt fī l-ghurfah bi-ḥaḍramawt, 1924–45, in Ṣāliḥ Bā Surrah and Muḥammad Daʾūd (eds.), *Wathāʾiq al-nadwah al-ʿilmiyyah al-tārīkhiyyah ḥawl al-muqāwamat al-shaʿbiyyah fī ḥaḍramawt*, Aden: Aden University Press.
Daum, W. (ed.) 1988 *Yemen: 3,000 years of art and civilisation in Arabia Felix*, Innsbruck: Pinguin-Verlag.
al-Dawlah, Ḥamūd Muḥammad. 1994 *Zawraq al-ḥalwā fī sīrat qāʾid al-jaysh wa-amīr al-liwāʾ* (Zayd al-Wazīr ed.; 2nd edition), Beirut: Manshūrāt al-ʿAṣr al-Ḥadīth.
Dayyān, Mundʿī and Sālim ʿAbd Rabbihi. 1992 *Jabhat al-iṣlāḥ al-yāfiʿiyyah*, Aden: Muʾassasat 14 Uktubar.
Deffarge, C. and G. Troeller. 1969 *Yemen 62–69: de la révolution "sauvage" à la trêve des guerriers*, Paris: Robert Laffont.
1972 Sud Yémen: une révolution menacée, *Le Monde diplomatique*, April.
Destremau, B. 1989 La République Arabe du Yémen: quel développement? *Cahiers de l'orient* 15/3, 103–16.
1990 *Femmes du Yémen*, Paris: Editions Peuples du Monde.
1991 Politique commerciale et développement; problèmes d'analyse (le cas du Nord Yémen republicain), *Cahiers du GREMAMO* 10, 209–23.
1993 L'économie du Yémen: quelle sortie de la crise? *Cahiers du GREMAMO* 11, 129–48.
Detalle, R. 1993a The Yemeni elections up close, *Merip* 185, 8–12.
1993b Les élections legislatives du 27 avril 1993, *Monde Arabe Maghreb-Machrek* 141, 3–36.
1994 Pacte d'Amman: l'espoir déçu des yéménites, *Monde Arabe Maghreb-Machrek* 145, 113–22.
1995 Esquisse d'une sociologie électorale de Sanaa, in G. Grandguillaume et al. (eds.), *Sanaa hors les murs: une ville arabe contemporaine*, Tours: URBAMA, Sanaa: Centre Français d'Etudes Yéménites.
1997a Ajuster sans douleur? La méthode yéménite, in F. Mermier (ed.), *Monde Arabe Maghreb-Machrek*, 155, 20–36.

1997b Ghadir and Nushoor in Yemen: Zaydistan votes for Imam ʿAlī, *Yemen Times*, 28 April.

Dostal, W. 1967 *Die Beduinen in Sudarabien: ein ethnologische Studie zur Entwicklung der Kamelhirtenkultur in Arabien*, Vienna: Ferdinand Berger.

1984 Squire and peasant in Tarīm. A study of "rent capitalism" in southern Arabia, in W. Dostal (ed.), *On Social Evolution: contributions to anthropological concepts*. Horn-Vien: Ferdinand Berger.

1990 *Eduard Glaser – Forschungen im Yemen*, Vienna: Österreichischen Akademie der Wissenschaften.

1996 The special features of the Yemeni weekly market system, *New Arabian Studies* 3, 50–7.

Douglas, L. 1987 *The Free Yemeni Movement 1935–1962*, Beirut: American University.

Dresch, P. 1989 *Tribes, Government, and History in Yemen*, Oxford: Clarendon Press.

1990 Guaranty of the market at Ḥūth, *Arabian Studies* 8, 63–91.

1995a The tribal factor in the Yemeni crisis, in J. al-Suwaidi (ed.), *The Yemeni War of 1994: causes and consequences*, London: Saqi Books.

1995b A fragment of the Yemeni past: ʿAlī Nāṣir al-Qardaʿī and the Shabwah incident, *Journal of Arabic Literature* 26/3, 232–54.

1996 A letter from Imam Yaḥyā concerning the Idrīsī, *New Arabian Studies* 3, 58–68.

forthcoming Colonialistes, communistes and féodaux: rhétoriques de l'ordre au sud-yémen, in P. Bonte, E. Conte and P. Dresch (eds.), *Tribus, parentèle, état en pays d'islam*.

Dresch, P. and B. Haykel. 1995 Stereotypes and political styles: Islamists and tribesfolk in Yemen, *International Journal of Middle East Studies* 27/4, 405–27.

Ḍubbāṭ aḥrār (Committee of Free Officers). 1978 *Asrār wa-wathāʾiq al-thawrat al-yamaniyyah*. Beirut: Dār al-ʿAwdah.

Farago, L. 1939 *The Riddle of Arabia*, London: Robert Hale.

Farouk-Sluglett, M. 1993 Problems of agricultural production in the Yemeni Tihamah, *Cahiers du GREMAMO* 10, 45–83.

Fayein, C. 1955 *Une française médecin au yémen*, Paris: Juillard.

1975 *Yémen*, Petite Planète series 49, Paris: Seuil.

1990 *Vies des femmes au Yémen; récits de Nagiba*, Paris: l'Harmattan.

Foreign Relations (various editors including J. P. Glennon and N. Noring). *Foreign Relations of the United States*, Washington DC: Government Printing Office.

Freitag, U. and G. Clarence-Smith 1997 *Hadrami Traders, Scholars and Statesmen in the Indian Ocean 1750s–1960s*, Leiden: Brill.

Friedlander, J. (ed.) 1988 *Sojourners and Settlers: the Yemeni immigrant experience*, Salt Lake City: University of Utah Press.

Gandy, C. T. 1998 A mission to Yemen, August 1962–January 1963, *British Journal of Middle Eastern Studies* 25/2, 247–74.

Gause, F. G. 1990 *Saudi-Yemeni Relations, 1962–1982: domestic structures and foreign influence*, New York: Columbia University Press.

Gavin, R. J. 1975 *Aden Under British Rule*, London: C. Hurst.

Ghamess, M. 1989 Les femmes et l'education, *Peuples Mediterranéens* 46, 151–4.
Gingrich, A. 1987 Die banū Munabbih im nordlichen Ḫawlān. Einige vorlaufige Ergebnisse ethnologischer Feldforschung im Nordwestern der Arabischen Republik Jemen, *Sociologus* 37/1, 89–93.
1988 Les Munebbih du Yémen perçus par leurs voisins: description d'une société par le corps et sa parture, *Techniques et cultures* 13, 127–39.
Glaser, E. 1884 Meine reise durch Arḥab und Ḥāschid, *Petterman's Mitteilungen* 30, 204–13 (trans. D. Warburton, 1993, as Yemen translation series 1, American Institute for Yemeni Studies).
1913 *Reise nach Ma'rib* (D. H. Muller and N. Rhodokonakis, eds.), Vienna: Alfred Holder.
GPC (General Popular Congress). 1982 *al-Mīthāq al-waṭanī*, Sanaa: no publisher listed.
Grandguillaume, G. et al. (eds.) 1995 *Sanaa hors les murs: une ville arabe contemporaine*, Tours: URBAMA, Sanaa: Centre Français d'Etudes Yéménites.
Grosgurin, J. 1994 La contestation islamiste au yémen, in G. Kepel (ed.), *Exils et royaumes: les appartenances au monde arabo-musulman aujourd'hui*, Paris: Fondation Nationale des Sciences Politiques.
al-Ḥabashī, Muḥammad. 1968 *al-Yaman al-janūbī siyāsiyyan wa-iqtiṣādiyyan*, Beirut: Dār al-Ṭalī'ah. [French edition 1966].
Ḥabshūsh, Ḥayyim. 1941 *Travels in Yemen* (S. D. Goitein, ed.), Jerusalem: Hebrew University Press.
1995 *Yémen* (trans. Samia Naim-Sanbar), Paris: Actes Sud.
Hādī, Nabīl. 1978 *17 Sā'atan tārīkhiyyatan 'ind bāb al-mandab,* Beirut: Dār al-Farābī.
al-Ḥajrī, Muḥammad Aḥmad. 1984 *Majmū' buldān al-yaman wa-qabā'il-hā* (Mashrū' al-Kitāb 1/16, 2 vols.), Sanaa: Wizārat al-I'lām wa-l-Thaqāfah.
Halliday, F. 1974 *Arabia without Sultans*, Harmondsworth (UK): Penguin.
1979 Yemen's unfinished revolution: socialism in the South, *Merip* 81, 3–20.
1983 The People's Democratic Republic of Yemen: the "Cuban path" in Arabia, in G. White, R. Murray and C. White (eds.), *Revolutionary Socialist Development in the Third World*, Brighton (UK): Wheatsheaf Books.
1984 Soviet relations with South Yemen, in B. R. Pridham (ed.), *Contemporary Yemen: politics and historical background*, London: Croom Helm.
1990 *Revolution and Foreign Policy: the case of South Yemen*, Cambridge: Cambridge University Press.
1992 *Arabs in Exile: Yemeni migrants in urban Britain*, London: I. B. Tauris.
Ḥamdī, Jamāl (with Rayshah Ma'mūn). 1964 series of seven articles in *Ruz al-Yūsuf*, Nos. 1883–1889, 13 July–24 August.
Hamilton, R. A. B. 1943 The social organization of the tribes of the Aden Protectorate, part 1, *Journal of the Royal Central Asian Society* 30, 142–57 (also *JRCAS* 29, 1942, 239–48); Social organization of the Aden Protectorate, part 2, *JRCAS* 30, 267–74.
(the Master of Belhaven). 1949 *The Kingdom of Melchior: adventures in Southwest Arabia*, London: John Murray.
(Lord Belhaven). 1955 *The Uneven Road*, London: John Murray.

al-Ḥarāzī, Muḥsin Aḥmad. 1986 *Fatrat al-fawḍā wa-ʿawdat al-atrāk ilā ṣanʿāʾ* (H. A. al-ʿAmrī, ed.), Sanaa: Dār al-Ḥikmat al-Yamaniyyah, Damascus: Dār al-Fikr.

Ḥawāṭmah, Nayyif 1968 *Azmat al-thawrah fī l-yaman al-janūbī*, Beirut: Dār al-Ṭalīʿah.

Haykel, B. 1993 al-Shawkānī and the jurisprudential unity of Yemen, *Revue du Monde Musulman et de la Mediterranée* 67, 53–65.

1995 A Zaydī revival? *Yemen Update* 36, 7–9.

1997 Order and righteousness: Muḥammad ʿAlī al-Shawkānī and the nature of the Islamic state in Yemen. Unpublished D.Phil. thesis, Oxford.

Heyworth-Dunne, J. 1952 *Al-Yemen: a general social, political and economic survey*, Cairo: Renaissance Bookshop.

Hickinbotham, T. 1958 *Aden*, London: Frank Cass.

Ho, Engseng. 1999 Yemenis on Mars: the end of the *mahjar* (diaspora), *Merip* 211, 29–31.

forthcoming Le don précieux de la généalogie, in P. Bonte, E. Conte and P. Dresch (eds.), *Tribus, parentèle, état en pays d'islam.*

Holden, D. 1966 *Farewell to Arabia*, London: Faber and Faber.

Hunter, F. M. and C. W. Sealey. 1909 *Arab Tribes in the Vicinity of Aden* (reprinted 1986), London: Darf.

Ḥugariyyah 1973 Hay'at taṭwīr al-ḥugariyyah: thalāthah sanawāt min al-bināʾ (pamphlet).

al-ʿInān, Zayd. 1983 *Mudhakkirātī*, Cairo: al-Maktabat al-Salafiyyah.

Ingrams, D. 1949 *A Survey of Social and Economic Conditions in the Aden Protectorate*, Asmara: Government Printer.

Ingrams, W. H. 1937 *Report on the Social, Economic and Political Condition of the Hadramaut* (Colonial No. 123), London: HM Stationery Office.

1963 *The Yemen: Imams, Rulers and Revolutions*, London: John Murray.

1966 *Arabia and the Isles* (3rd edition), London: John Murray.

Iryani, Horia. 1985 The development of primary education and its problems in the Yemen Arab Republic, in B. R. Pridham (ed.), *Economy, Society and Culture in Contemporary Yemen*, London: Croom Helm.

Ismael, T. and J. S. Ismael. 1986 *The People's Democratic Republic of Yemen: politics, economy and society*, London: Frances Pinter.

Ismāʿīl, ʿAbd al-Fattāḥ. 1978 *Thaqāfatunā al-waṭaniyyah min al-qadīm ilā l-jadīd*, Aden: Mu'assasat 14 Uktubar.

1986 *al-Turāth wa-l-thaqāfat al-waṭaniyyah; naṣṣ ḥiwār al-shāʿir adônīs maʿa ʿabd al-fattāḥ ismāʿīl*, Beirut: Dār Ibn Khaldūn.

ʿIzz al-Dīn, Najīb Abū. 1989 *al-Imārāt al-yamaniyyah al-janūbiyyah 1937–1947*, Beirut: Dār al-Bāḥith.

1990 *ʿIshrūn ʿāman fī khidmat al-yaman*, Beirut: Dār al-Bāḥith

al-Jabhah al-Qawmiyyah (NLF). 1965 *al-Mīthāq al-waṭanī*, agreed at the meeting of 22–25 June 1965, Aden: PRSY.

Jacob, H. 1923 *Kings of Arabia: the rise and set of the Turkish soveranty in the Arabian Peninsular*, London: Mills and Boon.

al-Janāḥī, Saʿīd Aḥmad. 1992 *al-Ḥarakat al-waṭaniyyah al-yamaniyyah: min al-thawrah ilā l-waḥdah*, Sanaa and Aden: Markaz al-Amal li-l-Dirāsāt wa-l-Nashr.
al-Jawharī, Shākir. 1992 *al-Ṣirāʿ fī ʿadan*, Cairo: Maktabat Madbūlī.
al-Jāwī, ʿUmar. 1975 *Ḥiṣār ṣanʿāʾ*, Aden: Muʾassasat Ṣawt al-ʿUmmāl.
n.d. *al-Ṣaḥāfat al-niqābiyyah fī ʿadan, 1958–67*, Aden: Muʾassasat 14 Uktubar.
Jibrīl, M. 1962 *Madīnat al-muhājirīn, ḥaḍramawt*, Cairo: al-Muʾassasat al-Miṣriyyah al-ʿĀmmah.
al-Jirāfī, ʿAbdullāh. 1951 *al-Muqtaṭaf min tārīkh al-yaman*, Cairo: ʿĪsā al-Bābī al-Ḥalabī.
al-Jirāfī, Aḥmad Muhammad. 1992 *Ḥawliyyat al-ʿallāmah al-jirāfī 1889–1900* (H. A. al-ʿAmrī, ed.), Beirut and Damascus: Dār al-Fikr.
Johnston, C. 1964 *The View from Steamer Point*, London: Collins.
Juzaylān, ʿAbdullāh. 1977 *al-Tārīkh al-sirrī li-l-thawrat al-yamaniyyah*, Beirut: Dār al-ʿAwdah.
1984 *Lamaḥāt min dhikrayāt al-ṭufūlah*, Cairo: Maktabat Madbūlī.
1995 *Muqaddimat thawrat al-yaman, 26 sibtimbir 1962*, Beirut: Manshūrāt al-ʿAṣr al-Ḥadīth.
Kerr, M. 1971 *The Arab Cold War: Gamāl ʿAbd al-Nāṣir and his rivals, 1958–70* (3rd edition), London and New York: Oxford University Press.
al-Khanbashī, Sālim Aḥmad. 1989 al-Intifāḍāt al-qabaliyyah fī muḥāfaẓat ḥaḍramawt khilāl al-fatrah 1951–61, in Ṣāliḥ Bā Surrah and Muḥammad Daʾūd (eds.), *Wathāʾiq al-nadwah al-ʿilmiyyah al-tārīkhiyyah ḥawl al-muqāwamat al-shaʿbiyyah fī ḥaḍramawt*, Aden: Aden University Press.
Klein-Franke, A. 1988 The Jews of Yemen, in W. Daum (ed.), *Yemen: 3,000 years of art and civilisation in Arabia Felix*, Innsbruck: Pinguin-Verlag.
Knysh, A. 1993 The cult of saints in Ḥaḍramawt: an overview, *New Arabian Studies* 1, 137–52.
Kopp, H. and E. Wirth. 1994 *Sanaa: développement et organisation de l'espace d'une ville arabe*, (trans. B. Blukacz-Louisfert and F. Blukacz), Sanaa: Centre Français d'Etudes Yéménites, Aix: CNRS (IREMAM).
Kostiner, J. 1984 *The Struggle for South Yemen*, London: Croom Helm.
Kruse, H. 1984 Takfīr und Gihād bei den Zaiditen des Jemen, *Die Welt des Islams* (n.s.) 23–4, 424–57.
Kuhn, T. 1996 Krisenprovinz Weihrauchland? Der osmanische Yemen in Urteil Reformer, 1879–1910, *Jemen-Report* 27/2, 4–9.
forthcoming Ordering urban space in Ottoman Yemen, in J. Hansen, T. Philipp and S. Weber (eds.), *Arab Provincial Capitals in the Late Ottoman Empire*.
Lackner, H. 1985 *P.D.R. Yemen: outpost of socialist development*, London: Ithaca Press.
Lambardi, N. 1947 Divisioni amministrative del yemen con notizzie economiche a demografiche, *Oriente moderno* 7–9 (26), 141–62.
Lambert, J. 1997 *La médecine de l'âme: le chant de Sanaa dans la société yéménite*, Nanterres: Société d'Ethnologie.
Ledger, D. 1983 *Shifting Sands: the British in South Arabia*, London: Peninsula Publishing.

Lefort, R. 1971 Révolution au sud-yémen, *Le Monde diplomatique*, February.
Leveau, R., F. Mermier and U. Steinbach (eds.) 1999 *Le Yémen contemporain*, Paris: Editions Karthala.
Lichtenthaler, G. 1999 Water management and community participation in the Ṣaʿdah basin of Yemen, unpublished preliminary report for the World Bank, School of Oriental and African Studies, London.
Lucet, M. 1995 Les rapatriés de la crise du Golfe au Yémen: Hodeidah quatre ans après, *Monde Arabe Maghreb-Machrek* 148, 28–42.
Luqmān, ʿAlī Hamzah. 1972 Education and the press in South Arabia, in D. Hopwood (ed.), *The Arabian Peninsula: society and politics*, London: Allen and Unwin.
1985 *Tārīkh al-qabāʾil al-yamaniyyah*, Sanaa: Dār al-Kalimah.
Luqmān, F. M. 1970 *Yemen 1970*, Aden.
Luṭfī, Ḥamdī. 1967 *Al-Thawrah fī janūb al-yaman al-muḥtall*, Cairo: Dār al-Kātib al-ʿArabī.
Mackintosh-Smith, T. 1997 *Yemen: travels in dictionary land*, London: John Murray.
al-Mahrī, Sālim Yāsir. 1994 *Bilād al-mahrah, māḍī-hā wa-ḥāḍir-hā*, Abu Dhabi: Dār al-Fajr.
Makāwī, ʿAbd al-Qawī. 1979 *Shahādatī li-l-tārīkh: khabāyā l-ghazw al-shuyūʿī li-janūb al-yaman*. Cairo: no publisher listed.
Maktari, A. M. 1971 *Water Rights and Irrigation Practices in Laḥj: a study of the application of customary and sharīʿah law in south-west Arabia*, Cambridge: Cambridge University Press.
Mandaville, J. 1984 Memduh Pasha and ʿAziz Bey: Ottoman experience in Yemen, in B. R. Pridham (ed.), *Contemporary Yemen: politics and historical background*, London: Croom Helm.
al-Maqbalī, Ḥusayn. 1986 *Mudhakkirāt al-maqbalī*, Damascus: Dār al-Fikr.
Markaz al-Dirāsāt al-Yamaniyyah. 1982a *Thawrah 26 sibtimbir*, Sanaa: Markaz al-Dirāsāt al-Yamaniyyah.
1982b *Thawrah 1948*, Sanaa: Markaz al-Dirāsāt al-Yamaniyyah.
1989 *Ḥiṣār ṣanʿāʾ: shahādah li-l-tārīkh*, Sanaa: Markaz al-Dirāsāt wa-l-Buḥūth al-Yamanī.
Martin, B. G. 1971 Migrations from Hadramaut to East Africa and Indonesia c. 1200 to 1900, *Research Bulletin* (Ibadan, Nigeria) 7, 1–21.
al-Maytamī, Muḥammad. 1993 Le marché du travail yéménite après l'unification, *Revue du Monde Musulman et de la Mediterranée* 67, 121–9.
1997 Crise du riyal yéménite . . . et spéculation, in F. Mermier (ed.), *Monde Arabe Maghreb-Machrek* 155, 45–54.
Meneley, A. 1996 *Tournaments of Value: sociability and hierarchy in a Yemeni town*, Toronto, Buffalo, London: University of Toronto Press.
Mercier, E. 1997a Aden à l'épreuve du foncier, in F. Mermier (ed.), *Monde Arabe Maghreb-Machrek* 155, 55–65.
1997b *Aden: un parcours interrompu*, Villes du monde arabe 3, Tours: URBAMA.
Merip = *Middle East Report*, Washington DC: Middle East Research and Information Project.

Mermier, F. 1991 Les souks de Sanaa, un monde bouleversé: changements économiques et recomposition sociale, *Cahiers du GREMAMO* 10, 145–66.

1997a *Le cheikh de la nuit, Ṣanʿāʾ: organisation des souks et société citadine*, Paris: Actes Sud.

(ed.) 1997b *Monde Arabe Maghreb-Machrek* 155 [guest-edited volume], Introductory essay, 'L'état en face à la démocratie', pp. 3–5.

1997c L'Islam politique au yémen ou la "Tradition" contre les traditions? *Monde Arabe Maghreb-Machrek* 155, 6–19.

Messick, B. 1978 Transactions in Ibb. Unpublished Ph.D. thesis, Princeton.

1993 *The Calligraphic State: textual domination and history in a Muslim society*, Berkeley: University of California Press.

Molyneux, M. 1991 The law, the state and socialist policies with regard to women: the case of the PDRY, 1967–1990, in D. Kandiyoti (ed.), *Women, Islam and the State*, Philadelphia: Temple University Press.

1995 Women's rights and political contingency: the case of Yemen 1990–1994, *Middle East Journal* 49/3, 418–31.

Muḥḍār, Ḥāmid bin Abī Bakr. 1983 *al-Zaʿīm al-sayyid al-ḥabīb ḥusayn bin ḥāmid al-muḥḍār wa-l-salṭanah al-quʿayṭiyyah*, Jiddah: ʿĀlam al-Maʿrifah.

"Muḥsin" (Muḥammad Saʿīd ʿAbdullāh). 1989 *ʿAdan: kifāḥ shaʿbi wa-hazīmat imbarāṭūriyyah* (2nd edition), Beirut: Dār Ibn Khaldūn.

al-Mujāhid, Muḥammad. 1997 *Madīnat taʿizz: ghuṣn naḍīr fī dawḥah al-tārīkh al-ʿarabī*, Taʿizz: al-Maʿmal al-Fannī li-l-Ṭibāʿah.

Mundy, M. 1979 Women's inheritance of land in highland Yemen, *Arabian Studies* 5, 161–87.

1983 Ṣanʿāʾ dress, 1920–75, in R. B. Serjeant and R. Lewcock (eds.), *Ṣanʿāʾ: an Arabian Islamic city*, London: World of Islam Festival Trust.

1985 Agricultural development in the Yemeni Tihama: the past ten years, in B. R. Pridham (ed.), *Economy, Society and Culture in Contemporary Yemen*, London: Croom Helm.

1995 *Domestic Government: kinship, community and polity in North Yemen*, Cambridge: Cambridge University Press.

Myntti, C. 1979 *Women and Development in the Yemen Arab Republic*, Eschborn: German Agency for Technical Co-operation (GTZ).

1984 Yemeni workers abroad: the impact on women, *Merip* 124, 11–16.

al-Nahārī, Muḥammad. n.d. *al-Barāmij al-dīniyyah fī l-idhāʿat al-yamaniyyah*, Cairo: al-Amal li-l-Ṭibāʿah.

Nājī, Sulṭān. 1979 *al-Tārīkh al-ʿaskarī li-l-yaman*, Aden.

1984 The genesis of the call for Yemeni unity, in B. R. Pridham (ed.), *Contemporary Yemen: politics and historical background*, London: Croom Helm.

Naʿnaʿ, Ḥamīdah. 1988 *al-Ṣubḥ al-dāmī fī ʿadan*, Cairo: Dār al-Mustaqbal al-ʿArabī.

Naumkin, V. 1985 Evaluation of socio-economic development in the People's Democratic Republic of Yemen, in B. R. Pridham (ed.), *Economy, Society and Culture in Contemporary Yemen*, London: Croom Helm.

Nini, Y. 1991 *The Jews of Yemen: 1800–1914*, Reading and Paris: Harwood.

Noban, Saeed. 1984 Education for nation-building – the experience of the People's Democratic Republic of Yemen, in B. R. Pridham (ed.), *Contemporary Yeman: politics and historical background*, London: Croom Helm.

Nuʿmān, Muḥammad Aḥmad. 1965 *al-Aṭrāf al-maʿniyyah fī l-yaman*, Aden: Mu'assasat al-Ḍabbān.

O'Ballance, E. 1971 *The War in Yemen*, London: Faber and Faber.

Obermeyer, G. 1981 *al-Īmān* and al-Imām: ideology and state in the Yemen, 1900–1948, in M. R. Buheiry (ed.), *Intellectual Life in the Arab East 1890–1939*, Beirut: American University.

PDRY 1978 *Constitution of the People's Democratic Republic of Yemen*, Aden: 14th October Corporation.

Peterson, J. E. 1982 *Yemen: the search for a modern state*, Baltimore: Johns Hopkins University Press.

Pieragostini, K. 1991 *Britain, Aden and South Arabia: abandoning empire*, New York: St Martin's Press.

Playfair, R. 1859 *A History of Arabia Felix or Yemen* (reprinted 1970), St Leonard's: Ad Orientem, Amsterdam: Philo Press.

Pridham, B. R. (ed.) 1984 *Contemporary Yemen: politics and historical background*, London: Croom Helm.

1985 *Economy, Society and Culture in Contemporary Yemen*, London: Croom Helm.

Prost-Tournier, J.-M. 1978 L'urbanisation du Yémen du nord, *Maghreb-Machrek* 81, 63–72.

Puin, G.-R. 1984 The Yemenite *hijrah* concept of tribal protection, in T. Khalidi (ed.), *Land Reform and Social Transformation in the Middle East*, Beirut: American University.

Qabā'il. 1974 ʿAlā ṭarīq al-taqaddum fī l-yaman: mu'tamar qabā'il al-yaman al-munʿaqad fī l-muʿammar, hamdān, 18/6/74 (pamphlet).

Qandīl, Nāṣir. 1986 *Hakādhā tafajjara al-burkān*, Beirut: Maṭbaʿat al-Ḥaqīqah.

al-Qāsimī, Khālid. 1988 *al-ʿAwāṣir al-ghinā'iyyah bayn al-yaman wa-l-khalīj*, Beirut: Dār al-Ḥadāthah, Sharjah: Dār al-Thaqāfat al-ʿArabiyyah.

Rashid, I. 1984 *Yemen Enters the Modern World: secret U.S. documents on the rise of the second power in the Arabian Peninsula*, Chapel Hill: Documentary Publications.

1985 *Yemen Under the Rule of Imam Aḥmad*, Chapel Hill: Documentary Publications.

Records = D. and L. Ingrams (eds.) 1993 *Records of Yemen 1798–1960* (15 vols.), Slough: Archive Editions.

Renaud, E. n.d. Ṣuwar min al-wāqiʿ, transcripts and translations of Sanaa radio series, 1975 (typescript).

1982 La vie culturelle en République Arabe du Yémen, in P. Bonnenfant (ed.), La peninsule arabique d'aujourd'hui, volume II, Paris: CNRS.

Renaud, E. and C. Fayein (eds.). 1979 *Poèmes de la révolution yéménite*, Paris: Editions Recherches.

Riḍā, ʿĀdil. 1969 *Thawrat al-janūb*, Cairo: Dār al-Maʿārif.

Rīḥānī, A. 1930 *Arabian Peak and Desert*, London: Constable.

Rodinson, D. 1984 Une économie qui se cherche: le capitalisme au Nord, in J. Chelhod (ed.), *L'Arabie du sud*, volume II, Paris: G-P Maisonneuve et Larose.

Rodionov, M. 1996 Poetry and power in Ḥaḍramawt, *New Arabian Studies* 3, 118–33.

Rossi, E. 1938 La stampa nell' yemen, *Oriente Moderno* 18, 568–80.

1939 *L'Arabo parlato a Sanaa*, Rome: Istituto per l'Oriente.

Rouaud, A. 1979 *Les yémen et leurs populations*, Brussels: Editions Complexe.

1984 L'émigration yéménite, in J. Chelhod (ed.), *L'Arabie du sud*, volume II, Paris: G-P Maisonneuve et Larose.

Rouleau, E. 1967 Le yémen: voyage à travers le moyen age, series of five articles in *Le Monde*, 11–16 May.

1972 L'étoile rouge sur le Yémen du sud, series of four articles in *Le Monde*, 27–31 May.

Sālim, Sayyid Muṣṭafā. 1971 *Takwīn al-yaman al-ḥadīth: al-yaman wa-l-imām yaḥyā* (2nd edition), Cairo: Maʿhad al-Buḥūth wa-l-Dirāsāt al-ʿArabiyyah.

1982 *Wathāʾiq yamaniyyah*, Cairo: al-Maṭbaʿat al-Fanniyah.

al-Saqqāf, Abū Bakr. 1996 *al-Waḥdat al-yamaniyyah: min al-indimāj al-fawrī ilā l-istiʿmār al-dākhilī*, London: Bareed al-Janūb.

al-Saqqāf, Mohammed. 1997 Banques islamiques: les enjeux politiques, in F. Mermier (ed.), *Monde Arabe Maghreb-Machrek* 155, 37–44.

al-Sarūrī, ʿAbd al-Raḥīm. 1987 *Mudhakkirāt ʿabd al-raḥīm ʿabdullāh*, Beirut: Manshūrāt al-ʿAṣr al-Ḥadīth.

Schmidt, D. A. 1968 *Yemen: the unknown war*. London: Bodley Head.

Scott, H. 1942 *In the High Yemen*, London: Macmillan.

Serjeant, R. B. 1962 Historians and historiography of Hadramaut, *Bulletin of the School of Oriental and African Studies* (London) 15, 239–61.

1979 The Yemeni poet al-Zubayrī and his polemic against the Zaydi Imams, *Arabian Studies* 5, 87–130.

1989 Dawlah, tribal shaykhs, the manṣab of the waliyyah Saʿīdah, *qasāmah*, in the Faḍlī Sultanate, South Arabian Federation, in Mooawiyah Ibrahim (ed.), *Arabian Studies in Honour of Mahmoud Ghul*, Wiesbaden: Harassowitz.

Serjeant, R. B. and R. Lewcock (eds.) 1983 *Ṣanʿāʾ: an Arabian Islamic city*, London: World of Islam Festival Trust.

al-Shahārī, Muḥammad ʿAlī. 1972 *al-Yaman: al-thawrah fī l-janūb wa-l-intikāsah fī l-shimāl*, Beirut: Dār Ibn Khaldūn.

al-Shamāḥī, ʿAbdullāh. 1972 *al-Yaman: al-insān wa-l-ḥaḍārah*, Cairo: Dār al-Hanāʾ.

al-Shāmī, Aḥmad. 1965 *Imām al-yaman: aḥmad ḥamīd al-dīn*, n.p. Dār al-Kitāb al-Jadīd.

1975 Yemeni literature in Ḥajjah prisons 1948–55, *Arabian Studies* 2, 43–59.

1984 *Riyāḥ al-taghyīr fī l-yaman*, Jiddah: al-Maṭbaʿat al-ʿArabiyyah.

Shamsuldin, A. 1993 Les échanges commerciaux entre les deux Yémen (1970–89), *Cahiers du GREMAMO* 11, 107–28.

Sharafaddin, A. H. 1961 *Yemen: Arabia Felix*, Taʿizz: no publisher listed.

Sharaf al-Dīn, Aḥmad. 1964 *al-Yaman ʿabr al-tārīkh* (2nd edition) Cairo: Maṭbaʿat al-Sunnat al-Muḥammadiyyah.

al-Sharjabī, Qā'id. 1990 *al-Qaryah wa-l-dawlah fī l-mujtamaʿ al-yamanī*, Beirut: Dār al-Taḍāmun.

al-Sharq al-Awsaṭ 1994 *al-Ḥarb al-yamaniyyah: khafāyā wa-alghāz*, Jiddah: al-Sharq al-Awsaṭ.

al-Shāṭirī, Muḥammad. 1983 *Adwār al-tārīkh al-ḥaḍramī* (2nd edition, first published 1972), Jiddah: ʿĀlam al-Maʿrifah.

al-Shuʿaybī, Muḥammad ʿAlī. 1973 *al-Yaman khalf al-sitār al-ḥadīdī* (2nd edition), Beirut: no publisher listed.

al-Shumayrī, ʿAbd al-Walī. 1995 *Alf sāʿatin ḥarb* (3rd edition, 2 vols.), Sanaa: Maktabat al-Yusr.

Stanzel, V. 1988 Marxism in Arabia: South Yemen twenty years after independence, *Aussenpolitik* 39/3, 265–77.

Stark, F. 1936 *The Southern Gates of Arabia: a journey in the Hadramaut*, London: John Murray.

Stevenson, T. 1993 Yemeni workers come home: reabsorbing one million migrants, *Merip* 181, 15–20.

Stitt, G. 1948 *A Prince of Arabia: the Emir Shereef Ali Haider*, London: George Allen and Unwin.

Stookey, R. 1978 *Yemen: the politics of the Yemen Arab Republic*, Boulder: Westview Press.

1982 *South Yemen: a Marxist republic in Arabia*, Boulder: Westview Press.

Stork, J. 1973 Socialist revolution in Arabia: report from the People's Democratic Republic of Yemen, *Merip* 15, 1–25

Swagman, C. T. 1988 *Development and Social Change in Highland Yemen*, Salt Lake City: University of Utah Press.

SWB = *Summary of World Broadcasts*, Caversham (UK): BBC.

Taminian, L. 1999 Persuading the monarchs: poetry and politics in Yemen, 1920–50, in R. Leveau, F. Mermier and U. Steinbach (eds.), *Le Yémen contemporain*, Paris: Editions Karthala.

al-Ṭayyib, ʿAbd al-Malik. 1991 *al-Tārīkh yatakallam* [no place of publication listed; printed privately].

1995 *Thawrat al-yaman: al-nafaq al-muẓlim* [no place of publication listed; printed privately].

al-Thaʿālabī, ʿAbd al-ʿAzīz. 1997 *al-Riḥlat al-yamaniyyah: 12 aghustus–17 uktubar 1924* (Jamādī al-Sāḥilī, ed.) Beirut: Dār l-Gharb al-Islāmī.

Townshend, C. 1986 Civilization or "frightfulness": air control in the Middle East between the wars, in C. Wrigley (ed.), *Warfare, Diplomacy and Politics: essays in honour of A. J. P. Taylor*, London: Hamish Hamilton.

Traboulsi, F. 1991 Les transformations des structures tribales depuis l'indépendance du Yémen du sud, *Cahiers du GREMAMO* 10, 125–43.

Trevaskis, K. 1956 Handbook for the Western Aden Protectorate, unpublished MS., Rhodes House (Oxford) MSS. Brit. Emp. s.367 4/3.

1959 The Western Aden Protectorate, unpublished MS., Rhodes House (Oxford) MSS. Brit. Emp. s.367 4/4.

1968 *Shades of Amber: a South Arabian episode*, London: Hutchinson.

n.d. private papers (Rhodes House, Oxford).

Trevelyan, H. 1970 *The Middle East in Revolution*, London: Macmillan.

Troin, J.-F. 1995 Géographie d'une 'explosion urbaine', in G. Grandguillaume et al. (eds.), *Sanaa hors les murs: une ville arabe contemporaine*, Tours: URBAMA, Sanaa: Centre Français d'Etudes Yéménites.

Tuchscherer, M. 1985 La littérature contemporaine en arabie du sud et ses aspects sociaux, in J. Chelhod (ed.), *L'Arabie du sud*, volume III, Paris: G-P Maisonneuve et Larose.

Tutwiler, R. 1987 Tribe, tribute and trade: social class formation in highland Yemen. Unpublished Ph.D. thesis, SUNY Binghamton.

al-ʿUbaydī, ʿAwnī. 1993 *Jamāʿat al-ikhwān al-muslimīn wa-thawrat al-dustūr al-yamaniyyah 1367/1948*, Amman, Jordan: al-Maktabat al-Waṭaniyyah.

ʿUmar, Jārullāh. 1989 The importance and position of political pluralism within the framework of political reform (typescript), memorandum submitted to the YSP central committee.

ʿUmar, Sulṭān Aḥmad. 1970 *Naẓrah fī taṭawwur al-mujtamaʿ al-yamanī*, Beirut: Dār al-Ṭalīʿah.

Van den Berg, L. W. 1886 *Le Hadramaut et les colonies arabes dans l'archipel indien* (reprinted 1969), Farnborough (UK): Gregg.

Van der Kroef, J. M. 1953 The Arabs in Indonesia, *Middle East Journal* 7/3, 300–23.

Van der Meulen, D. 1932 *Hadramaut: some of its mysteries unveiled*, London: John Murray.

1947 *Aden to the Hadramaut: a journey in South Arabia*, London: John Murray.

Van Hear, N. 1994 The socio-economic impact of the involuntary mass return to Yemen in 1990, *Journal of Refugee Studies* 7/1, 18–38.

Vom Bruck, G. 1999 Being a Zaydi in the absence of an Imam: doctrinal revisions, religious instruction, and the (re)invention of ritual, in R. Leveau, F. Mermier and U. Steinbach (eds.), *Le Yémen contemporain*, Paris: Editions Karthala.

forthcoming Le nom comme signe corporel, *Annales*.

al-Wāsiʿī, ʿAbd al-Wāsiʿ. 1928 *Tārīkh al-yaman*, Cairo: al-Maṭbaʿat al-Salafiyyah.

1948 *Tārīkh al-yaman* (2nd edition; reprinted 1991), Sanaa: Maktabat al-Yaman al-Kubrā.

Waterfield, G. 1968 *Sultans of Aden*, London: John Murray.

Watt, D. C. 1962 Labor relations and trades unions in Aden, 1952–1960, *Middle East Journal* 16/4, 443–56.

Wavell, A. J. 1912 *A Modern Pilgrim in Mecca and a Siege in Sanaa*, London: Constable.

al-Wazīr, Aḥmad Muḥammad. 1987 *Ḥayāt al-amīr ʿalī bin ʿabdullāh al-wazīr*, Beirut: Manshūrāt al-ʿAṣr al-Ḥadīth.

al-Wazīr, Zayd ʿAlī. 1971 *Muḥāwalah li-fahm al-mushkilat al-yamaniyyah*, Beirut: Muʾassasat al-Risālah.

Weir, S. 1985 *Qāt in Yemen: consumption and social change*, London: British Museum.

1991 Trade and tribal structures in North West Yemen, *Cahiers du GREMAMO* 10, 87–101.

1997 A clash of fundamentalisms: Wahhabism in Yemen, *Merip* 204, 22–6.

Wenner, M. 1967 *Modern Yemen, 1918–1966*, Baltimore: Johns Hopkins University Press.

1988 An economic history of Yemen, 1500–1948, in W. Daum (ed.), *Yemen: 3,000 years of art and civilisation in Arabia Felix*, Innsbruck: Pinguin-Verlag.

1991 *The Yemen Arab Republic: development and change in an ancient land*, Boulder: Westview.

Wilkinson, J. C. 1991 *Arabia's Frontiers: the story of Britain's boundary drawing in the desert*, London: I. B. Tauris.

al-Wishalī, Ismāʿīl. 1982 *Dhayl nashr al-thanāʾ al-ḥasan al-munabiʾ bi-baʿḏ ḥawādith al-zaman* (Muḥammad al-Shuʿaybī, ed.), Sanaa: Maṭābiʿ al-Yaman al-ʿAṣriyyah.

World Bank 1979a *People's Democratic Republic of Yemen: a review of economic and social development* , Washington DC: World Bank.

1979b *Yemen Arab Republic: development of a traditional economy*, Washington DC: World Bank.

Würth, A. 1995 A Sanaa court: the family and the ability to negotiate. *Islamic Law and Society* 2, 320–40.

YSP (Yemeni Socialist Party) 1986 *Critical and Analytical Document on the Revolutionary Experience of Democratic Yemen 1978–86*, Aden: no publisher listed.

al-Yūsufī, ʿAbd al-Raḥmān. 1976 al-Taʿāwun fī minṭaqat al-ḥugariyyah, *al-Ghadd* (year two) 1, 78–86.

Zabal, Sālim. 1965–6 Series of three articles, on Sayyūn (Aug. 65), Shibām (Dec. 65) and Tarīm (Feb. 66), in the series "I'raf waṭanak ayyuhā al-ʿarabī", *al-ʿArabī* magazine, Kuwait.

Zabārah, Muḥammad Muḥammad. 1956 *Āʾimmat al-yaman bi-l-qarni l-rābiʿ ʿashar* (3 vols.), Cairo: al-Maṭbaʿat al-Salafiyyah.

1979 *Nuzhat al-naẓar fī rijāl al-qarni l-rābiʿ ʿashar*, Sanaa: Markaz al-Dirāsāt wa-l-Abḥāth al-Yamaniyyah.

Zayd, ʿAlī Muḥammad. 1998 *Ẓahrat al-bunn*, Beirut: Dār al-Kunūz al-Adabiyyah.

al-Zayn, ʿAbdullāh. 1985 *al-Yaman wa-wasāʾil-hu al-iʿlāmiyyah*, Cairo: Maṭābiʿ al-Tawbājī.

Zulfah, Muḥammad ʿAbdullāh Āl. 1995 *ʿAsīr fī ʿahd al-malik ʿabd al-ʿazīz*, Riyāḍ: Maṭābiʿ al-Farazdāq.

1997 *Imārāt abī ʿarīsh wa-ʿalāqāt-hā bi-l-dawlat al-ʿuthmāniyyah*, Riyāḍ: Maṭābiʿ al-Farazdāq.

NOTE ON RECORDS AND UNPUBLISHED MATERIAL

British records on Aden and the Protectorate are surprisingly thin. Documents at the Public Record Office (PRO), Kew, are cited under PRO hand-list numbers: e.g. CO 725, CO 1015, CO 1055, FO 371. For the earlier period (pre-1921 for the hinterland, pre-1937 for Aden) the India Office Records are richer; these have just moved to Kew also and we must hope matter comes to light not on earlier hand-lists.

This material has been well trawled by Doreen and Leila Ingrams. The product is collected as *Records of Yemen*, which I cite as *Records*. I was fortunate enough to borrow the last eight volumes for ten days. The amount I could note was limited. The compilers are robbed of the honour due them by their publisher's exorbitant pricing policy and blithe disregard for depositing work with copyright libraries.

For those interested in further research, Rhodes House in Oxford has manuscript material from several of the Aden British; a second collection, including material from Ingrams, is at St Antony's College.

Index

Alphabetical ordering of proper names ignores the definite article, al-. Photographs of persons are indicated in **bold**.